Praise for *Facilitating Software Architecture*

Andrew groks architecture. Here is a book full of actionable wisdom, founded on broad experience, illuminated by a well-written narrative, and shaped in a manner that gets to the essence of what architecture is, what it is not, and how to make it real.

—*Grady Booch, IBM Fellow*

At its best, software architecture is evolved by everyone involved. Andrew's book provides a practical process to make that vision work: involving a wide range of people and keeping a faithful record of decisions.

—*Martin Fowler, chief scientist, Thoughtworks*

A fascinating dive into the often undiscussed act of decision making, with particular depth being given to the social aspects. Recommended for anybody looking to transition away from the traditional centralized power structures typically associated with software architecture.

—*Simon Brown, creator of the C4 model*
for visualizing software architecture

Controversially, I don't believe that "everyone can do architecture". Architecture is not a skill demonstrated by one individual. Architecture is the orchestration of practices that generate systemic support for thinking well together about software systems. In this book, Andrew tells us what those practices are, why they matter, and how to adopt them. Read the book. Prove me wrong.

—*Diana Montalion, systems architect, Mentrix founder,*
author of Learning Systems Thinking

This is a wonderful guide to the kind of decentralized and participative architecture decision making needed to steward the evolution of complex software-intensive systems.

—*Ruth Malan, architecture consultant, Bredemeyer Consulting*

In our rush to adopt the structural and heavyweight aspects of the architecture metaphor, we often overlook what architecture is about and who it's for: people. Architecture creates a place to live and work. It defines the experience of those who inhabit it. It has consequences in time and cost that affect those who create and those who use the software. In this book, Andrew reclaims this fundamental and human aspect of architecture that is so often neglected. He offers perspectives, principles, processes, and practices for architecture that enable people, their work, and their goals, rather than simply enabling technologies and technical structure.

—*Kevlin Henney, independent consultant, Curbralan*

Architecture for fast flow needs both "decentralized deciding" and "fast feedback at scale," and this book shows you how to navigate this vital sociotechnical approach. This book provides a coherent, easy-to-follow guide for everyone. Highly recommended.

—*Matthew Skelton, coauthor of* Team Topologies, *CEO and founder of Conflux*

Your software architecture is a representation of the decisions made to create it. Andrew shows you how to improve the underlying decision making of your architecture, and therefore the architecture itself, through collaborative techniques and processes. There is a better way to "do" architecture.

—*Jacqui Read, principal architect, author of* Communication Patterns, *trainer, and international keynote speaker*

Decentralized governance was one of the original characteristics of microservices, but what does that actually mean? In this book Andrew makes a brilliant attempt at answering that question. I think this should be on every technology leader's bookshelf.

—*James Lewis, director, Thoughtworks UK and author of the original microservices definition*

Every company I've worked with that values fast flow and independent teams struggles with trusting teams to own software architecture. Andrew's book provides clear guidance on empowering teams to take responsibility for architecture while building trust between teams and leadership.

—*Kenny Baas-Schwegler, coauthor of* Collaborative Software Design, *independent software architect, tech lead, and systems designer*

I had the privilege to participate in the first Architecture Advisory Forum (AAF), to see the magic in the making. A group of people who had never spoken to or understood each other before, quickly and seamlessly falling into the flow of the AAF. I saw technical decisions being made democratically and responsibly, arguments being solved with disagreement and commitments, and more than anything, I saw people converging naturally towards a common strategy and getting comfortable with responsibility towards themselves and others. This book is a ground-breaking contribution to our industry, and I wish it was on the desk of every technical leader.

—Vanessa Formicola, principal engineer, Flo Health Inc,
international speaker, community builder, social change advocate

There are many books that cover best practices when driving good software architecture practices. *Facilitating Software Architecture* is the first of its kind that really focuses on the most fundamental change agent of architecture, which is people and culture. It is grounded in the practicalities of enabling teams and organizations to evolve software architecture best practices in a safe and inclusive way. Every engineering leader should have this book in their physical or virtual library!

—Cassandra Shum, VP of Field Engineering, RelationalAI

We know that only when people work out their own designs will there be necessary motivation, responsibility, and commitment. And there is no better way than how Andrew proposes in this book. Architecture is something we all care about in software development, but many feel uncomfortable doing it. What Andrew describes in this book is a way to enable all to participate, and it is more important than ever before that we all do.

—Trond Hjorteland, IT consultant and
sociotechnical practitioner, Capra Consulting

Having applied these techniques in the real world, I can attest to their effectiveness. This book offers a practical and insightful guide for software architects navigating decentralized teams, building trust, innovation, and scalable architecture practices.

—Noush Streets, VP of engineering, Chainalysis,
ex-CTO of Xapo Bank

The most comprehensive exploration of the decision-making process in software development ever created—a must-read for all roles involved with creation of software.

—Sonya Natanzon, engineering director, Guardant Health
and international keynote speaker

This book is chock-full of a career's worth of software architecture experience and wisdom, couched within practical ways of applying it. Worth it for the detailed breakdown of the Advice Process alone. And yet it has so much more about how to build the foundations of trust and really do the work, in an approachable and light-hearted way. I found myself reading it cover to cover to deepen my own skills.

—JD Carlston, director of engineering, Stack Overflow

Facilitating Software Architecture introduces a fresh, decentralized approach to software architecture practices. With actionable insights, Andrew equips architects and developers to facilitate and engage in the architecture advice process, optimizing for decentralized, trust-based architectural decisions with accountable alignment.

—Susanne Kaiser, international keynote speaker
and independent consultant

Both a practical, simple approach to scaling and democratizing software architecture and a deep exploration of the "whys" that will help you avoid cargo cult failure.

—Rob Horn, technical principal, Thoughtworks

An innovative guide that challenges traditional notions of software architecture, this book champions a fresh methodology grounded in diversity, inclusivity, and empathy. It not only revamps how we think about software architecture, but also provides practical strategies for fostering inclusivity and empathy in architectural practices.

—Jen Wallace, lead developer, Thoughtworks

This insightful book is packed with real-life examples of how to handle architectural decision making, irrespective of your role in a team. As a tech lead, I found it particularly helpful in navigating the tech lead-architect relationship dynamic.

—Elena Alina Oanea, technical lead, Thoughtworks

This book takes a sociotechnical approach to software architecture that the world needs more of. Andrew clearly explains the need for and the role of leadership when "practicing architecture." A great concept that emphasizes the variety in architectural roles and their commonalities at the same time. This book won't be catching dust on your bookshelf, but picked up regularly for practical pointers.

—Evelyn van Kelle, coauthor of Collaborative Software Design,
behavioral change consultant, and socio-technical thinker

Facilitating Software Architecture

Empowering Teams to Make
Architectural Decisions

Andrew Harmel-Law
Foreword by Sarah Wells

Facilitating Software Architecture

by Andrew Harmel-Law

Published by O'Reilly Media, Inc., 1005 Gravenstein Highway North, Sebastopol, CA 95472.

O'Reilly books may be purchased for educational, business, or sales promotional use. Online editions are also available for most titles (*http://oreilly.com*). For more information, contact our corporate/institutional sales department: 800-998-9938 or *corporate@oreilly.com*.

Acquisitions Editor: Louise Corrigan	**Indexer:** Potomac Indexing, LLC
Development Editor: Rita Fernando	**Interior Designer:** David Futato
Production Editor: Clare Laylock	**Cover Designer:** Karen Montgomery
Copyeditor: Shannon Turlington	**Illustrator:** Kate Dullea
Proofreader: Piper Editorial Consulting, LLC	

November 2024:   First Edition

Revision History for the First Edition

2024-11-08:   First Release

See *http://oreilly.com/catalog/errata.csp?isbn=9781098151867* for release details.

978-1-098-15186-7

[LSI]

Table of Contents

Part I. First Principles

Part II.   Nurturing and Evolving Your Culture of Decentralized Trust

Part III.   Finding Your Way Through the Decision Landscape

Part IV. Centering the "Social" in Your Practice of Architecture

Foreword

We develop software very differently now than we did when I started out as a developer more than 20 years ago.

The changes that have happened—Agile, DevOps, and the move from project to product among them—have all involved increasing decentralization and increasing independence. Teams now generally release their own code, support their own systems, and decide how they are going to solve business needs.

But the one role that has been more challenging to sort out, in my experience, has been the role of the architect.

When I was building monolithic systems more than a decade ago, architects worked in a separate team, designing the architecture for the whole system, setting standards, and choosing which database, programming language, or deployment mechanism to use. There are several reasons why that doesn't work in modern engineering organizations: these decisions become a bottleneck, stopping teams from making progress, but also there is even less chance nowadays that a single decision will work for all teams.

But what's the alternative? You can allow teams to make their own architectural decisions, either by assigning architects to work hands-on with those teams or by making "architecture" a thing that people in senior engineering roles do (along with everything else). However, that can lead to a wide divergence in approaches. That can be risky: are all the different data stores patched and up to date? It can also be a waste of effort as many teams solve the same problems.

Andrew's architecture advice process is the answer. Teams still have autonomy to make architectural decisions, but the process means that they must seek advice from people who are affected by the choice they make and from experts, which reduces the chance that teams will make decisions that conflict with one another—or at least that they will do so unintentionally—or that several teams have to solve the same problem.

What I love about this book is that you can read the first few chapters and start using the process straightaway, and I would encourage that: following Andrew's recommendation of starting small, with a single team. However, the rest of the book anticipates that you may have difficulties and gives you a number of ideas for tackling those. After all, this is a small process that involves big changes.

Because the real center of what Andrew is proposing is that the architecture advice process can shape the culture we need, moving us toward an organization that optimizes for learning, autonomy, and a fast flow of value. This involves some people sharing the power to decide, which can be challenging. It also means others need to start deciding and being accountable for those choices, which is scary.

But it's worth doing, because the people who can best realize that there is a significant decision that needs to be made and the people who will bear the consequences of that decision are the people in the teams that will build that feature.

I was much more prepared to support my system in production once I could choose to move away from implementation choices that someone else had imposed on me: that meant choosing things that were easier to operate and where more people had relevant experience.

I will be recommending this process, and this book, to clients because it is a much more complete implementation of things that have worked for me in the past: let teams make decisions, make sure they talk to the right people, and then get out of their way. I think you'll be surprised at the effect this has on your organization.

— *Sarah Wells,*
independent consultant,
author of Enabling Microservice Success,
and chair, QCon London

Preface

If delivery of software were simply a matter of typing out lines of code, then unconnected individuals could achieve the same ends as *teams* of individuals of equal number and similar skills. This is not the case. Teams can and do build better software.

In sports, it is expected that abilities and experience will be diverse and that everyone will play their part. When a team combines their skills and focuses on a shared goal, they stand the greatest chance of winning.[1] The same dynamics apply in software development teams, where our goal is the sustainable delivery and evolution of a quality end product.

As a consultant, developer, and software/systems architect, I have been incredibly lucky to work closely with some brilliant software delivery teams. I have seen them in action, working within many different styles of architecture, using a broad range of programming languages, tools, and technology stacks, deploying a variety of approaches and practices, running on a cornucopia of runtimes, and supported by an abundance of cultures and organizations. I've learned an incredible amount from seeing them at work. They have been exemplars of the concept of "high-performing" teams.

I've also been lucky enough to have known, learned from, and—when I was *very* lucky—worked with some brilliant software architects. I've seen them think, create, deploy wisdom, and problem solve. But this was not what made them brilliant. What made them brilliant was how they listened, communicated, collaborated, co-created, and facilitated. This meant that the architectures they created successfully made it out into the world and ran as expected.

---

1 This applies even at a fundamental level. My son's rugby coach was fond of saying, "The ball always travels faster than one player can run," meaning that they should pass the ball between one another to gain an advantage over their opponents.

The delivery teams that taught me the most have always managed to maximize the skills and capabilities of the largest number of their teammates for significantly extended periods of time—what they did was sustainable and for the benefit of them all. The architects who taught me the most achieved exactly the same goal, but they delivered this value *across all teams*. In all cases, they were able to tap into the full potential power of software.

What were those teams doing that meant they succeeded? Equally, what were they not doing? It gradually dawned on me that the highest-performing teams, supported by the most collaborative architects, never seemed to be adversely affected by the incredible complexity of the architectures that they were building and running. In fact, many times when I watched this collaboration in action, it wasn't easy to spot who was the architect and who were the delivery team members. The blending of mindsets and roles was so extensive it almost felt *as if everyone were doing the architecting*.

Meanwhile, in the lowest-performing teams, there was rarely a lack of technical skill. Nor was there an absence of desire to work as a self-managing team. Why were they failing? What were they doing that was detrimental? What were they not doing that would have helped them? One key issue kept appearing again and again: the failing teams lacked a two-way relationship with the architecture. Instead, they were hindered by arms-length architects and their heavily guarded designs and other artifacts.

By observing both successful and unsuccessful teams and architects, I spotted patterns in ways of working, identifying what worked and what hindered them. With support, I've run experiments to see if we could optimize for the key parts of their shared mindsets, approaches, and practices that seemed to make everyone so collectively powerful. Consequently, I was able to extract a set of interrelated elements and other lessons that made the practices of the highest-performing teams accessible to everyone, which in turn returned the full potential power of software to all.

Marc Andreesen famously said, "Software is eating the world,"[2] because software, all software, has an enormous potential. Software enables us to do things faster, cheaper, and more efficiently. Software allows us to do things that otherwise would be impossible—incomprehensible, even. But although that article was published (at the time of writing) 10 years ago and spoke of the near future, software hasn't consumed everything in its path. This is because, though software has the power, that power is squandered, manifesting as complexity, rigidity, expense, and waste. Yet if we can address the challenges, the power is still available to us, in just the way it was when the article was written.

---

2 Marc Andreesen, "Why Software Is Eating the World" (*https://oreil.ly/OO3K5*), *The Wall Street Journal*, August 20, 2011.

Despite this potential power, far too many teams are begrudgingly working on half-hearted renderings of someone else's vision of a secondhand understanding of the problem they're trying to solve.

Quality software is created by cohesive, cross-functional teams who understand and have agency over their problem space and the designs used to tackle it. Quality software reflects the team's collective mindset and mental models, which are deeply influenced by the reality of their systems running in the wild. This should be everyone's future. This should be everyone's experience.

Sadly, this future is—to paraphrase William Gibson—unevenly distributed. Time and again, I've seen architectural ways of working, organizational structures, and corporate cultures that consciously, even intentionally, get in the way of this collective power of cross-functional teams. Ironically, these attempts at control exist precisely because the power of software when in failure modes is (rightly) feared. But the more they attempted to manage the downsides, the more they got in the way of the potential upsides.

This book aims to change the way we collectively practice software architecture, to offer everyone the chance to be part of a high-performing team. I'll share the practices and mindsets that I've seen work broadly, for both architects and developers. Architects particularly will learn a facilitation-based approach that has the potential to unleash the power of architect teams and their software. Developers will learn how to step up and make meaningful contributions to software architecture discussions as equal partners. This book will help everyone—architects and developers alike—to transition to this new approach, grounded in a set of core principles that will ensure, regardless of your individual circumstances, that you stay on the path to success.

As you build your skills during the course of this book, you will learn about the illusion of control you have over your architectures and running systems and about the power of learning and of teams when you let go. If you are an architect, you will also learn how to facilitate the collective, unleashing and growing its potential for the benefits of your shared architecture. If you are a team member, you will learn how to contribute to the architecture, both learning and teaching as you do so, maximizing the positive impact of everyone. Perhaps most importantly, everyone will learn about the centrality of safety and inclusion as well as the fundamental need for openness and trust.

Who Should Read This Book

This book is primarily aimed at the two groups I am trying to bring together: developers looking to take steps into architectural accountability and architects learning to add facilitation skills to their repertoire.

"Architects" in Software Engineering

Writing this book has taught me one thing: virtually every organization has a different idea of what an "architect" does in software, so for this book to make sense to my target readers, I need to define what I mean by the word.

Confusion arises because there are a wide variety of architect archetypes and as many different modes of engaging with the work of delivering and evolving software. This is why we talk about software architects, domain architects, solution architects, business architects, system architects, principal engineers, enterprise architects, IT architects, chief architects, and more.[3]

In this book, I am less concerned about what you call them than I am about the ranges of architectural remit and accountability. Being clear on those facts will allow you to translate what I say into the roles in your org.

First come those practicing architecture *within* (and *for*) multiple teams. They are commonly known as aligned[4] *software or solution architects* if they work with multiple teams and *team architects* or even *tech leads* if they are permanent members of a single team. Both possibly even have the opportunity to write some code that makes it to production. If you are one of these people or aspire to be, then you are target audience one for this book. In this book, I refer to these activities as architecture "within teams."[5]

Second come those practicing architecture *across* teams but within product suites or programs of work. They are commonly known as *system architects,* and if they do write code, it's unlikely it'll ever hit production. If you are one of these people, then you are target audience two for this book. In this book, I refer to these activities as "systems" architecture and architecture "across" or "between" teams interchangeably.

Third come those practicing architecture across the entire organization. They are commonly known as *enterprise, IT, or chief architects,* and their focus ranges across all technology systems in an organization, not just the ones built in-house. If you are one of these people, then you're not a target audience for this book, although you may want to recommend to those playing the first and second types of architecture roles that they check this book out as the practices it contains will help you achieve your goals too.

---

3 I'm *not intentionally* ignoring other flavors of architect, such as security architects and infrastructure architects. That doesn't mean there aren't parts of this book that you might find useful, but the dynamics of your worlds are different.

4 As in "aligned to a team."

5 If you are a member of a single team and practicing architecture, then you're well on the way to practicing what this book advocates for. To avoid conflating individuals with their roles, I refer to this as "the development team."

If you do have the word *architect* in your job title, then perhaps you can locate in these three types the role or roles you play. Perhaps you span multiple of them. The important thing is that you can translate. The important thing is that you are clear when I am referring to your role or roles.

In all likelihood, your organization is somewhere in its journey toward adopting the latest revolution in software delivery. It does not matter where you are on this journey. Neither does it matter what your specific architectural style, language or languages, and runtimes are.

You also don't need to do any preparation before tackling this book. I trust that you already know the painful details of your organization's architecture practice and the dark underside of the systems that are running in production. That is all you will need. Everything else you will learn within these pages and from your colleagues.

For this book to help, I ask that you are open to the experience, both of yourself and, equally importantly, of your colleagues. What you are about to learn *will* work for you if you are willing to change your outlook as well as your preconceptions about how software architecture is "done" and the skills and experiences of others. To get there, you need to be open to collaborating deeply and openly with your colleagues across your organization. You need to be ready to learn, and to fail, and to learn from that failure. It will be uncomfortable, but it will be worth it. You need to be willing to both let go of control and take responsibility, looking at things afresh but not forgetting what you know.

Why I Wrote This Book

Nicole Forsgren, Jez Humble, and Gene Kim's book *Accelerate* (O'Reilly) challenged all of us in the world of software engineering to do better and to deliver better. Specifically, to go faster *without impacting quality*. To deliver increased team independence without compromising the cohesion and quality of the resulting system.

In responding to this challenge, I experimented with a collection of practices. Some came from the world of software, others from elsewhere. I was inspired by the experiences of the people I'd met at the Java Posse Roundup open space event.[6] When I put these together, with client after client—made up not of rock stars but of developers and architects just like you and me—I was amazed how well they worked and how fulfilling they were to everyone who participated.

---

6 Now called the Winter Tech Forum (*https://www.wintertechforum.com*), this is the most amazing event, attended by the most amazing set of software professionals, that I've ever had the good fortune to attend.

Much of this experimentation followed the upheaval caused by the COVID-19 pandemic. Perhaps clients felt they needed to try new and different approaches to adapt to uncertain times. Whatever the reason, it produced fascinating results that I felt compelled to share with the world. I posted my initial thoughts in a Twitter thread (*https://oreil.ly/NsWfD*) that was surprisingly well received. Some of my Thoughtworks colleagues heard about the successes I was having and asked me what I was doing. In response, I wrote what became a blog post for Martin Fowler: "Scaling the Practice of Architecture, Conversationally" (*https://oreil.ly/FKjAY*). Once that was published, I was surprised yet again at the level of interest it generated. I began to talk about it at conferences and on podcasts. People approached me both to ask for further advice and to tell me about remarkably similar approaches they had arrived at themselves, completely independently of what I was doing. Others were experimenting in this area, too, and they wanted to talk about it.

While all this was happening, I was still working with clients, implementing various flavors of this approach with them while learning from others who were doing the same in their organizations. I researched why things were working and took note of ways it ran into trouble. It became clear that there was a lot that could be said about this fundamentally simple combination of elements. My notes accumulated, and my approaches became more refined. The sum of what I learned led me ultimately to write the book you have in your hands now.

My greatest hope is that this book keeps the experimenting, learning, and sharing going. What strikes me deepest about my experiences is how differently the elements and surrounding culture manifest themselves when they are set up. Although there is a core you must adhere to in order to get the most out of the approach I describe in this book, there isn't a strict "one way" to do it. Take what you learn here and adapt it to your needs. Even if only a small fraction of it works for you, share your experience with others. Please pass on what you've learned so that we might all benefit. The community pages of *https://facilitatingsoftwarearchitecture.com* are intended for this purpose.

Navigating This Book

This book is organized as follows:

- Chapter 1 describes the problem of centralized architecture practices in a decentralized world.
- Part I, "First Principles" (Chapters 2 to 6) covers the core aspects of a decentralized, feedback-centering approach to architecture.
- Part II, "Nurturing and Evolving Your Culture of Decentralized Trust" (Chapters 7 to 11) makes clear the dynamics arising from the core approach and introduces a series of supporting elements to ensure they are effective.

- Part III, "Finding Your Way Through the Decision Landscape" (Chapters 12 to 14) returns to the core practices and examines how to make them work best in your organization.
- Part IV, "Centering the "Social" in Your Practice of Architecture" (Chapters 15 to 17) finally takes a step back and looks at the social aspects of architecture practice that take center stage if you adopt this approach, sharing both pitfalls and practices.

Conventions Used in This Book

In this book, *italic* indicates new terms, URLs, email addresses, filenames, and file extensions.

 This element signifies a tip or suggestion.

 This element signifies a general note.

Supplemental Material

Supplemental material (additional practice, templates, further reading, and examples) is available at *https://facilitatingsoftwarearchitecture.com*.

O'Reilly Online Learning

 For more than 40 years, *O'Reilly Media* has provided technology and business training, knowledge, and insight to help companies succeed.

Our unique network of experts and innovators share their knowledge and expertise through books, articles, and our online learning platform. O'Reilly's online learning platform gives you on-demand access to live training courses, in-depth learning paths, interactive coding environments, and a vast collection of text and video from O'Reilly and 200+ other publishers. For more information, visit *https://oreilly.com*.

How to Contact Us

Please address comments and questions concerning this book to the publisher:

O'Reilly Media, Inc.
1005 Gravenstein Highway North
Sebastopol, CA 95472
800-889-8969 (in the United States or Canada)
707-827-7019 (international or local)
707-829-0104 (fax)
support@oreilly.com
https://oreilly.com/about/contact.html

We have a web page for this book, where we list errata, examples, and any additional information. You can access this page at *https://oreil.ly/FacilitatingSoftwareArch*.

For news and information about our books and courses, visit *https://oreilly.com*.

Find us on LinkedIn: *https://linkedin.com/company/oreilly-media*.

Watch us on YouTube: *https://youtube.com/oreillymedia*.

Acknowledgments

Writing books turns out to be harder than I imagined. It's also one of the most rewarding things I've ever done. Thank you to Diana Montalion for being beside me every step of the way, cheering me up when it felt impossible and calming me down when I got out over my skis. Thank you most of all for the purple wave of suggestions you unleashed when you saw what this book might just be.

This book is about the power of advice, and I had the best technical advisers ever. Thank you to Vanessa Formicola, Alina Balusescu, Jen Wallace, Trond Hjorteland, and Rob Horn for sharing so much of your time, experience, and expertise. This is a far, far better book thanks to you.

One of the first people to read the (nearly) finished article front to back was Sarah Wells. Thank you, Sarah, for grokking what I was trying to say and how I was trying to say it, and then capturing that so succinctly in your foreword.

The inspiration for the approach came from three sources. Ruth Malan was the first to inspire me. Ruth, your insight, defaulting to openness, community building, unbridled enthusiasm, and collaboration gave me a new way to think about the practice of architecture. Thank you.

Bruce Eckell and the Java Posse were the second source of inspiration. Until I struggled through the Colorado snow to my first Java Posse Roundup, I'd never seen what could be possible if you make space and let people self-organize. The conversations I had in Crested Butte over the years made me wonder how much I could get out of people's way and yet great things would still happen. Bruce, Dick, Carl, Tor, Joe, and everyone I met at those gatherings showed me. Thank you, everyone.

Alberto Brandolini was the third inspiration. Alberto, I doubt you have any idea how many sleepless nights I had after you told me that "it is the developers' assumptions that get shipped to production." Trying to figure a way to practice architecture that worked with this led me here. Thank you.

Inspiration in place, the first time all the elements in this book came together was at the start of the COVID-19 pandemic. When we were all huddled together over Zoom calls, I was lucky enough to work with Pete Hunter and the rest of the team at OpenGI. As this book testifies, Pete frequently saw the power and dynamics of this approach more clearly than I did. Thank you, Pete, for working on the alpha version of this with me. Thanks, too, to everyone at OpenGI for letting us experiment with you.

Thanks as well to Mel Mitchell and the rest of the Thoughtworks team who worked with me on that same project. You also contributed to the alpha version of this approach, but one person in particular told me to "write it down." Mel, thank you. Technically, this is all your fault.

"Writing it down" led to my article on the approach for Martin Fowler and my first real experience of being edited. Thank you, Martin, for bearing with me and offering yet more advice that gave structure to the approach as it is presented here.

That article led in turn to the next great ruggedizing of the approach. CTO Noush Streets and her team at Xapo Bank understood its power and suitability incredibly quickly but refused to compromise on their "remote always, async first" culture. It made me and my Thoughtworks colleagues confront yet again what the core was and how culture played an even more significant role. Thank you to everyone I worked with for not compromising and for demanding the highest standards of results.

The final boost to my belief that this approach might be generally useful was when Mathias Verraes and Nick Tune suggested we ask the 800-plus attendees of the DDD Europe 2022 conference what they thought about it and what advice they might have. The Everybody Keynote was the result. Thank you to them and the rest of the conference team as well as Gayathri Thiyagarajan and Diana Montalion for participating and Mike Rozinski and Dan Young for shepherding us into something amazing.

As the book took shape, I realized that it was going to take more than just an hour a day to write. Thank you to Pat Sarnake, Ashok Subramanian, and Shodhan Sheth for funding supplementary time to make sure I could hit my deadlines. Thank you to everyone who worked with me on projects, both Thoughtworkers and clients, and who worked around my absences.

In the spirit of the advice process, I asked for feedback as chapter after chapter made its way into the wild. I was bowled over by the amount I received, but Sonya Natanzon, Michael Gray, Dianing Yudono, J. D. Carlston, Indu Alagarsamy, James Brown, Samit Bico, and Romain Vasseur deserve special mention due to the amount of time they spent on it and the depth of thinking and insight they brought to bear. Thank you all, especially Sonya and Michael, who shared their experiences at conference after conference. I hope you can see your impact within these pages.

I also got the opportunity to share my progress with audiences of the Lead Dev Bookmarked, Happy Path Programming, and InfoQ podcasts. Thank you to Suzan Bond, James Ward and Bruce Eckell, and Thomas Betts for having me on and ensuring that I came across coherently.

Rita Fernando, thank you for being my development editor. You taught me how to write. Your patience was phenomenal, and your postcall notes were both a lifeline and a wonder to behold. We almost managed to hit your hard deadline. Thank you, too, for being with me right up to the point when you went off to work on something far more important. (Thank you as well to Corbin Collins for stepping in at the end.)

Melissa Duffield, thank you for taking a chance on this book based on a relatively sketchy pitch, and Louise Corrigan, thank you for whipping the pitch into shape and checking in with me as we went along. You were both co-conspirators in this project, and I hope you're as proud as I am of the result.

Clare Laylock, you picked up the baton, keeping my flagging energy going through production. Thank you. And Shannon Turlington, thank you for your patience and bringing way more attention to detail than I could ever muster to the final copy-editing stages.

It turned out that the experience of writing a book is deeply affecting in more ways than one. Thank you to Tricia Driver, Valentina Servile, Cat Morris, Amy Lynch, Juke Trabold, Javiera Laso, Krisztina Hirth, Sofia Katsaouni, Aki Salmi, Anne Macedo, Marit van Dijk, Andrea Magnorsky, and Kenny Baas-Schwegler for looking after me through the ups and downs (though you may not have known it).

Finally, thank you to my partner in parenting crime, Amanda, and to our beautiful joint projects, Charlie and Hattie. You made me cups of tea, stopped me thinking about the book *all* the time, did everything I didn't do because I was writing, and most importantly, reminded me why I did all this in the first place.

Centralized Architecture Practices in a Decentralized World

"Traditional" approaches to software architecture have become increasingly ineffective in the face of our rapidly evolving software systems. In this opening chapter, I'll describe how these problems originated with a series of fundamental changes—or revolutions—demanding further decentralization and increasing sensitivity to feedback. With these revolutions in mind, I'll then take you through the problems caused by the reliance of traditional architectural approaches on predictability and control. I'll conclude by setting out what an approach to architecture needs to incorporate, focusing on what is within our power to plan for, protect against, and respond to.

Let's begin by considering the value of software architecture, both as a practice and as an end result.

Both the Practice and the End Result of Software Architecture Are Essential for Success

What is *software architecture*? For Grady Booch, "[Software] architecture represents the set of significant design decisions that shape the form and the function of a system, where significant is measured by cost of change."[1] Martin Fowler has a similar take that can be paraphrased as software architecture being those decisions that are both important and hard to change.[2]

---

1 Grady Booch, "All architecture is design, but not all design is architecture" (*https://oreil.ly/ZqdmP*), Twitter (now X), November 11, 2021.

2 Martin Fowler, "Making Architecture Matter" (*https://oreil.ly/Ryi3S*), OSCON 2015 keynote address, July 23, 2015, 14 min., 3 sec.

I like these two definitions because not only do they encompass what software architecture is, they also highlight the greatest difficulty with the concept of "software architecture." Booch's definition leans toward the *end result* while Fowler's leans more toward the *practice*. In fact, the term *software architecture* can refer to one or the other, or both at the same time. Rather confusingly, we tend to use the meanings interchangeably when we talk about the software we build. For any software system to be successful, both the end result and the practice are essential.

Software Architecture Versus the Practice of Software Architecture

In this book, I'll differentiate the end result and the practice of software architecture as follows:

- The end result—the things that end up in code—is the "software architecture."
- The act of deciding which gets you there is "the practice of software architecture."

Many books have been written about that end result of software architecture and about the significant design decisions that shape the form and function of a system. New technologies are developed all the time that require changes to existing architectures or create entirely new ones. This is where patterns[3] and reference architectures[4] come into play, capturing proven ways to construct our systems.

You might assume that there would be an equal number of books about the practice of software architecture. Sadly not. This is because the way software architecture is practiced has changed very little over the years.

But the stakes are rising. Software architecture is becoming increasingly important as the complexity of our running software systems continues to rise. Our systems are larger, change more often, are more connected (both to things we own and things we don't), are used by more people more of the time, and are expected to never fail.

Although it is widely accepted that the practice of architecture *is* important *and* that having bad architecture should be avoided, only the end result has seen innovation and improvement over the years. For future success, we need to be open to evolving our practice of software architecture too.

---

3 Patterns in software have an interesting history, which we frequently misremember. I presented a lightning talk (*https://oreil.ly/ojFSL*) at DDD Europe 2021 on this topic.

4 Reference architectures purport to capture industry "best practice." The Open Group's IT4IT reference architecture (*https://oreil.ly/Y_89S*) is a good example of this.

This book redresses this imbalance. It describes an approach to the practice of architecture that reliably achieves and sustains the architectural end results that our software needs, maybe even improving the future of software development.

Let's begin by establishing the goals of good software architecture in our rapidly changing and unpredictable technological landscape. Systems with good architecture have:

- Individual parts that are coherent, cohesive, and aligned both to the domain and to business value
- Individual parts that are decoupled in the right way so that multiple independent teams can work on the overall system together and in parallel
- Half an eye on future evolutions, creating overall architectures that are sufficiently adaptable to change

Given these qualities, the definition of a suitable software architecture *practice* is trivial: it must deliver and maintain these "good architectures."

When appropriate approaches to the practice of software architecture are done well, I have seen them have a massive positive impact. You can see and feel it in the production of the software and the end results. Building and running code becomes efficient, predictable, easier, even joyful. When executed poorly, software architecture practice becomes wasteful, unpredictable, and a struggle—in short, not much fun.

Let's take this lens and use it to examine current software architecture practices, considering in particular how they cope with modern software architectures. (Spoiler alert: they don't fare very well.)

What Are the Practices of Traditional Architecture?

As I've said, the standard practices of software architecture haven't changed very much over the years; you'll probably recognize them as soon as I describe them. They're so ubiquitous that I am going to refer to them from now on as *traditional*. Although these practices fall under two extremes, which I'll discuss shortly, they share one common aspect. Traditional software architecture practices concentrate the power to make decisions in the hands of a select group: the people called *architects*. Architects are responsible and accountable for all significant architectural decisions.

Remember this, as it's crucial to this chapter's discussion.

Now for the two extremes of traditional architecture practice. To be clear, neither of these stereotypes ever manifests fully in reality, but the fact that our discipline has names for them—which we all recognize—means that they exist conceptually for all of us.

Ivory Tower Architects

On the one end, you have the ivory tower approach to architecture practice, illustrated in Figure 1-1. In this approach, multiple teams are building software and trying to flow. When a need for an architectural decision arises, they must seek it from the architect in the distant ivory tower.

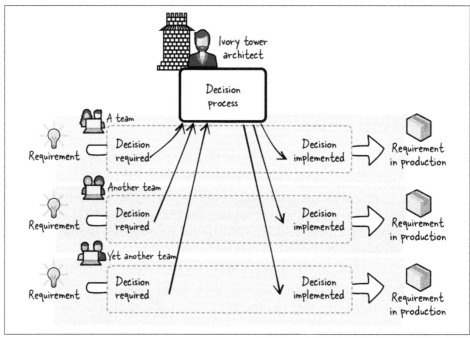

Figure 1-1. The ivory tower approach to practicing architecture

This approach tries to influence, even *control*, everything about both the parts and the whole. By this I mean it tries to have opinions on, and input into, individual software components that deliver specific features while also trying to look after all the components as they interact together. To achieve this, ivory tower practices look at everything from a variety of standpoints and perspectives, with a range of timescales in mind, and apply a series of constraints to keep the whole together, all the way to production.

The most significant failing of ivory tower architecture practices is that they overfocus on the whole at the expense of the individual parts and the teams that are trying to deliver and run them. This is necessary for them to be able to cope with all the variability. For example, ivory tower approaches mandate that everyone stick to a given architectural pattern, even when it doesn't fit in certain specific circumstances, because that pattern *ought* to make matters more predictable and thus—so the logic goes—easier to control.

Software architects practicing this ivory tower approach are consequently seen as above everything, all-knowing, and able to survey the whole scene. It is assumed that such architects have vast arrays of experience, traditionally manifesting as being superior in the organizational hierarchy—another reason they are viewed as "high up." These preconceptions are manifested in the term we use to identify this approach. *Ivory tower architect* implies that their architecture approaches are too far removed from the code to have a sense of the grubby, day-to-day reality.

Hands-on Architects

But surely being "down in the trenches" is also important? It is, and it is represented on the other end of the architecture practice spectrum: the hands-on, cross-team approach to architecture illustrated in Figure 1-2. Again, multiple teams are building software and trying to flow. When the need for an architecture decision arises, they must engage a roaming hands-on architect who meets them in their context.

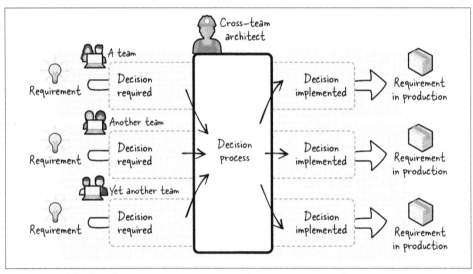

Figure 1-2. The hands-on, cross-team approach to practicing architecture

This approach reflects an architect's important determination to retain and prove their ability to code. The practice sees the work of these architects as happening "at the code-face," among the developers, moving from team to team, asking all the right questions and co-designing with team leads and senior devs. In direct contrast to the emphasis of the ivory tower approach, the hands-on approach prioritizes the experiences of individual teams and very much wants to make sure that the individual parts are deliverable.

Hands-on approaches require rushing around, spinning from team to team, never being anywhere quite long enough to do all the work that's needed. As a result, the overall system suffers. The overfocus on individual teams is this extreme's weakness because the "whole" is still of great importance, yet it is not treated as such. What is needed is an approach that can balance both "up-close" and "big picture" perspectives.

What's Wrong with Both Traditional Approaches?

Although these generalizations are intentionally polemical, they both fail for the same reason: they attempt to control the uncontrollable and predict the unpredictable.

I've practiced ivory tower approaches, and hands-on approaches too. I've also been a development lead trying to partner with both types, so I've seen how things can fall apart in different ways and from many angles.

As an architect working in the ivory tower, I've striven to keep both the big picture and the details in check. I've been the one trying to articulate the importance of fundamental information security and regulatory requirements (which we *had* to conform to for boring but existential reasons—not being compliant with various regulations can do that to a business) while a cool new library or approach is proving far more exciting to development teams.

As a jobbing hands-on architect, I've loaded my brain with all the context and domain information I can. I've moved from team to team, struggling to context switch, to bring to mind the vast number of details of their current focus, their history, the specifics of their part of the business domain, their specific pipelines and runtime needs, while listening to what they tell me about a particularly weird traffic blip, *while* trying to make sure the overall API we expose publicly has some degree of consistency.

In my experience, all software architects—no matter how they go about their practice— are sincere, applying their unique mix of the traditional approaches (and more) with the best intentions. But in doing so, architects are trying to achieve complete control because, regardless of their approach, they are responsible and accountable for the *entirety* of the architecture. By trying to juggle all expectations perfectly, they lead themselves into trouble.

With ivory tower approaches, this means having review boards, sign-offs, dedicated architecture functions, and straightjacketing frameworks. And the hands-on alternative? Close pairing, moving from autonomous team to autonomous team, trying to do all the required design in all the places it is needed. Neither works well.

Why not? Because, by design, ivory tower and hands-on architects are *at best* a drag on teams, and at worst, they lead to bad architecture and bad software.

With either ivory tower or hands-on approaches, when my architecture work is good and I communicate it effectively, the downside is simply that I slow teams down because I become a bottleneck—and that's the best outcome. With development teams expecting to move faster and faster, I can unintentionally block their flow, which means they sit idle, waiting for my input.

Frequently, the situation is worse still. As teams become increasingly independent and are able to deploy to production with greater frequency, they know far more about their parts of the system than I ever could as their architect. They know their requirements in more detail, they know their code better, they know their domain better, they know their pipelines and runtimes better, and they know their customers better. Consequently, I rely more and more on the teams to share the latest state of all this contextual information with me. The more they have to do this, the more it becomes impossible to think through everything required to play my role: that of representing the whole, the sum of all these independent parts.

I've striven to deliver software that meets the requirements, that delivers value to both the users and the business, and that evolves and changes as both needs and technologies evolve and change. I've tried incredibly hard to make both of the traditional architecture practices work, separately and together, but never with enough success to mitigate being a blocker and failing to be aware of every nuance of an increasingly complex system.

We find ourselves in a world where our software systems are made up of increasing numbers of independent, decentralized, and rapidly changing parts that are not always known or fully understood. Let's take a closer look at the kinds of software we build today and the ways in which we build it. With this clarity, it becomes possible to identify what qualities a suitable practice of software architecture needs to have.

Five Revolutions Unlocked the Power of Software

Change is a constant in the world of software. There is always a new tool, language, platform, technique, approach, pattern, antipattern, right way or wrong way, organizational model, or shift in values to keep up with. The desire to use or do the latest thing is so embedded in our software culture that we must frequently be reminded to actually deliver useful and valuable outcomes. In fact, change is such a feature of our lives that Chapter 13 is dedicated to tackling the challenges it offers.

Over the years, responses to this need and desire for change have surfaced as a series of revolutions that have altered our relationship with code and, consequently, our software architectures. Each revolution challenges key aspects of our software-creation ecosystem and offers us a new way of seeing the world before us and what is possible. (You might not be experiencing all—or even any—of these, but the opportunity exists for us all.)

There have been five revolutions so far (shown in Figure 1-3), but doesn't mean there won't be others in the future. (You can already see storm clouds brewing in the area of organization design. And who knows what machine learning might bring.)

 My use of the term *revolution* to describe the shifts in our relationships with code and software architecture is deliberate. You can think of a software architecture as revolving around an axis, which can have the effect of completely upending an established mindset. Although a rotation can bring us back to where we started, it will have caused us to view the world in a different way.

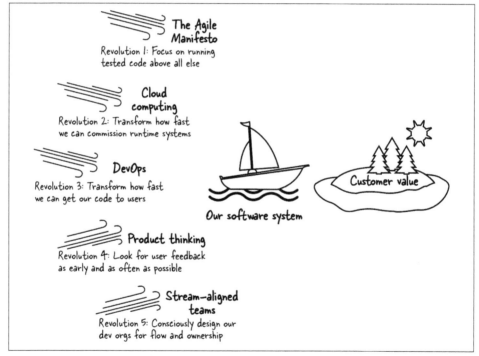

Figure 1-3. The first five software revolutions

The first revolution came with the Agile Manifesto (*https://oreil.ly/e7exd*). It encouraged us to return our focus to running, tested code[5] and trust in the humans doing this work. It highlighted the power of techniques such as test-driven development, pair programming, and continuous integration to help us achieve this.

The second revolution came with cloud computing. The increasing ubiquity and plummeting price point of network, storage, and compute cycles made us realize[6] that we didn't need to own the computers we ran our code on and that we could pay someone for time on theirs instead. This changed our perspective on just how fast we could set up and change our systems in production. No longer did we have to wait weeks (or months even) for a new server to be delivered in a box, unpacked, racked, cabled in, and an operating system deployed. After the second revolution, we could achieve the same thing within a few minutes, installed via the command line,[7] and our code could be running on it very soon afterward.

The third revolution came with DevOps and continuous deployment. It became clear that there was no reason to keep treating the people feeding and watering our cloud runtimes as having a different culture, a culture that we could interact with only via ticketing queues. This shift, which broke down artificial boundaries between roles in Development and those in Operations, reshaped just how soon "soon after the code is complete" could be and who might be initiating the deployments. Operations teams embraced the tooling that developers took for granted and used them to build, deploy, and maintain services, which in turn allowed delivery teams to self-serve all the infrastructure and pipelines that automated all the steps between production and our machines. DevOps and continuous delivery encouraged us all to break down the silos and see our systems running in production, learning from how they both succeeded and failed.

This direct exposure to our production-running systems drove the fourth revolution, which came from product thinking. Product thinking helped us see that there was no guarantee of problem-solution fit or product-market fit unless we heard from users. For example, when I seemed too confident in my work, my colleague Monira Rhami,

---

5 Evident in Agile Manifesto principles such as "our highest priority is to satisfy the customer through early and continuous delivery of valuable software"; "deliver working software frequently, from a couple of weeks to a couple of months, with a preference to the shorter timescale"; and "working software is the primary measure of progress."

6 You could argue it's *remember* rather than *realize*. Sharing of available compute cycles was a core concept in the days of the mainframe. The TV show *Halt and Catch Fire* (AMC, 2014) spent at least a whole season talking about this.

7 My first encounter with this dream was via the cover of *Automating Solaris Installations: A Custom Jumpstart Guide* by Paul Anthony Kasper and Alan L. McClellan (Prentice Hall). It depicts a single admin with their feet up on the desk, hands behind their head as automation provisions machine after machine with just the right software.

a product manager/CPO and ex-developer, would often challenge me by asking, "But how do you know your work actually works?" It was always a great point. Until my work was running in production and being used, I had no way of being absolutely sure of it. With product thinking, no longer did we have to build something and recklessly hope that it was valuable. Now we could write just-enough code, ship it, and prove the value from the feedback.[8]

Most recently, the fifth revolution of stream-aligned teams showed us that we were *still* getting in our own way. There was nothing so annoying as having two teams with conflicting priorities and imbalances of information delivering two halves of a feature on a shared codebase. Far better to put all the elements and information they required in the hands of a single team and let them get on with it. Feedback was improved yet again because the team owned the customer experience end to end, and it was far more direct.

Of the five, this last one had the longest uninterrupted gestation period—perhaps because it was the last to arrive and the one most extensively built on its predecessors. It was highlighted early on by people like Eric Evans in *Domain-Driven Design* (Addison-Wesley) and Donald Reinertsen in *The Principles of Product Development Flow* (Celeritas). James Lewis then made it increasingly actionable with his articulation of the microservices pattern (*https://oreil.ly/aMnRu*). Only recently, however, has the concept of having stream-aligned teams come to individual prominence, in great part due to the work by the DORA Report/Accelerate team, by Marty Cagan in his book *Inspired: How to Create Tech Products Customers Love* (Wiley), and by Matthew Skelton and Manuel Pais with their Team Topologies approach.

The idea of *flow* referenced in Reinertsen's book title, and also a constant theme in Team Topologies, is much beloved by people in the product world and refers to a fast-flowing river of value with nothing to get in its way. The search for flow means friction is constantly being removed, making feedback faster and more valuable.

Running throughout each of the software revolutions is the idea that nothing should impede a feature idea from getting in front of users. With flow, that feature can rapidly become a set of thinly sliced stories in a single team's backlog, then a commit to source control triggering a deployment that, within a matter of minutes or hours, could be in front of a user and either meeting their need (success) or not (failure). If we succeed, we can move on to the next incremental user story. If we fail, we find out why and course correct.

---

8 As you learn when you try to write a book, there is a far from tidy history to many of these ideas. One of the earliest in this area, but one that also prefigured many of the other revolutions, is documented in the 1986 *Harvard Business Review* article "The New New Product Development Game." (*https://oreil.ly/yEZJw*)

Diana Montalion calls the sum of these revolutions "the new physics" (*https://oreil.ly/ICdXo*), and that's the perfect term for it. Collectively, they undermine the Newtonian certainties of software development, and previously unimagined possibilities open up before us. When these revolutions are combined, months of work can be collapsed into minutes. Guesswork and hope can be turned into experiments, data, and facts. The power of running code in production and gathering feedback is more accessible now than it's ever been.

But the revolutions didn't make everything easier. Although they brought significant, rapid, and arguably positive change, they also left architects scrambling to adapt, struggling to hold everything together.

The Effects of the Five Revolutions on Architecture Practice

Although the software revolutions brought us the changes we needed and desired, they also brought us more architectural complexity. We have increasingly decoupled and autonomous parts of software systems, but they still must be able to work together as a cohesive whole. Additionally, the right domain logic (the real-world business rules encoded in the software) must belong exclusively and entirely to the right teams, and those teams must be sufficiently decoupled from all the others. All the while, "just enough" architecture needs to happen to enable all parts of the system to meet all the identified needs as well as change direction as needed. And *all this needs to take place while* listening to the feedback that the running systems provide from production.

Without knowing of an alternative, architects would be under the impression that they'd need to make do with traditional architecture practices, depending on the same hierarchies and adhering to the same traditional cadences, ceremonies, toolkits, and intervention styles. These traditional architectural practices are problematic because they are rooted in power and control. The entire arsenal of legacy architectural tools, processes, and techniques is geared toward controlling certain aspects and keeping that control in the hands of a chosen few so that everything can be managed. This has led to a clash between traditional architecture practices and modern architectures that embrace decentralization and reward adaptability.

Let's take the time to properly examine the effect that traditional practices have on the needs of modern software architectures.

The Rise of Decentralization

As a result of the software revolutions, our software architectures have become increasingly decentralized. Decentralization allows for more robust and future-proof systems. There are three fundamental aspects of decentralization that support our modern software needs.

First, "decentralization" is not "distribution." *Distribution* is when you take something whole and split it into parts, which you then spread around. When you do this haphazardly, hoping that it will help performance, you can do more harm than good. I'm referring to the kinds of distributions where components are sliced apart and put on separate servers with little regard to their relatedness. Let's say you distribute a monolith with a poor microservices structure. Suddenly, performance drops through the floor, timeouts are happening everywhere, (distributed) transactions are either taking ages or continually rolling back, data is probably in an unpredictable state, and you need to make changes to 17 different repositories to make a simple functional change.

This form of distribution is a bad idea because parts that were once close together could be placed elsewhere without verifying if the parts could handle the separation. To address this, you might put the parts on two different threads of execution, which are given two different lifecycles, and force them to stay in sync over an unreliable and slow network connection. This isn't ideal either.

Decentralization, on the other hand, is when you identify coherent and complete elements that could be isolated and run separately from the greater whole. An example of this might be where you can separate logic that creates orders from logic that fulfills orders, enabling them to be packaged and deployed as separate microservices. This allows them to have their own lifecycles and respond in ways that are appropriate to them and them alone.

Second, by decentralizing, you, as an architect or developer, are surrendering centralized control and accepting that things will need to be managed in a different way. If you split things up without surrendering overall control, you're not decentralized— you're just distributed. Anything less than a full commitment to decentralization will make your life harder, not easier. In fact, with distribution or partial decentralization, you need to be much more aware of where control *is* needed so that you can focus on it and protect it but also minimize it, allowing elements that can be allowed to change independently to do so.

Take the languages and versions of frameworks that teams use when adopting a microservices approach, for example. One of the *great* benefits of microservices is that teams can make their own choices. As long as the microservices can run on the corporate cloud platform, send logs and metrics to the monitoring frameworks, and don't break any open source licenses, then the teams should be allowed to choose their own. This means that teams can move at their own pace, freed from having to match the pace of the slowest team, which is, despite best intentions, stuck on a Java 1.4 JVM due to a dependency on an ancient Xalan jar, which is needed because the biggest customer can't upgrade its old SOAP API because its last developer left years ago.

Third, decentralization *will* increase *overall* system complexity. Complexity is not the same as saying something is "complicated." A complicated situation can be tackled, typically by simplifying things. A complex situation has the potential to tip out of control. A complex situation emerges without anyone intending it to happen—both good things (like network effects) and bad things (like cascading systemic failures, such as the 2008 credit crunch)—because everything is interdependent.

In our incredibly networked world, complexity rules our systems. We surrendered control of the parts of our systems that didn't increase our competitive advantage (also known as "undifferentiated heavy lifting") in the form of our data centers, our customer relationship management (CRM) solutions, our SMS notifications, our web frameworks, and our continuous integration (CI) engines. And why shouldn't we? Why should we build and maintain these things ourselves when they give us no unique value? To have a sense of "control" is not a sufficient justification. As such, we embrace complexity to reap the benefits.

There are three aspects to this: how decentralization is best for teams, how decentralization is best for modern software, and how the benefits of both are realized only if these two decentralizations are aligned.

Teams work best when decentralized

Ask any software development professional—fresh and keen or seasoned and maybe a little skeptical—and they can tell you about the many, many hurdles between their code and the production environment. Who put those hurdles there? Perhaps the fault lies in the organization and its power structure. Perhaps it's in management. Perhaps it's on another team. Perhaps it's priorities. Perhaps it's a colleague. Perhaps (infrequently, though you do hear it) it's themselves.

Whatever the source of these hurdles (real or imagined), what these developers are specifically talking about are couplings that block flow. These couplings typically take one of two forms:[9]

- Work couplings ("I'm waiting for them to do their thing so I can do my thing.")
- Permission couplings ("I'm waiting to be told it's OK for me to do this thing.")

---

9 There is a third, weaker kind of coupling—information coupling—but this does not block. It causes ineffi-ciencies in other ways. See Vlad Khononov's talk "The Fractal Geometry of Software Design" (*https://oreil.ly/rrvIb*) for more on this topic.

These couplings that block are frequently the remnants of centralized, prerevolutionary approaches and practices, and they hurt most when applied to decentralized organizational structures and software architectures. Therefore, teams should use decentralized practices that came about with the various revolutions; to do one without the other is a recipe for failure. How can you achieve this? It's all there in the revolutions.

The Agile Manifesto principles (*https://oreil.ly/zTlds*), for instance, encourage us to: "Build projects around motivated individuals. Give them the environment and support they need, and trust them to get the job done." Various Agile and Lean methods then hint at how we might go about this. Complementing this is the broad range of DevOps practices, such as continuous delivery, which puts the power of building and running our software firmly back in the hands of those who write it, without the need to coordinate with other teams nor being forced to work at the cadence of a centralized release manager or change advisory board (CAB).

By applying decentralized practices, build-and-run teams can now see firsthand their code being put to the test in production. Product thinking paired with this real-world feedback allow us to see our software from a different perspective, through the eyes of the user. This in turn enables us to ensure that our work actually provides value— enough value that someone is willing to pay for it. And if we find that the product we are working on isn't valuable, we can change gears and work on building things that actually are valuable.

In essence, we are able to align our teams to our business or our product, which is exactly what thinkers such as Mel Conway[10] and Eric Evans[11] suggested decades ago. My colleague James Lewis also has a nice way to express this: "The business and its organization should be isomorphic."

By employing tools and practices brought forth by each successive revolution, we are incrementally shortening the time between the writing of our code and the moment when our code will be executed by an end user in production, and in doing so, we are incrementally increasing the power and actual usefulness of our code. We are also stepping (consciously or unconsciously) toward independent, self-managing,

---

10 Mel Conway introduced his idea in his 1968 paper "How Do Committees Invent?" (*https://oreil.ly/4RJf6*). The whole thing is worth reading, but the sentence that is quoted over and over is as follows: "Any organization that designs a system (defined broadly) will produce a design whose structure is a copy of the organization's communication structure." This has now become immortalized in the Inverse Conway Maneuver (*https://oreil.ly/SjcDF*), which advocates for organizing your software teams along the lines where you want your software to be split.

11 Eric Evans famously wrote in detail about aligning teams to one or more bounded contexts in the final section of his book *Domain-Driven Design: Tackling Complexity in the Heart of Software* (Addison-Wesley). His goal was to maintain model complexity and keep cognitive load low for the multiple teams building the software. Part of the goal of this was to reduce coupling and therefore allow teams to be more independent.

self-organizing, and self-sustaining teams, with everything they need to get the right running, tested code into production while driving value and learning from mistakes. Like it or not, this is the future of most software systems.

When they are done right, all these new tools and practices are profoundly beneficial. I've been involved in transformation after digital transformation where we broke down Taylorist silos[12] and erected benign boundaries based on user segmentation and domain cognitive load.[13] I've seen firsthand that reduced work and permission coupling improves flow and delivers the best software the most efficiently. It is also sustainable. Teams working in this way are happier and less burned out.[14]

Modern software works best when intentionally decentralized

For software to meet our demands, it has almost always needed to be connected to other components, often a database over some form of network. Once our software was connected to that first external component, splitting out further elements for various reasons didn't feel like a great leap. First, we put client code down on desktop PCs, and then, with the rise of the World Wide Web, we moved frontend code to a new "web tier" and then all the way down to browsers. These leaps weren't decentralization, though. Not yet. Decentralization came when we discovered that we could also consume external independent services for more functionality.

With the benefits of these independent external services, it became clear that decentralization seemed like a sensible idea. If we could slice our systems into small, independent pieces, we could realize systems that were potentially less susceptible to catastrophic failure and other plagues of tight coupling. If we minimize the coordination of various parts, then everything and everyone doesn't need to be in sync or agree all the time. Admittedly, this kind of decentralization makes everything more complex, but that complexity can be bounded (for example, by putting code for

---

12 During World War I, businesses in the United States and United Kingdom began to apply a theory of scientific management first developed by Frederick Winslow Taylor between 1885 and 1910. Intended for use in the systematic training of blue collar workers on a large scale, this system analyzed tasks and broke them down into individual, unskilled operations that could then be learned quite quickly. Despite the fact that it never really worked and that, more important, intense role-and-responsibility siloing was entirely unsuited to knowledge work, the technique took hold in Western management circles and remains there in mental models today. For more background, see Peter Drucker's essay "Management's New Paradigms" in collections such as *The Essential Drucker*.

13 Trond Hjorteland has a great LinkedIn post (*https://oreil.ly/rTFQm*) and accompanying talk (*https://oreil.ly/_cYAM*), both titled "Good Fences Make Good Neighbors," that go into the benefits of these benign boundaries.

14 It should come as no surprise to find that Dr. Nicole Forsgren, Jez Humble, and Gene Kim not only identified that teams that adopt the practices they laid out in *Accelerate* (O'Reilly) are more efficient but that they are happier and less burned out, too. I'd encourage you to read the entire book to understand this in depth, but the summary flow chart (*https://oreil.ly/4sCRb*) from the book lays it out very clearly.

different services in different repositories), and we could then reap the benefits of availability, resilience, performance, and scalability.

In 2000, I worked at Sun Microsystems in Linlithgow, Scotland. Every day, I would pass under a massive sign with the slogan "The network is the computer." Although it was revolutionary for a vendor to have this vision back then, it's now the reality of our world as consumers of various networked services as well as software professionals.

These days, all the biggest and most powerful software systems take advantage of these architectures, and no one thinks twice about architecting one consisting of various autonomous-from-the-outset subsystems—systems that bring in third-party services and expose APIs to teams outside our firewall and organization. We can confidently use message queues and pub/sub patterns and ensure that, when distributed globally across multiple, virtual (cloud) data centers, the right elements are kept in sync, but no more than is necessary.

Decentralized teams and their software must be aligned

"Rubbish!" I hear you cry. "We moved to continuous delivery, and it made everyone's lives a living nightmare! And don't get us started on microservices…"

I understand what you mean. Building a decentralized architecture is hard work. (I spend my life helping clients with this precise problem.) It's even harder if teams are not decentralized in parallel with that architecture—and impossible when the traditional approaches don't support the practice of architecture to realize it.

Decentralized teams deliver and run decentralized software. Decentralized software is delivered and run by decentralized teams. If the two are not aligned, then teams will be in a constant state of conflict, and coupling will abound. Perhaps it's a tautology to say it. But what sounds like common sense is, in my experience, far from common.

In his 1968 paper (*https://oreil.ly/Zy0pL*),[15] Conway said that the human and organizational aspects of software delivery do have a massive impact, but (because we're technologists) we put all our focus on the software and hope that the human part will take care of itself. But we humans can subconsciously put up a fight, sticking to our old, Taylorist worldviews. Whether you're an architect or a software developer, this book will give you the tools to facilitate alignment and collaboration on software architecture practices between architects and teams.

---

15 This is the second time I've mentioned Conway and his 1968 paper. It's only four pages long. I'd recommend you take the time to read what is an incredibly influential and prescient study.

The Fall of Centralized Architecture Practices

In "Teams work best when decentralized" on page 13 I touched on how decentralized teams reduce coupling and, therefore, block less. In other words, they make better use of their available resources, such as time. The same is true of software architecture itself. Let's look at the inverse: overly centralized software architectures are blocking and therefore inefficient.

Blocking—the method of pausing execution of a task while waiting for some condition to be met—can manifest in a software system in many different ways and in many different parts. (Remember the "work and permissions couplings" I mentioned previously? This is the software architecture equivalent.) For example:

- At the network level when awaiting responses from HTTP endpoints.

- At the database level when rows (or worse) are locked.

- At the OS level waiting for a process call to return.

- At the cluster level waiting for a quorum to be established or a new leader to be (s)elected.

- At the deployment level, when your work is not packaged as a single independent deployable and instead must make its way to prod as part of a bigger whole, you must block. In this case, you wait for everyone's automated tests to complete and the next deployment window.[16]

As professionals concerned with building, running, and sustaining a quality product, we need to ensure value for money. Blocking gets in the way of that because blocking is a source of great waste. Blocking creates queues and is a warning that, while one small set of resources is probably working very, very hard indeed, many other parts of the system may be idle, tapping their virtual fingers (and perhaps timing out) waiting for their turn to come.

As with decentralization, there are three aspects to the failures of centralized architecture practices: the blocking of delivery flow, the failure to factor in sufficient feedback, and the fact they are incompatible with decentralized architectures.

Traditional architecture practices block delivery flow

Now let's turn our attention to the human element in traditional architecture practices. Centralized software architecture practices are a prime cause of blocked delivery flow.

---

16 This is actually straying into the organizational world, but the reason for the blocking is still a technical coupling one. If the systems were technically decoupled, the software elements could be deployed independently.

These blocks turn up as bottlenecks around architects and the decision queues that consequently form in front of them, impeding the flow of work. I've seen these blocks to delivery flow even in innovative companies and in highly effective teams where technical skills are not in question. In the end, it comes down to poor use of resources arising from unnecessary permission coupling—in this case, waiting for an architectural decision or approval of one that has already been decided.

Why do the traditional practices of architecture cause this blocking? I believe it's because although we technologists are happy to think and act creatively over and over again in the name of technical optimization, we rarely use the same skills to think critically about ourselves and how our practices might be leading to human coupling and use that insight to challenge the existing status quo.

Why are we only now feeling the pain caused by these permission couplings in traditional architecture practices? Because the flow rate of software delivery has increased rapidly and significantly. Prior to the first revolution (Agile), running tested code was not seen as the primary goal, so we had longer to think. Prior to the second revolution (cloud), we had a pretty good idea what the runtime platforms would look like months or years in advance, so we could incorporate that into our designs. Prior to the third revolution (DevOps), deployments were larger and less frequent, so we could work in bigger chunks. Prior to the fourth revolution (product), we could rely more on a set of (relatively) static functional and cross-functional requirements. And prior to the fifth revolution (stream alignment), teams were aligned along technical rather than domain lines, so we had to context-swap less when running between them.

The cumulative result of the software revolutions to date is that more and more teams expect to take greater numbers of their independent features more frequently all the way through to production almost immediately and without any undue friction; to them, it feels perfectly natural. This is great news for product managers, who always want users to get their hands on the software. This incremental ratcheting up of deployment cadences, across more and more independent teams, means that the practice of architecture is called on in many places, all at once, over and over again.

Yet the traditional architectural practices still require all decisions to be passed through the eye of the architecture needle, to gain the mandatory "responsible architect's approval." While the aim of this was to allow the architects to deliver on the three goals of good architecture (appropriately coherent and cohesive, suitably decoupled, and sufficiently adaptable), it also means that architects are swamped. You can see this represented in Figure 1-4.

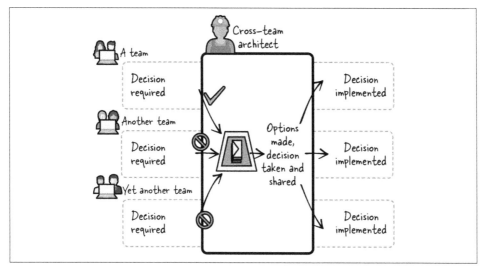

Figure 1-4. The blocking, serial nature of traditional approaches to architecture practice, illustrated here by the in-tray, racking up requests for the architect's involvement; the "tick" indicates the team the architect is currently working with, and the "no-entry" signs indicate the teams that also need input but are currently waiting

This means architects, who now are outnumbered by the amount of changes making their way to production on a regular basis, have two choices: do as little as possible and hope that the software teams deliver on good architectures on their own, or do enough to ensure the three goals are met in each and every change and block the flow in the process.

Architects trying to do architecture in the traditional ways are now the biggest blocker in more and more organizations because their practices cannot cope with the volume, variety, and cadence of changes brought about by the five revolutions given the size of systems today. (And that's without even trying to keep up with the pace of technological change.)

Traditional architecture practices fail to factor in sufficient feedback

Blocking is the first way that traditional architecture practices fail, but it is not the only one. They also famously fail to factor in sufficient feedback for the architects who use them (see Figure 1-5).

At the beginning of this chapter, I talked about how the ivory tower extreme of architecture practices fails to factor in sufficient feedback from teams. These practices contain painfully few built-in mechanisms to gather feedback that rolls up to architects and subsequently affects their decisions.

Hands-on architecture approaches came about in great part as a direct response to this problem after practitioners heard the howls of pain from teams and moved to remedy their problems. Hands-on practices have architects visiting teams that need their assistance, doing some co-design with team members, and perhaps even some pair programming on a bit of skeleton code. By doing so, they may experience how easy or hard a new feature is to implement in the existing codebase, and consequently, they are open to the feedback from the code.[17]

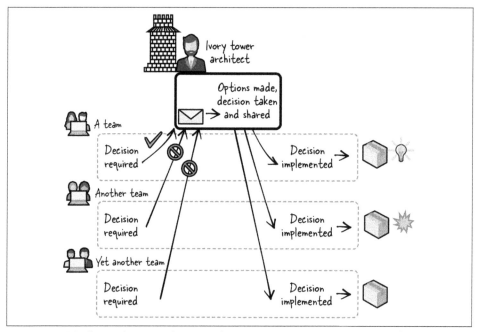

Figure 1-5. Traditional approaches to architecture practice are not aware of much of the feedback available arising from running systems, such as usage data and insights (the light bulb) and failures (the explosion)

This is a vast amount of information to ignore, and in the remaining sections of this chapter, I'll explain why it's *essential* to factor in feedback when decentralized software is being built by decentralized teams.

---

17 Even if the team is practicing DORA Elite levels of continuous deployment practice. By *DORA Elite*, I'm referring to the four levels of engineering effectiveness introduced by Forsgren et al., first in their annual "DORA State of DevOps" reports and subsequently in their book *Accelerate*. Of the four levels, Elite was the best. It meant you were in the top bracket across all surveyed in lead time for changes (short), deployment frequency (large), change failure rate (low), and mean time to recovery (short).

Traditional architecture practices are incompatible with a decentralized world

While we can build better systems faster as a result of the software revolutions, we can also deliver distributed software, which potentially exposes us to catastrophic failure modes, triggered by systems and individuals we have no awareness of, let alone control over. Software architecture is frequently the source of both success and failure.

Not only that, but a well-architected system can be hospitable to build and evolve, self-healing, elastically scalable, and incredibly resilient—able to operate even during partial failure. A poorly architected system, on the other hand, can be unmaintainable, debt ridden, expensively underperformant, and terribly brittle.

In a perfect world, hands-on architecture practitioners would be able to split their attention across all teams, giving them all individual attention, and still keep an eye on the architecture as a whole. In a perfect world, ivory tower architecture approaches would factor in feedback from everyone and everything. But we don't live in a perfect world, and ivory tower and hands-on architecture practices are both limited by their methods of engagement. Within a decentralized system, they both need to deal with all the independent moving parts and all the team relationships as well as address frequent changes to everything and anything.

Attempting centralized architecture approaches in a decentralized world is an impossible task. An alternative is needed.

What Must Any New Practice of Architecture Provide?

Whatever the approach, we need architectures that deliver on the three goals of good architecture. They must be appropriately coherent and cohesive, suitably decoupled, and sufficiently adaptable.

We need to go back to a blank sheet of paper on the drawing board and imagine other ways to achieve these ends. Specifically, we need a completely new—complementary—system where our architecture practices work with the dynamics and cadences of both our teams and our software systems, rather than fighting them. And as we have seen, this new system must have two key aspects: it must be decentralized, and it must incorporate feedback at its core.

It needs to be decentralized to allow independent teams to decide on architectures with minimal coordination. This means more architecture is happening in parallel. If you can do more architecture, you can unblock the writing of more code, optimize flow of delivery, and consequently have more of your architecture running.

It also needs to provide everyone with direct and rapid insight into the emergent properties of this architecture as it runs. This information must then be "fed back" directly into both architects and decentralized, independent teams, allowing everyone to cut through the complexity, understand it, and respond to it in terms of further architectural decisions and implementations.[18]

A new approach to architecture must factor in certain forces to be truly successful. Although no approach can protect against the forces of chaos, it should:

- Embrace uncertainty
- Allow for emergence

Let's work through each force, starting with what architecture practices cannot ever achieve.

No Approach Can Protect Against the Forces of Chaos

No architecture practice can protect against chaos. When I use the term *chaos*, I mean in the context of physics. According to the *Oxford English Dictionary*, chaos is "the property of a complex system whose behavior is so unpredictable as to appear random, owing to great sensitivity to small changes in conditions."[19]

I'm sure that definition of *chaos* sounds familiar to many architects and developers alike. Neither the architectures you conceive nor your teams that build them could be described as "predictable." Perhaps "appearing random" feels like a stretch, but I bet that if you were asked to list out all the factors that *might* have an impact on each and every system, and *then* tried to enumerate the potential ramifications of all of them, and *then* tried to think about the interactions of the results of all those interactions, you'd end up with way more than anyone could cope with. And those are only the factors you could think of. Things are combinatorially complex. Add just one more thing and the number of relationships it has with all the other existing things explodes.

What if we then asked your colleague? Would they come up with a few relationships that you'd forgotten? Inevitably.

It doesn't take many independent parts to unleash something far too complicated to reason about exhaustively, let alone predict how it is going to operate. Therefore, any new approach to architecture must not attempt to exhaustively predict how systems will operate and protect against all potential ramifications.

---

18 If this reminds you of techniques and approaches like John Boyd's OODA (observe, orient, decide, act) loop, sense and respond, build-measure-learn, continuous delivery, and everything laid out in the DORA State of DevOps report's four key metrics, then you're on the right track. My point is that we need to bring the practice of software architecture into line with all these other techniques.

19 *Oxford Dictionary of English* (2010), under "chaos."

Architectures Should Embrace Uncertainty

Decentralized architecture, as a combination of apparently simple elements, including independent teams and their independent software modules, gives rise to uncertainty. Where does that uncertainty come from? Variability. *Variability*, as I'll discuss in more detail in Chapter 13, refers to the unknowns in software development that need to be addressed—unknowns that are present *throughout* a system's cycle of evolution.

Consider this: you have a system that is made up of a collection of interacting components. These are not only the components of the software that you're building but also the teams that are building them, the tooling they use to deploy them, the processes used to work together to build and run them, the infrastructure they build and run on, and the external, third-party dependencies that the software depends on. These are all important parts in what is commonly referred to as the *sociotechnical system* that is engaged in building and running the software.

What Is a Sociotechnical System?

A *sociotechnical system* is a concept that recognizes the interaction between social and technological aspects in workplaces. It was originally coined by Eric Trist, Ken Bamforth, and Fred Emery during World War II, based on their work with English coal miners.

These days, with the rise of technology, the Interaction Design Foundation describes a *sociotechnical system* (*https://oreil.ly/CrYmh*) as "one that considers requirements spanning hardware, software, personal, and community aspects. It applies an understanding of the social structures, roles and rights (the social sciences) to inform the design of systems that involve communities of people and technology."

Even taken alone, each part is neither wholly understandable nor predictable. Each can be a source of variability. Combined, they get far worse because when you interact with something, you act on it, but it also acts on you. It's a two-way action, one that changes both parties.

Perhaps even now you are thinking, "But if I have two components, and one calls the other, I can predict the outcomes of that operation in my head." At this point, I need to highlight a most important concept that gives rise to system complexity.

Let's take an artificially simple scenario of A and B interacting. In this formulation, "A causes something to happen in B" is *linear* thinking. What happens in reality is that the consequent actions of B will also result in *something happening back in A*.

For example, let's imagine we're talking purely about a technical system: a synchronous interaction such as an HTTP GET. After it sends the request, A will be waiting

---

for B to respond. If B has what A wants, then A will receive it, probably in the form of a "200 OK" response with a payload. If it does not, then A will have to respond to those eventualities too: "404 not found," "500 internal server error," and so forth.

Even under this "normal operation" scenario, you can see that there are a few things going on. We have to add only a few other possibilities for things to get complicated. What if B takes a long time to respond, and before it does, A performs a retry? B is now (potentially) performing the operation for A two times over. Does it give A two of the things it requested? Or does it give A the same thing twice?

Perhaps, instead of a retry, A stops waiting and goes off to try another way to achieve its goal. That means that when B eventually returns the thing to A, A isn't around to do anything with it. What does B do then? Does it care? Does it put some resources back in the pool? Does it even know that A didn't care any more?

By asking these questions, we are opening our complicated, artificial, tech-only world up to the sociotechnical world around it. Why did B take a long time to reply? Was it because it was already loaded with other requests? Similarly, why did A stop waiting? Was it because its needs were met elsewhere? Or did it simply get bored? You can see that, even from this incredibly simple example, there's a lot that we need to think about when things interact, and our systems are never this simple.

But there's more. If we add further well-understood components to the picture, each of them has the potential to interact with all the others in a myriad of different ways, and maybe not even directly. Here's an interesting exercise to try: introduce some latency to a single part of any system you currently run. It doesn't matter if the part is trivial or if it's on the periphery. See what happens. You might be surprised at how simply slowing down one thing can break seemingly unrelated things.[20]

Any new approach to architecture must acknowledge—even incorporate—information from as many of these component interactions as possible to respond to the variable, unpredictable eventualities that inevitably arise.

Architectures Should Allow for Emergence

What could be more surprising than coming across properties in a software system that you didn't design? Properties that didn't arise from a single part and instead come into being because of the interaction of multiple parts?

This phenomenon is generally called *emergence,* which can be described as follows: when an entity is observed to have properties its parts do not have on their own, properties or behaviors that emerge only when the parts interact in a wider whole.

---

20 It might not come as a surprise to learn that "Latency Monkey," which does exactly this, is a less famous member of the Netflix "Simian Army" of chaos engineers.

Emergence can manifest in two different ways, which are distinguished as *strong* and *weak*. Both are important in how we architect our systems.

Strong emergence is where we live and work as software professionals every day. It is the phenomenon where a new, higher-level entity is created by the combination of multiple, separate elements. This higher-level entity *emerges* from the combination of these individual parts. A car is a good example of this, or a human body, or a distributed software system.

Weak emergence also happens to us all the time, but it is different in two key aspects: it is only self-evident after the fact, and the individual parts remain independent when it acts. Let me give you a real-world example to help you grasp this idea.

I once worked on a system that exposed APIs to a number of well-known online retailers, such as eBay. Our APIs allowed eBay's sellers to buy postage-paid shipping labels as per their customers' shipping requests. Our APIs were simple, as were the few microservices that sat behind them. My team felt smart because, when planning, architecting, and performance testing, we had the demands of Black Friday in mind. We knew traffic around that time would be the greatest our system would have to endure, and we did a bunch of stress testing specifically to ensure we could be confident the system would be able to cope.

What we *didn't* know—and thus didn't plan, architect, or test for—was the more regular, far lower volume, and, frankly, much less exciting behavior cycle of eBay sellers. It was this client behavior that gave rise to some simple but interesting emergent behavior that we could not have predicted.

eBay sellers in the UK, it turns out, tended to make their auctions end sometime during the weekend, and then to catch the first post on Monday, they would buy the shipping labels from us on a Sunday evening. This meant we would see a spike in requests regularly every Sunday. The graphs were beautiful to behold, but that wasn't the emergent part.

For some labels, the seller would want to include a tracking number. Tracking numbers are a finite resource, so we needed to be doubly careful that we didn't hand the same number out on two stamps. You can imagine the confusion if a purchaser looked to see where their parcel was and saw it headed to someone else's house, purely as the outcome of some race condition. Consequently, it's easier to create a pool of tracking numbers and then hand them out as required.

One day, a month or so after go-live, we were conducting our regular maintenance checks and took a look at the tracking numbers database. It had *way* more tracking numbers in an unavailable state than we thought it should (based on how many tracked parcel labels we knew we'd sold). We'd been bleeding tracking numbers, but how?

Upon closer examination, we realized that there were whole ranges of tracking numbers in the database that were stuck in the "reserved" state. These were the tracking numbers that were provided for use in labels but the confirmation of their usage had never been returned. When we looked deeper, we could see that the reserved timestamps corresponded with the Sunday-evening postage peaks, and looking *even* closer, we saw that these were happening at the start of the ramp-up of requests. What was happening?

It turned out to be the result of a "clever" thing we'd done: we built in an elastic scaling capability for our services so that we would have the right number of instances running when we needed them. What was happening was that, as we scaled all the services rapidly, the system would issue more requests from client microservices than the tracking number service could cope with. Some of these requests would time out, and the calling client microservices would consequently issue retries. Those retries would reserve another tracking number, and everything would then proceed as planned, ultimately marking this new tracking number as "used." There was one small issue. The failed requests left the tracking numbers they'd been using in a "reserved" state. We'd forgotten to build a mechanism to put those reserved tracking numbers back into the pool if no one came back to mark them as "used" within a certain time.

These chunks of reserved tracking numbers in the database were an emergent property of the running of this simple set of components. I'll not go into the fix, but it was a simple one. (You're probably in your head right now telling me how you'd do it.) Rather, let's focus on the three things you should take away from this example.

First, once you see them, weak emergent effects are not hard to understand. (When observed, emergence rarely is.) What is surprising is that, prior to seeing it, the possibility of it had never even entered your mind.

Second, it's not hard to work with it once you see a weak emergent effect in operation.

Third, the emergence in this example happened precisely because we believed we'd thought of all eventualities—and we'd thought of a lot of them. What we saw was caused by the interaction between the elements we had put into the system and the users.

You can map this anecdote to the definition that I gave for *emergence* earlier. First, the fact that emergence creates in systems "properties its parts do not have on their own" is the predictable reserved-but-not-reclaimed pattern we could see in our data store. Second, "emerge only when the parts interact" is the result of a set of factors: the rate of the auto scaling, the nature of the response times from the tracking number service, the duration of the request timeout, the subsequent retries, and the fact that we never thought to reclaim the tracking numbers. All of these played their roles in the pattern we saw.

We could not have architected for this specific weak emergence in advance. You'll notice that we did think of things—the failures, for instance—and had put in retries and the need to scale instances horizontally based on rising load, but those in turn had created effects in combination with other elements. Despite your best efforts, weak emergence will happen again and again, both where you expect it and where you don't.

The more you chase things, the more unforeseen emergent events will come to the surface in the form of variability from the expected functioning. This is because the systems we build operate in unpredictable ways, and these emergent effects will always happen. It is not just hard to foresee all possibilities—it is impossible.

So we should stop trying to predict how our systems will run in the wild. Instead, any new approach to architecture should optimize for running architecture in systems in production as soon as possible and respond to the emergent effects as they arise.

Conclusion

My goal in this chapter was to describe the pain that traditional approaches to architecture practice cause. I took you through the challenges of trying to impose traditional centralized architecture practices in a world that favors decentralization.

As decentralization increases, traditional architectural practices incrementally overindex on aspects that are less and less likely to succeed and underindex on what needs to be happening more and more.

Traditional software architecture practices cannot cope with either revolutionary delivery cadences or emergence. We need to stop thinking slowly and linearly because the systems we build are rapid and nonlinear. We need a new way to approach architecture.

This new approach to architecture should incorporate decentralization and rapid, constant feedback. It should acknowledge that chaos and complexity are inevitable, and it should accept that emergence cannot be fought, only embraced.

In Chapter 2, I'll discuss what must lie at the heart of all approaches to software architecture: architectural decisions. It is only by understanding decisions that alternative ways to practice architecture begin to make sense.

First Principles

The opening chapter of this book offered both a revolutionary explanation for why the traditional approaches to the practice of software architecture are feeling increasingly hard and a new approach to resolve it. The first part of this book will now describe a way to practice architecture in this postrevolutionary world.

Chapter 2 kicks us off by looking at the key aspect of how *decisions* affect how we practice architecture: specifically, the types of decisions, when they are significant enough to pay attention to, and when they aren't.

The problem defined, Chapter 3 goes on to describe all of the traditional *approaches* for deciding at scale before evaluating them in light of our current need: decentralized deciding and fast feedback. None of the traditional *options* could support both of these, but the analysis clarifies the requirements for a decision process that could.

Chapter 4 then introduces the *architecture advice process*: an approach that optimizes for both decentralized deciding and fast feedback at scale.

But how might you make such a change, and what might the *consequences* of such a change be? Chapter 5 considers *adoption of the advice process*: what you need, where to start, challenges you will likely need to overcome, and confidence concerns that will likely arise.

Chapter 6 then proceeds to tackle these concerns, taking the already established concept of *architectural decision records (ADRs)* and showing how they are an essential tool for trust building and organizational learning when rolling out the advice process.

By the end of Part I, you'll understand the basics of how the advice process works and how it is underpinned by the social contract. You'll be aware of the role of decisions in software architecture and how ADRs are an essential, trust-building and learning complement to that practice. You'll then be ready to consider how additional elements can support your decentralized architectural practice and center feedback.

CHAPTER 2

To Practice Architecture Is to Decide

We need now to dig into the fundamental element that underpins any approach to software architecture: decisions. This chapter will define clearly what architectural decisions are. Chapter 3 will then cover how we decide, individually and in groups.

Before I start, I'd like you to do something for me. Close your eyes. Imagine a software architecture decision being made. When you open your eyes again, consider the following:

- What images came to mind?

- Was it you or someone else or several people doing the deciding?

- Was the decider "high up" in the organization and "handing down" the decision? Or were they below you? Or were they a peer?

- What age was the person? Were they older, younger, or a similar age? Did you even notice that?

- What tech skills do they have? Are they the same as yours, or are theirs stronger or weaker? Have they programmed? What was the language? Is that a language that you know? Have they run their code in production? At what scale?

- Were they from the same background as you? What about their outlook and experience—were they the same as yours? If they were not the same, in what ways were they different?

Keep your answers in mind as you go through this chapter and explore what makes an "architectural" decision important. Along the way, I'll highlight the common assumptions about decisions that can cloud our thinking. You may be surprised at how your current vision of deciding in software architecture has changed.

Decisions Are the Core of Software Architecture

Regardless of which approach you use, to practice software architecture is to work with decisions. Software architectures are full of decisions—so many decisions that you may not always realize they're there. When building software, you need to decide how you want something to be structured, how you want the process to work for that something, and so forth. You even need to decide if your team should use resources from a third party, such as an open source library.

Software architectures are in this respect the sum of all architectural decisions made during the entirety of their development lifecycle.[1] The rise of evolutionary architectures[2] means that architectural decisions are happening over and over again, throughout the lifespan of the system, eternally and unpredictably. That's a lot of decisions, all piled up one on top of the other, each an ossified record of the power structures and feedback loops (or lack of them) that got it there.[3]

Therefore, it's critical that everyone, those doing the architecting and those writing the code, has a firm grasp of what a decision *is* in software architecture and *how they come about*. Having such an understanding fosters a better alignment across teams and helps everyone make better choices. There are a few steps on this journey, and the first step is to be clear about what makes something an architectural decision as opposed to simply a technical decision. As Figure 2-1 shows, all architectural decisions are technical decisions, but not all technical decisions are architectural ones.

---

1 To be clear, I'm talking specifically here about decisions that are architectural and not decisions that have architectural impacts. That's not to say that the latter don't have a significant impact.

2 See *Building Evolutionary Architectures* by Neal Ford, Rebecca Parsons, Patrick Kua, and Pramod Sadalage (O'Reilly).

3 I wrote a Twitter thread about the topic: "Thoughts on the anthropology of software (power and freedom special edition)" (*https://oreil.ly/lFGmX*).

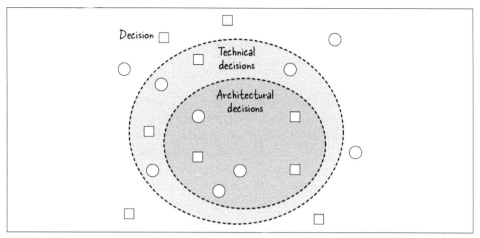

Figure 2-1. All architectural decisions are technical decisions, but not all technical decisions are architectural ones

What Constitutes an Architectural Decision?

The *Cambridge Dictionary* defines a *decision* as "a choice that you make about something after thinking about several possibilities."[4] So what's an *architectural* decision?[5]

A quick web search will turn up *many* definitions of what software architecture is, and almost as many definitions of an architectural decision. But of all the definitions out there, I've found that Michael Nygard's, from his 2011 blog post "Documenting Architecture Decisions" (*https://oreil.ly/qnsXK*), has been the most useful to me when practicing software architecture, primarily because it's simple to understand and easy to remember.

He states: "…'architecturally significant' decisions:[6] *those that affect the structure, non-functional characteristics, dependencies, interfaces, or construction techniques*" [emphasis mine]. This definition lists five criteria that identify an architectural decision. Let's add a little more detail to each in turn.

---

4 *Cambridge Dictionary*, "decision" (*https://oreil.ly/zL1sl*), accessed April 28, 2023.

5 Other decisions might be product decisions, financial decisions, hiring decisions, organizational structure/staffing decisions, and so forth. While all are important, it's only architectural decisions that I'm concerned with here.

6 I'll come back to the significance of architecturally significant decisions a bit later in this chapter. Just consider the definition as a whole for now.

Structure

First, structural decisions are architectural. This seems self-evident, as it refers to the arrangement of the parts of a software system, what each does, and how they interact (or not).

The more decentralized an architecture, the more evident the "parts" are, not least because the interactions between them are typically over a network (via HTTP or a message queue, for example). However, the structural "parts" aspect applies equally in other architectural styles. "Parts" are just as much the modules in the "modular monolith" as they are a collection of microservices, and there are still connections between them, though these are less obvious within runtime function calls.

Cross-Functional Characteristics

As you work on any piece of software, you will discover that you cannot capture all the characteristics (or requirements) using a purely functional format. There are characteristics you need from your systems that simply won't fit into a standard, single-function user story[7] or use case[8] format. Some requirements simply don't define a specific instance of something. What, for example, about performance requirements? And security? And regulations? And scalability? And operability? And usability? And resilience? And cost to operate?

I could go on. Rather than specifying behaviors of things, these types of requirements allow you to judge the operation of the overall system.

These characteristics are also widely referred to as "nonfunctional requirements" or "quality attributes." Those two terms are not without their problems.[9] Nygard refers to them less problematically as "nonfunctional characteristics," but there's still the "non," which implies a lack of something. In this book, I'll use the term *cross-functional characteristics* that are specified with cross-functional requirements (aka CFRs) as I believe it more accurately represents needs I have fulfilled that apply *across a system*.

---

7 The best intro to user stories can be found in Chapter 6 of Jeff Patton and Roy McCrerey's *User Story Mapping* (O'Reilly, 2014).

8 Use cases were commonly used before extreme programming (XP) popularized user stories. First proposed by Ivar Jacobson at OOPSLA 1987, use cases were core to diagramming notation UML and the rational unified process (RUP). They are a more heavyweight, documentation-driven way of capturing user requirements for software.

9 The problem is that some of them are arguably functional—some regulatory requirements, for instance. My Thoughtworker colleague Sarah Taraporewalla coined the term *cross-functional* (*https://oreil.ly/PmE4t*) not only to avoid this problem but also to combat the issue that "non" gave people the impression that these requirements were somehow less important than the functional requirements. Now both terms are in use, largely interchangeably. Another one popular among the older generation is FURPS+. Again, it's not great (the "+" is kind of a copout), but at the time, people mostly knew what was meant.

A decision that responds to these types of needs is also architectural. The architecture of a system that targets a concurrent user count of 10 compared with one that targets tens of thousands of concurrent users would be vastly different.

Dependencies

I like to think of *dependencies* as things your system interacts with *that you do not control*. This lack of control may be because this system is a service provided by a third party. Or it's a platform that you run on (such as the container provided by a framework like Drupal, or a runtime .NET Common Language Runtime, or an operating system). Or even if it's an API offered by a team in another department of the same company. All of them create the same issue: you have little to no control over their work backlog and the priority of items on it. So you need to think about how you connect to and communicate with dependencies, and the decisions that result are architectural.

Interfaces

Interfaces are the flip side of dependencies, and they are equally, yet differently, important. Unlike a dependency, an *interface* is when your software is being consumed by another party. When you are exposing an interface, you are the one who has people depending on you to achieve their goals. Although you have full control over your backlog, you must be careful here. Even small changes to your APIs can break your consumer's integrations, forcing them to make changes. Consequently, decisions that affect the interface your system exposes to others are architectural.

Relationships Between Systems Can Be Two-Way

Sometimes your system and another will be mutually dependent. Your system will be consuming an interface on a system that is doing the same back to you. If that sounds complicated and a bit of a nightmare to manage, you're right—it is. Multidirectional relationships can rapidly become hellish because everyone needs to think about their architecture from both angles.

Construction Techniques

Finally comes *construction techniques*, which is possibly why I love Nygard's definition of architectural decisions so much. Nygard was one of the early proponents of architecting for "build and run"[10] in his book *Release It!* (Pragmatic Bookshelf), so it's no surprise that he would acknowledge construction techniques in his definition.

In the intervening decade or more since the beginnings of each of the software revolutions I described in Chapter 1, more and more learnings have been piled into both the tools and the techniques that software is built and released with. As a consequence of changing construction techniques, the architectures of our systems themselves have changed.

How so? Let me explain.

It was back in 2005 when I first saw the impact of evolved construction techniques. I had joined a J2EE-based project,[11] and the code was broken into modules in ways that would be called "hexagonal," "onion," or "ports and adapters" architecture (*https://oreil.ly/81DWm*). This meant that there were explicit "domain" packages that had no dependencies on the standard Java EE libraries. Why had we done this? For testability. In those days, spinning up a J2EE server locally on your dev machine to run some automated tests could take 25 minutes. Most of the "smarts" were in these domain packages. This is what we wanted to test the most extensively, and to achieve that, we needed the tests to run quickly. By isolating these packages, we could spin up the tests for the key elements without having to spin up the associated infrastructure. It worked. When working on functionality in the core, we could work in a red-green-refactor, test-driven development style, with a 10- to 15-second feedback loop. Rapidly and safely.

Since 2005, other extreme programming (XP) practices (*http://www.extremeprogramming.org*) have become standard (continuous deployment in particular[12]), realizing the benefits of the "new physics." Now we can get code all the way to production and in front of customers incredibly rapidly, and incredibly frequently. The benefits of this are well known, and I touched on them in the discussion of the five revolutions in Chapter 1. The point is, to be able to continuously deploy your software, you need

---

10 This concept is widely accepted to have been popularized by Werner Vogels, Amazon CTO, in a 2006 interview (*https://oreil.ly/3EfOD*) with ACMQueue. In it, he stated: "The traditional model is that you take your software to the wall that separates development and operations, and throw it over and then forget about it. Not at Amazon. You build it, you run it. This brings developers into contact with the day-to-day operation of their software. It also brings them into day-to-day contact with the customer. This customer feedback loop is essential for improving the quality of the service."

11 The project was based two blocks up the road from the site of the Buncefield explosion (*https://oreil.ly/TmCnb*), so it's memorable in more ways than one.

12 See *Continuous Deployment* by Valentina Servile (O'Reilly, 2024) for everything you need to know about the topic.

---

to use certain construction techniques, and you need to make certain architectural choices to be able to work in this way. For example, using a tool like LaunchDarkly (*https://launchdarkly.com*) to manage release toggles will never be a feature that is exposed to your end users (it is arguably a failure if they ever notice its presence), but it is something that affects your code.

Using feature toggles, continuous deployment, and therefore pipelines—and much, much more—comes under the heading of "construction techniques," and such decisions are architectural because they change how we shape our software.

Should I Care Where Platforms, Languages, Frameworks, and Libraries Sit?

While you can debate whether choices of platform, language, frameworks, and libraries best fit the structure or construction technique criteria, they are clearly important, wherever they sit under Nygard's five criteria for architectural decisions. In most cases, the argument could be made for both. In some cases, they might even come under the cross-functional characteristics heading. Irrespective of how you choose to classify them, choices of platforms, languages, frameworks, and libraries definitely fit the definition of architectural decisions.

Some Examples of Architectural and Nonarchitectural Decisions

As discussed, architectural decisions have to meet one or more of these five criteria: they have to affect structure, cross-functional characteristics, dependencies, interfaces, and/or construction techniques. Let's practice making these determinations by looking at the following lists, which show architectural decisions and nonarchitectural decisions.

Architectural decisions

Structure

How to split a module and what the new boundaries will be

Which teams will own which services (While this is an organizational design/staffing decision, it is now widely accepted that this will have a direct impact on the resulting structure)

Cross-functional characteristics

The format everyone will use to write their logs and where these logs will be sent for collection

How you will horizontally scale (or not—other forms of scaling are available) various aspects of your system

Dependencies
> How to integrate with a new third-party API

Interfaces
> How to expose functionality or data via an API or message queue (either to another team you are working with or to an unknown future third party)

Construction techniques
> Which contract testing framework to use

> How to use release toggles

Dependencies, likely structure, and quite possibly cross-functional characteristics
> An upgrade to a new major version of a framework you are using[13]

Dependencies and most likely cross-functional characteristics
> Which type of virtual compute primitive to use from your cloud provider

Nonarchitectural decisions

Not cross-functional characteristics
> Which tuning parameters to pass to your virtual machine's garbage-collection routine. (This will be expected to change over the life of the system. While you might architect things so that you have a great deal of flexibility in this area, the changing of these settings is not an architectural decision.)

> Whether you horizontally scale to 5, 7, or 30 instances of part of your system. (This is simply the side effect of the system being scaled.)

Not interfaces
> Which customer segment you will target from a set of possible options. (This is a business/product decision.)

Not construction techniques
> Which IDE developers should use. (This should have no impact on the architecture of the system. It is an individual developer decision.)

> Deciding whether developers pair program on a user story. (This is a team practice decision. They may choose to pair more on architecturally significant user stories, however.)

> What naming convention you want to apply to the folders and files. (This should have no impact on the structure of the system.)

---

13 I realize that you have probably had the opposite experience. This is a case of failing to adhere to the Semantic Versioning principles (*https://semver.org*). It states, at the very top of the site, that *major* versions are when a framework makes incompatible API changes.

Not dependencies or construction techniques

Which unit testing library you are going to use. (How you architect your system for unit testing is unlikely to change if you change your specific unit testing library, though the tests themselves will undoubtedly change.)

Which performance testing tool you are going to use—again, this is outside the system. (While you might architect in a way to make performance testing easier, the choice of software to drive the load is not an architectural decision.)

Who Makes These Architectural Decisions?

Before we continue, let's return to our visualization exercise. Who did you picture as making the architectural decisions in the previous subsection? You probably envisioned an architect or staff or principal engineer for most of them. But for others, such as the contract testing framework, it could actually be someone on the development team—a quality assurance engineer (QA), for example. Take note of this. Architectural decisions can be made by anyone, not just those with "architect" in their job title.

Next up, let's refine our criteria for architectural decisions to focus on the ones that are *significant*.

Architecturally Significant Decisions

When software systems are constructed, delivered, run, and evolved, architectural decisions are happening all the time, but not all of them have the same impact.

Although decisions made by architects *ought to be* architecturally significant, it's important to understand that developers can make significant architectural decisions, too. That means you can't determine if a decision is worth paying attention to simply based on the involved parties or as a result of how long it took them to decide.

Let's sharpen the five architectural decision criteria from before so that they define architecturally *significant* decisions.

What Makes an Architectural Decision "Significant"?

Just as all technical decisions are not architectural, not all architectural decisions are equally important or impactful. See Figure 2-2.

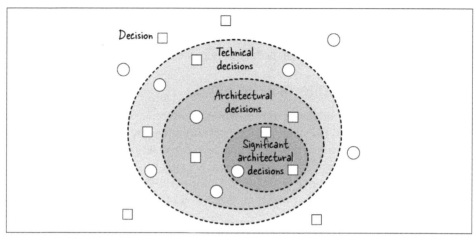

Figure 2-2. Not all architectural decisions are "significant"

You can determine if an architectural decision is significant if it meets more focused versions of the previous criteria—structure, cross-functional characteristics, dependencies, interfaces, or construction techniques—in an outstanding way. It's somewhat straightforward to identify a significant architectural decision based on three of the criteria (dependencies, interfaces, and construction techniques) because the magnitude of their impact is reliably predictable, so let's start there.

Your architectural decision is significant if you add:

- A completely new dependency, or (for an existing dependency) you upgrade by a major version with the same vendor, or there is a complete vendor change

- A new API to your interface, or you make any change in your API that would constitute a major version upgrade for your consumers[14]

- A new construction technique to a production environment (such as canary releases or blue-green deployments) or as a step in the pipeline(s)

It's trickier to identify a significant architectural decision based on the remaining two criteria (structure and cross-functional characteristics) because the magnitude of their impact is harder to quantify. Significant structural architectural decisions

---

14 Semantic Versioning (*https://semver.org*) has a nice way of thinking about when something is a "major version change" or not.

typically relate to either the *placement of function* (where some logic or responsibility for something is located) or the decision to start (or stop) using a new design pattern or a higher-level architectural pattern.

Design Patterns

By *pattern*, I'm referring to widely known and reusable solutions for commonly observed problems in software structure. By *design pattern*, I mean the concept that entered the widespread software development consciousness with the publishing of *Design Patterns* by Erich Gamma, Richard Helm, Ralph Johnson, and John Vlissides (O'Reilly) in 1994. Further works built on this, such as the *Pattern-Oriented Software Architecture* series (Wiley), Martin Fowler's *Patterns of Enterprise Architecture* (Pearson Education), Eric Evans's *Domain-Driven Design: Tackling the Complexity at the Heart of Software* (Addison-Wesley), Gregor Hohpe's *Enterprise Integration Patterns* (Addison-Wesley), and Bill Wilder's *Cloud Architecture Patterns* (O'Reilly). All these books introduced not only more design patterns but also architectural patterns. I highly recommend that you check them out, although there is no need to commit them all to memory. I certainly haven't.

So an architectural decision is significant (in a structural way) if it involves locating some key logic or responsibility in a specific place or a decision to start or stop using any one or more of the established design patterns described in the books listed in the "Design Patterns" sidebar.

Finally, we come to the hardest of the five criteria to define: those decisions that affect cross-functional characteristics. I mentioned previously how the term *cross-functional characteristics* covers a broad and disparate collection of nebulous concepts, but that's not why it's difficult to define what makes a cross-functional characteristic significant. They're difficult to define when the cross-functional requirements behind them are poorly defined. Once you clarify those CFRs, the cross-functional characteristics will be easier to define, and their significance will be a lot easier to state.

So how do you obtain this clarity of definition in CFRs? State your intended cross-functional requirements exactly as you would any other requirements: by scoping them clearly, articulating their value, and defining their acceptance criteria.

Unsurprisingly perhaps, a nice way to do this is with the standard user story form. First, for the value:

EXAMPLE

"As a [ROLE]…I want to [ACTION]…so that [VALUE]."

And then the acceptance criteria:

EXAMPLE
"Given [CIRCUMSTANCES]…when [EVENT]…then [OUTCOME]."

Once you have taken the time to achieve this level of detail, you stand a fighting chance of knowing if something is significant. (I'll return to this means of capturing CFRs in much greater detail in Chapter 8, but this is sufficient for now.)

An architectural decision is significant if it alters our ability to meet one or more CFRs. For example, assume I have the following CFR:

EXAMPLE
As a customer
I want my search results within 500 milliseconds
So that I can find what I want quickly
Given the site is experiencing normal levels of search requests
When a customer submits a search request
Then the system responds 99% of the time with valid search results within 500 ms

If I am making a decision that will endanger my ability to meet the acceptance criteria, then it is significant.

Taken together, an architectural decision is therefore "significant" if it meets one or more of the five criteria for a decision to be architectural.

What Shouldn't Be Considered Regarding Architectural Significance?

It's time to look at the flip side: what *shouldn't* be considered regarding architectural significance?

Let's compare two examples.

First, imagine a developer is working on some code, and they see that a dependency is out of date but only by a bug-fix version. They decide to update it by running the build script, but what they don't realize is that this accidentally upgrades a bunch of other transitive dependencies at the same time, and one of those dependencies has changed their open source license from MIT (which the InfoSec department is fine with) to GPL v3.0 (which they're not fine with because of it's so-called viral nature).[15]

Second, imagine an architect following a long, detailed, and technically involved process considering the decision to move a core part of a system from a relational to a document data store (specifically from MySQL to MongoDB). In doing this, they involve many experts, do some tests, and conduct a great deal of research, even engaging both the vendors in a "bake-off"[16] competition to see how their products perform under realistic data volumes and load profiles.

So what can be learned from these two examples? There are three lessons.

The first lesson, which I've been alluding to this whole time, is that anyone can decide on something architecturally significant. Although architects most often decide, they aren't the sole source of decisions; developers can decide, too. You can't determine if a decision is significant simply based on who the involved parties are. Therefore, both of these examples are architecturally significant, irrespective of who was involved. (The theme of how everyone can decide is central to this book and will pop up time and time again.)

The second lesson is that the length of time taken in the decision process is irrelevant. The long, drawn-out process to select a new data store to replace some existing MySQL one is irrelevant. It is distinctly possible that in other circumstances, this decision might be taken by a CTO or their chief architect in a few seconds, purely based on their personal prejudices and preferences. Likewise, the instantaneous nature of the "decision" to use the GPL-licensed dependency would have been no more or less significant had it been subjected to days of scrutiny. Both these examples are architecturally significant, irrespective of how long they took to decide.

The third lesson is that a decision doesn't need to be deliberate for it to be architecturally significant. Again, recall the accidental addition of the GPL-licensed dependency. This change was an accident. It would be easy to miss because nothing would tell you it happened. The build will still work, and the code will still do what it's supposed to.

All these elements are irrelevant with regard to the decision's significance. Both examples are architecturally significant, irrespective of the awareness of the decision the responsible parties had.

---

15 In this case, the avoidance of the GPL v3.0—or even all "viral" open source licenses—ought to be captured as a CFR and ideally tested for in the pipeline.

16 A *bake-off* is a colloquial term for a contest between companies to win a contract. It has since been made famous by the UK TV show *The Great British Bake-Off* (confusingly known as *The Great British Baking Show* in North America).

Architectural Significance in Relation to Deployed Software

So we have our criteria for significance: outstanding decisions regarding structure, cross-functional characteristics, dependencies, interfaces, and construction techniques. We also have clarity on factors that are irrelevant: who is deciding, how long the deciding takes, and whether it was conscious or not. But it is important to bring to prominence another aspect hiding behind them all. In this revolutionized world, decisions are only significant when you bear in mind how they relate to deployed software: either in relation to a system's path to production or its qualities when it gets there.

This might seem arbitrary, so let me explain. Recall the example of the developer who added a new GPL-licensed dependency that reached production. Imagine now, that before they updated their dependencies, the developer added a dependency scanner to the pipeline (which undertook the build, validation, and deployment). This scanner would catch the license violation and fail the build. The transitive dependency would never reach production. This conscious and significant decision on the part of the developer meant that the "accidental" decision wasn't significant. The architecturally significant decision to add the scanner and configure it to capture GPL-licensed transitive dependencies, on the other hand, was significant.

What if you're not yet delivering anything to production at all? In those circumstances, you should look out for decisions that are actively getting in the way of your software making its way into production. Those decisions are significant in a negative way.

I say this because, up to the point that your architectural decisions are reflected in deployed software, they aren't yet decisions at all: they are *aspirations, the code merely a collection of schematics.* In these circumstances, I'd seriously recommend you get your architecture into production as rapidly as possible. There is always a way to manage this, except in the *most challenging circumstances,* and 99.99% of us don't face these. (I'd encourage you to constantly be asking "How can we ship this right now?" rather than "Why can't I ship this?") If you need new or different decisions to do so, then so be it. At this point, you might realize some of your architecturally significant decisions are actually getting in the way of this. If you don't try to get to prod, then you have no means of knowing about this negative aspect.

Recall the experience I shared earlier where the development team had used domain-driven design techniques to structure the code so that the majority of it could be tested locally and without any J2EE server being started up? That benefit made its way through to the pipelines, too. If this decision had gone another way, and testing both locally and in the pipeline had been hard, then that would have been considered significant. Significantly bad, but significant all the same. The subsequent decision by developers to use the hexagonal architecture to allow local testing, which could also be run in the pipelines, was instrumental in getting the code out into production.

Prior to it being in production, the hoped-for benefits of the J2EE server at runtime were just that, hoped for and not yet realized, but their negative impacts at build time were being mitigated.

It is for this reason that I consider the construction techniques criteria of architecturally significant decisions as important as all the others. Construction techniques ensure that focus is given to this important aspect as much as to any of the other four criteria. This serves to balance out, at least in part, the bias the others have away from the runtime.

Decisions About Product and Team Alignment

To keep this chapter focused, I've intentionally ignored two sources of influence on architectural decisions:

- Product management/the business
- Whoever decides on the alignment of teams to work

It is unarguable that a product decision can have a direct impact on software architecture. The same can be said for a staffing or team-alignment decision.

To avoid confusion, consider these decisions that affect software architecture *as if they were architectural*. Treat them in the same way as all other architectural decisions, and the approaches that I will lay out for facilitating these are entirely applicable. A product manager can take decisions that have an architectural impact, but in an ideal world, they will be conscious of this and involve the relevant parties when they do so.

Some Examples of Significant Architectural Decisions

Architecturally significant decisions are impactful because they meet one or more of our five enhanced criteria: they affect the structure, cross-functional characteristics, dependencies, interfaces, and/or construction techniques. They also get into code.

Let's close with some more examples of decisions. This time, all of them are architectural, but only the decisions in the first list are significant while the decisions in the second list are not. It's a great exercise to think about some decisions you have been part of recently. Ask yourself: were they architectural or merely technical? And if they were architectural, were they significant?

Architecturally significant decisions

Structure
Developers in a team decide to refactor their code to extract a micro-frontend.

Cross-functional characteristics
An infra developer adds an API gateway in front of the public services. No authentication, rate limiting, or any other interventions are enabled. It is a simple pass-through for now.

Dependences and likely cross-functional characteristics
An architecture committee decides to change the type of virtual compute primitive the company is going to use from its cloud provider.

Interfaces
An architect updates a REST API to remove an optional parameter that some consumers might be using.

Construction techniques
A QA decides which contract-testing framework you are going to use.

Not architecturally significant decisions

Not significant structure
A developer refactors a class to extract a private method.

Not significant cross-functional characteristics
A developer refactors some code without changing the structure, which removes a bottleneck, allowing the throughput to double. (Note that if the reverse of this decision happened, and consequently, a CFR was missed, then it would be significant.)

Not significant dependencies
A developer cleans up a build script to remove a number of dependencies without changing the functionality of the system.

You upgrade to a new minor version of a framework you are already using. (If it truly is a minor version change, this should be undetectable to all the code that consumes it.)

Not significant interfaces
An architect updates a wiki page to remove an optional parameter from an API that (they have validated) none of its consumers are using.

Not significant construction techniques
An infra developer deploys a developer portal that allows all teams to share their services and APIs.

Not All Decisions with an Architectural Impact Start as "Architectural" Decisions

You might have read the examples of decisions in this chapter and disagreed with how I've categorized them. It might help to know that (1) I wholeheartedly acknowledge the architectural impact of nontechnical decisions, and (2) I very much agree that some technical decisions, while not significantly architectural, ought to go through some kind of formal (or at least conscious) decision process.

Conclusion

Why have I spent a whole chapter laboring the point of architectural significance? First, practicing architecture successfully in a postrevolutionary world means that lots more decisions are happening. Knowing what decisions are "architectural" amid all that is important and knowing which of those decisions are "significant" are critical for focusing time, effort, and resources.

Second, it is important to acknowledge the power of developers, knowing or unknowing, in affecting the running architecture of a system. Against all the criteria of significance, developers can (and do) make architecturally significant decisions, and that's to be welcomed.

If our architectures are composed entirely of decisions, then we need to know which ones to pay particular attention to. I also stressed that, although being in deployed code isn't strictly speaking a criterion for architectural significance, decisions that impede this step being taken early and often are significant *in a negative way*. Up to the point a decision is running, you are simply guessing as to its suitability. Stop guessing, start deploying, and learn from the feedback.

Before you move on, think back to the visualization exercise you did at the beginning of the chapter. When you closed your eyes and pictured who makes the architectural decisions (significant or not) in your organization, did you see a single person, the architect? Or were you picturing a collective of people?

Chapter 3 will take this view and address two more questions: "What are the standard approaches to deciding at scale?" and "What are the characteristics of an 'ideal' decentralized, feedback-centering decision process?"

Decisions at Scale

Chapter 2 clarified what makes a decision an architectural one and, more importantly, what makes an architectural decision significant. It's now time to get a firm grip on the *act* of deciding and various ways to approach it. Specifically, we'll answer:

- What are the standard approaches to decisions at scale?
- What are the characteristics of an "ideal" postrevolutionary decision process?

Despite the fact that we all make many decisions a day, few of us are cognizant about how we go about it. This chapter will remedy that. I'll start simply by presenting a generic decision process that applies to *all decisions*. You'll gain an understanding of the steps involved, which I'll return to again and again throughout this book. You'll then move on to consider decision processes when more than one person is involved. You'll see how the processes compare and, more important, how suitable they are for a revolutionized world.

Decision Processes

Let's take a break from architecture for a moment and focus on the practice of arriving at decisions in general terms. Let's start with an example of a personal decision of the kind many of us likely make on a daily basis. (Bear with me. I'll get back to architectural decisions in the next section, but for now I want to provide clarity on a fundamental aspect underlying *all* decisions—even the ones where you are choosing a beverage for yourself.)

I'm standing at the counter of a coffee shop. I'm parched and want a drink that is tasty and thirst quenching. I need to decide what to order. Once I decide and pay for the drink, the barista will make it for me. This process is illustrated in Figure 3-1.

Figure 3-1. A naive view of a generic decision process ("deciding") in context (the required need for the decision and the subsequent implementation of the result)

Although this is overly simplified (have you *seen* the myriad options at some coffee shops?), it serves to demonstrate a high-level, three-stage decision process: (1) a decision is required, (2) the decision happens, and (3) the decision is implemented. Let's take a closer look at each stage.

Stage 1: Decision Required

The first stage of the decision process is identifying the need for a decision. Sometimes this will be obvious, and sometimes it won't be. In "What Shouldn't Be Considered Regarding Architectural Significance?" on page 42, stages 1 and 2 happen without the decider realizing. If the decision is conscious, then this is where a need is identified. In my example, after I entered the coffee shop, I realized I had to decide what to order.

Stage 2: The Act of Deciding

The middle stage of the decision process is where the work of deciding happens. When you "decide" something, you are actually performing *at least* two steps: you are discovering, crafting, and assessing your possible options; *and* you are *then* selecting one of those options to act on. That selected option is your decision. On top of these first two activities, you may have a third: communicating your decision to others so it can be implemented. Simply put, when you are "deciding," you are in fact making a set of decision options, taking a decision to select one of them, and then (possibly) sharing that decision. See Figure 3-2.

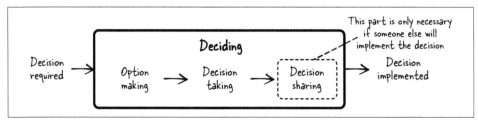

Figure 3-2. A more realistic view of a generic decision process

Let's dig into these activities individually now, starting with making options.

Step 2a: Making your set of decision options

In this first decision activity, you are *making* a list of possible options to choose from. This "making" step brings together the available information, doing the work to identify and shape the options to select from. This is a distinct step, even when the options are already laid out in front of you. In the coffee shop example, this is the time I spend making myself aware of everything I might like on the menu, mentally adding, of course, the possibility of not ordering anything, which is also available as a course of action. (I might also have a desire to go off menu and ask for goat's milk to see if they have it.)

This option-making step is where everyone seems to believe the hard (and exciting) work of software architecture lies. In many regards, that's true. Whenever I talk to colleagues and clients about the practice of software architecture, the focus of conversation is always this crafting of several possibilities. (In fact, all too often the "several" part is forgotten, but we'll get to that later.)

After all, this *making* is the time where you need to know about a myriad of architectures, technologies, and patterns—in fact, the more you know, the better. You need to know how these elements fit together and how they achieve this in such a way that meets the current and future requirements of your software system.

But this is not the only source of hard architectural work in this option-making step. To solve a problem or seize an opportunity, you first need to understand it and its context. What is the situation right now? What has been tried in the past? Who are the stakeholders, and what are their needs? What are the constraints? Are they really constraints? Are any of the constraints in tension or even direct conflict? Is doing nothing a viable option? What would happen if you did? All of these are inputs to consider when crafting your potential courses of action.

Taking all of this together, there is potentially much work put into a decision, even before we select one of the available options. But the next step, the "taking" of one of these options, is as—if not more—important.

Step 2b: Taking your decision

After you make your set of possible options, you are ready to "take" your decision by explicitly selecting one of them to act on. Using my coffee shop example, I might determine that I'm in the mood for something with milk and made with tea, and decide to take a matcha latte.

The decision-taking step can take far less time than option making, but it has to happen. A development team may deliberate on the details of a single option for days or weeks, yet it may take a split second for the decider to think, "Yes, that's what we'll do." While the timescales in decision taking may be far shorter than in decision making, the impacts are equal, if not greater. This choice point is a critical one—quite probably *the* critical one in the decision process when it comes to software systems. It is also where a great deal of the power lies.

Unlike caffeinated beverages, software architecture falls into the realm of "wicked" problems (*https://oreil.ly/O4HTN*), which is to say, problems without clear "right" or "best" solutions. In this world, the "taking" of a decision can have significant consequences because there are always pros and cons, whatever option you select. The trick/luck/skill is in picking the one with the smallest negative and largest positive impacts in your circumstances. It is the gravity of this that can lead to people's reticence or inability to take decisions. Ironically, despite the comparatively small effort involved compared to option making, the decision-taking step can be feared and avoided or postponed by many. (I'll spend half of Chapter 13 on this very topic.)

Step 2c (optional): Sharing your decision

After the taking of the decision, rapidly or otherwise, there is sometimes a third step in the option-making/decision-taking subprocess, one often glossed over because it seems self-evident. After a decision is taken and right before the decision is implemented, the decision needs to be shared with the relevant people. If the option makers and decision takers are not the same as the implementer, or even if more people need to be made aware of the decision, the selected option must be shared. So in my coffee shop example, after I decide to order a matcha latte, I need to then tell the barista, "I'd like a matcha latte."

Despite the potentially obvious nature of this (how can the barista make my drink if I don't tell them which one I chose?), I never fail to be amazed when I see this step either completely ignored or just mishandled in the world of software. This is the hidden weakness—the Achilles' heel, if you will—of many decision processes. A decision that is not shared with those who will implement it isn't a decision at all, and the efforts made during the decision-making and -taking process will be partially or totally wasted.

Even a decision that is poorly shared results in significant issues: either because those who will implement it don't have the necessary information or they do, but they don't agree with the decision.

Stage 3: Decision Implemented

The decision is implemented, and hopefully, it makes its way rapidly and smoothly down to production. The barista whips up a matcha latte, you pay for it, and then you enjoy the result of your successful decision process.

Where Does the Power Balance Lie in Decision Processes?

Given this detailed framing of decision processes, let's think about where we place the privilege with regard to decisions in software.

The majority of the power in a decision process lies with the decision taker because they select the option that will be progressed and reject those that will not. Despite the fact that decisions need not be taken by architects, the most significant, highest-profile decisions in traditional approaches to architecture typically are.

Yet for this power to be exercised, options must be crafted: they must be *made*. Consequently, power lies in the option-making step, too. There are a few different types of option making: where you are in uncharted territory options-wise, where there are various well-known solution options to enumerate, and where a decision's significance is missed and, consequently, only the most obvious option is considered.

In the first of these, a great deal of effort is required to come up with one or more of the options. If a new path is being forged, and the standard approaches and patterns simply won't cut it, this can be hard, creative work. (Imagine, for example, the time when your favorite design pattern was being created. At that point, they didn't have a book to turn to for an answer. They had to come up with a solution on their own.)

The second instance is the most common, and the option-making work is simply enumerating and understanding, which doesn't take as much effort—all the options seem self-evident, and intuition may well come into play—but even here, some degree of mental effort is necessary to bring the options to mind ready for the subsequent taking. Think back to the coffee shop for a second. Even here, I have a choice of sizes of cup, types of milk, flavor of syrup, and more. I don't need to create any of these options for myself as they are all laid out on the various menus in front of me, but I do need to combine them into a set of valid options I might choose to order.

The remaining times, only a single option is brought to mind, perhaps only partially thought through and described. I would hope that in these circumstances, the decision isn't an architecturally significant one. Decisions that are made semi- or unconsciously have a making step like this.

In these three types of option making, the proportion of power that is being brought into the making step is decreasing. It is greatest in the first instance, when new paths are being forged and options being made out of virtually thin air. It is virtually nonexistent in the last instance. Depending on the decision at hand, any of them can be appropriate. What is important is to recognize this and put in the appropriate amount of effort.

All too frequently in my experience, insufficient emphasis is placed on the power contained in the making step, and too much on the taking. Why might this be the case?

Traditional Architectural Approaches Insufficiently Expose Teams to the Option-Making Stage of the Decision Process

Unfortunately, in the world of traditional software architecture, where much option-making and decision-taking power rests with the architects, development teams frequently only witness architects taking decisions, or even worse, hear about them secondhand. You might say that, at least from the teams' perspectives, the decisions are taken *for* them (or perhaps taken *away* from them). Teams almost never get to witness any of the act of option making at all. And all of this depends on whether the architect in question feels comfortable about it or not.

This is worst in the ivory tower: little insight is available into the deliberations that may have gone into the decision because it happened without the team's involvement and without them being able to witness it taking place.[1]

Even with hands-on architects, it can appear to teams that architectures and the decisions around them emerge from the heads of architects fully formed, perhaps tweaked a little based on conversations, but the majority of the option making is unspoken and unshared, or overly bureaucratic, or both. This happens because in the traditional approaches, little value is placed on getting architects to talk out loud and explain their thought processes: to explain their thinking, their route to the solution option, and the decision to select it.

This is why taking a decision still feels like the natural way to express the entire practice of deciding for many developers and others outside the world of architecture. The options seem to pop up fully formed from the minds of architects, and the work of the decision is simply to pick one. The option-making stage, however, is where so much of the architectural thinking work happens.

The option-making stage is the part that people know and respect when they see architects at work. But even here, development teams rarely see the options because they are not made explicit. This is why, in my opinion, those in development roles may find it daunting to move into the architecture space. If a design appears to spring from the mind of an architect fully formed, how might I, as an inexperienced developer, ever learn to pull off such a feat?

---

1 I once arrived on a project, my first as a consultant, to be met by an architect wielding a PowerPoint slide deck full of various diagrams. They had finished their part of the work. "The design is done," they confidently stated, "the rest is implementation," and they headed off to their next assignment.

Decision Processes at Scale

So far, I've covered things from the perspective (both inside and out) of a single person making, then taking, and finally sharing a decision.

There can be a certain bliss to making options and taking a decision that only you care about and that only affects you, which only you have to understand, implement, and live with. Perhaps that's why architects and developers alike have side projects.[2]

Unfortunately, once other people enter the picture, the ease of deciding rapidly evaporates. You now have to consider things like how other people are affected by success or failure and whether they need some convincing. You also have to bear in mind how failure affects the timescale, who needs to be involved with the implementation and what they need to know, and so on. Everything about the decision process gets more complicated.

For all these reasons and more, decisions at scale, when more than a single person is involved, are hard. You can't avoid this; software development is a group activity. So you need a way of thinking about—and talking about—deciding scale.

Standard Approaches to Decisions at Scale

Decisions at scale are often challenging because there is a lack of clarity as to who is and isn't involved in a decision process. The roles and powers of the participants may be unknown as well.[3]

As I take you through the various approaches to decisions at scale, I want you to pay attention and ask, "Are the powers to initiate a decision in this approach centralized or decentralized?" and "What is the speed at which it allows options to be made and decisions to be taken and subsequently shared?" These questions are important because once I've introduced all the approaches, I'll evaluate each of them against both criteria.

For clarity, I've grouped the approaches into two categories.

Centralized decision processes
- Autocratic
- Delegation
- Consultative

---

2 I know you do—we all do. It's one of the things that keeps architects and developers together culturally. The impulse (compulsion?) to have side projects is shared by architects and developers alike. Side projects allow us to learn new skills and exercise existing ones, and they are fun to do.

3 For this, I've leaned heavily on thedecider.app, which does a great job at listing out standard decision processes and clarifying their pros and cons.

Decentralized decision processes

- Consent

- Democratic

- Consensus

For completeness, there is also the avoidant decision process.

Keep the Key Steps of the Generic Decision Process in Mind

Remember to keep the distinctions between option making, decision taking, and sharing clear in your mind as you read the following sections because the various processes differ largely in when and how they involve people in each of these activities.

Option making
  When you craft a set of options

Decision taking
  When you consider and then select an option

Decision sharing
  When you communicate your selected option to others

Centralized decision processes

Centralized decision processes all begin with a single individual who holds all the power to decide. Different flavors of centralized decision processes arise from how that person chooses to use that power.

Autocratic decision process. Let's start by adding group involvement to a single-person decision process. In an *autocratic* decision process, there is a single option maker/decision taker and a group that implements the decision. See Figure 3-3.

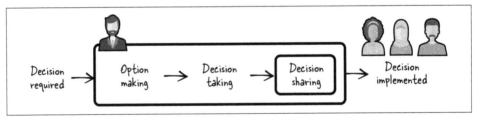

Figure 3-3. The autocratic decision process has just one individual making, taking, and sharing the decision

With this approach, there is one person who both makes options and takes *all* the decisions. No one else is empowered to do so. Everyone else's job is to implement the decision, and so sharing the decision here is vitally important.

An example of an autocratic decision is where a new chief architect joins a startup and decides, after no consultation with others, that the company will move from Amazon to Azure for their cloud services.

This method can be incredibly fast for individual decisions and, in certain circumstances, very powerful. It can also lead to disaster. Perhaps the decision was a terrible one, or even if it was suitable, it was poorly communicated, and therefore, the implementation never stood a chance. It can also be very slow overall, as all decisions go through a single person, making them a bottleneck.

Delegation decision process.   Next comes the *delegation* decision process (Figure 3-4), which is a variant of the autocratic method. Here, the autocrat delegates their decision to someone within a wider group who is better placed to make options, take the decision, and (if the delegated decider is not also the implementer) share it.

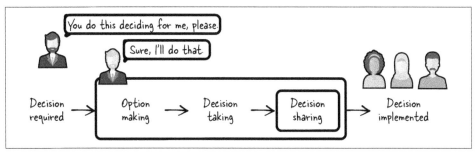

Figure 3-4. The delegation decision process still has just one individual making, taking, and potentially sharing the decision, but this person is not the same as the person doing the delegating

An example of a delegated decision is one where the previously mentioned chief architect realizes they don't know enough about the current state of Amazon cloud offerings and so enlists their lead Infrastructure architect to make and take the decision for them.[4]

This method is potentially marginally slower than an autocratic approach, as the delegate needs to be found and briefed per decision. However, if the delegate is appropriately chosen, it can lead to better choices and, if the chosen person is in or closer to the right teams, better implementations. It's still a potential bottleneck, though, as the number of people doing the deciding remains small.

---

4 In order to scale, many open source programming languages and other significantly sized endeavors, such as the Linux kernel, have a decision-making approach known as "benevolent dictatorship" (a phrase coined by Eric S. Raymond in his essay "Homesteading the Noosphere" in *The Cathedral and the Bazaar* by Eric S. Raymond [O'Reilly, 2001]). This is equivalent to the delegation model described here, although delegated decision privileges can be revoked if the dictator disagrees with a specific decision.

Consultative decision process. An alternative to delegation is the *consultative* decision process (Figure 3-5). Here, the decision taker is again the same person as in the autocratic method—the chief architect of the previous two examples—but now they actively go out to a group of their choosing and seek inputs during the option-making stage.

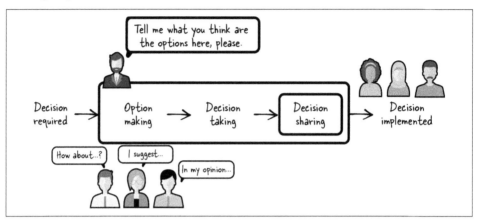

Figure 3-5. The consultative decision process still has an individual taking and sharing the decision, but now others, at the request of the decision taker, provide input into the option making

For example, rather than delegating to a chosen cloud infrastructure expert, the chief architect simply consults them, along with a few of the development leads they used to work with and a QA.

With the consultative process, the autocrat is not obliged to listen to any of their consultees' inputs, but they do potentially benefit from them, shaping the options and choice accordingly. Perhaps they change very little from what the consulted parties provide.[5]

This method is slower than both the autocratic and the delegation approaches, but it can benefit from the expertise of a wider group. The downside is that whole groups with valid expertise can be shut out completely, never even asked for their input, because the decision taker selects who to consult and who to ignore.

All these centralized decision processes focus power in a single, named individual: either an autocrat or their delegate. Consequently, they are potentially individually very fast because decisions are taken by a single individual and require no agreement.

---

5 This, so I understand, is how Apple works. See the last point ("A top-down culture is not as bad as we think") from Andrea Pancheco's *Medium* post, "What I Learned as a Product Designer at Apple" (*https://oreil.ly/bZFJ4*).

However, this same single, fixed decision-taking individual means that power is centered in one place. Speed has been achieved at the expense of decentralization of control.

Let's look now at methods that prioritize power sharing.

Decentralized decision processes

In Chapter 1, I sketched out the practice and consequences of decentralized architecture. It should be clear to you that none of the centralized decision process options I just described will deliver in those circumstances (though that doesn't stop people from trying). What are our options if we start to crack apart that power center? What happens when we start to involve others in the decision-taking parts of the process?

Consent decision process. The smallest step away from a centralized decision process is to use the *consent* process (Figure 3-6). In this approach, the option maker and the decision taker are still the same individual person, but once the decision is taken, others in a far wider group can block it in the form of a veto, also called a *paramount objection*.

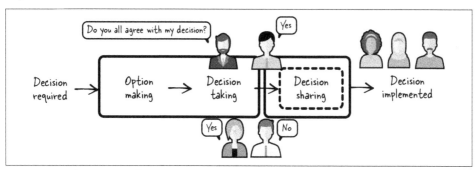

Figure 3-6. The consent decision process has a single individual both making options and taking the decision, but the decision is only passed for implementation if everyone consents to it

Put very simply, the veto means that, after a decision is taken, there need to be no paramount objections raised against its implementation. If a person in the group does not agree with the selected option for some reason, they deploy their veto. This veto can offer significant power to individuals.

For example, the option maker and decision taker is again the chief architect. This time, they are picking a programming language for the new set of microservices. They select Java 8 for this because, despite being end-of-life for almost a decade at time of writing (see endoflife.date (*https://endoflife.date/java*) to find out how old it is at time of reading), it's the last language they coded in. They then ask all the development team leads for their consent.

If one or more vetoes are used, then the decision is blocked, and the decision taker must return to their previously made options and either choose a different one or try to change an option such that all objections are withdrawn and no more are put forward. The decision is taken and implemented.

As I said, this is a significant shift of power, although not a complete one. Vetoers do not have the power to either directly make the options or take the decision, but they can block progress after that. In our example, the development leads were not asked what language they would have suggested instead of Java 8. Consequently, this approach is open to abuse by those who may deploy their veto with no intention of withdrawing it until they get exactly what they want. At best, this can slow things down and at worst, grind things to a halt.

On the upside, the decision-sharing element is unnecessary, or greatly reduced, as most people involved in the implementation are already part of the process.

Democratic decision process. The next step into the world of decentralized power is one many of us *ought* to know well: the *democratic* decision process (Figure 3-7).

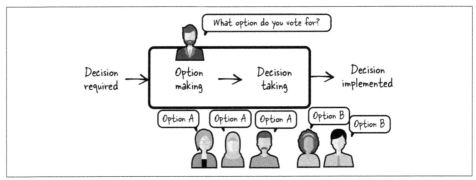

Figure 3-7. The democratic decision process presents a preselected set of options to a vote; the option with the majority of votes is the one that is implemented

Direct Versus Representative Democracy

When I use the word *democracy* here, I'm referring to the Athenian idea of *direct* democracy, not *representative* democracy. In a representative democracy, individuals cast votes to select someone who will *represent them* in the decision-making process. This is, for example, how many parliaments around the world work. In a direct democracy, individuals cast votes or use some other means to *directly indicate* their preference from a selection of options put in front of them. There may even be options to not vote at all or to indicate ranked preference. In direct democracy, your vote is directly related to the decision at hand. "Should we do this or that?" "I voted for this, but 54% of those polled voted for that, and so that's what we went with."

A democratic process for making decisions in software architecture again entails a single individual making all the options but then presenting these options to the entire group,[6] who each vote on their preferred option. The option that gains a majority of votes is the one selected—in the democratic process, the group is taking the decision.

Returning to the previous example where a new programming language is being selected, the chief architect would lay out a set of options: Java 8, COBOL, Lisp, and Rust. These would then be voted on. If the chief architect is feeling particularly magnanimous, they might extend the franchise to all developers who will be working on these new services, not just the team leads. They would then each have a single vote to indicate which of the languages they would prefer.

Consequently, the consent-process problem of a single vetoer blocking a decision is removed. Now it's down to the majority.[7] However, this itself can give rise to problems because in a democratic decision process, the majority can ignore a minority even though that minority may have some very valid objections. This also cuts in the other direction, where the (ignored) minority feels little to no ownership of the selected option and therefore is disinclined to implement it.

With regard to decision sharing, as with the consent process, this step is either unnecessary or greatly reduced, because again, everyone is (potentially) involved at the decision-taking point and is aware of what needs to be implemented.

Consensus decision process. There is one final step down the path to decentralization of power that we need to take. For many, it is the farthest step away from the centralized-power model: the *consensus* process (Figure 3-8). It also seeks to resolve many of the inherent issues I just highlighted in the democratic approach.[8]

---

6 Yet again, the parallels with political democratic models are too juicy to ignore. Who gets to vote? Is it a team? Is it all the team leads? Is it every developer? Are other roles (QA, business analyst, product manager/owner, delivery/project manager, Scrum master, infra engineer) allowed to vote, too?

7 Majority is typically set at "more than half," but sometimes for bigger decisions, things like "supermajorities" (e.g., more than 60% or 70%) can be employed. Another factor sometimes brought in is the need for there to be a majority of *all eligible to vote*. This means that, if 40 out of 100 vote in favor of something, and 35 out of 100 vote for something else, it is still not carried if the majority needs to be drawn from the full 100.

8 Just to be clear, I am in no way saying that democratic approaches are fatally flawed, but we ought to be way more aware of their shortcomings. Democracy fundamentally solves a scaling problem when applied at a state level. That scaling problem may not exist within the engineering division of an organization.

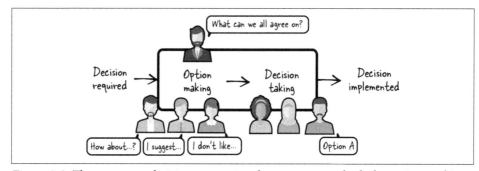

Figure 3-8. The consensus decision process involves everyone at both the option-making and decision-taking stages, the latter happening when everyone agrees or no overpowering objections remain

Consensus-based decisions involve everyone in both stages of the decision process, both in the making of options, which allows for everyone's needs and viewpoints to be taken into account, and then in the taking of the decision of which option to select.[9]

In our example, the chief architect involves the developers of the new services in the shaping of the options (they come up with Kotlin, C#, TypeScript, Rust, and Pony), which are then discussed in depth before one is eventually agreed to.

Consequently, this goes a long way toward leveling out the power across everyone in the group as well as providing the possibility for everyone to be involved and listened to at both stages. Although this sounds great, consensus-based deciding can take forever to arrive at a conclusion, and there is often a significant danger that the conclusion reached will be a catalog of lowest common denominator compromises. Is it a good thing if no one is upset but the resulting architecture is a catalog of compromises?

More fundamentally, a consensus-based approach requires that everyone feels equally able to be involved and to share their viewpoints and opinions. Too often, people who decide are unaware of who they are excluding. They commonly conclude that those who don't participate don't have anything to contribute or will surely agree with the opinions of those who do participate. You can spot this when you see assumptions such as "they were there—if they had wanted to contribute, or if their idea was a good one, then it would have been incorporated." When this happens, you are failing to take advantage of the benefits this approach offers you.

---

9 The canonical work on the details of how this can work in practice is the classic RFC "On Consensus and Humming in the IETF" (*https://oreil.ly/1V5fN*) by Pete Resnick. A nonsoftware view on a similar approach can be found in David Graeber's *The Democracy Project* (Random House), page 209. There are also parallels here with participative democracy (*https://oreil.ly/zGJwT*) and citizens' assemblies (*https://oreil.ly/q_u6t*).

Avoidant decision process

While the consensus approach was the last step on the decentralization-of-power path, there is one more "process" I ought to include: the *avoidant* approach. To many, this is not a process at all, but deciding not to decide is as much a choice as any other. In fact, I know some architects who factor this into every decision they make, although they would be thinking, "What if we did nothing?" This is a good thing. Hardcore Agilists will also be familiar with the adage "Defer decisions until the last responsible moment." It's the same thing, but you can't base a design on never taking any decision ever. When the time comes and a decision *needs* to be made, then you'll have to fall back on something other than avoidance.

Returning to our example for one last time, avoidance would likely be detrimental. All the services are currently written in Java 6, which *everyone* hates. By avoiding deciding on a new language entirely, everyone continues to suffer.

Decision Processes in a Revolutionized World

With that survey of standard decision processes complete, let's evaluate them for suitability with modern architectures. As described in Chapter 1, this world requires speed of response and decentralization of decision rights. As such, decision processes should be able to rapidly respond and be decentralized with regard to the power to decide. I've plotted all of the standard decision processes (apart from avoidant) on the graph in terms of speed and centralization of power in Figure 3-9.

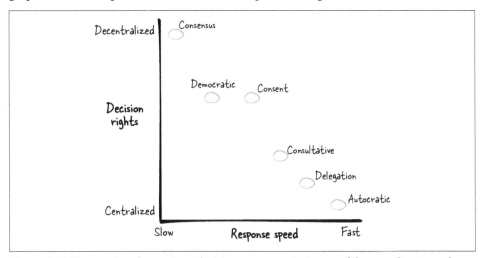

Figure 3-9. Comparing the various decision processes in terms of decentralization of decision rights and speed to respond

The graph shows how the standard decision processes compare with regard to the degree of power decentralization and speed at which they can respond with a decision. There are a few points I need to make clear. First, the points plotted here show the "best" possible result that any process could achieve regarding the revolutionized ideal. For example, you can see that the consensus approach is maximally decentralized as it involves everyone in both the making and the taking. However, because of the maximum involvement of participants in both steps, it is the slowest with regard to ability to respond rapidly with a decision, even when both the making and taking steps are performed efficiently without either dispute or debate.

Taking the other extreme, you can see that the autocratic process is the opposite on both fronts. It only ever involves the same solitary person, so power to decide is very centralized, but because no one needs to agree, or even be listened to, it also has the ability to respond the fastest. Remember, the points are plotted as the "best" they can be with regard to the two ideals. If an autocrat is a ditherer, unable to make any decision at all, then their dot would drift back to the left.

Notice that there are two areas of the graph that have no decision methods in them at all: "slow and power centralized in one/a few" (bottom left) and "fast and power decentralized across everyone" (top right). I doubt anyone would argue for an approach that was centralized and slow; that is the scenario of the dithering autocrat mentioned in the preceding paragraph. That has no benefits at all—not for our purposes, at least. But what about decentralized and fast? Is that possible, and is that desirable? To unpack that, let's consider the two factors needed in a decision process that would be optimal in the revolutionized world. Armed with that information, we will be in a position to imagine the best process.

What makes a decision method fast to respond?

First, let's ask: what is it about the fastest-response decision processes that make them fast?

Autocratic decisions, the fastest as plotted, involve a single individual in both the making and the taking, without any input from others. Delegation decisions are the next fastest and involve two people: the autocrat who delegates the decision and the person delegated to make and take the decision. (The delegate might decide not to use an autocratic method to determine their decision, but we're talking about the fastest alternatives here.)

After this comes consultative decisions. While the number of individuals involved in the option making could be significant (a number as large or as small as the decider desires), the decision taker is under no pressure to implement the advice they receive because it is simply that: advice. No option-making or decision-taking power has been delegated, and there is no need to reshape things to placate advice givers. In all cases, rapid turnaround on decisions can be achieved if required.

To provide the counterpoint, consider one more process: consent, which can be a sticky thing. In the consent decision process, a group rather than an individual has influence on decision taking, and this can play out in a number of ways.

Consent decisions *can* be fast. When trust in the option maker and decision taker is high, consent from teams can sometimes be preassumed to be given in all circumstances. Why? Because when everyone feels the decider is closely attuned to their opinions without having to ask, the number of people needed to be explicitly made happy is zero.

However, this is a relatively rare occurrence. When trust is lower, the presence of vetoes inevitably leads to decreased speed of response. The greater the number of vetoes, the greater the likelihood of a slower process. While I have no concrete data, in practice this truly feels like a logarithmic scale, where, beyond a certain number, there is a likelihood that there will always be at least one veto, and in such circumstances, the decision speed is effectively zero.

Consequently, the key factor in a decision's response speed is the number of people who either contribute directly to the taking of a decision or can object to that decision after it is taken. The lower the number, the faster the optimal response speed.

What makes a decision method decentralized in decision rights?

Second, let's ask: what is it about the most power-decentralizing decision methods that make them so?

As with speed to respond, decentralization is not a good thing in and of itself. A quick glance back at Figure 3-9 shows that with the standard approaches, increasing the decentralization of a decision method correlates with a slower decision speed. However, decentralization is also self-evidently powerful, in part because it brings increasingly more minds to bear on an increasing number of problems, *simultaneously*.

Let's consider the various standard decision processes again, considering who is involved and how. Up first is consensus. In this approach, everyone is potentially involved in the option making, which is only reduced if some choose not to contribute. The same number of people are potentially involved in the taking, too.

Consent and democratic processes are worth comparing side by side. In both cases, only one person is involved in the option making. The democratic process is slightly more decentralized in that everyone is involved in the decision taking, whereas this step in the consent process remains centralized. At first glance, this appears to be less decentralized.

However, if a veto is deployed in the consent process, the vetoer gets the opportunity to state the nature of their objection. To get a decision passed in this process, the option maker and the decision taker must somehow incorporate the vetoer's feedback into their next attempt to pass a decision. For this reason, I plotted the consent and democratic processes in Figure 3-9 as equally decentralized, though for different reasons.

Finally, it's instructive to consider the consultative process. Here, the number involved in the selection is minimal—one person—but the number involved in the creation of the options can potentially be vast: as many as the decision taker deems necessary to get the best outcome.

In her book *The Age of Surveillance Capitalism* (PublicAffairs), Shoshana Zuboff discussed how, while it's important to think about who is involved in the making and taking of decisions, it's equally important to think about who initiates the decision process and selects who is involved in it. She expressed this very succinctly, asking both "Who decides?" *and* "Who decides who decides?"—meaning that it is important to think about not only who participates in a decision process but also who can initiate a decision in the first place. This is where the consultative approach stands out because, while it can *potentially* include many people in the option making, the overall power sits fully with the singular decision taker.

Consequently, the key factor in a decision process's decentralization with regard to decision rights is the number of people who are de facto entitled to initiate and then contribute to the taking of decisions. The greater the number and the deeper their involvement, the greater the decentralization.

What are the requirements for a decision process fit for the revolutionized world?

Just as the DevOps revolution challenged the adage "You can have fast or stable but not both" (as categorically disproven by Forsgren and colleagues' *Accelerate* research), let's entertain the possibility that a decision process that is both fast to respond and decentralized with regard to decision rights might be possible. If it was, what are the requirements such an alternative decision process ought to meet?

1. First, it must *involve the appropriate people in decisions* while keeping this number as small as possible.

2. Second, it must *optimize the entitlement to initialize, make options, and take decisions.*

3. Third, it should *prioritize trust* so that people feel the need to involve themselves in decisions where they have a stake.

4. Fourth, it should *minimize the need for explicit sharing.*

There is at least one decision process that meets all these requirements. It's the topic of the next chapter.

Conclusion

Software architecture is wholly composed of the implementation of decisions, and because software is delivered, run, and evolved by groups rather than individuals, it's important to have a handle on how we approach deciding collectively. This chapter took you on a deep dive into the various ways to approach architecture decisions at scale.

I cast light on decision processes, starting with the basics all such processes share before showing you what forms such processes can take at scale. You looked at standard approaches to this and then thought about what kind of approach would work for a fast, decentralized, feedback-centric world. We'll talk about this mythical approach in Chapter 4.

CHAPTER 4

The Architecture Advice Process

In the previous chapter, I talked about how these days decisions at scale need to be both decentralized and fast. I then showed how none of the various traditional decision processes could offer everything we needed, being either too slow or overly centralized.

In this chapter, I'll introduce you to the architecture advice process—a simple yet powerful approach to deciding that is both decentralized and fast. I'll explain how this process meets all four requirements for a modern decision process by involving the right number of people, optimizing the entitlement to initiate decisions, prioritizing trust, and minimizing the need to communicate decisions. I'll also take you through two examples of it in action so that you have a better understanding of its mechanics and can see how you and others can participate in it openly and effectively. I'll close by discussing the widespread positive impacts the advice process can have on both your software and your organization's culture: not only removing blockers and increasing feedback but also promoting healthy, equitable communication. I'll also show how the process delivers software architectures that evolve more fluidly and responsively. I've described these benefits in some detail so that you'll know them when you come across them.

First, let's remind ourselves *why* we need a faster, decentralized decision process.

The Need for a Faster, Decentralized Decision Process

There are clear challenges when it comes to using traditional approaches to architecture. When using ivory tower approaches, I found that I couldn't focus on the relevant details. With the hands-on alternatives, I struggled with stepping back to see the bigger picture. And I failed miserably trying to be the best at both. I realized I was always stressed for three reasons:

- My accountability and responsibility in decision processes meant I was blocking or at least impeding team flow.

- My architectures might not be fit for purpose: I was unaware of how existing systems were running and the nuances of the current implementations.

- My architectures might not be getting into production and staying there: I was failing to communicate them effectively.

All three of these were entirely due to the way architectural decisions were being made and taken: with me at the center, responsible and accountable, irrespective of whether my approach was an ivory tower or a hands-on one.

I asked around, speaking to colleagues, ex-colleagues, and clients, and discovered that although I wasn't alone in feeling this way, no one had a solution. Is there a way to make architecture less about the responsibilities associated with a job title and more about architecture as a collective practice? Might there be an alternative approach that could take architects out of the critical but stressful decision path while still maintaining the practice of architecture at the core? Could there be a decision process that locates decisions in the right place, involving as few decision takers as possible (i.e., be fast), while allowing as many different individuals to make and then take those decisions (i.e., be decentralized)?

There is, and it sits in the coveted top-right quadrant of the speed/decentralization graph in Figure 3-9. It has the potential to remove all three stressors of the traditional approaches in one fell swoop.

The Architecture Advice Process: One Rule, Two Advice-Offering Groups, and One Contract

In Dennis Bakke's book *The Decision Maker* (Pear Press), he describes an "advice process" that he devised at AES, a Fortune 200 global power company. It's an incredibly simple, trust-centering process that is applicable to all flavors of decision making, including those that involve software architecture. As such, I call my version an *architecture* advice process.[1]

---

1 You can read about general advice processes that are applicable to all decisions, not just software architecture ones, on the Reinventing Organizations wiki (*https://oreil.ly/omiTf*), which supports the book *Reinventing Organizations* (Nelson Parker) by Frederic Laloux.

In the architecture advice process, there is a single rule: anyone (a development team member or someone playing a cross-team architecture role) can take (select a decision option) and communicate an architectural decision as long as during the option-making stage, they seek advice from:

- Everyone who will be meaningfully affected by the decision
- People who have expertise in the area in which the decision is being taken

This seeking of advice is a social contract that balances the rule. That contract is upheld by ensuring that the required advice has been sought, listened to, and understood. Once the contract is met, the decision taker is free to select the option of their choice and appropriately communicate it to the relevant parties. See Figure 4-1.

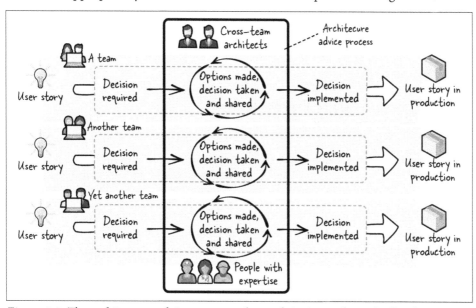

Figure 4-1. The architecture advice process, where advice is sought and offered on in-flight decisions, initiated by either teams or cross-team architects as software flows to production

Being both fast and decentralized, the advice process (I'll drop the "architecture" part of the name from now on) sits in the top-right quadrant of the response-speed/decision-rights graph I shared in Chapter 3, now updated in Figure 4-2. This might seem like a bold claim. Let's unpack it a little.

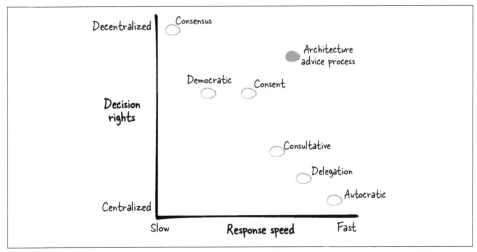

Figure 4-2. Updated graph comparing the various decision processes in terms of decentralization and speed

The Architecture Advice Process Is Fast

I'll start with speed. First, recall from Chapter 3:

> The key factor in a decision's response speed is the number of people who either contribute directly to the taking of a decision or can object to that decision after it is taken. The lower the number, the faster the optimal response speed.

In the advice process, the number of people involved in and accountable for the taking of the decision is one (or one team-sized group), and the number of people who can object—and effectively block the taken decision—is zero. That's a pretty small number, and it's the reason why the advice process is so fast!

Not only that, but during the preceding option-making step of the process, those driving the decision are seeking advice—but importantly, not permission—from those affected by it and those with applicable expertise.

Therefore, the need for broad consensus—or indeed any form of broad agreement—is avoided, and the advice process can reap the speed benefits of the autocratic, delegation, and consultative processes, which circumvent this issue in the same way.

It's for this reason that I've placed the new architecture advice process dot on the graph in Figure 4-2 just slightly to the right of the consultative process with regard to speed. This is to reflect the fact that it probably involves the same number of people as the consultative approach but with the added sense of urgency because the responsibility for the decision comes directly from those who need it, with zero intermediaries.

A few words on how the number of advice offerers affects the speed of deciding might help.

First, the greater the number of "meaningfully affected parties," the more people decision takers are obliged to seek advice from. While this sounds like a drawback, it actually sets up a valuable reinforcement dynamic: to make fast decisions, teams will look to reduce the number of affected parties they must turn to for advice. The simplest way to do this is to more sharply define a decision to reduce (or remove) the impact on others. This nudges teams to continually validate good system boundaries, rewards decoupling, and reduces the scope of the decision. (I'll go into all these topics in greater detail in Part II of this book.)

And "those with expertise in the area"? Structuring decisions to avoid engaging experts is something you don't want to do, but the architecture advice process changes the interaction dynamics here, too. Decision takers no longer need to convince experts of the reasons for a decision, so a rich conversation can take place from the beginning, with the sole goal of seeking and sharing knowledge and experience.

With the option-making and decision-taking steps covered, what about the third step: sharing the decision? In a centralized process, this sharing stage is another weak point. If a decision taker doesn't share their decision with those who will implement it, nothing happens; all decision-process efforts were for nothing. If they share it but poorly, the implementation may bear little or no resemblance to the decision that was taken.

With the advice process, the people who make and take the decision are also the ones implementing it. The sharing step is simply getting back to the affected parties and experts and letting them know what the decision taken was. This is simpler because everyone was previously involved. It's also derisked because poor communication at this stage won't affect the implementation.

The Architecture Advice Process Is Decentralized

The main issue with traditional architectural decision processes—and hence in both the ivory tower and hands-on architecture approaches—is that their "center" is fixed. It is always occupied by a fixed group of named individuals: the architects responsible and accountable for the overall architecture.[2] You can see this represented in Figures 4-3 and 4-4. All significant architectural decisions in both traditional approaches must pass in front of the architects, at least for approval, and frequently much more.

---

2 This is a likely contributor to the gradual rise of architects up organizational hierarchies. Despite the fact that they occupy what might be considered a *glue role* (a term coined by Tanya Reilly (*https://oreil.ly/gu-df*)), their "in-between" focus gradually became seen as "across" and then "above"/"on top of."

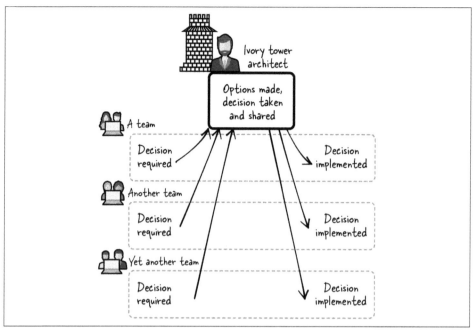

Figure 4-3. When using ivory tower approaches to architecture, all development teams must defer to the architects for decisions, at least in the form of their approval

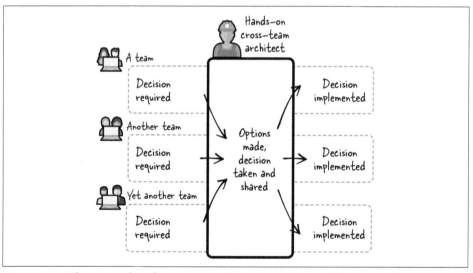

Figure 4-4. When using hands-on approaches to cross-team architecture, all teams must still defer to architects for decisions to be taken

In contrast, the advice process locates the center around whoever needs it, whenever it needs to be there. (This "center" can even be in multiple places at once.) Therefore, it meets the key need for optimal decentralization (I'll come back to the ramifications of this again and again throughout this book):

> The key factor in a decision process's decentralization with regard to decision rights is the number of people who are de facto entitled to initiate and then contribute to the taking of decisions. The greater the number and the deeper their involvement, the greater the decentralization.

The essential words here are "de facto entitled." The biggest downside of the *most* decentralized decision processes (such as democratic or consensus) is that they are *always* maximally decentralized; *everyone* is *always* entitled to contribute to the taking of *every* decision. Consequently, even in circumstances where everyone is aligned and on the same page with regard to consensus, simply letting everyone be heard on every topic can be at best long-winded. This happens because everyone feels obliged to participate, contributing what they can to both the making of the options and the taking of the decision. Why? Because if they stop participating, then they will be seen to not care or not know enough to offer opinions. At the extremes, what you find is that while everyone has an opinion, no one takes decisions. In these circumstances, not only decision speed but also accountability suffer.

Again, an advice process flips this. (As the renowned systems thinker Russell L. Ackoff would no doubt remind us, an advice process does not solve a problem—it resolves it.) There is now one decision taker, but that decision taker arises from the collective, wherever and whenever a decision is required. With the advice process, no one needs to seek permission to initiate this. As per Zuboff's book *The Age of Surveillance Capitalism*, when deciding, it's important to consider both *who* decides and *who decides* who decides. With the advice process, the answer to both questions is "whoever feels the need to." It's for this reason that I placed the new architecture advice process dot on the graph in Figure 4-2 between the democratic and consensus processes with regard to decentralization, reflecting both that anyone can take a decision if they see the need but that decision won't have everyone involved in it.

So what about involving the right parties in the option-making and decision-sharing stages? The responsibility for both lies with the decision takers, which is the topic of the next section.

The Architecture Advice Process Gives Rise to a Social Contract

The core of the advice process gives rise to a mutual agreement, a social contract, which comes into play whenever a decision is required. If we were to write out this contract, it would say:

We trust others to make and take decisions, on the understanding that they put in the hard work, listen, and think about their decision's impact on everyone and everything else. We in turn trust that others will do the same for us.

There are two parties in this contract:

The decider
This is the person (or when it's a team, one of their members, most likely the tech lead) who initiates the process because they have a need for a decision.

Those offering the advice
These are the people who represent the affected parties and those with expertise.

The key that holds everything in balance is that everyone in the sociotechnical system, those building and running the software, could be called on to play either of these roles. Today, I could be a decider, seeking advice from others. Tomorrow, I could be an advice offerer, providing my wisdom to others. What I want for myself, I need to be able to offer to others. Perhaps this feels like a flimsy platform on which to build something, but remember that we are already engaged in a collective endeavor: the construction of a complex system with many interconnections and emergent properties. In such an environment, it makes sense to play by the rules of the game. To play well, I need others to trust me, and I need to trust them.

How do I build up this trust? By involving the appropriate people in my decision via their advice (I'll cover how to identify these people in Chapter 5), by listening to and understanding that advice properly, by taking that advice into account in the options I shape and select when taking the decision, and by ensuring that the right people know about a taken decision by sharing it appropriately.

Trust is a big topic, and nurturing and protecting trust as you collectively practice architecture is a theme you'll see throughout this book. For now, it's sufficient to be aware of its central role and how it manifests in the form of the advice process's social contract. You now have enough detail on the process to see how it works in practice.

Two Examples of the Architecture Advice Process in Action

Whenever I present the architecture advice process to clients, colleagues, and audiences at conferences, the description on its own always elicits strong emotions, both positive and negative.

On the one hand, you have developers who have felt the pain of being simultaneously blocked and berated for not getting the latest feature into the hands of users quickly enough. They typically greet the whole idea with open arms. On the other hand, some software and systems architects treat the architecture advice process as a potential silver bullet;[3] they're too experienced to accept it without question, but they're willing to give it a try, evaluating experimenting with it as soon as possible.

But not all developers welcome the idea as enthusiastically. This is usually because not everyone feels as ready, willing, and able to take on the responsibility and accountability that the advice process entails. Some architects, those whose job it is to worry about the overall system, about coherence and predictability, and about nebulous things like cross-functional characteristics, tend to experience vertiginous flashes of panic as images of multiple teams, all headed off in completely different directions, arise.

You might be experiencing one, some, or all of these emotions yourself at this moment. That's no bad thing. It means that you're at least open to the idea of change.

These uncomfortable emotions arise from the advice process's apparent simplicity. To many, it feels a little *too* simple. This comes from the tendency to think that for something to be important, it also has to be complicated.

If you are feeling this, remember the concepts of complexity and emergence. Surprisingly complex (and responsive) things can arise from very few and relatively simple elements when interconnected in a dynamic environment. The same thing happens here with the architecture advice process: you'll be amazed how transformative adopting the advice process can be. Not only for your architecture practice but also for the resulting software and systems architectures, and the social dynamics of the teams that build and run them.[4]

With this in mind, I'm going to share a pair of stories to let you get a feel for how the process runs. They not only demonstrate the versatility of the advice process but also show how the process looks from different viewpoints. For that reason, I'll keep coming back to them throughout this book, so it might make sense to add a bookmark (digital or otherwise) so that they are easy to find again. The stories show:

- How a development team member might follow the process to address a need they are experiencing
- How an architect might do the same with regard to something related to the overall system architecture

As you read these two tales, pay attention to the social contract and who the different parties are: decision maker/taker and advice offerers. Watch to see how the members

---

3 Because they've been working in software too long to know this is never the case. If you've not yet treated yourself to it, I recommend you check out Fred Brooks's essay "No Silver Bullet: Essence and Accidents of Software Engineering" in *Computer*, vol. 20, no. 4, pp. 10–19, April 1987, doi:10.1109/MC.1987.1663532.

4 Principle 11 of the Agile Manifesto (*https://oreil.ly/qP6dZ*) states: "The best architectures, requirements, and designs emerge from self-organizing teams."

of the advice-offering groups change depending on the decision at hand. Try to think about which party you might be in both types of scenarios. Also think about what the others are doing and contributing, and try to be aware of how it might feel to do so. You can refer back to Figure 4-1 for a visual representation of the advice process in action.

Story 1: A Development Team Decides to Use Release Toggles

The first story starts, as the majority of decisions do, with a team facing a challenge they want to resolve. Their organization uses the architecture advice process.

This team works with a product manager who is always pushing to deliver features to their users with less and less delay.[5] Luckily, some of the team had read *Accelerate*[6] and learned that by moving to a trunk-based delivery practice,[7] they could eliminate pull requests altogether and consequently improve on their lead time for changes and deployment frequency metrics, and (most important) they could do it safely. A worthy goal if ever there was one.

Enthusiastic to learn new things, the team did their research and realized that to make this possible, they would need to make a small, localized, but significant architectural change: some form of release toggle. The question they had in front of them was: what would this release toggle implementation look like?

So let's recap. The team is in need of a solution right now that lets them disable their unfinished code while still pushing directly to the trunk and deploying regularly to production. To do so, they need a significant architectural change involving some form of release toggle. This issue is blocking them from delivering as fast as the product manager needs them to.

The team has loads of local, specific, and up-to-the-minute detail on their need. They know all about the state of their codebase. They know what their running services are like, what they do, how they do it, and what kind of infrastructure their services run on. They know their backlog and what is coming up next, and they know the state of their existing pipelines, testing strategies, and other automation. Perhaps most important of all, they know about the skills they have as a group and what they are and aren't comfortable with.

---

5 The product manager is right, by the way. Code that is written but is not in use isn't delivering value. Donald G. Reinertsen calls this *design-in-process (DiP) inventory*. We'll see exactly why this matters in later chapters.

6 This is the third time I've mentioned *Accelerate* by Nicole Forsgren et al. in this book so far, and it may not be the last. If you haven't gotten the hint that I highly recommend reading it, maybe this third mention will be the charm. Go read it.

7 *Accelerate* suggests that you adopt this practice, but the best place to find out *how* is in Valentina Servile's *Continuous Deployment* (O'Reilly).

In this first story, who do you think is the decision taker? And who do you think is the option maker? I'll let you think about it while you read and give you the answers at the end.

The team started by investigating the options, doing some design work, and landing on what they felt was the best option for them: simple boolean checks in code. This can be considered their "draft decision."

It was at this point that they decided to seek advice. First, members of the team listed and spoke to the "affected parties":

EXAMPLE

Checklist: People to seek advice from about our feature toggle

Teams that consume our APIs:

☐ Team Yan

☐ Team Tan

☐ Team Tethera

It was self-evident to them that these people would be their peers in other delivery teams whose lives would be changed as a consequence of the release toggles being implemented. It wasn't very hard to sit and think, "Who would have extra work to do as a result of us implementing this decision?" as well as "Whose freedom to act/flexibility to make changes unimpeded might be curtailed as a result of this?" It didn't matter if their proposed decision *would* have such an impact. What was important was that the team thought about who *might* and then went to speak to them.

These impacted teams provided an incredibly useful and visceral "outside but still here-and-now" perspective on the proposal. They provided valuable context and detail that the deciding team was only slightly aware of. The key point that multiple impacted teams raised was the fact that these toggles would effectively "hide" unfinished services that they were developing and testing against. How would they test with the proposed solution? This was a great piece of information that the deciding team had simply not thought of. They noted it, vowing to figure out how to incorporate this need into their design.

The deciding team wasn't being reckless or uncompassionate here. As soon as they were reminded of this fact, they realized just how problematic their original proposed change would be. They might get their features to production faster, but these other teams were building services for the same end users, just for later stages of the journey. By moving faster with their original, preadvice design of boolean toggles in code, the overall benefits would be small to none—perhaps they would even make things worse overall.

So why had the team not thought of this themselves? Because putting yourself in *everyone else's* shoes is difficult to do. It comes down to human psychology. Someone who is having something removed from them is far more alert to that fact than someone who might be doing the removing. This is because the person affected knows what they need and how much they need it far better than anyone else. This is one of the great powers of the advice process: all you need to do is think of the people and then let them tell you what this will mean to them. Instead of trying to put yourself in someone else's position (as other approaches to architecture can do), the advice process engages with these parties directly and involves them explicitly. It's a much more effective way to make good decisions.

At this point, the team already knew they had to return to the drawing board with their design, but before they did so, they chose to speak to the other advice-offering group: the parties with expertise. What insights would they have to share?

In many circumstances, "expertise" translates to "past experience and/or wider horizons on the decision." We'll dig into each of these in detail in Chapter 12. For now, it will help to think of these "horizons" as matters like longer time periods, broader scopes, greater risk awareness, deeper understanding of cost implications, and wider understanding of the impact on people and skills in other areas of the organization as well as general organization, business, market, and industry understanding.

In our story, the experts initially identified to speak to were a systems architect, the lead QA, and a different product manager for another part of the product who had experience with release toggles. The team spoke to them each in turn.

EXAMPLE

Checklist: People to seek advice from about our feature toggle

Teams that consume our APIs:

- ☑ ~~Team Yan~~
- ☑ ~~Team Tan~~
- ☑ ~~Team Tethera~~

People with expertise:

- ☐ Fiona, the systems architect
- ☐ JB, the lead QA
- ☐ Monira, the product manager

The architect turned out to be a great first port of call. Not only did she have a wealth of opinions, but she also had experience working with a form of release toggle back when she was a developer. She pointed out that not everyone had the same idea in mind when people used the term *toggle* and pointed them to an article on feature toggles (*https://oreil.ly/YD8-u*) that the team had not previously seen to help them disambiguate. After the team had read this, they realized they had been lucky—they really did mean *release toggle*—and they had also learned that they should think about making their implementation temporary. The architect backed up their advice with tales of all the dead code that was left in the codebase when her project had used them. This was a key piece of advice and one that was very simple to incorporate into the decision, whatever the selected option. In doing so, all options were improved, and technical debt in the form of redundant code could be managed, saving the team a lot of time in the future. This is an example of an expert providing "farsight" (looking farther into the future) advice.

The architect suggested that the team talk to the lead infra engineer. They'd be able to provide advice on environments, permissions, and access rights. The team agreed to set up a chat with them. But first, they had a scheduled meeting with JB, the lead QA.

EXAMPLE

Checklist: People to seek advice from about our feature toggle

- ☑ ~~Team Yan~~
- ☑ ~~Team Tan~~
- ☑ ~~Team Tethera~~

People with expertise:

- ☑ ~~Fiona, the systems architect~~
- ☐ JB, the lead QA
- ☐ Monira, the product manager
- ☐ Yinka in infrastructure (suggested by Fiona)

JB had some great points, too: specifically, a concern that toggles would make testing more involved. They explained that with release toggles in place, testing would have to ensure that features (1) did work when toggled on, (2) did not work when toggled off, and most important, (3) didn't interact with one another in weird, unpredictable ways when some were on and some were off. Despite this, the lead QA, JB, was also very excited. They knew the risk-mitigating benefits of being able to make many small releases of code as opposed to one large one. (No prizes for guessing that this quality expert had provided an example of "greater risk awareness" advice.)

Next, the team sat down to talk with Yinka, the lead infra engineer, who was kind enough to have an impromptu chat with them despite feeling a little ambushed. That conversation, although initially a little fractious, validated what Fiona, the systems architect, had pointed out: if the toggles were in code, then to change one toggle—for example, to enable a feature for an internal showcase demo—the team would have to submit a code change and trigger an entire run of the pipeline.

While it would work, the infra engineer Yinka wasn't shy about sharing his feeling that this was a pretty heavyweight approach, but when questioned, he explained how the team's goal could be better achieved with toggles controlled by environment variables, which could then be changed without redeployments. "This would be easy for the team to implement," Yinka said, "as we're already using this approach for some of our infra configurations, and it has the added benefits of not giving me and my team any more infrastructure to look after, such as databases or more elaborate products." Yinka even concluded by telling the team about a colleague to speak to when it came time to implement. In the course of this slightly difficult but enlightening conversation, the infra engineer had provided examples of both "deeper understanding of cost implications" (with regard to time taken to swap toggle settings) and "wider understanding of the impact on people and skills in other areas of the organization" advice.

There was one final expert to seek advice from: Monira, the product manager from another department who had experience using release toggles. The team kicked off the chat with her by summarizing everything they'd learned from the prior conversations. Monira validated it all and didn't have much advice to add. She did, however, point out a final benefit of the environment-variable approach: it would allow the team to safely, and with little notice, demo to her colleague, the team's product manager, or clients. When the team asked how, Monira explained that the toggles could be used to turn on a specific feature or set of features for such impromptu demos and then turn them off again afterward, with little overall disruption to the team's planned work and without blocking environments for multiple hours while the toggle was enabled and then disabled. The team loved this. It would allow them to smash the expectations of their product manager, who only really wanted to understand users' needs (and therefore build the best product possible) without much disruption. A win-win situation.[8] Yet again, advice had broadened the horizons of the team. This time they had benefited from an adviser's "understanding of cost implications" as well as their insights into what the market would tolerate in the form of clients' willingness to get incredibly early views on in-development features.

---

[8] You can see from this that product managers deeply and intuitively understand the concept of early feedback. Here, they were hoping to get this before a feature was even completed. What better way to find out what users think *and* prevent waste in the form of the team continuing to build anything unwanted?

Checklist: People to seek advice from about our feature toggle

- ☑ ~~Team Yan~~
- ☑ ~~Team Tan~~
- ☑ ~~Team Tethera~~

People with expertise:

- ☑ ~~Fiona, the systems architect~~
- ☑ ~~JB, the lead QA~~
- ☑ ~~Monira the product manager~~
- ☑ ~~Yinka in infrastructure (suggested by Fiona)~~

Armed with all this incredible advice, the deciding team went back to their design and made significant changes. They followed the advice of the infra team member and decided to use environment variables for their toggles, and they checked to see if this meant they would have to request any significant changes to their delivery pipelines. It didn't. They also decided to track the existence of toggles for stories in their Jira tickets, which would allow them to see what toggles were in use and, importantly, what they were used for. This last idea came from the business analyst in the team who knew Monira, the product manager, would appreciate being able to know at a glance and without disrupting the team what was demo-able.

The team's final act was to get back to everyone they had sought advice from to let them know about their decision. This was easy and quick because those involved already had a lot of the context, and even the affected teams who didn't know about the shift to an environment-variable-based solution knew about all the context of the decision and so needed little extra information. They were also pleased at this new easy-on/off solution as it meant they could get access to the in-development services far more rapidly when they were needed.

Now that the advice process is complete, I can tell you who the option makers and decision takers were. The answer for both is "the team." The reason they are the decision takers is because they are the ones who felt the need for the decision and who initiated the advice process in order to take it. And why are they the option makers? Because they are the ones making the options (with help in the form of advice from the advice offerers whom they are obliged to engage).

I hope the benefits of the advice process are clear from this first story. The deciding team ended up in a far better place than they would have been had they gone with their initial design, which they came up with on their own. This is in great part because the advice process provides a basis for combining a wide variety of data and viewpoints: near and long term, local and systemwide, upstream and downstream. It's an incredibly powerful mix.

It's worth being explicit about the fact that not all of the advice a decider receives may change their planned approach, but every piece does contribute toward making them aware of the full scope and impact of their pending decision. In exposing the decider to this, in the context of their real need that arises from their real-world circumstances, the advice process is a great catalyst for learning. In this tale alone, the team learned more than they ever expected about types of toggles and their uses, about the past experiences of the architect, about the thought processes of QA (developers could always benefit from thinking more like QAs), and about how infra contribute to building and running their systems and how they are reticent to take on more things to look after. Most important perhaps, the team collectively built their human network across the organization. The more times they made decisions using the advice process, the stronger this was to become.

For these arising-from-teams decisions, the traditional architectural dynamics are flipped on their head; previously, decisions were taken outside teams, then handed to them to implement. Now with the advice process, teams have a stronger voice *and* are exposed directly to their peers and the consequences of their decisions. They have, in the words of the Netflix culture deck,[9] both "freedom and responsibility."

Story 2: An Architect Decides to Unpick a Workflow Problem

Over the course of software delivery, especially in these days of constantly evolving architectures, a majority of decisions arise in the fashion of my first story. But not all of them. What about decisions that address those needs for cross-cutting decisions and decisions that arise from the nature and evolution of the system as a whole? Who raises those questions in the advice process? These decisions inevitably come from people playing roles outside of any single delivery team. In most (but not all) cases, these are roles we traditionally think of as "architecture." This type of decision is the focus of our second story. As you read it, pay attention again to the social contract and who the different parties are. It'll help make the story clearer.

Picture the scene: delivery has been up and running for a few years now, and a mature product is in place. It has an established customer base, supported by a set of robust and predictable microservices. Predictable, that is, in all places but one. One microservice has slowly become both a delivery and a performance bottleneck as well as a single point of failure.

---

9 It never fails to amaze me that Netflix published this so early on in the company's life. I've taken inspiration from it many times and stolen a few ideas from it, too (*https://oreil.ly/HjnaT*). You can see the latest version (*https://oreil.ly/HLqJz*) as well as previous versions (*https://oreil.ly/qH-Wp*).

It wasn't supposed to be this way. The service in question had begun life as a simple component built by a single team to externalize a few key decision points of their workflow logic. Because it was solidly built, well tested, and, most of all, easy to consume and extend, other teams started to put some of their workflows into it. This isn't an uncommon occurrence. Over and over, I've seen the place where it's easiest to put complex logic be the place where it ends up, whether that was the best or right place or not.

Time passed, and as the company's product became more popular, the user needs it was supporting became more complex. This subtle but definite change in overall product philosophy also changed the demands placed on the underlying services.

The workflow microservice began to take more and more of the strain. Because of its high-quality implementation and ease of extension, it coped admirably. Sometimes, for example, a team needed more than the basic workflow support, so the team that owned the workflow service gradually extended it. It worked. Everyone managed to deliver their stories rapidly, and product managers were happy.

But slowly, problems began to arise.

Teams had been noticing for a while that very occasionally, an individual user's journey would act strangely: they might jump forward a few steps, or jump from one flow to another, or (worst of all) potentially gain access to subflows they shouldn't be able to access. While this wasn't great, what was worse was that these failures were hard to replicate and therefore difficult to fix.

As the company's overall product became more and more successful, the load on all the services increased, and these "blips" in workflow functioning became more frequent and increasingly harder to replicate. It became clear where the root cause of the problem lay: the workflow service. Over time, what had been seen as a reliable and useful tool was slowly becoming a liability.

This isn't an unusual evolution—I see it over and over again, and let me be clear: what the workflow subsystem was doing now was *far* outstretching the original design goals of the team when they first developed it. It's no wonder then that things were beginning to creak at the seams. This superservice was now performing a lot of different jobs, many of which simply hadn't been considered at the outset because the need wasn't there. There was a reason for this: when the system was originally designed, no one thought user journeys would get so complex. In fact, one of the original selling points of the product was that it was simple, straightforward, and to the point; it worked the same everywhere. The only reason this service had been brought to life in the first place was to allow minor changes to the user-journey flow to be deployed without updates to the mobile app. But as we all know, even if it's only from our experiences as consumers, products don't stay the same for long these days, so the product began to incrementally evolve in a different direction, one that was more individually tailored to users, and the underlying services evolved incrementally to support this.

The signs that the architecture was the problem rather than simply a lack of testing or low code quality first became clear to those in architecture roles. Because they considered matters across the entire system, they were in a position to aggregate all the individual instances of failure, while teams were quite likely aware only of the ones that affected them, so the architects could see a possible pattern emerging. Their longer experience had taught them to stay alert for bad smells, and this service was increasingly the source of troubling odors.

The smell that tipped the balance from observing and offering advice into architecture changes and deciding was work coupling. Teams were being blocked in delivery of their features while they waited for the team that owned the workflow service. The reason? They needed minor enhancements in the underlying service to allow their features to work.

At this point, a systems architect decided that something needed to be done, and as you would expect, she went about this using the architecture advice process, playing the role of the decision maker and taker and seeing the relevant advice inputs. She put together the following list:

EXAMPLE

Checklist: Teams to seek advice from about detangling workflow

Those affected by the decision:

☐ Team Ichi (backend—currently owns the repo with the code)

☐ Team Ni (backend)

☐ Team San (backend)

☐ Team Yon (backend)

☐ Team Go (mobile: iOS/Swift)

☐ Team Roku (mobile: Android/Kotlin)

Their initial focus in seeking advice was to (1) establish the current design of the workflow service *as it existed in the code*, and (2) find out what each of the teams was trying to use the workflow service for. As I've already mentioned, it turned out that the code was clean, and the design was explicit and well tested. Unsurprisingly, the code was doing a *lot*. What the architect uncovered with regard to the second line of investigation backed this up. By looking at the combination of the code and the team's needs, the architect could see that there were three usage patterns being supported.

Some teams were still using the system as originally designed: purely as a workflow engine, directing the users to the next steps in their journeys. These teams didn't put any of the logic of each step in the workflow; for that, control would be passed back to the mobile user and the app in their hand. This was the first usage pattern.

This original design explicitly did *not* hold the state of individual user-journey flows. However, as journeys had become more involved, more and more complex business logic had started to be duplicated in both the iOS and the Android version of the app. As a result, the decision had been implicitly taken to put this logic in a single place. By "implicitly," I mean it had arisen during the course of coding and not been identified as an architecturally significant decision.

It was significant, though, and it was acted on appropriately. The duplicated logic for these flows had been removed from the Swift and Kotlin codebases and located instead back in the workflow service. This decision made a lot of sense from many angles. This was the core business logic, and it was important to the business too because of the increased user expectations. Writing it in two places was a clear violation of the DRY principle.[10]

In the refactored workflow engine underpinning all these journeys, there was an implicit assumption that these shared, backend business logic steps would be stateless–that is to say, when they were called, they would have all the user state needed to operate passed into them, and all the information needed for the mobile apps to proceed would be passed out of them. Nothing would be persisted. Consequently, other teams were then able to use it in similar ways. All these teams were the second usage pattern.

Finally came the third usage pattern. When the systems architect spoke to these teams, she discovered that, rather cleverly, the teams had realized that they could build on top of the platform provided by the workflow service and add their own cross-request state persistence features. They'd managed to circumvent the "no persistence" rule.

Yet again, the teams hadn't done this simply for their own gratification or out of laziness. These teams had foreseen that all this passing of state back and forth, especially in some of the less mature mobile marketplaces, would slow things down, ruining overall user experience. (In the future, this would most likely have been the case, but it wasn't an issue yet.) This local optimization had pushed the workflow service as far as it could go and, in certain edge cases, farther. It also meant that something like session

---

10 This was the *real* DRY (don't repeat yourself) principle: the issue here was duplication of knowledge, not simply of code. These were key business rules, so having to code and test them twice was opening the teams up to undue risk. The best explanation of this I've ever found is in Mathias Verraes's blog post "DRY is about Knowledge," (*https://oreil.ly/5ELAc*) which does a great job of disambiguating Andrew Hunt and David Thomas's original explanation in *The Pragmatic Programmer: From Journeyman to Master* (Addison-Wesley)

stickiness would need to be implemented if the workflow service ever scaled up to multiple instances, which would have an impact on options to scale.

The systems architect now had a good view of all the forces at play in this decision. Fundamental to her thinking was acknowledging that the workflow service was now meeting multiple needs. Some it had been designed for at its core, and some it hadn't. What was amazing was that in most cases, it was coping admirably.

EXAMPLE

Checklist: Teams to seek advice from about detangling workflow

Those affected by the decision:

- ☑ ~~Team Ichi (backend—currently own the repo with the code)~~
- ☑ ~~Team Ni (backend)~~
- ☑ ~~Team San (backend)~~
- ☑ ~~Team Yon (backend)~~
- ☑ ~~Team Go (mobile: iOS/Swift)~~
- ☑ ~~Team Roku (mobile: Android/Kotlin)~~

People with expertise:

- ☐ Cassie, the mobile SME

The architect now had the information she needed to engage the experts, bringing in one of the organization's global mobile subject matter experts (SMEs). In the ensuing conversation, it became clear that this kind of evolution is not uncommon where patterns aren't initially as distinct as they might be in the web world. What is more, the nature of mobile deployments, and the fact that teams can have multiple versions of their clients in the form of the mobile apps out there in the wild running in parallel, compounds issues.

Cassie's first piece of advice was to acknowledge the various forces at play and the needs of the various teams. Second, she suggested addressing these needs individually. Third, she suggested that some of the problems might not need to be solved right now; instead, the teams that were experiencing them should simplify their implementation while starting in parallel to investigate relevant third-party and open source solutions.

Checklist: Teams to seek advice from about detangling workflow

Those affected by the decision:

- ☑ ~~Team Ichi (backend—currently own the repo with the code)~~
- ☑ ~~Team Ni (backend)~~
- ☑ ~~Team San (backend)~~
- ☑ ~~Team Yon (backend)~~
- ☑ ~~Team Go (mobile: iOS/Swift)~~
- ☑ ~~Team Roku (mobile: Android/Kotlin)~~

People with expertise:

- ☑ ~~Cassie, the mobile SME~~
- ☐ Patricia, the newly hired mobile developer with experience of Kotlin Multiplatform
- ☐ Gayathri, the backend dev who remembers enterprise service buses[11]
- ☐ Isha, the QA who worked on an Apache Camel workflow system

This then led the architect to go speak to Patricia, one of the newly hired senior devs on the Android Mobile team. The company that Patricia had just left had famously faced similar issues around duplication of business logic. They had a great chat about the pros and cons of different approaches to solving this. The architect kept in mind the fact that the circumstances this company was facing were slightly different, but there were great insights around available frameworks, tooling, practices, and developer experiences to make this work.

Finally, the architect knew that Gayathri, one of the more-experienced backend devs, had been around in the days of enterprise service buses, and in another part of the business was Isha, a QA who had worked on a heavily workflow-oriented system based on Apache Camel (*https://camel.apache.org*). The architect chatted with both of them, sharing with them both the current usage patterns of the subsystem and the benefits and pitfalls of various types of standard patterns that this was approaching. In doing so, the architect drew together a decision that would, if not make everyone

---

11 *Enterprise service bus* (aka ESB) was a pattern favored in the early 2010s that got out of control and became a place to mislay and then lose your organization's key business logic. (See the ESB tech radar blip (*https://oreil.ly/CE1-6*)). The "smart endpoints, dumb pipes" (*https://oreil.ly/69g45*) pattern emerged in response to this.

entirely happy, be right-sized for the organization and aligned to its future direction as well as one that maintained investment in the homegrown workflow solution.

EXAMPLE

Checklist: Teams to seek advice from about detangling workflow

Those affected by the decision:

- ☑ ~~Team Ichi (backend — currently own the repo with the code)~~
- ☑ ~~Team Ni (backend)~~
- ☑ ~~Team San (backend)~~
- ☑ ~~Team Yon (backend)~~
- ☑ ~~Team Go (mobile: iOS/Swift)~~
- ☑ ~~Team Roku (mobile: Android/Kotlin)~~

People with expertise:

- ☑ ~~Cassie, the mobile SME~~
- ☑ ~~Patricia, the newly hired mobile developer with experience of Kotlin Multiplatform~~
- ☑ ~~Gayathri, the backend dev who remembers ESBs~~
- ☑ ~~Isha, the QA who worked on an Apache Camel workflow system~~

The systems architect was now in a position to make her decision proposal. It comprised three independent parts:

- Some simple refactorings of the workflow service to firm up usage patterns, making it explicitly easier to use this service to do the things it was good at, and harder or impossible to make it do things it was poor at. These refactorings focused on protecting the statelessness of the service above all else. The architect proposed that this be developed using an "inner source"[12] approach to allow teams to put their flows into the workflow service codebase without having to rely on the team that owned it to do it for them.

---

12 See the report by Danese Cooper and Klaas-Jan Stol, "Adopting InnerSource," for more information. Fundamentally, it espouses using techniques that are used to run open source projects: codebases and backlogs everyone can see, documentation on processes for those outside the core committers to submit features, bugs, code, etc.

- Identify an element of shared cross-platform business logic that is well understood and tested in the workflow service. Take this and reimplement it using Kotlin Multiplatform, providing libraries that can be consumed directly by both the iOS and the Android apps. The architect hoped that this would allow this code to be written once, but that this approach would avoid the need to have this shared code running in the backend, instead packaging it with the iOS and Android releases directly.

- Refactor the stateful, performance-optimization workflows to make them stateless. At the same time, instrument the journeys to capture real-world data on the journey times and volumes of data being shipped over the wire. Use this to look into solutions such as realtime backend databases for mobile (such as Firebase Realtime Database (*https://oreil.ly/wSP8X*)) and backends for frontends (such as GraphQL (*https://oreil.ly/8koxp*)).

The next step before taking and then sharing the decision was for the architect to go back to each of the teams and seek their advice on this draft decision, particularly how it might be rolled out. This time, the architect brought everyone together so that the scope and interdependence of everything would be self-evident to all concerned. This was crucial because the implementation of big architectural changes is as important as the architectural design itself. By doing this, everyone involved learned even more about the specifics of what was planned, and an incremental strategy that could be pursued team by team was worked out.

It helped that the decision had been split into three parts. These could be tackled independently and at a sensible pace. All the teams knew what they would get as a result, what their roles in the refactorings were likely to be, and when it would all happen. They also provided some further pieces of advice, based this time on the teams' capacity for this extra work, the skills and predisposition to learn new things in each team, and any early warnings of potential difficulties. The architect factored this advice into the decisions and supported the teams that required further investigations while helping the others get to work on their elements. Finally, the architect was able to take this involved yet incredibly important decision with the support of all the teams.

The necessary refactorings were implemented slowly, steadily, and safely. Milestones were celebrated by everyone as they were reached. Because everyone understood the overall goal, teams could call in the architect when unpredicted events happened. The product managers supported the change as they could see, step by step, that the numbers of defects their customers were experiencing were decreasing and the speed at which their teams could implement new features was beginning to recover.

You will, I hope, have noticed that the dynamic of this outside-team-initiated advice process is different. In this mode, those concerned with the overall systemic architecture (the roles almost inevitably played by those of us with "architect" somewhere in our job title) have a mechanism to work out in the open, establish dialogue, and build trust and understanding across all teams within the sociotechnical system.

This is where the power of the advice process comes in yet again. The architect pursuing this change had to recognize that they depend on the teams to deliver the necessary implementations. She had to listen to the teams as part of the contract (a great way to get right-now detail) and make coherent arguments for the benefits of their change. This has a balancing effect. No longer could arbitrary, wide-reaching decisions be taken without at least some attention being given to the teams that would bring them to reality.

The Centrality of Advice

I hope that you're starting to get a feel for how the advice process works. As it becomes more familiar to you, it's important to keep in mind what advice is and how it shifts the power to decide. Everyone participating in the advice process needs to understand the value of advice, which advice is pertinent to a specific decision, and how advice affects the decision process.

Advice Is Suggested Direction Plus Reasoning

The concept of *advice* can be a tricky one to grasp. *Advice* is frequently confused with *opinion*, and opinions are things that we software development professionals seem to have many of. It's an incredibly important distinction, though, because in the advice process, opinions are a near enemy of advice.

Near enemy is a Buddhist concept, best thought of as a counterfeit that appears to offer the same value as the real thing but is, in fact, harmful. For example, needy codependency is a near enemy of love.[13] From a more technical perspective, a DevOps team is a near enemy of a DevOps mindset, and a top-down-imposed Agile transformation is a near enemy of Agile teams.[14]

Why is a DevOps team a near enemy of a DevOps mindset? By its very nature, a distinct team "doing" DevOps is fundamentally missing the point of the DevOps movement, which came into existence to *break down* silos between Dev and Ops (hence their proximity in the name), with goals that include improving communication and building in feedback loops. A separate team to achieve this clearly flies in the face of these goals.

---

13 You can read some other general examples in "This Column Will Change Your Life: Near Enemies" (*https://oreil.ly/qfIDR*) by Oliver Burkeman.

14 Gayathri Thiyagarajan and I filled an entire presentation with the near enemies of domain-driven design called (unsurprisingly) "Combatting the Near Enemies of Domain-Driven Design" (*https://oreil.ly/QFtoK*).

And how is a top-down-imposed Agile transformation a near enemy of Agile teams? Well, the Agile Manifesto principles (*https://oreil.ly/i2xr7*) remind us that "The best architectures, requirements, and designs emerge from self-organizing teams" and "Build projects around motivated individuals. Give them the environment and support they need, and trust them to get the job done." Sadly, these principles are the exact opposite of a directive from senior management to "be Agile." You know things are really getting out of hand when things like standardized tools and ways of working are rolled out by a team that isn't itself involved in the delivery of software.

Now that the concept of near enemies is clear, let's turn it on advice and opinion, and see why the latter is a near enemy of the former.

Merriam-Webster has the most appropriate definition of *advice* for our purposes: "a recommendation regarding a decision or course of conduct: counsel."[15] According to this definition, advice is directly related to decisions. No surprise there. The "recommendation" and "counsel" parts are what I want to focus your attention on. When advice is offered, we get both the direction recommendation *and* the reasons behind it—the benefits of experience. That means the advice recipients get the advisers' perspectives and perceived outcomes that a potential course of action may or may not lead to. That can truly be incorporated into the decision process.

For example, some advice might be offered regarding which build of the OpenJDK to use in a new project. Now, there are a lot of builds available, and the choice can be overwhelming (the latest list is maintained on the OpenJDK Wikipedia page (*https://oreil.ly/AUE34*)). Advice received might be: "I would use this build because not only does it have licensing terms appropriate to our company's standards but also because their releases always keep up with the upstream OpenJDK from Oracle, and they have a great wiki as well as an active community who responded rapidly to us when we asked them for help on a weird issue we had."

You get the idea. Not only do we have a suggested build, but we can also see *why* the adviser reached their conclusions. Knowing this, we can then consider if these reasons are relevant to our circumstances and reflect a sufficient understanding of the decision we are engaged in.

How does this compare with *opinion*? *Oxford Learner's Dictionaries* defines opinion as "your feelings or thoughts about somebody/something, rather than a fact."[16] Clearly, an opinion might still be targeted at a decision ("about something") and might come in a form that *initially* sounds like it might be advice: "do this" or "don't do that." Both advice and opinion can begin in this way, but after that shared beginning, they diverge, which is where the near enemy opinion lurks. The key differences are two-

---

15 *Merriam-Webster Dictionary*, "advice" (*https://oreil.ly/3U_ge*), accessed August 14, 2024.
16 *Oxford Learner's Dictionaries*, "opinion" (*https://oreil.ly/kuqpO*), accessed August 14, 2024.

fold, both stemming from an opinion's lack of a "why." First, opinions lack supportive reasoning, or to put it more simply, they lack facts. They tell you which direction to go in but not why that direction is best. Second, opinions might also be driven by feelings or emotions, which quite likely are submerged and implicit. The lack of associated facts is a clue to this.

If we return to the example of advice that I gave earlier, this time phrasing it in the form of an opinion, you will be able to see the difference: "I would use this OpenJDK build because it works better. It's faster, cheaper, and higher quality."

You can see we still have the direction ("Pick this one, not any of the others") but the reasoning is absent. *Why* is that build better? *Why* is it faster? *Why* is it cheaper? *What about it* is higher quality? For a decision maker seeking advice, these opinions are damaging because they do not provide the real juice of the offerer's experience. The adviser hasn't shared their supporting reasoning, their "whys."

Architectural decisions are always "it depends" decisions; the trick is to figure out what the decision "depends" on, and advice helps with that greatly. Opinions lack this key aspect, and omitting it makes it harder for the decider to benefit from the offerer's experience.

All is not lost, however. If you are lucky, you might be able to tell that there's an unvoiced feeling motivating the opinion, and you can get to it via some questioning. In our OpenJDK build example, the advice seeker could probe with appropriate "why" and "how" questions, and perhaps this would be enough to turn the opinion into advice by supplementing it with supportive reasoning. You might not always get this, particularly when the opinionated person is unaware of their bias, or is aware of it but is ashamed to admit it.[17] However, even this information is valuable as it signals the presence of a near enemy, which can be handled carefully.

Why do I say "carefully"? By not sharing the "why" of advice and instead restricting involvement to the raw statement of opinion, opinion offerers can be attempting to retain power for themselves, whether they know it or not. If advice offerers are struggling, for whatever reason, asking "why" can boost the process and forge a path to the advice. Underlying it all may be the fear arising from a lack of trust. That's perfectly understandable, and I'll come back to this topic again and again in Part III, but while it's front of mind, let's have an initial look at the shifts in power dynamics right now.

---

17 As a former employee of Sun Microsystems, I was raised to have an unthinking bias against everything Microsoft. Even when it was clear I was in the wrong, I would stick to my opinions. This bias ran so deep that it persisted for years after I left the company, and even after the company ceased to exist. These days, I still have a remnant of that bias (Sun was my first employer after all, and it was the heady days of the first dot.com bubble), but I am aware of it, and I can express it out loud. This allows advice seekers to separate the advice from the opinion and get what they need. I also quite like joking about it.

Advice Powers Up Option Makers and Decision Takers

When you gather advice, useful or otherwise, you expand the knowledge and experience base that informs your decision. You are hearing what others would do in your circumstances, but not only that—you are hearing what they would be thinking or asking themselves if they were in your shoes, and most importantly, you are hearing *why* they reached the conclusions they have.

Recall the opinionated adviser in the previous subsection. Imagine now that we'd followed up their opinions with a bunch of questions, and that, excited by the prospect of being asked to expand, they did. Sharing just a little of their experience, they talked about how they had worked on a project that used a pre-OpenJDK version of Java, and it had caused them no end of problems. Biggest of which was the fact that they had been forced to rely on a small team of part-time committers to fix the bug requests they logged, which had been many. They told how they had tried to take control of matters by submitting patches and pull requests but to no avail. The core committers were disinclined to offer anyone outside their immediate circle commit privileges. As a consequence, the adviser had gained a distrust of open source projects that were maintained by teams, not subsidized full-time by a commercial company. Even then they were skeptical, reasoning that the company would always prioritize their own needs over those of the community.

Mapping advice onto your specific circumstances powers up your decision, either because you now have supporting reasoning from others or you now have a more cleanly defined context, options, and consequences. Thinking critically about whether you are receiving "advice" or simply opinions really helps in this. It also helps to ask questions, transforming opinions into advice. Both ensure that you really listen and really understand by interrogating advice you identify and isolating the parts that are useful, even if they are mixed in with elements that don't apply to the circumstances at hand. You can tell which is which from the supporting facts and the reasons why because they allow you to differentiate what is applicable from what is not.

With this counsel available, you become (potentially, at least[18]) greater than if you were simply thinking and acting alone. However, you—the decider, the one who has initiated this decision and who is responsible and accountable for it—are still the only one in the driving seat. As long as you have lived up to your end of the social contract, fulfilling your obligation to seek all the relevant advice and making sure you understand it, you are entitled to take any decision you need, including if this means acknowledging *but putting aside* the aspects of the advice that are not pertinent to your decision.

---

18 Barry O'Reilly (the residuality theory one, not the Lean Enterprise one) is in the process of proving this mathematically. See his paper "An Introduction to Residuality Theory: Software Design Heuristics for Complex Systems" (*https://oreil.ly/n7bN2*) (*Procedia Computer Science*, vol. 170, 2020) for more information.

Offering Advice Does Not Make You Accountable—Taking Decisions Does

Let's be clear: as the decision taker in the advice process, you are not only responsible for a decision but also accountable for it. The permission that the advice process confers to make and then take decisions is a powerful one indeed, but for that reason, it can sometimes be a bumpy road.

This unhitching of this locus of power can be particularly tough for architects who are traditionally used to being in the driving seat of *all* decisions. Watching others taking the wheel and steering the technical direction can feel uncomfortable, especially when the decisions don't go the way they would take them, against their offered advice. Even if intellectually, architects and other leaders, right up to the executive level (CTOs and CIOs, for example), understand that this transfer has taken place, it can be emotionally hard to let go, especially when it has been your role's raison d'être (and quite possibly a motivation for pursuing the career of architect in the first place).

For some traditional architects, feelings around this change in role are self-evident, while for others, they are not so conscious. Either way, it leads to problems when an architect is unwilling (consciously or unconsciously) to let go of their sense of accountability. You will see it arising (either consciously or unconsciously, in yourself or in others) in the offering of opinions rather than advice, even more so when there are difficulties clearly articulating the "why."

When this happens, it helps to remember that in the new world of the advice process, the responsibility of advice seekers/decision takers is to understand all the advice they can get their hands on, and the advice offerers will now want those who are newly accountable to have as much information as they can provide. This dynamic super-charges the advice seeking—least because of the social contract, but also because there is little to gain in taking a poor decision when a better one might be achievable. Furthermore, if opinions are offered, then it is beneficial to the advice seeker to deploy questions to find out what is behind them *because they are accountable for the end results* (both the decision and, if they are in a team, the resulting implementation). If there are useful elements for them, then they can access them. If this power is going to transfer, then it had better transfer properly and fully, with the advice seeker aware of all the concerns that the advice offerer has.

There is a great benefit to this transition to the advice process. Recall the two scenarios demonstrating the advice process in action from earlier in this chapter. Story 1 showed that *some* decisions were now moving into the realm of the teams—they initiated the decisions, made and then took them, and implemented them. They were accountable. In the old world, even if an architect had merely been along for the ride at every step of the way, merely nodding and agreeing to every suggestion the team might have, effectively rubber-stamping everything, at the end of it all, the architect would still be accountable, not the team. This happens with the traditional architecture approaches over and over again right now. It's happening in your organization (either explicitly or implicitly). How *can* an architect possibly be responsible for everything these days? And yet, because of the ways that things are currently set up, they are.

Now bring to mind the second story. There, the cross-team architect initiated the process, so *they* remained accountable for that decision, even though the teams were, as always, the ones who implemented it. Again, that is as it should be. In a world where multiple teams have roles to play and no single team is doing even a majority of the work, you need someone outside the teams to make sure the best outcomes are achieved. As I made clear, the architect still depends on the teams to implement their elements, but this was always the case. If you are an architect, do you really, *truly* believe everything you told teams to do ended up in production, in the way you told them to do it?

Of course not.[19]

The Importance of Conversations

However you approach it, the first thing to bear in mind is that the advice process places great value on conversations. It therefore should come as no surprise to hear that the influential architect Ruth Malan presciently noted that for an architecture to be successful:

> It is very much about ensuring that conversations that need to be happening are happening—not always initiating them, nor always helping to focus or navigate them, but ensuring they do happen and guiding when needed.[20]

The advice process is robust precisely because it operates in this way. As a decision process, it decentralizes power so that anyone can initiate a decision. It opens up space for conversations to happen around the making of those decisions and requires that you have conversations with the right people. Malan's "needed conversations" are the heart of the advice process.

However, it's quite possible that the approach still feels a little too loose for you, and I can sympathize with that. Many software professionals, myself included, have, in part at least, gravitated toward software because of the certainty and concreteness of code.

---

19 In fact, I *hope* teams have never simply coded up my designs unthinkingly. Some of my most memorable nightmares have arisen from something I forgot to even worry about suddenly springing to mind, and when I spoke to the dev lead of the team at work the next day, they let me know that they had already spotted it and updated the design accordingly.

20 Ruth Malan, "How is Software Architecture Created?" (*https://oreil.ly/uD5zs*), updated July 18, 2020.

All this talk of "advice" and "anyone can take a decision" feels a tad too close to anarchy.[21]

Let's unpack that a little because it's important. I want to acknowledge it and provide reassurance, too, with Malan's centering of conversations as our touchstone.

The Significance of Trust

There is a fear regarding trust that may have been circling your mind as you've been reading this chapter. With client after client, I encounter architects who don't trust development teams and development teams who don't trust architects. In fact, I frequently see development teams who don't trust one another either as well as architects who are at odds with one another.

However, trust *within* development teams is usually quite high, and this indicates to me that trust is possible to achieve and sustain in today's organizations. The reason this can happen within teams is because, in the majority of cases, there is a shared goal and a mutual dependency on the successful delivery of its associated outcomes.

By deploying the advice process, you are both establishing and subsequently relying on a broader trust network. Is *that* possible? If you are unsure if your organization can achieve and sustain this, then I encourage you to have faith—just because you may not see it now doesn't mean it is an impossibility. It's just that traditional practices prevent it from arising.[22]

Remember as you read this book, whoever you are and whatever your role, you are worthy of trust. It follows that if you are, aren't others? If particular problematic individuals spring to mind who you feel are unworthy of trust, I'd challenge you to ask "why not?" Perhaps you disagree with one another. In that case, use the advice process to work with them—at least trying to seek their advice—safe in the knowledge that you can ignore their advice if you choose to. Perhaps they are actively secretive or destructive; I will spend whole chapters in Part II and again in Part III to help you identify and resolve this (both personally and as a collective). For now, bear in mind that such people will be a problem, no matter what approach you take to the practice of architecture. A problem that your organization will need to address.

---

21 I use this word advisedly. When people use the word *anarchy* in general conversation, they typically mean a state of disorder. That couldn't be further from the anarchist's own definition. Ironically, the advice process is in many ways a textbook implementation of anarchistic organizing in that it follows Paul Goodman's definition: "Authority is delegated away from the top as much as possible, and there are many centers of decision and policy-making. Information is conveyed and discussed in face-to-face contacts between field and headquarters" (quoted in *Patterns of Anarchy: A Collection of Writings on the Anarchist Tradition*, eds. Leonard I. Krimerman and Lewis Perry (Anchor Books, 1966), 379–380).

22 I've argued elsewhere (*https://oreil.ly/nFIvO*) that the single-mode, traditional organization structure fundamentally prevents other ways of collaborating from arising.

Once again, this demonstrates the power of conversations, and *conversation* is precisely the right word. Conversations aren't adversarial, they're not a battle, and they don't seek to have a winner and a loser; they're not a zero-sum game. Conversations are interactions that take place between equals. They are about the back-and-forth exchange of information and, dare I say it, building of trust and understanding. They are about co-creation of something shared: both software and trusting relationships. There can be no pulling of rank in the advice process.

By centering conversations, you aren't only solving your problems of architectural processes that block and fail to factor in sufficient feedback. You're also potentially uncovering a better way to do architecture.

Conclusion

In this chapter, I introduced you to the architecture advice process: a decision process that embodies a fundamental shift in software architecture practice. The advice process is built on the core idea of allowing everyone to make options and take architectural decisions, with appropriate input from others, and a social contract that supports this. This seemingly small change eliminates decision bottlenecks, optimizes feedback, and catalyzes a healthy culture of trust and learning.[23]

Hopefully, the architecture advice process sounds like something you want to experiment with. Chapter 6 introduces an essential complementary element, and subsequent chapters offer further optional supporting elements to establish and bolster trust, but for now, let's look at three different ways that you can roll out the architecture advice process, start these conversations, and transform how you go about practicing architecture within your organization.

---

23 It's small, but it's a key leverage point, hence its power. See Donella Meadows's article "Leverage Points: Places to Intervene in a System" (*https://oreil.ly/aDZvf*).

CHAPTER 5

Rolling Out the Architecture Advice Process

Now that you have an idea of how the advice process works and what it looks like in action, you may be wondering how to start implementing it in your own team or organization. In this chapter, I'll share how you can start experimenting with and then adopting the architecture advice process depending on whether you currently hold any decision-taking power or not. I'll also cover early-stage challenges you might face before addressing confidence concerns that you might encounter with this approach.

Far from being weaknesses, these confidence-challenging concerns will help you get to the core needs of your architecture practice and set you up for the additional decision process elements (one essential plus an optional four supporting) that you might need to start those conversations and build trust in the social contract within your organization.

First Steps

All journeys to the architecture advice process start somewhere, but that somewhere depends on what architectural role you currently play in your organization and what decision rights that offers you.

If You Already Have Decision-Taking Power

If you are an architect, you're in luck. You already have some authority to gather options and take decisions. Given this, the best way to experiment with the advice process is by adopting it openly as a personal practice, telling everyone what you are doing, and sharing your hypothesis that this will help you decide better and raise awareness of the advice process generally. What this means practically is the next time you see the need for a decision arising, you can initiate the decision process and start by splitting your activities explicitly into the three steps of the advice process.

In the first step, actively go out and seek advice regarding the challenge that needs a decision and gather the options. Explain what role the person you are interacting with is playing in the process. Direct them here and to Chapter 4 if they are curious and want more information.

Once you have collected all the advice that the social contract obliges you to, you can move to the second and third steps of taking and sharing the decision. As the architect who initiated this decision, it is possible that you are already empowered to do both. If you are, make the process clear that you have followed to get to the decision in hand.

If, even though you have some decision power, you are not empowered to take the decision entirely on your own—perhaps you have to take it to something like an Architecture Review Board (ARB)[1] for agreement with the rest of your architecture peer group—then you can share the decision you have made and subsequently are proposing to be taken. As you do this, emphasize the advice elements, particularly the advice that you incorporated directly into your decision and the advice that you explicitly decided not to. If more comments arise, treat them like advice as well, asking "Why?" if they come in the form of opinions, making sure you understand them, and then either explicitly incorporating or ignoring them (and if it's the latter, explaining why). If it's possible, invite those who offered you advice earlier to observe this review session. It will help them to see you modeling the process and upholding the social contract.

However the decision goes, ensure that you share the decision outcome with everyone who has been involved and then with all the advice offerers. In my experience, everyone who witnesses this process in action is impressed, given the quality of decisions it leads to.

If You Currently Lack Decision-Taking Power

If, on the other hand, you don't currently have the power to take architecturally significant decisions—maybe you are a member of a development team or part of any other team that acts collectively—you can still experiment with the advice process by modeling its fundamental aspects.

As with the approach for architects given in the previous subsection, experiment by following the process and letting people know you are using it. You will need to be clear about the fact that you are not actually taking the decision because you are not allowed to do so. Instead, your team will be preparing a decision and taking it to the responsible

---

1 An *ARB* is a group of governing architects who meet regularly to ensure that only decisions that support an organization's architectural framework and strategic goals are passed. The best definition of what ARBs are and their responsibilities, staffing, and ways of operating can be found in the excellent book *The Art of Scalability: Scalable Web Architecture, Processes, and Organizations for the Modern Enterprise*, 2nd Edition, by Martin L. Abbott and Michael T. Fisher (Addison-Wesley Professional). I'm not suggesting you set one up, but if you have one, I hope it follows their suggested modus operandi.

decision taker. Your hypothesis for this experiment is that you will prove or disprove that the responsible decision taker (most likely an architect outside of your team) will be comfortable with the decision your team prepares for them to take. You might even hypothesize something like "we are confident we can make and take a similar decision to our decision taker."

As you do this, ensure that you are identifying and properly seeking advice from all the people you are obliged to under the advice process's social contract. Remember that conversations are key. Talk with those who have architecture experience, not only to seek their advice on the decision but also to find out who else they would involve as advice offerers. Definitely seek advice from the person who would be both making the options and taking this decision in traditional architecture approaches. This is usually the most aligned architect.

Once your options are prepared, you should do one last thing before handing them over to whoever is actually responsible and accountable for the decision: provisionally select the decision option that you would have chosen if you were the decider and make this clear to the decision taker. Think about your reasons for selecting your option and articulate the results clearly.

Then take your recommendation to the authorized decider and present it to them as if they were an ARB: take them through what led you to the need for the decision, the options you considered, the pros and cons of each, and the advice and whom you sought it from.

When you present your selected decision option, relate it back to the relevant advice, both supportive and countering. If you engaged the decider earlier for advice, you likely know what option they preferred at the time, so take the opportunity to highlight whether your selected option matches what you perceived as their preference. Whatever option you have selected, back it up by referring to the advice you received, acknowledging where there were differences and how you have addressed these.

It's unlikely but possible that the decider will disagree with your selection. If they do, take the opportunity to discuss in more detail what led you to take a different direction. Perhaps you misunderstood their advice, or they didn't give you all the information you required. Ultimately, the architect still holds the power to take the decision, so you must defer to them rather than picking a fight about it. They may not initially trust your and the team's ability to decide. This can be for various reasons, including emotional ones. (I will examine the personal, emotional side of deciding for all parties in Chapter 13. You might be surprised how much nonintellectual stuff is going on in our heads as we perform this critical act.)

Through this experiment, the hope is that the decider sees five things: (1) your team is keen to both make options and take decisions, (2) you are doing this in a conscientious way, (3) they are still involved in the process, (4) their experience and perspective is valuable, and (5) this is a safe and effective way to decide—and perhaps better than what they would achieve themselves using their current approach.

The goal is that the currently accountable decider (and other technical leadership roles) gains enough trust in the team and the advice process to let you adopt it fully and keep making options and taking your own decisions. They will likely want to see you take a few more decisions through the process as they build up their trust in your team's ability to decide and in the advice process. They may also want to start adopting the process themselves. What you want to get to is the point where the process is properly up and running and the architect surrenders their power to take decisions entirely. You might have to move through a period of rubber-stamping of decisions prior to that, however.

Regardless of Where You Begin, Start Small

So far we have talked about individual teams and individual architects responsible for decisions across a number of teams. What about those with even more architectural decision-taking power? The chief architect or the CTO or whatever the title is of the person in your organization who decides what the approach to architecture decisions is. If you are this person and are free to move everyone over to the advice process immediately, I would still suggest that you take a gradual approach. This is a big change on a lot of levels and for a lot of people. There are a lot of unknowns, and a lot of new skills will need to be learned and old skills unlearned.

The advice process will affect everything in your current sociotechnical system: how software is developed, the means to deliver to production, the levels of trust in your culture, and much more. (I'll go into this in detail in Chapter 17.) Although it is simple, the advice process has the potential to change much in your organization for the better. Neither you nor I can predict how it will play out, so it's best to give it the freedom to run, but in a way where you can watch it, nurturing it as needed.

Start small by—you guessed it—running experiments. Your hypothesis could be: "we believe that by following the architecture advice process, we will get an increased number of better decisions made faster with fewer drawbacks or implementation problems." To run the experiment or series of experiments, pick one or more teams (no more than three) and an appropriately aligned architect or two who are willing to try out the advice process. If you are lucky, these teams will be ones who are already motivated to participate in finding a better way of practicing architecture because they are facing permission-blocking challenges, and those with a broader architecture view will already be working highly collaboratively and in sync with the teams.

Brief the teams and the architects fully about the experiment and what you expect them to do. You might want to point them to Chapter 4 to familiarize themselves with the process. As they carry out the experiment with their first decisions, ask them to explicitly communicate their actions to everyone involved. This not only brings awareness to the experiment but also informs others of what is expected of them and how they fit into the advice process.

It works well to time-box this trial period. A few months is typically sufficient to find out how this process fits into your organization. The initial novelty will have worn off, and teams and those with a broader architectural perspective will have settled into using it as "how we do architecture." At the end, hold a retrospective[2] to learn as much as possible. Hopefully, absolutely everything went well, and at the conclusion, you will be confident to roll out to more, or perhaps all, of the remaining teams. Even if it didn't go well, you will know what additional steps are needed to make sure a future rollout stands every chance of success.

However you roll out the advice process, I strongly advise you to remember:

- This approach centers conversations between equals.
- Both responsibility and accountability now lie with whoever initiates and takes a decision.
- Trust and learning are central.

These key facts seem pretty simple, but because of the size of the change, you can encounter a variety of challenges as you roll out the advice process. It's to this topic that I'll turn next.

Overcoming Early-Stage Challenges

As your adoption of the advice process spreads, you'll likely encounter challenges. The following are four root causes of early-stage challenges that I see over and over again:

- Miscommunicating about the architecture advice process: what it is, how it works, and what it changes
- Neglecting to engage with all the advice offerers
- Missing out on valuable information because you didn't ask "why"
- Failing to explicitly acknowledge the shift in accountability

Let's look at each in turn.

---

2 Regular retrospectives are a very powerful tool for learning, trust building, and continuous improvement. For more, see *Agile Retrospectives: Making Good Teams Great* by Esther Derby and Diana Larsen (Pragmatic Bookshelf).

Explain the Architecture Advice Process to Everyone Involved

For the advice process to be successful, everyone involved needs to know how it works, what the various roles are, and how power in the form of responsibility and accountability has shifted. When you first experiment with the advice process, it's natural that there will be some initial confusion from both the people you engage with for advice and spectators. You can confront this directly by communicating the process early and clearly.

Start with a presentation of the facts to everyone who will be involved, including those who are currently responsible for how the architecture decision process works. This presentation must cover what the architecture advice process is, how it works, who is involved, and what the key benefits are. Following this, you should be clear about your experimental hypothesis and scope. Finally, make it clear what you are hoping to learn from the experiment. It works really well to put this all on a piece of paper (it need not be any more than a few lines per item) or a few slides if you want to use images. However you tackle it, allow adequate time for questions. They might not have many at the outset but then think of questions after you start to run the process with them, so make sure you leave the door open.

Once the concepts and mechanics of the advice process are understood by everyone involved, you can move on to your experiment proper. Keep an eye out for indications that the process may have been misunderstood. Where misconceptions arise, jump on them fast to prevent confusion.

Source Advice from the Right People

The next challenge that can undermine your experimentation with or adoption of the practice is missing people who should be sought out for their advice.

Those who are used to playing architecture roles are least likely to miss advisers because, as the traditional option makers and decision takers of architectural decisions, they tend to cultivate a mental model of who to engage in which decisions—with regard to both those with expertise and affected parties. But this doesn't mean that traditional architects don't have blind spots, too. If you are such an architect, then when you're thinking about seeking advice, take the time to make sure you're engaging all the right people, even if you think they might not have any new information to offer you. That's for them to decide when you engage them for their advice.

For any given decision, the social-contract-meeting advisers are likely to be the same. You should always source the relevant advice, speaking to the same affected parties and those with expertise. However, the content of the conversations may differ depending on who is deciding. It is also no bad thing to seek additional advice if a decider feels it is necessary. There is a strong element of learning that runs through this process, and that's great. The reason this happens is because not everyone is as experienced in the ins and outs of all aspects of software and systems architecture as well as the art and science of deciding. As long as the core people are involved as required by the process, there is no shame or harm in bringing in extra people. It is by doing this that less experienced deciders can gain the support and experience they lack, learning as a side effect.

It should come as no surprise that when development teams first start taking decisions, they may have only a partial knowledge of who to consult in your organization. In this case, one of the first people you should speak to is someone with architecture experience. Explicitly ask them (on top of any advice they might offer themselves): "Who should we seek advice from?"

Traditional architects can be stressed because they both need to be in too many places at once and aren't privy to much of the information required to decide well. The advice process alternative helps those self-same architects be in many places at once, surfacing the key information in decisions at hand, without taking the decision power or accountability away from them. It's an easy way for teams to build confidence in option making, too, because option making is where a great deal of the learning takes place, and with the advice process, it can now be done safely. In the worst-case scenario, a team realizes that they don't like stepping up and taking this responsibility, which is perfectly fine. In the advice process, teams are under no obligation to do their own deciding. They can rely entirely on those with existing architecture skills if that is their preference.

When teams do begin to step up, this process of teams tapping traditional architects for their organizational literacy is a powerful move. It not only allows those architects to get out of the way of development teams, plugging them directly into their network in an effective and efficient way, but it also enables teams to learn about the organization from many more angles than those that they are usually exposed to. This allows everyone who is deciding to be exposed to broader organizational perspectives, such as strategic direction and how aligned to it or not your decision is. Sometimes, for example, a decision will fit cleanly under an existing product decision, and the individual or individuals with broader architectural viewpoints and remits can simply offer advice along these lines. Other times, a pending decision can raise challenges or previously ignored options that might now offer business benefit. Chapter 9 will discuss this in detail, but for now it's enough to be aware of it.

There's one final tip I'd like to share that can both smooth the rollout process and further increase trust in everyone participating. As decisions are being made and advice is sought, incrementally build up a checklist for your organization that shows who has expertise in which areas. Is information security (InfoSec) affected? Talk to the CISO. Getting close to personally identifiable information (PII)? Engage Mary who works on the data team and Mariana in legal. Is there a potential change to the user onboarding flow? Talk to your UX lead. Thinking of adopting a new cloud service?

Chat with Kris, the cloud architect. Thinking about a change to your API? Speak to all the leads of the teams who are your consumers.

Sometimes, as a consequence of this checklist, the resulting list of advice offerers for a given decision can be a long one. That's fine. Some decisions are large ones, and the advice scope is a clear indication of both size and importance. Sometimes, decisions can be made smaller in scope, and many consequently are. Other times, the sheer number of folks affected will make the decision taker(s) think again. Is this thing that might make their life a little bit easier really worth the effort of consulting all those people? Or can they split this large decision into multiple smaller decisions? When decisions do proceed, they are frequently right-sized purely as a matter of expediency. Again, there is a lot to say about the art of splitting decisions, enough to fill Chapters 13 and 14 in fact.

Ask the Right People and Find Out "Why?"

The third challenge to successful experimentation with or adoption of the architecture advice process is failing to get to the valuable advice. This comes from failing to speak to the right people and missing out on the juicy supportive reasoning by failing to ask "Why?" with regard to the advice you received.

Dangers of seeking advice only via established, hierarchical relationships

When seeking advice, it can be easy to slip into engaging only those with whom you already have established relationships. This poses problems when those individuals offering advice are used to a traditional, hierarchical power dynamic (both formal or informal). As a consequence, they may be inclined to slip into command, direction, opinion, or anything that has to be followed. This isn't advice, and despite giving the impression that the process is being followed, it is in danger of falling into a "near enemy" trap.

To counter this, remind the advice offerer that you are only seeking advice and that you, the decider, are accountable. If anything other than advice is offered, you can deploy skills such as asking "Why?" to get to the advice beneath. Remember, the advice offerer has no power over your decision at all, even if they do not accept that fact. Freed from the need to agree with what they hear about your proposed decision, they may engage far more seriously. Consequently, the depth and breadth of advice received are greater. Decisions don't tend to suffer as a consequence either. Neither does their learning.

Seek advice from those with conflicting views

One of the obvious benefits of seeking advice from others is that they see things differently from you and communicate that different perspective to you. As we just saw, there are dangers in seeking advice only from those whom we are already comfortable interacting with, in areas that we simply admit we don't know about. But advice should be sought equally from uncomfortable sources because if you always favor the former over the latter, you will be missing out.

By being open to the advice of others, making sure you understand their points of view and the reasons behind their advice, your decision may well become stronger. This strength derives from gaining assurance that your decision gives the advice offerer no cause for concern *or* the advice offered is directly relevant and can be fed into the decision, strengthening it.

Antagonistic advice giving is actually so powerful for these reasons that some decision processes incorporate it as a matter of course.[3] With this in mind, potentially destructive advice can be encouraged from everyone, even (especially?) those who are a proposal's strongest supporters. At the least, it offers different perspectives, and frequently, it challenges your own potentially blinkered views, forcing you to scrutinize them. Even if nothing changes as a consequence, it is still reassuring to know that a decision withstood such scrutiny and survived.[4] Either way, it really helps to think about the value of disagreement when seeking advice from those whom you are less comfortable with as it provides a distance between them and you without sacrificing the wisdom they might impart. (I'll go into such approaches in more depth, starting with personal practices in Chapter 12 and group practices in Chapter 15.)

Make Who Is Accountable for Each Decision Explicit

Whenever I first introduce the concept of the architecture advice process—whether to an architect or to a developer—their biggest concern is that others might act selfishly without there being any means to rein them in—for example, taking a decision that benefits only themselves and flies in the face of all advice suggesting that it will be bad for others. This fear often arises because the associated shift in accountability has not been made explicit.

If you take on the responsibility to decide, you are solely accountable

As I covered earlier in this chapter, the advice process means that decision takers are not only responsible for their decisions but are also accountable for them. For

---

3 Known by terms such as *ritual dissent* or *red teaming*, this kind of advice offering gives all involved the permission to really try to shoot holes in any decision and associated proposal for the benefit of the overall end result. They are all a little like Michael Nygard's "evil test harness," from his book *Release it!*, which does everything it can to break your software.

4 If you're thinking of some of the best group design sessions you have experienced as a team member in the past, when everyone felt 100% safe to criticize the idea and therefore work together to truly get the best, most robust, non-group-think-y idea they could, you've experienced a self-organizing, organically arising version of this technique already.

traditional architects, this is nothing new—it has always been the case—but for teams stepping up and taking decisions, it must be made clear.

Knowing that I am accountable for my decisions and that others know I am accountable serves as a significant bolster to the social contract and associated trust. It means that decision takers are even more motivated not only to seek the appropriate advice but also to listen to it, understand it, and incorporate it or explicitly dismiss it given the decision at hand. In doing so, they will be exposed to the sum total of the knowledge that is available to them at that point in time.

According to Ruth Malan's definition of effective architecture practice, explicit accountability guarantees that conversations are happening, whether others are required to be involved or not, and that when required, appropriate and timely guidance can be provided.

Taking this to its logical extreme—the worst-case scenario in everyone's fears—if a decision is still taken that goes against all advice, I would ask: would this selfish deciding have happened anyway? I would argue that it would. If selfish deciding is happening under the advice process, it is simply brought out into the open where it can be addressed. Most frequently, this comes down to a lack of understanding or (and this is important) a unique insight that only they are party to. If either lack of understanding or unique perspectives is the case, then the process can help with that. If it is purely down to malign intent (and I have never, ever witnessed this, but I am willing to countenance that it might occur), then alarm bells will sound, and other organizational mechanisms can kick in beyond those governing software delivery; those mechanisms ultimately can remove the person from the organization.

Not everyone is ready for accountability

It's fair to say that not everyone will feel ready or willing to take on the responsibility of option making and decision taking. This is perfectly understandable and acceptable. There is nothing in the advice process that *obliges* anyone to become a decider. If this person were a traditional architect, it should again raise significant alarm bells as the responsibility of deciding is, for all intents and purposes, the remit of architecture, and again there will be organizational mechanisms beyond software development to address this. If this person is, however, in a development team, they can still see the need for a decision and bring it to someone else or see if they want to initiate the decision process. That person can then decide if there is a strong enough motivation to act.

Yet again, let's return to Malan's centering of conversations in the practice of architecture. Conversations are taking place, most likely needed conversations, and off the backs of these, decisions and actions are being taken. In the postrevolutionary world, this is essential, but in any software delivery program, the power of this is incredible. Whether everyone is involved in the deciding or not, the entire sociotechnical engine is participating in not only the action of software delivery but also the sensemaking of the feedback arising from the resulting software. There is also a path for learners to take steps *should they feel so inclined*. Confidence in nondeciding team members may eventually increase, perhaps after having witnessed the advice process working one degree removed from them, and when they are ready, they can follow it for themselves. And if no one feels the drive to take this path? That's fine, too. The option to do so remains open.

Confidence Concerns Arising from the Architecture Advice Process

When I first introduce people to the advice process, I'm often asked questions that are mixed with excitement and trepidation. In listening to their early-day concerns, I've noticed that the trepidation stems from a lack of confidence that surfaces itself in themselves, in others, and in the social contract of the advice process. I'll describe them in the following sections. See if any of them resonate with you.

Lack of Confidence in Your and Others' Deciding Skills

The most prevalent issue that arises when adopting an advice process has to do with a lack of confidence in people—both in yourself and in others. Faced with a new responsibility, everyone naturally feels some uncertainty if they have to exercise a previously underutilized skill. In the case of the advice process, this can cut both ways: you may worry that you are unable to decide well, or you may worry that others may not make good options nor take decisions.

It is my experience that most people gaining comfort with the advice process experience a mix of both. That's healthy. Deciding *is* important, but it's also hard, as well as one of those skills that only improves with practice and experience.

To the architectural-decision newcomer, veteran architects may seem like they are auto-magically good at deciding, but it's an illusion, built through years of practice. A new architecture practitioner *can't* expect to have those skills yet, and deciding well *will be* more difficult. It is beneficial to acknowledge this skills gap, whichever side of it you sit on, and work to strengthen these skills widely.

New deciders feel more comfortable with their practice if they have a place to receive support from others. It's like having a safety net or a spotter, lending them the confidence to practice their new decision power in increasingly significant situations.

If this place of support were available, it would offer the means to openly build confidence in the skills of yourself and others. Everyone would be able to see that not only is everyone going through all the required steps, but also they are performing each step with due care and attention and to the best of their abilities.

Lack of Confidence in Advice Seeking and Offering

The second lack of confidence is voiced less often, but it's equally a cause of concern for many. Again, it arises from the advice process's social contact and the centrality of trust.

This lack of confidence concerns the transparency of advice rather than the decisions that result. Specifically, it's hard to build trust in others when you have little to no idea who was involved in the advice giving, what the advice offered was, and whether the advice seekers disregarded or even just misunderstood the advice they received. This is because there is no way of knowing if the people consulted had the required expertise, if they were biased, if key advice offerers were left out, or if their contributions were disregarded.

Trust is *far* easier to maintain if everyone can see who was consulted (and, by extrapolation, who wasn't) and what their advice was (and wasn't). With a mechanism to provide such transparency, the process gains the space to operate, and mutual trust can build.

Lack of Confidence in Knowing Everything That Is Happening

The third lack of confidence doesn't relate to trust in others. Instead, it arises directly from the consequences of decentralization. One of the few benefits of the traditional, blocking approaches was that there was one group in the middle of all the deciding: the architects. Being in the center of it all meant that at least one group was aware of everything that was going on architecturally, and if anyone wanted to know the current state of affairs, they could approach a member of this group and receive an update.

With a decentralized architectural approach such as an advice process, there is no group in the center that does all the deciding *because there is no center* (though there will still be those playing cross-team architecture roles). Decisions are made in many places, and there is no built-in way of tracking everything that is happening. What's more, when things are working well, there will be a lot more decisions because the bottleneck of the traditional approaches is removed.

The need to know what is happening is increased in decentralizated compared to traditional approaches. Both architects and development teams need to have some idea of the context their systems are running in as well as potential changes that might be coming their way. While it's not necessary for everyone to know everything about everything, it is essential to have a way to find out everything about any specific decision, should the need arise.

Taken together, these three areas where your confidence may be lacking are important. I'm not about to tell you, "Just trust me and get over it." In fact, I'm about to show you how to mitigate all three of them.

Conclusion

I've presented three approaches to rolling out the architecture advice process depending on who you are and the deciding power you currently hold. Then, I discussed the reasons why starting small is essential before considering likely early challenges you will face and the concerns many may have about how your practice of architecture will now work.

These concerns arise because, while the architecture advice process is incredibly powerful on its own, in the fast-moving, ever-evolving, knowledge-rich, and power-offering world of sociotechnical systems, it is not sufficient. To be successful with the advice process–based approach to decentralized deciding, you need one more core element, which I will cover in the next chapter: architectural decision records.

CHAPTER 6

Architectural Decision Records

Although the architecture advice process will transform your organization's decision processes, I always combine it with at least one further element: architectural decision records (ADRs). They are the best way I know to mitigate the three confidence deficiencies that I discussed in the previous chapter: in your and others' deciding skills, in the advice seeking and offering, and in knowing everything that is happening.

I consider ADRs the essential add-on to an advice process base model, supporting and enhancing all its key aspects. ADRs help everyone make better decisions, and advice seeking and sharing happen in the open. Best of all, ADRs maintain a transparent, accessible history of all decisions for everyone, including the supporting advice. That helps build and maintain trust *and* is a great resource for learning.

In this chapter, I'll use two examples to illustrate how writing ADRs supports your decision process. I'll show how the structure of ADRs can be used to understand the context of decisions and as a means to think in a structured way about your various options and their consequences. I'll also demonstrate how ADRs provide invaluable support to the smooth running of the advice process, regardless of how you choose to manage and maintain them throughout their productive and valuable lifecycle.

Let's introduce ADRs, starting with where they sit within the advice process.

Introducing Architectural Decision Records

ADRs support the *entire* decision process: considering the challenge or problem that requires the decision, making decision options, taking the decision, and sharing the result. Figure 6-1 shows this for the advice process approach.

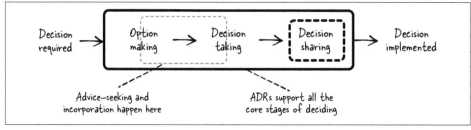

Figure 6-1. The place of ADRs in the advice process

ADRs are not new. They were mentioned significantly in a paper by Jeff Tyree and Art Akerman (*https://oreil.ly/XxyJr*) in 2005 before being popularized by Michael Nygard in a blog post (*https://oreil.ly/YKQ7r*) in 2011.[1] In that post, Nygard showed how to appropriately document the thinking behind a decision in an evolving software system. ADRs fit well with the various trends emerging from the five revolutions, and consequently, they steadily gained in popularity, with many variants of the ADR format emerging.

Further ADR Resources

ADRs have given rise to the popular site Architectural Decision Records (*https://adr.github.io*), which covers their history and heritage and provides links to resources, tools, and variations. The topic also warranted most of a chapter in Mark Richards and Neal Ford's *Fundamentals of Software Architecture* (O'Reilly).

So what are ADRs? ADRs are short documents (with a target length of about two pages' worth of text, not counting diagrams or recorded advice, hence the reason why many people refer to them as "lightweight ADRs") that tend to follow a typical format. Each ADR records a single architectural decision that has been taken, along with appropriate supporting information.

Like all records, ADRs are *immutable*: written once, read many times, and never updated once accepted. As soon as the decision of an ADR is decided, it does not change. Consequently, even though people will sometimes want to go back to a decision (perhaps offering additional advice on an ADR or questioning the decision after it is taken), you cannot. If you think about it, it would make no sense to go back in time and change your historical record. Instead, ADR decisions can be *superseded*,

---

1 What follows in this chapter remains essentially faithful to Nygard's original outline and doesn't materially contradict any of the other ADR sources. When I do add, change, or extend something, I'm transparent about it.

indicating that one ADR has been overridden by another subsequent decision and so is unlikely to be evident in the codebase.

This is important because knowing a software system's decision history is powerful. If something *was* the decision, even if it isn't any longer, that tells you a lot about the issues and priorities that were top of mind *at the time* a decision was taken. Immutable decisions—complemented by subsequent ADRs, which supersede them—maintain this record.

Bear this in mind when reading and digesting ADRs. Taken together as a group, they tell an essential story of a software system, steps and missteps alike—something that should be relatively simple if an ADR library is maintained. I'll share how to do that later in this chapter, when I move to considering ADRs as a group rather than individually.

But let's stick with discussing a single decision for now and walk through a completed ADR. Not only will this familiarize you with their structure and the importance of each section, but it will also show you how ADRs keep readers informed of the details of all decisions being made in their organization.

The Structure of an ADR

No matter what tool is used to publish them, ADRs are structured with the reader rather than the writer in mind (but this should be true of any design documentation). For that reason, reading an ADR is much more straightforward than writing one. Used to support an advice process, completed ADRs have at least the following sections in the order given in Table 6-1.

Table 6-1. Common ADR sections

Section name	Description
ID and Title	A unique identifier and a very short summary of the decision itself (e.g., "ADR001—Use AKS for Kubernetes Pods").
Status and Date	State of the ADR document, typically "Draft," "Proposed," "Adopted," "Superseded," and "Retired."
Author	The person (or team) who wrote the ADR and is therefore accountable for it.
Decision	The decision taken described in a few sentences, frequently bolded or italicized so it stands out.
Context	The forces and current contextual circumstances that brought about the decision.
Options considered	Each considered option is described briefly, with pros and cons. Typically, the option proposed/adopted comes first in this list.
Consequences	The ramifications of selecting each option, both positive and negative.
Advice	The raw outputs from following the advice process. This is where all offered advice is recorded. It includes the name and role of the advice giver and the date the advice was given.

In this section, I'll take you through an example of a completed ADR that records the decision taken after the completion of an advice process, and I'll explain each section in more detail. The example is based on a real-life ADR from an ex-colleague, Wisen Tanasa, and records how they decided to shorten the IDs for various business entities exposed through their REST API.

As you read, think about how each section may help mitigate the various issues you and others might have with the advice process. If you want to look at the completed ADR on its own, head over to the Git repository that accompanies this book (*https:// oreil.ly/TaCJH*).

Title

First comes the title, which is a short statement that conveys the essence of a decision. In the current example, the title makes clear that the decision was taken to shorten inventory IDs using the Nano ID library:

EXAMPLE
Shorten Inventory IDs with Nano ID

Descriptive titles like this are incredibly helpful. Readers can see the gist of the decision in a single short sentence, without even having to open the ADR itself.

This title format also means that when you view a list of ADRs, you can parse the decision history at a glance. This isn't the case if the title is vague. "Inventory IDs," for example, wouldn't do it. You'd need to click in, have a read, and find out that they were going to be short. When the decision is in the title, that's not required.

Meta-Elements

The first meta-element is also visible from outside the ADR because it's typically included in the title: the ADR ID (in the example, its "ADR002"). IDs must be unique because, although an ADR's descriptive title is helpful, its ID eliminates all ambiguity.

Including the identifier in the ADR title means that it's easy to see and organize by in your overall list of ADRs:

EXAMPLE
ADR002—Shorten Inventory IDs with Nano ID

The remaining three meta-elements are inside the ADR and are typically shown at the top of the record: status, date, and author.[2]

In the current example, these meta-elements are as follows:

EXAMPLE
Status: Accepted
Date: 2020-03-25
Author: Wisen Tanasa

The status tells the reader where the ADR (and by extension, the decision it records) currently lies in the decision process. There are a number of statuses, and I'll go into them in depth later in this chapter. For now, just know that the status of this example ADR is "Accepted," which means the decision has been taken. (The status can be anything that means "this decision has been taken," but "Accepted" seems to be the de facto standard.)

The date corresponds to when the ADR's status was last changed. For example, if the status is "Accepted," then the date indicates when the decision was taken. The date is important because it means you can place the decision in a timeline. Remember, ADRs are point-in-time artifacts, and once they are completed, they effectively become immutable, just like an entry in an event log.

Finally comes the author: the person accountable for the decision and the point of contact for any questions about it. This author is usually either an architect or a team lead, but a whole team could be listed on the ADR if the decision was a collective effort. This can be extremely useful when looking for SMEs to offer advice on other decisions, for example.

Taken with the title, the meta-elements quickly give the gist of a particular decision. In the example, we know that Wisen Tanasa took the decision to use Nano ID to generate shorter inventory IDs on March 25, 2020. That's a pretty powerful summary.

Decision

The Decision section is intentionally sparse. It is a declaration of intent, stating the next actions for those who will implement the decision. It tells you which option was selected during the decision taking but nothing more.

---

2 Only the status is featured in Nygard's original post, though I'm not alone in adding the other two.

In the current example, the Decision section is as follows:

EXAMPLE

We will create shorter inventory IDs with random generated letters and numbers (option 1). This will involve Nano ID with the following configuration:

Building ID
- ID Length: 6
- Characters: 23456789ABCDEFGHJKMNPQRSTUVWXYZ

Space ID
- ID Length: 8
- Characters: 0123456789ABCDEFGHIJKLMNOPQRSTUVWXYZabcdefghijklm-nopqrstuvwxyz

Provider ID
- ID Length: 5
- Characters: 0123456789ABCDEFGHIJKLMNOPQRSTUVWXYZabcdefghijklm-nopqrstuvwxyz

---

It is notable what the Decision section *doesn't* include: neither the problem it solves, nor any mention of the options that didn't make the cut, nor the consequences of the selected option and why it was selected. Again, this is to support the person reading the ADR after the decision has been taken. After reading the Decision section, they may have the answers they need—if you are a developer about to start coding, for example. If that is the case, you can stop now and open your IDE.

If you want to know extra details, however, you can keep reading. Those details are provided in the following three sections, starting with the context.

Context

The Context section provides the facts surrounding and driving the decision as they were known to the decider or deciders and the advisers at the time. A Context section tells the reader why the decision matters and gives an idea of the circumstances that were on the mind of the person or team doing the deciding. Readers can also discern what the deciders weren't thinking about at all based on their absence from the Context section.

The Context section is lower in my ADR approach than you'll find it in other templates. This is because I believe the decision itself is more important to the first-time reader than the background that brought it about. That's not to say that this background isn't important, but you shouldn't have to read or skip it if you want to get straight to the details of the decision.

The Context section of the current example ADR is as follows:

EXAMPLE

Our inventory IDs are currently generated. For example, our building IDs look like:

22cadcb6-00e5-4baa-a701-785854fc2a9e.

As we scale our inventory, the length of these ID strings will increase. They are already too long. We would like our IDs shorter, so the seekers' UX is better:

- They can type the ID into the browser if they are printing the building page.
- They can share the URL easily without a URL shortener.
- These are the decision criteria:
  — Short
  — Low collision probability (see: *https://oreil.ly/MXqWZ*)
  — Unambiguity—0 (zero) and O (capital o) must not be confused
  — Cost of implementation

This gives you just enough history about the situation *at the time of deciding* as well as the perceived forces at play. These forces likely include any applicable requirements (most likely cross-functional, but it's not unusual to see functional requirements called out, too) as well as technical, sociotechnical, and organizational information. You can see these expressed in the intention to make the seekers' UX better and all the decision criteria, such as cost of implementation.

Options

Next comes the Options section, which details the options considered during the decision process.[3] It is important that this section details not only the decision path taken but also the paths considered *but not taken*. Having only one option is a bad smell in ADRs because there is always more than one option in a decision.

---

3 The Options section is again an addition to the basic Nygardian format but is found in most standard alternatives.

Remember, ADRs represent a point in time. At the very least, there is one option to do something and another to do nothing, although the futility of inaction may have been partially broached in the Context section.

In our case, the current ADR example has five options:

EXAMPLE

1. (SELECTED) A4VHAOFG: Random generated letters and numbers with Nano ID
2. 123456: Automatically generated sequence ID
3. Canvas: Manually generated ID
4. BBBB2221: Pretty generated letters and numbers
5. Canvas-A4VH: Combination of building name and generated ID

There are a few things to note about these options. Each one is numbered, meaning they can be clearly referred to (e.g., Option 1) elsewhere in the document. (I also give them names, which can be used shorthand in the ADR, too.) The first option listed is traditionally the one that was selected because that's just where readers expect the "preferred" option to be placed.[4]

Note that each option is only lightly described. Sometimes an ADR author may feel the need to describe one or more options in more detail, perhaps even with a diagram or two.

Finally, note what is not included. There is nothing in this section that talks about the consequences of selecting each of the options. That comes next.[5]

Consequences

The Consequences section details the reasons why the selected option was chosen and why the other options were not. In some ADR templates, the Consequences section contains only the reasoning for the selected option. In others, the reasoning behind not choosing the other options is also included. The second approach is my preference because it means that the ADR is a complete record of all the pertinent

---

4 If the decision process hasn't been completed yet, then you might not know what to put at the top of the list. Luckily for me, you're reading a decision that has been taken.

5 Sometimes I structure my ADRs slightly differently, with a Consequences subsection for each of my options. This has the benefit of putting the consequences right next door to the introduction of the option but the drawback of making it nigh-on impossible to take in all the options considered at a glance. I've stuck with my default in this chapter as it tends to work best most of the time.

details of the decision. It is also exceptionally important when using ADRs as a decision-support tool (as you'll see when we get to the section on writing ADRs).

The current example has options as follows:

Option 1: (SELECTED) Random generated letters and numbers with Nano ID

- Selected because we don't have to provision any infrastructure, as the ID can be generated with the Nano ID library (*https://oreil.ly/942I5*)
- Selected because we can use it in our serverless architecture
- Selected because the chance of an ID collision is low. Even if we generate one building ID per hour, we have only a 0.001% probability of a collision. This is acceptable, and we don't think that we'll have one building ID per hour.
- Selected despite the fact that we may produce profanity words, but the likelihood of this seems incredibly low, and IDs will clearly have been randomly generated to external consumers.

Option 2: Automatically generated sequence ID

- Rejected because it will be too costly to implement. It requires new infrastructure to be provisioned as we're adopting serverless architecture.

Option 3: Manually generated ID

- Rejected because it requires too much human intervention.
- Rejected despite this being able to guarantee both no collisions and no profanity words.

Option 4: Pretty generated letters and numbers

- Rejected because we couldn't find a free and appropriately licensed open source library that supported this.

Option 5: Combination of building name and generated ID

- Rejected because we can prepend a slug if we're concerned about the URL.

There are a few elements to highlight here. First, for the selected option, you can see that there are both benefits and drawbacks, the latter being the most important. Drawbacks are the things to look out for, or the risks and issues to mitigate when the decision is implemented.

The other options in this example only have drawbacks, specifically only the "killer drawbacks" that include the reason (or reasons) for the option being dropped from consideration. There may be benefits in rejected options, too, but less often. Usually, this is when the author wants to make clear the compromise that was made in the selection.

Advice

The final section of the ADR, Advice, is a simple bulleted list of contributions from advice offerers.[6] I've found that it helps to have the advice in the format [Advice] ([Advice-giver's name, role]) with some idea of the date it was offered.

You can see this in the last part of the example ADR:

EXAMPLE

- Have we thought about the possibility of auto-generated profanity in the auto-generated text? It could be bad for our reputation if this happened. (Monira R., Product Manager, 23 Mar 2020)

- What's the possibility of ID collisions with each option? Have we looked at generating them in a database? It's a good way to offload the responsibility of making sure IDs are unique. (Hanna A., Infra team, 20 Mar 2020)

- Does making it human-meaningful matter, or just human-readable? (Rebecca F., UX, 23 Mar 2020)

- Can we list out all the places where we'll need to use this ID? (Izzy H., Tech Lead from another team: Site Search, 24 Mar 2020)

- Will the IDs be exposed publicly? We must think about leakage of internal data models and generation modes as it might broaden our attack surface. (Pete H., InfoSec, 23 Mar 2020)

- What are the licensing concerns with the various options? Will any of them cost us more money as we scale? If they're open source, what license are they under and are they actively maintained? I ask because I once got bitten by this at a previous company. We have a [CFR (linked)] that states which licenses are allowed. (Alina B., Architect, 20 Mar 2020)

The advice here comes directly from the advice offerers. What is most important is that the Advice section captures these different voices and perspectives in their raw, unfiltered form. The process of mining and extracting this advice for incorporation

---

6 The last section is not only an addition to the Nygardian format but to all versions. It's where the advice process lives.

into the body of the ADR is part of the act of deciding, and there is a whole section on that later in this chapter. For now, notice that by comparing the two—the advice and the rest of the ADR—you can get an idea of how much the former informed the latter.

This raw advice alongside the ADR itself levels up ADRs into a great learning resource for your current and future colleagues where they can see how decisions came about and were shaped. They can also consult Advice sections to see who best to seek advice from in future decisions.

Experiment with Your ADR Template

I always find the elements I listed in the previous section—title, meta-elements, decision, context, consequences, and advice—to be essential. Not only that, the order in which they appear and the bias in this toward the reader over the writer are important given the central role they will play in building trust and organizational learning.

But I don't think this is always everything you need. Experiment with adding and removing sections. As you do, always remember who your audience is: contributors and future readers. Lightweight ADRs are called that for good reason. Despite the act of writing, every part of them should be beneficial, not a burden.

You can tell if your template isn't fulfilling its remit for your organization when sections start being completed half-heartedly or are left empty altogether. Add sections that you predict will support everyone in deciding but be prepared to be proven wrong.

Drafting an ADR to Support Deciding

Now that I've shared what I think a completed ADR should look like, I'll take you through another decision, but this time, I'll write this second example ADR as I go. My goal is to show you how each section supports deciding in an advice-driven decision process.

The example decision I'm going to use arose from a project to build a set of shared payment and subscription services.[7] This decision took place as we in the team were thinking about changing subscription-payment details. For historical reasons, we *really* wanted to make sure failure scenarios didn't result in customers being double-billed.

---

7 It comes from a project I worked on a number of years ago with my then-colleague Gayathri Thiyagarajan. We presented the project as a case study at Devoxx UK, and if you're interested in the background, you can watch the whole talk on YouTube (*https://oreil.ly/IUP4k*). We introduce the overall case study at 14:19, and the decision I'm using for the example is discussed starting at 18.58 and reprised at 31:13.

As I step you through the stages of the decision process—in this section and the two that follow ("Using ADRs to Facilitate the Advice Process" on page 136 and "Taking Your Decision and Completing the ADR" on page 146)—you'll notice that I'm not tackling the ADR sections in the order they appear in the template. Not only that, but I'm visiting some sections multiple times. This is because I'm not simply using an ADR to "record a decision." Rather, I'm using the act of writing to understand my need and context, to make my options and consider their consequences, to seek and understand my advice, and when that is done, to take my decision.[8]

As I progress, try putting yourself in my shoes. Bear in mind that I am the decider, writing the ADR *to help me decide*. As with all decisions, when I start, I don't know what the decision outcome will be. The act of writing is helping me get there.

Step 1: Create Your Empty ADR and Set Its Metadata

The first task in any ADR-supported decision is to create a new ADR file from your template. If you don't have one, you can use the starter template that you can download from the GitHub repository for this book (*https://oreil.ly/zYWDe*).

Once created, I immediately add a self-evident placeholder title such as "(DRAFTING) Changing subscription payment details" (don't spend too much time on it) and a unique ID (e.g., ADR-003). This announces to everyone that this is an ADR at the start of its decision process.

 ADR titles should *ultimately* state the decision that has been taken. But when you're at the start of the decision process, you don't yet know what this is. Therefore, it's perfectly fine for an ADR title to change multiple times up to the point a decision is taken.

For the remaining metadata elements inside the ADR, set the status to "Draft"[9] and the date to today. Your last piece of housekeeping is to add your name (or the name of the team you are representing).

Here's what this looks like for the second example ADR at this earliest stage:[10]

---

8 British journalist, author, strategist, broadcaster, and activist Alastair Campbell calls this "thinking in ink."

9 This status is not part of the Nygardian approach (most likely because he conceived of ADRs as records, entirely postdecision). However, this status is present in other ADR approaches.

10 You can see this second example ADR in its entirety, including all the change sets, on the GitHub repository that accompanies this book (*https://oreil.ly/QHfff*).

Title: ADR-003—Changing subscription payment details

Status: Draft

Date: 2023-10-28

Authors: Andrew Harmel-Law and Gayathri Thiyagarajan

 Having your ADR template set the default status to "Draft" and your date to the creation date means that no ADR author ever has to rely on their own self-discipline when they first create the document. It's a simple way to make sure these fields always get populated.

Admin done, you're ready to begin the process of writing-supported deciding.

Step 2: Write the Context

The Context section is where you make clear (to yourself and future readers, both before and after the decision is taken) why a decision is required. Architectural decisions are always "it depends," so it's essential to know what the decision depends *on*—the circumstances that led to it being necessary. The Context section of an ADR is the place where you state this clearly and hence where all decision journeys begin.

For that reason, as soon as you have the metadata and placeholder title in place, jump down to the Context section, gather your thoughts, and start writing. Leave the Decision section blank for now. We'll come back to it later.

Writing the Context clarifies your awareness of both the issue at hand and the key factors that affect it (the things that the decision "depends on"). These factors can be other teams, other parts of the software system, cost, available skills, tooling (including pipelines), and more. It's impossible—and unnecessary—to be exhaustive, but as I highlighted in this chapter's first example ADR, applicable requirements (both cross-functional and functional) are essential when considering the context. Associated technical, sociotechnical, and organizational facts are also potentially important.

Crafting the context *always* shapes and clarifies my conception of the decision I am working on. For this reason, I consider the Context section—along with the Consequences section—to be the two most important sections of the ADR when deciding. (I'll provide various strategies for approaching this in Chapter 12 so that you can realize the full benefits of context writing for deciding.)

I find it useful to begin drafting a Context section with a brain dump. Jot down everything you know that has led to your needing a decision at this point. Don't worry if something is directly pertinent or about writing beautiful prose—just try to get down all the forces, constraints, and important historical steps that are at the top of your mind. In the second example ADR, the first draft of the Context section looks as follows:

EXAMPLE

These are new service(s).

Existing services are Spring Boot Microservices architecture running on Java 1.8 and Linux (Red Hat Enterprise Linux) VMs.

We support one-off payments AND recurring payments/subscriptions.

We don't want to be PCI compliant—don't handle financial information.

Actual payment services (debit/credit transactions and setup of recurring payments) will be provided by a third-party payment services provider.

Services are "white-labelable." Shared Payment Services will be backend only—screens to be provided by companies consuming the services, e.g., ecommerce checkout journeys or from the payment gateway itself.

This third-party payment services provider might change in the future.

Shared Payment Services store, manage, and publish payment and subscription info to other business systems (CRM, data warehouse, etc.).

We don't want the customer to have to worry about the fact there is a third-party payment provider; that's our internal decision.

Fail in favor of the customer.

How do we ensure we never have two active mandates in place at the same time for a single customer?

How do we ensure the customer always has a valid subscription mandate in place?

This roughest of drafts captures everything I could think about the current situation at the time: what was needed and what had to be avoided. As you write the context, you should only think, "What is the problem?" and not wonder, "What's the solution?"[11]

With all this raw information available, it's time to focus and clarify. What do future readers need to understand the current state? I then remove any extraneous details. If I

---

[11] If you want to get into the headspace of a company that has innovated again and again, largely by thinking about the problems they needed to solve rather than the preexisting patterns they needed to apply to solve them, look no further than Adrian Cockcroft's QCon 2023 presentation "Microservices Retrospective: What We Learned (and Didn't Learn) from Netflix" (*https://oreil.ly/6tg8J*).

sketched diagrams to understand the problem, I consider adding legible versions, especially if I'm looking at structure or placement of function. For example, a simple diagram can be useful for showing the main moving parts, including those that are under the team's control and those that aren't—something that's key to weighing the options.

At the Start, Diagrams Just Need to Be Functional

Try not to get hung up on presentation at this stage of writing an ADR. As long as a diagram illustrates a point, don't worry too much about the format. For example, a photo of a hand-drawn diagram on a whiteboard can be just as effective at this thinking stage as the same diagram created in a drawing app. Of course, if you find yourself having to make changes or add more detail, then perhaps you might move it into a diagramming tool, considering a slightly more formal notation.

However you craft your Context section, you should stop occasionally and self-check that it has the required detail to give potential advisers the information they need to offer their best advice. You will find that the simple act of writing with an adviser audience in mind helps surface elements for the context that you may otherwise have missed or disregarded and frequently leads to more rounded, balanced decisions. Consequently, if potential advisers come to mind as you write the context, jot their names or roles down so that you don't forget to involve them later.

After polishing it, our example ADR's Context section looks like this:

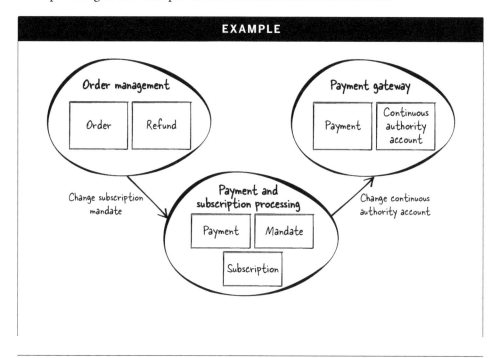

We are creating a new set of payment and subscription processing services to enhance our market offering. Our only consumer at the moment is the in-house Order Management System, though we hope there will be other consumers in the future.

To avoid PCI compliance, we consume a third-party Payment Services Provider.

Our new services are backend only. All consumers will provide their own screens leading up to the payment. Payment screens come from the Payment Gateway.

The riskiest part of subscriptions is when bank details are changed: the Payment Provider API requires separate REST calls to cancel, create, and activate mandates. It is essential that clients are never double-billed for subscriptions but also that we don't give products away for free unnecessarily.

Finally, once I feel I have the main parts of the Context section in place, I'll update the title of the ADR so that it now asks the question that the taken decision will answer. This means the placeholder title in our second example becomes "ADR-003—How do we handle subscription changes so the customer isn't mischarged?" This communicates the fact that we are now beginning to understand our problem space but also that I am still very much in the thinking stage.

Ad Hoc Advice When Writing the Context

Writing the context needn't be a solo or team-only effort. Though this is not explicitly mandated by the advice process, it can help to seek advice on the Context section, even before you've written anything else. As I discussed earlier, the Context section is where you really get the chance to understand the problem space. Advice can apply to this as much as it can to the various solution options.

If you do seek advice at this early stage, make sure to let the advisers know where you're up to in the decision process so that they focus where you are looking for input and don't get confused.

Step 3: Make Options and Gather Their Consequences

Options and their consequences are useful when ADRs are decision records, but when ADRs are decision-support tools, they're essential, helping both you and your advisers to think. Therefore, once you're satisfied that the initial contents of your Context section succinctly reflect the challenge that your decision is aiming to address, it's time to make the options set, gathering the consequential pros and cons of each.

To keep matters simple, jump down your template again, skipping the Options section for now, and work in the Consequences section. You can move back up to the Options section once everything in the Consequences section settles down.

Begin this options collection with those options you already know about—it's quite possible that you had one or more solutions in mind from the moment you realized that a decision was required. If you did, jot them down first, but don't stop there. Consider the "do nothing" and "not yet" options, too. Also use your Context section for inspiration and don't be afraid to sharpen that further if this thinking leads you to greater clarity on the problem.

Making a set of decision options typically involves a good deal of creativity, and I encourage you to approach it with that mindset. If you're like me, your first pass at things will again come rushing out in an unstructured, disordered fashion, options and their associated pro and con consequences spilling out all mixed up. That's fine if they do. Just get them down. You can tidy them up for readers later.

On the other hand, you may be very disciplined and methodical, working incrementally through all the aspects you can think of. Or perhaps you like to conduct a bunch of research, finding out about how others have solved the problem and getting inspiration from them. However you go about it, the key is to remember the problem space you described in your context; it'll keep you and your options focused on the task in hand.

Whatever your approach, the general goal is to get these early, possibly messy, possibly simplistic ideas for options out of your head and on paper, screen, wall, or whiteboard. Once they've been captured, you don't have to worry so much about forgetting any of them. This practice of capturing everything allows you to be confident that you have been exhaustive. Continue until you have nothing more to note that is pertinent.

As you make your options, try not to favor one over another or write pros and cons to simply validate your biases. (There are likely more biases than you are aware of. I'll go into the most important ones and how to be aware of them in Chapter 12.) When you entered this decision process, you may already have had an inkling of the most likely best option. To avoid overfocusing on this, capture it but don't elaborate on it. Not yet. Do that last.

Embrace this creative freedom but don't get lost in it. What you are seeking is to give each of your options the appropriate level of detail to make it clear to you and others *why they are under consideration given your context*. If you do find some useful information, make sure you make your sources clear, ideally by linking them directly with a URL. Think about the longevity of these links. This ADR will live for a good number of years, so find a source that is likely to persist, such as a book, official documentation, or a well-known authority on the subject.

How Many Options Should I Make?

While having a single option is a bad smell (there is never only one way to go with a decision—that simply shows a lack of imagination), you don't want to end up with too many options either. I've seen ADRs with more than 10. It screams "impending analysis paralysis." So what does a good number of options look like? Two is a minimum, and between three and five is a nice place to aim for. (I'll dive deeper into options and how to unleash your creativity in Chapter 12.)

The following is my initial brain dump for the second example ADR's Consequences section. You'll see that my initial thought was to cancel the existing mandate first,[12] then create and activate the next. My second thought was the reverse of this, which I knew would have a bad consequence of potentially double-charging the customer, but it was an option. My third thought came a little later, when we were drawing the interactions out and thinking a little more about how things might fail and how we could recover (there were three separate calls to a third-party API, after all).

The full brain dump for the options and consequences are as follows:

EXAMPLE

NOTE: How will we recover from failures? Manually or automatically?

1. Cancel the existing mandate, then create and activate the new one.
   - Blocks returning to the client until all three requests succeed.
   - Risk of having no mandate in place if the creation or activation fails. This is "fail in favor of the customer" but might cost the company money.
   - Missing or inactive mandates could be fixed with a customer-support process.
2. Create and activate the new mandate, then cancel the old one.
   - Blocks user journey for initial attempts, then returns.
   - Doesn't lose the company money.
   - Blocks returning to the client until all three requests succeed.
   - Risks having two active mandates (old and new) if the cancellation fails. This is "fail in favor of the company." How frequently do we think this will happen?

---

12 A *mandate* is a domain term from banking. It means you have given express permission for someone to operate your bank account. In this scenario, this permission is to take the subscription fees on a monthly basis. If your ADR has a few such domain terms, it can be nice to link to a glossary.

3. Cancel the existing mandate, then create and activate the new one, async retries if "activate" fails.

   - Same as Option 1, but with async retries to "activate."
   - Blocks for initial attempts, then returns.
   - Risk of having no mandate is virtually eliminated.

After you have your initial brain dump and sketches, keep working them through, fleshing them out into proper options with detailed consequences. This method of writing things down and drawing them out helps significantly in the decision process. It helps you think through and around the problem, using your context as cues. You need just enough detail in specific sentences to exercise your mind.

In the updated Consequences section from the second example ADR, the last option has become the first because, after some research into domain-driven design aggregates (*https://oreil.ly/C4vDH*) and best practices for maintaining subscription invariants ("always have one active mandate"), it felt like it would give the cleanest implementation, even in failure mode. It's also been generally polished to ensure it's legible for advice givers, and the diagrams we drew to think things through have been included.

EXAMPLE

NOTE: How will we recover from failures? Manually or automatically?

1. Cancel, then create and activate mandates—async retries if "activate" fails.

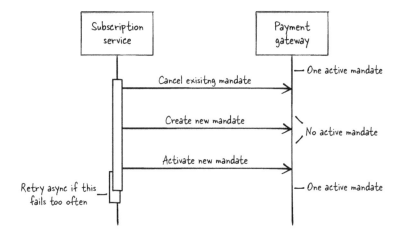

   - Blocks for first few attempts at activation, then returns to client.
   - Risk of having no mandate is virtually eliminated.

---

2. Cancel, then create and activate mandates.

- Same as Option 1, but without the async "activate" retries.
- Blocks returning to the client until all three requests succeed.
- Risk of having no mandate if the creation fails. This is "fail in favor of the customer" but might cost the company money.
- Missing or inactive mandates could be fixed with manual support processes.

3. Create and activate, then cancel mandates.

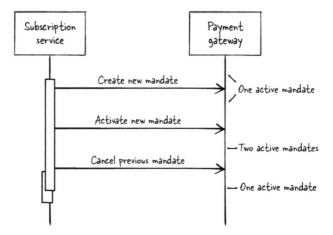

- Blocks returning to the client until all three requests succeed.
- Doesn't lose the company money.
- Risks having two active mandates (old and new) if the cancellation fails. This is "fail in favor of the company." How frequently do we think this will happen?

A Note on ADR Sections

I sometimes structure my ADRs to have a Consequences subsection for each of my options. This has the benefit of putting the consequences right next door to the introduction of the option but the drawback of making it nigh-on impossible to take in all the options considered at a glance. It's for that reason that I've gone for the "listing the bare options separately first" approach in this chapter. While it's repetitive, it again helps the ADR reader focus and digest the wealth of information that the Consequences section brings.

Step 4: Propose a Selected Option

Finally, once you think you have a comprehensive set of options and a related set of consequences, both pro and con, you can (if you feel confident) provisionally select one.

Should You Provisionally Select an Option or Not?

There are a couple of reasons why you might or might not want to include a provisional selection. Although it may seem like you're trying to influence your advisers, provisionally selecting an option tells them where to direct their focus because it flags your current preference. On the flip side, if you're in a position of authority, you *may not* want to include a provisional decision because the anchoring effect of authority can be strong—typically far stronger than those in authority are aware. Anchoring effects mean others tend to agree with you because of your position rather than anything else. Avoid this by not selecting an option.

This is what the team did in the "Story 1: A Development Team Decides to Use Release Toggles" on page 78 example in Chapter 4. They were pretty set on using simple boolean checks in code because it worked for them. But remember, it wasn't where they ended up after they had collected and processed all the advice.

Even if you don't make a selection, many advisers will assume that your preferred option is the first on your list. Make sure they don't overfocus on what they know or assume to be the selected option, however. Remind them to offer advice on all options if they desire and suggest new ones as well as things relating to the context. The entire ADR is open for advice.

If you do take a draft decision, make sure you update the status of the ADR from "Draft" to "Proposed" and flag the option you've picked (writing "provisionally selected" next to your preferred option will suffice). Doing both makes it clearer to readers that you have made a provisional selection. If you're not taking a draft decision, then leave the status as is.

Whether you're taking a draft decision or not, don't waste time writing up the Decision section. It'll still be empty at this point. There will be enough in the Options to support advice offering.

Returning to the second example decision, I am confident enough to take a draft decision. Our updated ADR now looks as follows:

Title: ADR-003—How do we handle subscription changes so the customer isn't mis-charged?

Status: Proposed

Date: 2023-11-01

Authors: Andrew Harmel-Law and Gayathri Thiyagarajan

…

Consequences:

1. (PROVISIONALLY SELECTED) Cancel, then create and activate mandates—async retries if "activate" fails

…

Having got this far, and with your decision process and associated ADR well on its way, it's time to move to the advice-seeking phase.

Using ADRs to Facilitate the Advice Process

As well as helping you think about a decision at hand, ADRs give you a way to organize and capture the advice you gather throughout a decision process. They also help ensure that you've sought advice from everyone you are obliged to in a way that's transparent to all.

Before I talk about how to set up the Advice section of an ADR, let's discuss how and when to seek advice generally.

When and How to Seek Advice

Remember, there is no "best time" to seek advice. You don't need to wait until the explicit advice-gathering part of the advice process. Although there are no hard and fast rules, there is some strategy for when, how, and how often you seek advice.

Early in the decision process

You can seek advice as soon as you have the first draft of your Context section, a placeholder title, and nothing else. Asking earlier on in the decision process gets more minds on the whole extent of the problem—a nice way to build trust and confidence. If this is how you choose to approach your decision, you are looking for others to not only propose options to you but also offer their advice on the options and the surrounding context. It can help to remind advisers that they should watch out for personal bias toward their preferred options.

This is the way that the architect in Chapter 4's "Story 2: An Architect Decides to Unpick a Workflow Problem" on page 84 approached matters: they first engaged teams to find out how the workflow component was designed and how it was being used. In this case, it was a perfectly sensible approach, especially as the affected parties had a lot of contextual information that was essential to capture.

Later in the decision process

Alternatively, you may wait until you have your Context, Options, and associated Consequences sections and a draft Decision section before seeking advice. Engaging later can get you sharper, deeper commentary focused on the decision your ADR pertains to. You can even ask for advice on the drafted Context, Options, Consequences, and Decision sections of the ADR itself. In fact, it can help as the advice seeker to encourage this explicitly.

This is the way the team in Chapter 4's Story 1 tackled things, and again, it's perfectly valid. You see this a lot with decisions that come from teams who understand that the implementation of the decision rests entirely with them.

As teams become increasingly skilled in deciding, many optimize for smaller decision scopes because there is less work to implement and less intrateam coordination. This is a very good thing that Chapter 13 will cover in more depth. For now, it suffices to say that the best decisions are those that are the quickest to implement, deploy, and collect feedback from. Smaller decision scopes are the best way to achieve that.

But how do you know if your small scope is possible? Advice is a great way to validate this quickly. Recall the draft decision in Chapter 4's Story 1. There, the deciding team *thought* they would not affect any other teams with their in-code, boolean-toggles approach. When they received advice, however, the teams that consumed their APIs advised that this approach *would* affect them, which then highlighted the benefits of other options, such as the environment-variables method suggested by the infra team member.

Advice can relate to any part of the decision

It's hopefully clear by now, but it bears repeating: advice *could and should* pertain to any section and to metatopics. As you and others learn how to seek advice, you will get a feel for when the best time is to do this.

Advice can be used to generate new things (such as more options), provide greater detail (such as sharpening the contents of the Context section), validate or contradict (for example, additional pro and con consequences against existing options), and even split the decision into multiple, smaller-scoped, and potentially staged decisions. It's very decision and individual/team specific.

More than once and when necessary

You are not restricted to a single advice session with a given individual. You can go back to them as often as you need. Recall that both the example decisions in Chapter 4 place conversations at the heart of an advice process. Recall also that Story 2 had multiple interactions with the affected teams, some more involved and collaborative than others. The key factor for the decider to bear in mind is the focus on a solid decision that you understand and can get behind, one that maintains the shared trust you are all cultivating so carefully.

But don't forget: one of the key goals of an advice process is to speed up decision making. Again, I'll spend a lot more time on this in Part II, but for now, it's enough to know that making incremental progress and learning from the feedback that results is better than spending forever trying to take the perfect decision.

Make sure you get the advice you need but beware of becoming stuck in the advice-seeking phase. I'll come back again to ways to spot this decision paralysis in Part III, but for now, it's sufficient to point out that you should be aware of it and try not to fall prey to it.

Setting Up the Advice Section

Before you gather advice, you need to know who to gather it from. In an advice process, you know you need to approach two groups: the people who will be affected by the decision and the people who have relevant expertise. Ensure that you really put the effort into finding all those who will be affected directly as the most valuable advice will come from them.

Capture these people/teams in a bulleted list in your Advice section. This is what the list looks like in our second example ADR:

EXAMPLE

- Monira R., Product Manager
- Hanna A., Infra team
- Rebecca F., UX
- Vanessa F., Tech Lead from the Order Management team
- Pete H., InfoSec
- Alina B., Architect

You may even want to include why the person is on the list. Consult "Source Advice from the Right People" on page 106 for more details.

With this in place, it's time to gather the advice.

Gathering Advice

Set up meetings with the advice givers. Make explicit to potential advisers that you are following the advice process and which of the two advice-offering roles they fulfill. Use the ADR to focus your conversation with the advice giver.

Sharing your ADR in its current state is a great way to set out your thinking around a decision *prior* to an advice conversation.[13] It sets up the conversation, making clear what you have and (by omission) don't have in mind. If you are headed in a direction that the advice offerer thinks is completely wrong, that will likely be evident, and they should bring it to your attention. If you are missing something fundamental and vital, that will be evident as well. If your idea is sound but you are missing some additional supporting information, that will also stand out. You're priming the conversation by showing not only *what* you are thinking about but also *how* you are thinking about it.[14]

The advice that arises from a conversation that is supported by an ADR—whatever its state of completion—is almost inevitably better advice than one that isn't. Not only that, but additionally recorded "in the raw" in the Advice section, the advice is a superb supplement to the ADR as a *record*. ADRs without the addition of the Advice section are decision summaries *after the fact*. They are a lossy form of compression of the entire decision process. With the Advice section, ADRs become not only a record of the advice process but also a learning resource for the future. This learning can arrive in the form of retrospectives or could simply be developers and architects later wondering how the current state of affairs came about or even how this decision was worked through. Both are incredibly valuable.

To make things easier for the advice giver, offer to be the note taker during the advice-giving session. Try sketching diagrams too if it helps clarify and focus matters. This way, you will have a reason to listen more deeply, you will understand better, and you will be more motivated to respond with clarifying questions rather than simply

---

13 Sometimes organizations call this advice-gathering process "requests for comments" (aka RFCs (*https://oreil.ly/ nVTha*)). Thoughtworks has a "lightweight approach to RFCs" (*https://oreil.ly/yrtoM*) on the Technology Radar. I have never felt the need to separate the deciding from the recording of a decision into different documents.

14 Used in this way, ADRs function very much like the famous Amazon six-pagers (*https://oreil.ly/t_C05*). These are memos circulated prior to meetings that are read in silence during the first 10 minutes of the session. Jeff Bezos, the founder of Amazon, has described these (*https://oreil.ly/m6Cq5*) as "the smartest thing we ever did." Just like six-pagers, ADRs "create the context for what will…be a good discussion." Unlike six-pagers, they do not need to be complete, nor should they be as long as six pages. (Two pages, minus the advice, is still the target length for ADRs.)

reacting to what you heard. This kind of active listening is a skill, and although it can take time to develop, it's worth the effort as you maximize the value you can gain from the advice shared.

After the advice-giving session, add the notes to the Advice section of the ADR. Then, share the ADR plus the notes with the advice giver for validation. I recommend using the negative-assurance method. When you share the ADR, explain that if the adviser sees nothing wrong with the notes, they have no further action. Otherwise, they can make corrections up to the decision-taking point, resulting in their intent being accurately captured.[15] Or they can ask you to fix it on their behalf. It's important to do this while the decision is still open, before it has been taken, so that the benefit of the advice can be gained.

Whether you take the notes on the advice you receive or not, the advice offerer is accountable for ensuring it accurately ends up in the Advice section of the ADR. If you are the author and add it, make sure you loop back with the advice offerer, so they can check that you caught their intent clearly and completely. "Clearly and completely" is key here. The ADR Advice section needs to be an accurate record.

At the end of the advice-gathering process, the second example ADR has the following validated content in its Advice section:

> **EXAMPLE**
>
> - How quickly will we be able to respond to the customer when there is a failure at the Payment Provider? How confident can we be that they will never be double-charged? (*Monira R., Product Manager*)
> - We have some uptime stats on the third-party Payment Provider's service. It's not great. They have at least one failure a month, frequently losing service for more than five minutes at a time. (*Hanna A., Infra team*)
> - How much will we be able to tell the customer about what's going on when Payment Provider failures happen? What information will we be able to share with them, and can we reassure them that their experience (and bank balance) will not be impacted? (*Rebecca F., UX*)

---

15 The proceedings of the UK Parliament are recorded in something called Hansard. Hansard is the "substantially verbatim" report (*https://oreil.ly/U_UVS*) of what is said. But it might not reflect the actual words that were used at the time. This is because there is a window of opportunity for *nonsubstantive* speaking errors to be corrected (*https://oreil.ly/bWCt3*) before Hansard is published. This is inspired by that approach. In both cases, the speaker (member of parliament or advice offerer) is the most motivated of everyone involved to have an accurate record.

- Will this complicate our team's integration with your payment and subscription processing service? Will you be able to hide this from us? Also, have you thought about the retry schedule for the async retries? (*Vanessa F., Tech Lead from the Order Management team*)

- We need to ensure that we don't store any PCI data (card details, etc.). See this [CFR]. (*Pete H., InfoSec*)

- Can you update the diagram in the Context section to show there are three separate calls to the Payment Gateway? Does the order of API calls always have to be "create," then "activate"? Can you "cancel" in the middle? Being able to rely less on chained API calls makes us more robust. Also, we pay per API call to the third-party Payment Provider, and they are very good at collecting this fee, whether their service works or not. Exponential backoff schedules are good for this. Also think about observability (see this [CFR]) and make it easy to keep track of failed (and hopefully auto-recovered) subscription changes. (*Alina B., Architect*)

Now that we have met our obligations under the social contract and sought and understood (and recorded) the relevant advice, what are we to do with it?

Updating the ADR to Reflect the Contributions of Others

It's now time to consider how the advice affects your ADR. While under an advice process, the decision taking is in the hands of the team or the individual who initiated this decision process and no one else, deciders are still obligated by the social contract to consider each point of advice received.

Even if you are still sure that the best option is self-evident, go through every piece of advice one last time. The best way to do this is to revisit each section of your ADR in light of the advice and make relevant updates:

Add further information
Enhance the Context, Options, or Consequences sections. Take this opportunity to include advice and options you don't agree with or even like. Remember, you are in control of the decision taking, so there is no need to show bias or favoritism. Be transparent.

Clarify
If information in your ADR was misinterpreted by advice givers, fix it. Take this opportunity to make sure the ADR text is as clear as it can be so that all readers will be able to understand it in the future. This happens a lot in my experience. The opportunity to both sharpen a point for the decider and meet a need for readers is a gift.

Acknowledge advice

It helps to show in the main ADR text when you received some advice but decided not to change your decision as a result. (I'll share a technique for explicitly stating this in an updated Consequences example.)

One of the key strengths of advice is that it mitigates your blind spots. If during the process of making ADR updates, it becomes clear that you didn't understand a piece of advice sufficiently—for example, to solidly and explicitly reject it—feel free to go back to whoever offered it to you. If on the other hand, you are finding it hard to state why you are rejecting something, I'll share exercises for building your metacognition skills with exercises in Chapter 12.

This act of editing makes your ADR better because it forces you to engage directly one last time with the advice you have received, but this time in the safety of a more private space. It also transforms your ADR into a solid *record* of the decision process. By explicitly putting the advice that you feel is relevant into the ADR body, you give it the appropriate recognition. You also remove the need for others to read the entire document to benefit from it. Remember, future readers may read only the title of your ADR, or they may just consult the Decision section or indeed stop after the context has been laid out. This ADR updating isn't simply housekeeping.

The advice in the example resulted in a number of updates to the second example ADR. Let's step through the document and see how it was affected.

First, the Context section: on advice from Alina, the architect, the diagram was updated to reflect the three calls that need to be made to the payment gateway compared to one in the original. The diagram description was changed, too. Furthermore, prompted by Vanessa from the order management team, a note that "the new services must hide the complexity of the Payment Gateway API" was added. Finally, Hanna from infrastructure's experience with the payment gateway's stability was reflected in a note: "They don't meet their SLAs. Conversations are currently underway with alternative suppliers."

Here's what the Context section looks like now (additions are bolded, and the interaction with the payment gateway in the first diagram has been split to show the three types of requests):

Note the single integration with the Order Management systems and the pair of integrations with the Payment Gateway.

We are creating a new set of payment and subscription processing services to enhance our market offering. Our only consumer at the moment is the in-house Order Management System, though there may be other consumers in the future. **All consumers will provide their own frontends. The new services must hide the complexity of the Payment Gateway API.**

To avoid PCI compliance, we consume a third-party Payment Services Provider, **but they don't meet their SLAs. Conversations are currently underway with alternative suppliers.**

The riskiest part of subscriptions is when bank details are changed: the Payment Provider API requires separate REST calls to cancel, create, and activate mandates. It's essential that clients are never double-billed for subscriptions but also that we don't give products away for free unnecessarily.

Finally comes the updated Consequences section, which is where the most postadvice updates have taken place. Appearing first now is the new option that came from the architect Alina's advice to think about calling the Payment Gateway API in a different order. This entry is fleshed out with a diagram and thinking about failure modes and messages to the user in light of advice from Monira, the product manager, and Rebecca from UX. Their advice showed that not only was this new option the best way to ensure that no one lost any money, but it was also the best way to be responsive and transparent to customers when failures did occur. Last, we added a little more detail about payment card industry (PCI) data in failure scenarios in other options based on the timely reminder from Pete in InfoSec. To summarize, other retry options would not be possible as it would mean we would have to keep a temporary copy of payment details, which would make us liable for PCI contraventions.

Here's what the updated Consequences section looks like now ("NEW OPTION" is the new addition, and more details have been added to the other options, which are bolded):

EXAMPLE

1. (NEW OPTION) Create, then cancel, then activate mandates. Async retries if "cancel" or "activate" fails.

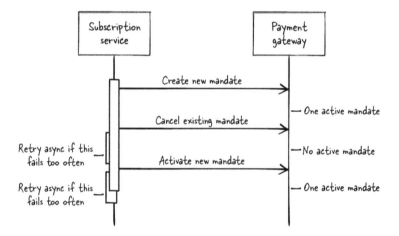

- "Create" call is the only one that contains PCI data, and if this fails, we can tell the customer immediately.
- Failures in "cancel" and "activate" calls can be retried async without any PCI data, ensuring there is always an active mandate.
- Async retries can exponentially back off, reducing API usage costs without making the customer wait.
- All these key transactions can be monitored.
- Risk of having no active mandate when a payment isn't entirely eliminated. Mandate creation failure can be flagged to customers immediately.
- Doesn't lose the company money.

---

2. (DESELECTED) Cancel, then create and activate mandates. Async retries if "activate" fails.

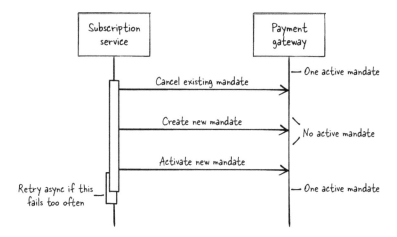

- Blocks for first few (configurable) attempts...
- **Async retries ensure activation after the fact.**
- Risk of having no mandate...
- **Failures in mandate creation can be logged for customer service follow-up.**
- **Two active mandates cannot happen.**
- **Doesn't lose the company money.**

3. Cancel, then create and activate mandates.
    - Same as Option 2 but without the async "activate" retries.
    - Blocks returning to the client until all requests **complete**.
    - Risk of having no mandate if the creation **or activation** fails. This is "fail in favor of the customer" but might cost the company money. **Chances of Payment Provider failure based on previous experience are not insignificant.**
    - Missing mandates would be fixed with a **customer support process as we can't store bank details.**

4. Create and activate, then cancel mandates.

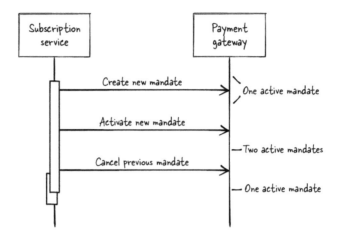

- Blocks returning to the client until all three requests succeed.
- Doesn't lose the company money.
- **This is not "fail in favor of the customer."** Risk of having two active mandates (old and new) if the cancellation fails. **Chances of failure based on previous experience are not insignificant.**

With all this in detail and the collective thinking in place, you're now ready to move to the final two stages of the decision process.

Taking Your Decision and Completing the ADR

Having gathered and considered your advice without prejudice—from those affected and experts—you're now ready to take the decision. The ADR is in perfect shape to support both the "taking the decision" and "sharing the decision" stages of the decision process. Little work remains to be done regarding the decision process, but it is important work nonetheless.

Select the Decision Option

By this point, you are likely clear in your mind what your selected option will be. The ADR needs to be updated as follows:

1. Write your Options section from the Consequences section.
2. Move your preferred option to the top of your list (if it's not already) and write "Selected" next to it.

3. For each of the upsides of the selected options, express them in the format "Selected because…" and for each of the downsides of the selected option, express them in the format "Selected despite…"

4. For all the upsides on each of the rejected options, express them in the format "Rejected despite…" and for all the downsides on each of the rejected options, express them as "Rejected because…"

The Options section of the second example ADR can now be written up as follows:

1. (SELECTED) Create, then cancel, then activate mandates. Async retries if "cancel" or "activate" fails.

2. Cancel, then create and activate mandates. Async retries if "activate" fails.

3. Cancel, then create and activate mandates.

4. Create and activate, then cancel mandates.

The Consequences section is also updated accordingly:

1. (SELECTED) Create, then cancel, then activate mandates. Async retries if "cancel" or "activate" fails.

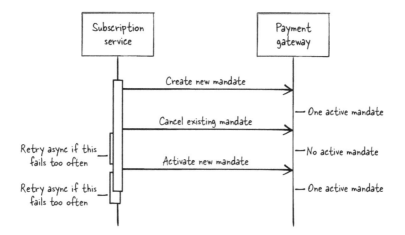

- Selected because the "create" call is the only one that contains PCI data, and if this fails, we can tell the customer immediately.
- Selected because failures in "cancel" and "activate" calls can be retried async without any PCI data, ensuring there is always an active mandate.
- …
- Selected despite the risk of having no active mandate isn't entirely eliminated, though it is handled automatically without human intervention.
- …

2. …

Before moving forward, look back at your updated Options and Consequences sections for a confidence check. Are you comfortable taking this decision? Seeing it written out makes it more "real," causing new gut reactions. While this check can be a simple tidying-up exercise, it can also give you a reason to pause and even change your mind. Feel free to have one last rethink. Remember, "taking" a decision is simply selecting one option from a set of options, but it is also intended to have a significant impact.

This final confidence check can sharpen both your thinking and the content of the ADR. If a drawback doesn't stand a real chance of being a problem, you shouldn't include it. For example, the concern that the format for a manually generated ID might be hard to agree on became irrelevant when this option was deselected. If it's not clear if something will or won't happen and cause an impact, however, you should include it.

If this prompts you to go back and make changes, go for it, but remember that taking architectural decisions is both hard and a significant responsibility. There is no "right" solution, only the best option that you know is open to you right now, given the current circumstances. Don't let yourself get stuck at this stage. Remember that your decision is backed by all of the advice you've gathered during the advice process. (I know this can be hard, especially when you are new to deciding. Chapter 12 will have tips and techniques for you to avoid falling into this trap.)

Once you are satisfied with your taken decision, you need to update/complete the remaining sections of your ADR.

Write Your Decision Section and Update Your Title

At last, you can write your Decision section: a short, punchy summary as described earlier in this chapter. It's common to see them composed of noun phrases in the form: "We will…".

While you are there, update the title to contain the decision, too. If you find it hard keeping the Decision section focused and to the point, it can help to write the title first. Then you have that as a hypersummary and your selected option as the full details. Your Decision section is somewhere in the middle of the two.

The second example ADR now has this title and new Decision section:

EXAMPLE

Title: ADR-003—Change subscription mandates without costing the customer or the company money

Decision:

Mandate changes will be handled by Payment Gateway calls in the following order: (1) create new, (2) cancel existing, and (3) activate new (Option 1).

Failures in mandate creation will immediately be flagged to the customer. Failures in mandate cancellation or activation will be retried asynchronously, backing off exponentially to balance the time out of sync with the cost of API calls to the Payment Gateway. Customers will be informed by email when this completes. All mandate change steps will be logged for monitoring.

A single "change subscription mandate" endpoint will be exposed to Subscription service consumers.

Change the ADR Status to Accepted

Finally, update the ADR status to "Accepted" and change the ADR date. I've sometimes seen teams retaining a history showing the dates when each status was achieved. This is fine, but it's extra.

The metadata for the second example ADR now looks as follows:

EXAMPLE

State: Accepted

Date: 2023-11-04

Authors: Andrew Harmel-Law and Gayathri Thiyagarajan

The completed ADR can be seen in the GitHub site that accompanies this book (*https://oreil.ly/zUs-N*). The Git change history for the ADR file corresponds to the change steps that this chapter has worked through, too.

With the decision taken and recorded in the ADR, you have completed the penultimate stage in your decision process. But there's one last thing you need to do.

Share the Decision

As you know, the final stage in the decision process is to share your decision with those who will implement it. Do this by sending out the completed, adopted ADR to everyone who was involved in this decision's advice process. This might generate more advice, but it's important to make clear at this point that it's too late: the decision has been taken and is about to be implemented.

You've now seen how ADRs support all stages in the decision process. ADR statuses have been used to give readers and advice offerers some idea of at what point the decision is in this process. Let's now move on and consider these statuses in more detail.

The ADR Lifecycle

As with any record, ADRs have lifecycles. ADR statuses reflect not only the status of the decision at hand but also the status of the ADR as an individual record in the evolving story of your overall architecture. In this section, I'll take you through the statuses most commonly used for ADRs as well as a few uncommon ones you may want to try.

Standard Statuses: Draft, Proposed, Accepted, and Superseded

Figure 6-2 shows all the standard statuses: draft, proposed, accepted, and superseded. Most ADR approaches use these or their equivalent, although "Draft" is implicit in some approaches. I include "Draft" in my ADR template because, when deploying an architecture advice process, it pays to clearly communicate the current state of the decision, especially as we are relying on transparency to build and maintain trust. ADRs stay in this state until a provisional decision is taken, which moves an ADR to a "Proposed" state. While an ADR is in either of these first two states, the advice seeking is taking place. Once all the advice has been provided and the qualifiers satisfied, then the final decision can be taken and the ADR status changed to "Accepted." The final standard status is "Superseded," used to indicate when a further, separate decision has been taken that invalidates or deprecates the current ADR.

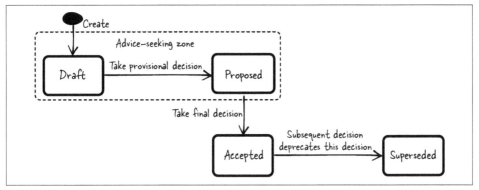

Figure 6-2. State-transition diagram showing the lifecycle of an individual ADR

Remember, ADRs are immutable. Once decided, they exist in the historical record of your architecture. The decision has been *taken* and is *being acted on*. It's too late to go back in time and take a different decision. You are making the decision *on top of* the previous one, overriding some or all of it. Perhaps this separate, subsequent decision undoes what the original decision did (as when a $20.00 debit to your bank balance after a $20.00 credit returns it to the previous state). More likely, you decide to replace the existing thing with something new and different. Both of these types of decision will result in the original decision being marked as "Superseded" (and ideally linked explicitly to the new ADR to aid navigation, but that's really a topic for a later section and I'm getting ahead of myself).

For example, imagine you have a historic ADR describing the design of a public API, its name, parameters, and mode of operation. Time passes, and there is a need to update the API. These changes are documented in a new ADR that replaces the previous one. This new ADR refers back explicitly to the original ADR, which is moved to the status "Superseded." This tells future readers that it is no longer an up-to-date reflection of the system's architecture.

Nonstandard ADR Statuses

The four standard statuses covered will probably be sufficient for most circumstances, but what if they're not? In this subsection, I'll introduce two nonstandard statuses that I've occasionally found useful when working with clients with specific needs and one that comes up but that I've not found useful. I'm not sharing them to encourage their use, but I do want to illustrate this extension point to help ADRs better fit your needs.

Expired status

The first nonstandard status is "Expired," shown in Figure 6-3. I've used this with a number of clients when a decision is time sensitive and they want to revisit it after a certain period of time has passed. For example, perhaps they had a need to deliver a product to market, and at the time, only one of the cloud providers, a nonpreferred vendor, offered a specific managed service, though their preferred provider had it roadmapped. A time-bounded ADR could be written stating that the decision had been taken to go with this first vendor rather than waiting for the preferred vendor to come to market, but that in a stated period of time (e.g., three or six months), the original ADR decision would expire and the decision would be revisited, possibly with the end result that the product would be migrated back to the preferred cloud provider.

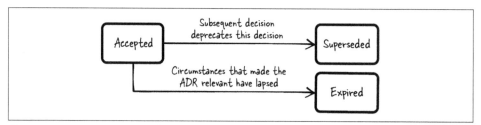

Figure 6-3. State-transition diagram showing where the experimental status "Expired" sits

This status was a nice addition in the circumstances as it made it clear when a decision was scheduled for revisiting, in the form of a new ADR, but that such a revisit might not yet be top of the priority list. It also clarified that the new decision might be to just keep things as they are if the current decision still stood. This communicated well at the executive level, too, especially when a lot of change was happening all at once and senior folks were concerned that corners were being cut (when in fact they were not).

Retired status

The second nonstandard status is "Retired," shown in Figure 6-4. I've used this when engaged in significant amounts of legacy remediation work. In these circumstances, while many of the decisions will simply be "Superseded" as new versions of old features are put in place, sometimes things just come to the end of their natural life and there is no replacement, or not a direct one anyway. In these cases, it is nice to be able to mark the ADR that documented them as "Retired" along with the system it pertains to.

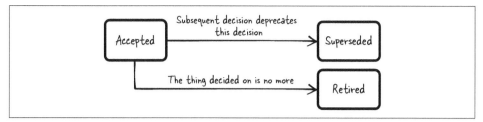

Figure 6-4. State-transition diagram showing where the experimental "Retired" status sits

Rejected status

One experiment that has failed for me in the past is a "Rejected" status. The argument goes that teams and architects will want to see when a decision was proposed but, after consideration, was rejected.

It's an interesting viewpoint, but "Rejected" puts the wrong spin on matters. What you really have in these circumstances is a decision to do nothing and stick with the status quo. In this case, you will have an ADR with a status of "Accepted," with the chosen option being "keep going as we are" or similar and a title that reflects this. In short, you get the same benefits without the addition of any further complexity of another status option. If the decision really was adopted but then someone (typically someone senior) decided on another course of action, then this original decision will be superseded by a new ADR that documents the decision to do nothing.

Hopefully, these three examples illustrate how you *might* add your own statuses. Even if the default ones work well for your organization, take time to consider how these three nonstandard ones (and others of your own invention) might affect your current system, both positively and negatively. Even if you decide not to change anything, you'll at least have a better understanding of your current system.

Managing ADRs

As your advice process starts working, you'll have many ADRs at various statuses that will then need to be managed. You'll want to keep them all in one place (that's why having unique IDs is so important). In this section, I'll take you through some tooling options. But first, no matter where you keep your ADRs, you need to bear some fundamentals in mind.

Fundamental Aspects of Managing ADRs

In his original article about ADRs (*https://oreil.ly/Otixv*), Micheal Nygard made two short but important points about managing ADRs:

- We will keep ADRs in the project repository under *doc/arch/adr-NNN.md*.
- We should use a lightweight text formatting language like Markdown or Textile.

His principle here is that ADRs are written in formats familiar to developers and stored in developer tooling, such as a wiki or source control. This tooling has key benefits that we may not always be conscious of. First, they allow multiple people to collaborate, most likely asynchronously, on a shared work item, keeping a public record of who did what and when. Second, perhaps due to the "heads down" nature of a significant part of our work, they all integrate well with various messaging systems such as chat and email, allowing us to know that something has been created or updated *without having to repeatedly check*. When using ADRs as part of an architecture advice process, you want these benefits, too.

Nygard's suggestion to use developer tooling and not architect tooling was also important because it mitigated against a legacy failure mode. While traditional architecture tooling applications are incredibly powerful, access to them (e.g., Rational Rose, Rational Software Architect, even Visio) was not evenly distributed. These tools also required a significant amount of skill to use. All this placed a barrier between those who created and owned the architecture (the architects) and those who implemented it (developers)—a barrier we are breaking down with this decentralized approach to the practice of architecture.

ADRs, combined with more accessible, lower-fidelity tooling that appeared to let everyone contribute to architecture diagrams, broke away from that (tooling like PlantUML (*https://plantuml.com*), C4 (*https://c4model.com*), and Mermaid (*https:// mermaid.js.org*) has done great work here, but there are others). It's for this reason Nygard suggested the location for ADRs that he did, and it's important that you follow suit.

Nygard suggested using rich text files in source control, and another popular option is on a wiki. I'll quickly consider those first, highlighting a few aspects to get right if you use either of these options, before I introduce my own personal preference: work ticketing systems.

ADRs on Wikis and Rich Text Files in Source Control

If you are looking to use a wiki for ADRs, make sure the ADRs are in a location alongside the other developer documentation where they can be discovered by those teams building and running the systems. Don't put them in the architects' space where few developers ever venture. This just adds unnecessary friction and additional cognitive load.

The alternative (and other predominant way to manage ADRs) is to use markdown (or similar) files, one per ADR, stored in the source code repository alongside the code and configuration. This alternative is popular, and pull requests can be used during the "Draft" and "Proposed" stages, with a merge resulting in a move to "Adopted." Again, resist the urge to put these in a "blessed by architects" repository or somewhere architects have superpowers for the same reasons as before.

ADRs in Work-Ticketing Systems

You can also manage ADRs using your work-ticketing system (e.g., Jira or Azure DevOps). Creating a new "ADR" work item template with fields for all the ADR template elements (except for the advice, which goes in the comments) and associating your chosen status workflow can be done easily.

This approach can be controversial for some who believe that ticketing systems should be reserved solely for work items that go on backlogs (valid, if a little puritanical). However, the additional benefits of work-ticketing systems are threefold:

Status, ID, author, and date are raised above simple sections in the template.
You saw earlier how important the status field can be. Work-ticketing systems allow you to put type constraints around many fields, which makes it easy to specify what data they should contain, and more importantly, most tools these days make completing them easy by suggesting and autofilling lots of them (also updating, such as when someone leaves the organization).

Alerting can be more targeted.
This is a direct result of the first benefit, because richer type information is available. Async alerting can be based on, for example, the change from one status to another, the update of a specific field, or the addition of a comment.

ADRs can be queried in many ways.
Again because of the richer data fields, queries can be set up that, for example, select ADRs of certain statuses, or are authored by specific teams, or fit within a certain date range. ADR lists can therefore be displayed in wiki pages with embedded queries, removing the need for constant updates.

However you choose to manage ADRs—in a developer wiki, as files in a repository, or in a work-ticketing system—one thing is of paramount importance: back up your ADRs because you don't want to lose them. As they grow in number, they form an increasingly valuable collective resource that everyone can rely on to be informed about what decisions are in flight and being taken (the third and final lack of confidence from the previous chapter). Such a resource must be curated, which is the final topic of this chapter.

> ## Start Simple
>
> It's perfectly OK to start simple and then swap over to a more complicated tool when you need to. The top-level narrative can make this clear. You can even use an ADR to record it, though technically this is not "architecturally significant."

Curating ADRs

So far, I've dealt with ADRs individually, but there is an important aspect to bear in mind: ADRs are more than a set of individual parts. Considered *collectively*, they tell the story of your architecture, and you want to ensure that this story is as accessible and digestible as possible.

As soon as you have your central location for storing your ADRs set up, I recommend that you take the final steps to make the contents of this area as easy to consume as possible. This unlocks the final aspects of the ADRs' power: as a historical decision library and record of your systems' history.

This ADR curation will likely entail:

- Creating an architectural change-log page (probably on your wiki) to contain the links to the curated ADRs
- Listing all the nondraft ADRs on this page, arranged in reverse-chronological order, newest first
- Ensuring that all the ADRs have a unique ID
- Using titles that make the decisions clear
- Giving everyone in the company access to the page, even if it's only at a read-only level for those outside the technology part of your organization

With this decision library wrapping around your ADR collection, you now have your architectural "change log." As long as you set up the page and let everyone know its purpose, it will largely self-manage (especially if you put ADRs in a work-ticketing system since your change-log page can then simply contain a query), but it might occasionally require some checking and tidying up to ensure that it's complete from the point it was started and in the right order.

This change log is a superb resource. Actively encourage new joiners or transfers from other parts of your organization to consult it during their onboarding to familiarize themselves with your architecture and culture. Those looking to progress in their career and take on more architectural responsibility can consult it, too, even before they feel confident enough to take the big step of driving or even participating in a decision process themselves.

Both these use cases may very well find that the change log in its raw form is a little hard to digest. For that reason, it might be worthwhile investing in either a summary or a highlighting of the key ADRs or both. How will you know what your key ADRs are? They will typically be the ones that had the broadest impact (intentionally or unintentionally, positive or negative, consciously or unconsciously).

The creator of these summaries or highlights will most likely be someone with a remit that is cross-team: most likely someone playing a cross-team architecture role. Creating a summary is harder work as it not only involves crafting new content and distillation, but it also requires keeping an eye on things overall as they change (which they will be continuously doing). It can, however, be incredibly powerful work. You might choose to supplement it with high-level diagrams and links to key parts of the codebase. It might even bring in other elements, such as a domain-driven design vision statement (see Chapter 15 of *Domain-Driven Design: Tackling Complexity in the Heart of Software* by Eric Evans). It can become the basis for a real hub of knowledge.

Highlighting key ADRs is simpler and lower maintenance. What you're looking for here are the pivotal ADRs that appeared at forks in the road of the architecture. They need not always be for paths taken. I've worked with more than one client who looked at a certain direction incredibly carefully before rejecting it and sticking to the path they were on. This is an important decision and should be highlighted as much as a decision that took an architecture from being entirely synchronous toward being async and event driven.

Conclusion

In this chapter, I discussed how ADRs are an excellent tool to help make better decisions, to seek and offer advice in the open, and (when taken collectively) to know what decisions others have taken and are in the process of deciding. I also showed how, even though ADRs should always be set up for readers, their structure supercharges the advice process. Finally, I highlighted how ADRs, when placed at the heart of developer tooling and appropriately curated, can form the basis for organizational learning.

While this single additional element complements the advice process, opening up a space for it to start working and for trust between all parties to develop, it doesn't remedy all concerns. In Part II of this book, I'll introduce four supporting elements, each of which mitigate specific issues you might encounter. But before that, the next chapter will consider the signals I look out for and the thought processes I typically engage in when thinking about adding anything, because more than anything you want to make sure your advice process has space to breathe.

PART II

Nurturing and Evolving Your Culture of Decentralized Trust

In Part I, you learned about combining the architecture advice process with ADRs to form the basis of a collective practice of architecture. In Part II, we'll take this a step further by looking at the elements that can support your decentralized architectural deciding by nurturing and evolving your culture of trust.

Chapter 7 begins by taking a step back, exploring how *power centers and governance are reset* when the advice process is introduced. It considers where accountability for decisions moves (to the decision initiator and taker) and how the space it opens up for a *culture of trust* to develop needs to be consciously protected.

But how? With one or more optional supporting elements. In the remaining chapters of Part II, I describe a number of these supporting elements. Each of them acknowledges a particular systemic need you might be experiencing. As with the architecture advice process and ADRs, these supporting elements are deceptively simple, and the chapters that present them incorporate discussion about what they *might* contain and how they *might* land, fit, evolve, and potentially become redundant.

Chapter 8 introduces the first supporting element, which flips standard architectural sign-off meetings into an *architecture advice forum*: a focused space for conversations, advice, transparency, trust building, and group and organizational learning.

Chapter 9 then shines a light on a pair of areas frequently overlooked in other approaches to the practice of architecture: minimal viable agreements aligned to the organizational vision and goals. It introduces a pair of supporting elements to make this real: first covering the bare minimum "what not how" of *cross-functional require-ments* before showing how an *actionable technology strategy* can provide alignment and focus shared efforts.

However, tech strategy can be at too high a level to inform individual decisions, so intermediary levels of support might be needed. The final two supporting elements provide these.

Chapter 10 describes team-sourced *architectural principles*: how to capture them, how to use them in decision processes, and how to keep them relevant in light of feedback from decisions being taken.

Finally, Chapter 11 introduces a *technology radar*. It offers a means of regularly sweeping your organization's entire technology landscape to capture the current cli-mate of experiences, insights, and learnings from everyone, representing the resulting guidance in a consumable and digestible form. Yet again, the chapter describes how to fold this into individual decision processes and update it in light of taken decisions.

By the end of Part II, you will have learned multiple decentralized ways to achieve accountable alignment—all in ways that nurture and evolve your culture of decentral-ized trust.

CHAPTER 7

Replacing Hierarchy with Decentralized Trust

Replacing your existing approach to architecture with the architecture advice process is a significant change. In Part I, I described *how* it affects your software architecture practice and *who* practices it. In summary, the architecture advice process:

- Creates a space for decentralized deciding, supporting, and governing the process as it happens

- Restores flow to delivery of software and bakes in fast feedback

- Unlocks latent skills and develops hidden talents through individual and team learning

ADRs are a core element for the success of the advice process in the postrevolutionary world. You need both the advice process and ADRs to succeed at this alternative approach to software architecture practice. As essential as the architecture advice process and ADRs are, though, they may not be sufficient on their own.

This chapter describes how responsibility and accountability for architectural decisions shift when using the advice process. I'll show how the advice process replaces traditional architectural governance, but I'll also explain how it is still compatible with wider enterprise architecture frameworks. I'll then describe how the social contract and ADRs' explicit nature forge a path between the two extremes of recklessness and reticence, opening a space for architecture practice. I'll cover the qualities of that space created for the practice of architecture, an open space for a generative culture of trust and learning. While acknowledging that this space can be threatened by mistrust, I'll describe how you can prevent that outcome by understanding how trust can be nurtured, even as your organization changes and grows. Finally, I'll set you up for the four remaining chapters of Part II, each of which suggests an additional supporting element. The recommendations you will read in each are optional, but I encourage you to understand them all, so you can use them when you need them.

These are all consequences of adopting the architecture advice process and ADRs. Let's begin by understanding the nature of that paradigm shift—not only what has been added but, more important, what has been taken away.

Responsibility and Accountability Have Moved

The architecture advice process redistributes *responsibility and accountability* for decisions. Traditional approaches to architectural decisions give power to a fixed set of individuals who both "decide" and "decide who decides." Those people are responsible for their decisions and are accountable for them. When they delegate the responsibility to others ("deciding who decides"), they still retain accountability for the outcomes.

Under the architecture advice process, anyone writing an ADR can decide and communicate an architectural decision as long as they seek advice from those impacted and people with relevant expertise. The decider is now accountable as well as responsible for their decisions because they decided that the decision was needed. That decider can technically be anyone.

The architecture advice process points toward a further "great revolution" and creates a new space for the practice of software architecture. The power redistribution directly replaces many existing architectural governance processes, practices, ceremonies, agreements, artifacts, checks, and balances. Indeed, you may currently be responsible for them. If you are, what does that mean for you?

I'll first consider the advice process's relationship with "traditional" governance practices. Then, I'll help you get comfortable with this surfacing of the thinking practice of architecture by considering it from three angles: how it increases the value of standard enterprise architecture frameworks, how it mitigates risk, and and how it encourages self-organized adoption.

Most Traditional Governance Practices Become Obsolete

The architecture advice process points toward a further "great revolution" because it replaces your existing governance practices with two very simple core elements. You are in many ways starting again. But not entirely. Resetting isn't forgetting.

The advice process calls into question many traditional supporting practices. You no longer need Architecture Review Boards with their "signoffs" and "approvals." Architectural principles will no longer be plucked from the minds of a select few. You won't rely on thoughtlessly mandated software frameworks and runtime platforms or spreadsheets full of wooly and untestable "cross-functional requirements." You don't need to refactor tons of architectural documentation, which is rarely consulted and never updated. Instead, you draw a line and start again.

I'm not suggesting that you bin everything. Just as with code in a repository, you should pull out the information and artifacts you need. In fact, you'll see how past artifacts and ceremonies can be used to seed replacement equivalents in the form of a regular forum for advice seeking and offering, a set of testable CFRs, a way to meaningfully align to tech strategy, architectural principles that actually assist in deciding, and a radar that collects the real experience of delivering and running the systems and their architecture.

You won't lose access to all the architectural knowledge, expertise, wisdom, and experience everyone has accumulated. The architecture advice process will allow far more of these riches to make their way into your software—which is ultimately where they ought to be.

Despite replacing many traditional *approaches* to practicing architecture, this new alternative doesn't reduce the amount of architecture being performed. It doesn't remove the need for people who are skilled in architectural thinking. In fact, we have brought the practice closer to the surface, unburdening those practicing it, and leading to more architecture "happening," not less. The process ensures that those skills are grown, shared, visible, and, most important, impactful.

The Advice Process Is Compatible with Existing Enterprise Architecture Frameworks

If you're concerned that enterprise architectural frameworks such as The Open Group Architecture Framework (TOGAF) will clash with an advice process, you needn't worry. The advice process is compatible with the latest flavors of these frameworks. They, too, have had to respond to the forces of the five software revolutions. The Open Agile Architecture (O-AA) framework, for example, makes this clear on its page on governance (*https://oreil.ly/K20ad*) where it actually calls out the first (Agile) and implicitly the third (DevOps) and fifth (stream-aligned) revolutions:

> In Agile organizations there are fewer standards and processes. Those that remain are defined differently…Instead of being specified as a set of tasks or activities to accomplish, standards…now…express policy intent.

It goes on to say that approaches to governance must address the "social system" and "organizational culture" (what I've been calling "sociotechnical"). It acknowledges that Agile ways of working "challenge classical IT governance." To solve this, it intentionally moves accountability and authority closer to the code: "align decision-making authority with accountability" where "authority" is the power to act and "accountability" is to be liable for the outcome of decisions.

This is precisely what the architecture advice process plus ADRs enable. The pairing also makes this alignment explicit, incorporating detailed audit trails.

Even without an additional framework, such as O-AA, the combination of advice process with ADRs provides a framework to monitor, direct, and record architectural work. You'll also see in Parts II, III, and IV how they directly address social systems and cultural issues. Most importantly, however, they transparently place responsibility and accountability next door to each other.

Explicit ADR Accountability Is a Check to the Reckless

The architecture advice process's rallying cry of "anyone can make and then take an architectural decision" is both incredibly powerful and potentially alarming. But it doesn't lead to a free-for-all, one of the fears that many used traditional governance approaches to mitigate.

Accountability comes along with responsibility, and this keeps in check the more single-minded decisions. Everyone first seeks the appropriate advice, listens to it carefully, and assimilates it properly.

In ADRs, the author—be that an individual or a team (represented by a tech lead or named delegate)—is now the one responsible and accountable. This is where accountability lands. The "author" being named on ADRs makes this clear. System-wide decisions initiated by those working across teams ought to fall to, and come back to, the architect who drove them. Meanwhile, the more focused, within-team decisions necessarily belong to the lead of that team (or the team collectively, if that is how they choose to organize). These individuals are best placed to take on this responsibility; they understand the "architecture" running in production.

The dynamic that is set up between those practicing cross-team, cross-system architecture and those practicing within-team architecture is a fruitful one, but there's no guarantee of who will take on each set of decisions.

Teams Are Not Obligated to Decide

What happens if no one in any team wants to step up and decide? While the advice process and ADRs offer the *permission* to decide, they do not oblige anyone to do so. Even if you adopt this process, those with a cross-system architectural perspective might still be making the majority of the decisions *if that is what everyone is comfortable with*. Architects in these circumstances are still obliged to follow the advice process for all decisions, and write everything up in publicly shared ADRs as they do so, and (most importantly) keep an eye out to see if teams want to make decisions for themselves and support them appropriately when they want to.

The Architectural Practice Space Opens Up

It is my experience that, at client after client, with team after team, architect after architect, this revolution in approach to architecture is a welcome and freeing change. It removes accumulated drag and bloat from the practice of software architecture and allows everyone to focus on what is required to build, run, and evolve their systems. What is more, the space created for this practice of architecture allows everyone to focus on the software and the value it delivers, taking decisions they require *when* they require them. However, your collective practice *might* require additional supporting elements on top of the advice process and ADRs to ensure that happens.

If you picture the architecture advice process as a room, it's rather minimally furnished and uncluttered. The floor is clear, and you can do whatever you need to within its walls. The space is ready to be filled with a culture of trust and learning. But trust is a fickle thing.

By contrast, the "traditional" architecture practice space doesn't leave much free space at all. Cluttered with meetings and forms, and restricted by bottlenecks and signoffs, there was little room for either trust or learning to develop.

The urge to repopulate the practice space with traditional clutter will be strong. Care and attention will need to be paid to keeping your practice space clear but also filled with a generative[1] and supportive culture. That takes work.

In a utopian world,[2] the advice process and ADRs would give you all the practice space you need; they would be your "just enough." The architectural practice space would be filled with a positive and inclusive culture of trust and learning among individuals and teams. In such a world, nothing else would be required to protect the decentralization and catalyze self-organizing.

But trust can be fragile. It can fail to grow if you don't protect the space it needs. Not only that—trust can be smothered when restricted too much.

To maintain a delicate balance of *just enough* standard practices and formal agreements, you'll likely need supporting elements that nurture and evolve your culture of trust and learning without being too restrictive.

---

1 The term *generative culture* comes from Professor R. Westrum's work on a typography of organizational cultures (*https://oreil.ly/0QiWF*). It was adopted by the DORA State of DevOps report as the description of the optimal culture type.

2 "But Andrew, utopias don't exist!" I hear you cry. You're correct, but bear with me as I examine why they fail.

In later chapters I'll describe:

- A regular face-to-face place to seek, offer, and discuss advice effectively and efficiently (Chapter 8)
- A means of capturing, articulating, and testing shared cross-functional requirements complemented by an actionable technical strategy (Chapter 9)
- A set of principles to ensure that everyone understands the strategic focus (Chapter 10)
- A means of capturing lessons learned and offering guidance so that problems only have to get solved once (Chapter 11)

Before we get to that, let's ensure that the nature of the architectural practice space and the culture of trust that needs to fill it are clear in your mind.

Keeping Space for a Culture of Learning and Trust

As soon as you use the advice process and ADRs to make room for the practice of architecture, your organization's culture will naturally flow into the space, with all of its unique blend of positives and negatives. It will rush in to fill the gaps between the new processes and structures. For better or worse, this will happen without you doing anything to make it happen. This inflow of culture will directly affect the trust everyone will have in these new processes, deciding structures, and most important, one another.

Why does this happen? My favorite definition of *culture* (because it is concrete and actionable) is by Edgar Schein. He says that culture is: "the pattern of basic assumptions...a given group has...to cope with its problems."[3]

Culture is an ad hoc element. Unlike organizing elements such as the advice process and ADRs, culture doesn't explicitly dictate things. But culture does drive behavior, setting the precedent for how everyone lives and interacts within and between the structural frameworks, and this can have both positive and negative aspects. Let's first look at two extreme examples that demonstrate how trust (or lack of it) affects architectural decisions before moving on to consider how this relates to culture.

Two Examples of Trust (or Lack of It) in Action

First, imagine an organization where the tech stack is incredibly homogenous, despite there being nothing explicit that mandates it. This stack is just the set of platform primitives, languages, libraries, frameworks, and tools that the team has gathered

---

3 Jeffrey K. Liker, *The Toyota Way: 14 Management Principles from the World's Greatest Manufacturer* (McGraw Hill, 2004), 299.

around over time, and the unspoken assumption is that it will stay like that. This is a good thing. It's easy to hire, easy for people to move around the organization, predictable (though perhaps not optimal) in terms of cost, and more.

Now, imagine the opposite at another organization. Its systems are being unnecessarily extended and embellished by developers for a scale, flexibility, and availability profile that's never anticipated by the business model. This comes from an unvoiced assumption that this is "good engineering," which in turn arises from a lack of confidence in the ability of other teams to provide robust integrations. Not only this, but everyone is scared to decide, or even admit that they agree with decisions taken by others. Needless to say, it's really hard for new joiners to get productive on the codebases, and rotations never happen.

In both cases, the teams have made assumptions about others in practicing their architecture. The first group assumed everyone was competent in the tech stack. The second group assumed the architecture of others was unreliable.[4]

In the second example, the consequences are problematic. It isn't so much a culture of low trust as one of fear. This organization needs many of the supporting elements I will explore in the remaining chapters in Part II.

You Can't Assume a Culture of Trust and Learning Will Appear

All my other professional experiences have fallen between these two extremes. Where are you? Picture removing all of your current architecture practice and governance and replacing that with an advice process and ADRs in your organization. Imagine how a set of assumptions, unwritten and enforced socially, could fill the architectural practice space, tackling problems that arise in a positive or negative way.

If I cannot expect my peers to make the appropriate decisions without intervention, then my trust in them will fail to flourish. The same is true of everyone in the sociotechnical system working collectively to build, run, and evolve the software.

Atrophying trust can exacerbate negative aspects in your culture. Information might be hoarded, perhaps even withheld, and in worst-case scenarios, disinformation might be spread. Decisions can be slowed or blocked entirely purely as a means of exerting some form of control, even though it manifests as inaction. In such circumstances, a positive, high-trust culture will not fill the architectural practice space.

A Culture of Trust and Learning Must Be Carefully Nurtured

For decentralized approaches to work, trust must be protected, nurtured, and most important, given space. Trust is strongly connected to an organization's culture, but to

---

4 The Westrum organizational model is the one used in *Accelerate*. Chapter 3 of that book covers it in detail.

have "high trust" does not mean the complete absence of supporting elements like explicit agreement, supporting processes, checks and balances, or predictable artifacts. Starting from a position of lower trust does not mean it cannot be developed by careful cultivation.

Which supporting elements are required to nurture and sustain trust among everyone in your organization *without* getting in the way of flow? Figuring this out should be on everyone's mind. The answer depends somewhat on organizational size. Trust changes as an organization grows without taking any steps to protect and nurture it.

Understand the Changing Dynamics at Different Org Sizes

A small organization with a high trust and an explicit transparent culture may only need to adopt the process and use ADRs to contain decisions. I've known some early-stage startups that operated in this way without even being aware of it.[5] However, for the vast majority of us—and for those near-utopian startups when they start to grow—there needs to be some explicit form of intervention

Let's consider the gradual reduction in trust that many startup companies inevitably experience as they grow.[6] These so-called scale-ups, ones that weren't founded on a cult of personality or culture of fear, are a great example. They have a high-trust, low-ceremony culture that disappears gradually, often for nebulous reasons. ("We used to be able to…" and "it used to be so much easier to…" are phrases you hear a lot when working with scale-ups.)

The fact that the original collaborators are small in number and self-contained rather than part of a larger organization is essential here. I've had this experience a number of times. While I wasn't involved in all architectural decisions, we were collectively working on the same relatively small system. With basic forms of work division and open communication, we didn't need much beyond the visible progress of the work at hand to know if the right decisions were happening and, importantly, that they were all aligned. What was striking was how effortless it all felt to decide and implement, how much everything flowed, and how great that felt. When you speak to people with positive startup experiences, they frequently refer to similar experiences.

Gradually, as matters get more complicated and everyone stops knowing everything, the means of deciding and of keeping a historic record of the resulting decisions changes.

---

5 Though as you scale up, you may find this is harder to maintain. Even the simple fact that larger groups of humans tend to break into subgroups means that what is a step too far today might be necessary tomorrow.

6 See the "Bottlenecks of Scaleups" (*https://oreil.ly/cDCts*) article series for lots more.

High trust in small groups

What these positive experiences had in common was that everything was just-in-time and ad hoc. Decisions were made for self-evident reasons, and the results were understandable (perhaps because everything is agreed on by everyone, unless people actively recuse themselves from the decision process due to confidence that they will add nothing further). What's more, we knew we could ask about or challenge anything we wanted.

When everyone is focused and knows the goal, people get on and get things done. They frequently go outside their job roles, taking responsibility as and when required.

The strong culture of trust is the predominant means of ensuring that the right things happen in the right ways at the right time. When this proves to be insufficient, things are supplemented by just-enough formality (aka process). Relationships are personal as opposed to formal because everyone knows one another. There is no need for anything more complicated.

We also had a pretty good idea of our collective mission. The systems we were working on were small, well bounded, and coherent. They were understandable to all of us, and there was no need for other teams to be formed. Both the cognitive and social loads were relatively low (toxic, deceptive founders notwithstanding; Netflix has an entire subgenre of documentaries and docuseries dedicated just to them).

In a culture of collective ownership and commitment, you can get away with being informal. Take the decision processes, for example. Sometimes, a decision might be taken autocratically; other times, it would be made by consensus. Sometimes, you unknowingly get close to the architecture advice process in your approach. No one really thinks about an explicit "decision process" because everything is happening organically. The trust is an implicit understanding that the right way of going about things will be chosen and the right people will be involved.

The chances of getting this wrong because of miscommunication are low (everyone is usually in the same room or on the same Zoom calls all the time), and the cost when things do go wrong is low, too. No other teams are affected; no other plans get pushed out. Relationships that are high trust already can be rapidly and easily restored with lessons because of the high safety levels.

In all cases, the group was in control of everything it needed to deliver on its mission. There was never anyone outside the group to give "approval" for anything, and when we wrote things down, it was for our own benefit, not anyone else's.

A lot of the satisfaction and enjoyment (dare I say fun?) of these types of experience come from the fact that they are so *productive*. It's not entirely by accident that the word *flow* is used to describe not only organizations but also individuals performing optimally (the "flow state"). Getting things done *feels good*.

Upsetting the trust balance

Despite all these positives of self-organization and trust, it's incredibly easy to disrupt such team flow states. I've seen it be as simple as adding one more person to a team. When a team is at its size limit, adding a single individual can tip the delicate trust balance significantly.

I'm not talking here about the "forming, storming, norming, performing" process that happens when anyone joins a team, no matter what its size. When that person is not the "one too many," the effects are temporary. Eventually, you get back to "performing" (and high-performing teams like the ones I'm describing typically get there faster).

What I'm talking about are the instances when you add one more person, and because of the dynamics of groups, something destructive rather than reconstructive is set in motion. The team starts to split.

To be very clear, there is no need for anything else to have changed. Not the software, not the customers, not the mission, not the goals, not the reporting structures or organizational hierarchy. Nothing. Simply adding one more person to a team of a certain size kicks off this train of events. The new person doesn't even need to be slightly toxic—they could be a lovely individual—but the gradual splitting will happen.

Growth-triggered distrust

A gradual splitting within a collective might not be immediately obvious, it might not occur where you expect it to, and it will probably not rend things completely asunder. (Which might be unfortunate. The more transparent the rupture, the easier it is to spot and then resolve). There is no sudden and complete cleaving that happens when two teams are formed by splitting a single team.[7] This is a gradual weakening, a tearing, and it usually takes place *along lines of interpersonal trust*.

This phenomenon is not restricted to software teams. It's not even restricted to for-profit businesses. It's universal and was best described by the political scientist Jo Freeman in her 1972 paper on power relationships within feminist collectives called "The Tyranny of Structurelessness" (*https://oreil.ly/FFXYY*).

---

7 See Heidi Helfand's *Dynamic Reteaming* (O'Reilly, 2020) for more details on how to achieve this move safely.

Freeman observed that groups always start out with an ad hoc anarchism,[8] an assumption that there is no need for any kind of rules-of-order mechanisms to govern how everything works. People just sit down and work things out. When groups are small, this is exactly how it begins. However, as numbers increase, informal cliques invariably begin to form, and small groups of friends begin controlling information and access to resources, setting agendas, and wielding power in all sorts of subtle ways.

This splitting manifests in the formation of one or more in-groups (the "informal cliques") and one or more out-groups within a single team. There is a subsequent unequal sharing of the power and influence: the in-group gets more, and the out-group(s) get less.

The addition of the new joiner can set in motion group dynamics that were already in the group but until then had been balanced. The power and influence were reasonably equitable, until they weren't.

The changes will not be equally evident to everyone because the impact will not be felt equally across the group. Plus, they will be gradual—the dynamics might take some time to shift. If you're part of the in-group (the one retaining the power), then you won't notice it unless you are watching very, very carefully. Even then, it's inevitable that you will have blind spots and underestimate the importance of certain shifts. If you are part of the out-group, you will be painfully aware of the change.

If the entire group listens to everyone else and trusts their perceptions, they can become aware of this shift. Armed with this awareness of collapse in trust, the collective can then move to remedy it.

Adopt Supporting Elements to Protect the Space for Trust

A maximal-trust, high-performing, zero-structure utopia is not possible at any significant size (by which I mean "more than two Agile teams"). The vast majority of systems we build these days are simply too large to be tackled by a single team. When you get beyond the size of a group in which everyone can know and trust everyone else, then some structure is needed. But what structure? And how might you know when you need it?

Freeman proposed a number of formal elements to counteract the problems she highlighted when there is zero formal structure. Since that time, other thinkers and organizers have contributed to this thinking. The core of these is a formal decision process, and associated with this are mechanisms to ensure information transparency and alignment of activity toward the shared goal.

---

8 I could swap this for "self-organization" because that's what Freeman means, but it's important to retain her language as the spirit of anarchism as a form of organization flows through this entire book. It's the basis that underpins trust organizations for a start.

We have both. The formal decision process is the architecture advice process, and the means for sharing information transparently are our ADRs. It's possible to imagine how in some circumstances these alone can be sufficient, but not in many. To quote David Graeber,[9] the architecture advice process and ADRs are designed to "make the crowd smarter and more imaginative than any individual participant. It is indeed possible to do this, but it takes work." And the larger the group, the more supporting elements may have to be put in place.

The next four chapters of Part II introduce a number of these optional supporting elements: an architecture advice forum, testable CFRs and complementary actionable tech strategy, team-sourced architectural principles, and an in-house technology radar. But before we get to them, I'll spend the remainder of this chapter setting you up so that you adopt the right ones, in the right way, at the right time, because you almost certainly don't need them all—at least not immediately.

Protecting the Architectural Practice Space

If you are not careful, any additional element that supports the architecture advice process and ADRs can suck the oxygen out of the space that ought to be left for culture and trust. Think about those well-intentioned traditional architecture practice elements that this new approach clears away: the Architecture Review Boards, architectural principles, reference architectures, and more. They all sound like they're there to help, but the way they traditionally manifest means they inevitably end up being used to restrict, to deny, to basically say "no" and reduce trust.

This need not be the case. Carefully introduced, the right kind of supporting elements can encourage and bolster appropriate cultural developments without destroying any of the nascent trust you just unlocked.

All the elements, core and supporting, that I cover in Parts I and II of this book are consciously intended to be like the architectures they support: individually simple but capable of combining in many complex ways, giving rise to emergent behaviors. Most importantly, they will be responsive to all the key differences that make your business and your software and your teams unique.

---

9 David Graeber, *The Utopia of Rules: On Technology, Stupidity, and the Secret Joys of Bureaucracy* (Melville House Publishing, 2015), 201–202. The original quotation is: "Activist decision-making process is, instead, designed to make the crowd smarter and more imaginative than any individual participant. It is indeed possible to do this, but it takes a lot of work. And the larger the group, the more formal mechanisms have to be put in place."

There Is No Standard Prescription for the Supporting Elements

While there is no standard prescription for your specific supporting elements, they must take account of everyone's collective skill sets and motivations, the focus and goals of the teams they work in, the software being built, the way it is being run, the people and companies they're partnered with, the market and customers, and the company that organizes and funds all of this.

Supporting elements must also account for the fact that these factors are constantly interacting, changing, and evolving in unpredictable ways. This means that as your organization changes, the supporting elements—their number and nature—will likely change, too.

This is why I cannot be prescriptive about what your supporting elements should be or how they ought to be deployed, adapted, and removed. What I can offer is the means of diagnosing and prescribing your own interventions.

Make Any Supporting Element Yours

For your organization to thrive in a revolutionized world, you need to collectively adopt a culture of learning on an organizational level. To do this, everyone needs to be able to learn new ways to practice software architecture and let go of old ones.

Organizational learning is the cultivation of an optimization mindset when it comes to what, when, and how you adopt supporting elements as well as the culture that arises around them. You need to optimize the flow of decisions and integration of the resulting feedback.

To achieve this, an organization must continually consider itself and how it functions, learning from what is observed and making continual changes to how everyone collectively operates. If flow is good: optimize. If flow is bad: reduce, ameliorate, remove.

Check Your Motivation Before You Add Anything

As you consider adding a supporting element of any kind and in any form, there is a trap waiting for you. Adoption of *any* supporting elements is an active process. Don't simply adopt them blindly. You might not need some of them at all.

Remember, you are looking to *actively protect* the space for architectural practice that you have opened up. By adding a supporting element without good cause, you might actually be unconsciously moving farther away from the mode of organization you want, drifting back toward a "traditional"—hierarchical, low-trust, bureaucratic—system of organizing. (This is a manifestation of a subconscious need to control, predict, look busy, and not "throw away what we had before." You'll likely hear all these objections being raised as everyone becomes comfortable with this new sociotechnical system.)

I was reminded of this drift-to-bureaucracy tendency in myself when I suggested to the CTO of a client that we should set up a weekly face-to-face meeting to speed up offering advice on ADRs. Up to this point, I had firmly believed that this practice was as equally essential to this new system as the advice process itself and ADRs. Until, that is, she pointed out that, as a meeting, this was in direct opposition to their existing always-remote culture of maximizing asynchronous communications and protecting focus time.[10]

Her challenge made me check myself and question my motivations. Was this ceremony really necessary for success? Or was I simply recommending it because I had convinced myself that it was "best practice"? I wasn't sure, but I was glad of the challenge—something that happens more frequently when the level of trust is higher—because it forced me to return to the reason *why* I thought this was required. Did the reason match up with the needs that the CTO and I believed we could discern in the organization? It turned out that some elements of it were important, but the default pattern I was intending to implement could be changed significantly.

Consequently, we spent a portion of time looking at the needs that the meeting in question was designed to address. Did this organization need them? Yes, it turns out they did. (It was one of the main reasons we had been engaged to help.) Were there alternative ways to address the same need that were more in tune with the preexisting culture? We thought we might have identified some, so we experimented. As a direct result of these experiments, we learned. This learning was then embedded in the organization as a regular weekly meeting, but lasting 30 minutes rather than 60, with a focus on awareness and clarification rather than work—work that could be done asynchronously either in advance or after the meeting itself. In making this change, the organization itself could be said to have "learned."

This is a tiny example of institutional learning based on a prioritization of focus and flow. We did change how things worked, and we did add a new element, but in a way that added only what was needed and that had a positive rather than negative impact on the existing culture. There are many other examples. Let's turn now to one of the most famous because it highlights brilliantly the mindset needed to drive this organizational learning.

---

10 This had a practical as well as a philosophical angle: the company was fully remote and had been since its inception. Finding times when everyone would be free was hard. Graeber puts it beautifully: "Bureaucracy tends to expand according to a kind of perverse but inescapable inner logic. The argument runs as follows: if you create a bureaucratic structure to deal with some problem, that structure will invariably end up creating other problems that seem as if they, too, can only be solved by bureaucratic means....A slightly different version of the argument...is that a bureaucracy, once created, will immediately move to make itself indispensable to anyone trying to wield power, no matter what they wish to do with it. The chief way to do this is always by attempting to monopolize access to certain key types of information." (*The Utopia of Rules*, 149–150)

Netflix: An Example of the Flow-Finding Mindset

It's a cliche to mention Netflix as a company to copy, but there are lessons to be learned from how they focus their attentions and how they think about the problems they observe, most notably from their ex-Chief Talent Officer, Patty McCord.

In her book *Powerful* (Silicon Guild), McCord shares how she was challenged by Netflix's CEO and founder Reed Hastings to nurture and protect the unique "Freedom and Responsibility" culture that Netflix would become famous for. They too wanted to move fast (in everything across the company, not just in their software architecture practice and governance), and to do so, they wanted to empower and trust everyone who worked there. McCord notes they didn't want to unconsciously start with "best practice," instead looking to "what it takes to deliver a fabulous end product to customers."

With that as the core of their organizing philosophy, they rapidly realized that "policies and structure can't anticipate needs and opportunities," but they *could* get in the way of team flow. So they started experimenting with removing them. As McCord says, "We experimented with every way we could think of to liberate teams from unnecessary rules and approvals." They gave the staff at Netflix back their power but also increased their level of responsibility.

There are many famous examples, but Netflix's approach to expenses is illustrative. One day, after running a number of experiments, McCord stood up in front of the entire company and said, "I'm going to get rid of our expense policy, and I'm going to get rid of the travel policy, and I want you to just use good judgment about how you spend the company's money." When I heard about this, I felt there was no way it could be true. "That will never work," I thought, but I've been at open spaces with *many* Netflix employees over the years, and I can testify to the fact that this is *totally* the way things run, they take it seriously, and it works.

While Netflix's specific practices aren't guaranteed to be suitable outside of the company, this liberation mindset is widely applicable, not least in the area in which we are engaged: architectural practice. It pays to bear in mind what McCord advocates for: "operate with the leanest possible set of policies, procedures, rules and approvals because most of those top-down mandates hamper speed and agility." Note that she says "leanest possible set" here, not "none." Remember what Jo Freeman said regarding trust at scale: the complete absence of any policies, procedures, rules, or approvals (our "supporting elements") does not produce optimum results for the organization as a whole.

That is the flow-finding mindset: a mindset that keeps a whole-org focus as it continually looks to discern the leanest set of supporting elements to optimize architectural practice. It's one that, when adopted collectively, does the most to help organizational learning proceed smoothly.

Beware the Siren Songs of Certainty and Predictability

As humans, we find comfort in certainty and predictability, whether it's a secure place to sleep, a guaranteed meal, or the reliability of an accurate shared document or a process that guarantees the same result every time. As such, we drift toward bureaucracy as a source of certainty, even of tidiness. While that's rarely the case in reality (unless predictably interminable handoffs, disconnectedness, blame diffusing, and innovation crushing is the kind of predictability you want), we still do it, over and over.

It's easy to add things because they fit our problem/solution mindsets. See an issue? Do a thing to fix it. See another issue? Do another thing to fix it. Individual instances of this approach frequently make sense, but the end result is ossifying. It seizes up the system. Bureaucracy slowly replaces the space and need for trust. We know that things might have been made a little worse than they could have been and that our freedom might have been curtailed, but it's a sacrifice we'll gladly make for a guarantee that nothing else is going to go dramatically wrong elsewhere.

So think like the CTO from that always-remote company. Challenge yourself: is this element in question necessary? Am I looking for certainty for its own sake? How will it work with what we already have (both organization and culture)? In what form ought we to adopt it? Do we need to make subsequent changes to it? Will it break anything we already have in place? Did it create a new bureaucracy? Do we still only have what is sufficient, or is it superfluous? Remember, the goal is to maximize the flow of delivery of quality software and learn from the feedback this generates.

Experiment to Find Your Organization's Flow

By adopting the architecture advice process plus ADRs, you've cleared your architectural practice decks and are ready to find flow. You've taken the first step on your liberation journey and redistributed both the power to decide and the power to decide who decides.

On their own, an advice process and ADRs are as lean as you can get. The question then arises, "How can you make sure you optimize this trust-centering, advice-based approach to architecture without breaking any of its fundamental attributes?" Patty McCord again:

> Discover how lean you can go by steadily experimenting. If it turns out a policy or procedure was needed, reinstate it. Constantly seek to refine your culture just as you work to improve your products and services.[11]

---

11 Patty McCord, *Powerful: Building a Culture of Freedom and Responsibility* (Silicon Guild, 2018), 13.

Therefore, experimentation is the approach—experimentation with the number and nature of supporting elements you have in place. As with all experiments, it's good to start small, run one at a time, and be as happy with what you learn from failure as you are with success.[12]

Conclusion

This chapter discussed how the advice process and ADRs point toward a possible further great revolution. This revolution most importantly clears a space for the practice of software architecture and a culture of trust and learning that actively supports it. Nurturing this culture in an ever-changing organization involves protecting this practice space, understanding the dynamics of trust, and valuing organizational learning. To help your organization evolve, I discussed experimenting with optional supporting elements.

The rest of Part II introduces a number of these supporting elements to be experimented with individually and as required. The list isn't exhaustive. I am sure you can come up with some of your own, but these are the ones I've found most useful.

With that in mind, let's move on to the first supporting element: an architecture advice forum.

---

12 An experimentation approach I've found particularly suitable is BOSSAnova. Details on how to use it, including some example probes, can be found on the website that accompanies this book (*https://oreil.ly/PVvu8*).

CHAPTER 8

An Architecture Advice Forum

The architecture advice process is intentionally lightweight, even when supported by ADRs. Although you could just use those two core elements for your decentralized architecture practice, you may want to consider bolstering it with supporting elements (but, as discussed in the previous chapter, be deliberate about which ones you include).

You might well be worried that practicing the advice process will take up too much time, and even more so if you add supporting elements. That it might lead to a *lot* of conversations. You're not alone. I've heard this from others. Might a regular meeting, focused on the seeking and offering of advice and the transparent practice of architecture, be a good thing? Or would it fall into the trap of most meetings?

In this chapter, I'll introduce the first of four optional supporting elements that can help optimize your architecture advice process: an architecture advice forum. It's a meeting, but don't let that put you off; it's an intentionally simple affair. I'll begin by describing what it does, how it's structured, and how to run one. I'll also take you through both the social dynamics it surfaces and the benefits it offers, so you know what to protect and nurture when you notice it arising. I'll close with a discussion of how to roll out your advice forum, supporting your organization's growing culture of trust.

Introducing the Architecture Advice Forum

Simply put, the architecture advice forum is a regularly recurring space and time for open advice conversations about pending architectural decisions. It supports the advice process without changing it. It is *not* there to review or approve decisions. Nor is it a forum where consensus is sought.

The purpose is threefold. First, it brings the practice of the architecture advice process into the open. Second, because of this transparency, it builds trust. Third, as a result of increasing trust, learning can take place.

Because the forum is for advice process conversations, the attendee list is very important. The core invitees are a union of the two advice-offering groups:

- Delegates from each team using the architecture advice process (playing the role of "affected parties")

- Those most frequently turned to for their domain knowledge (playing the role of "those with expertise")

Each individual piece of advice is sought, offered, and perhaps discussed in the open in front of all the other attendees. Consequently, an advice forum is one of those rare meetings that benefits from a large number of attendees, even when not everyone actively contributes. This might not be your experience of traditional architecture gatherings. Let's see how an advice forum differs.

A Simple Standing Agenda

In contrast to the diversity of expertise and perspective arrayed at advice forums, the order of business is very simple. My basic standing agenda (available as a template in the GitHub repo that accompanies this book (*https://oreil.ly/9Qo_a*)) is as follows:

- Advice conversations around each new "Proposed" (and perhaps "Draft" if it has enough to it to gather meaningful inputs) decision, presented by those making the decision and captured ahead of time in the form of an ADR

- A revisit of other decision statuses (timeboxed, both to limit the window for incoming advice and to allow for revisits of decisions that might so far have been made with spare inputs)

- Any other business (AOB)

Give Advice Discussions for Individual ADRs the Time They Need

I don't put time bounds on each agenda item. There are so few items, and the duration of each depends on the nature of the decisions arising. I do, however, make sure that each element gets the time required, within the bounds of the meeting time slot.

How an Advice Forum Differs from Traditional Architecture Meetings

I'll be explicit once more: an *advice forum* is not simply a new title for one of the traditional architecture meetings I've mentioned in previous chapters, meetings typically known as Architecture Decision Forums (ADFs) or Architecture Review Boards (ARBs). There are three fundamental differences: there is no "approval," the attendee group is wider, and conversations take place in the open.

First, there is no "approval." The architecture advice process reigns. Decisions brought to the advice forum are still owned and taken by their originators. The only thing other attendees can do is offer advice. Nothing about the advice forum relieves the deciders of any of their obligations under the architecture advice process, nor does it transfer the power to make and take decisions in any way. Remember, the advice forum is simply and solely a refactoring to optimize the core elements. Just like a code refactoring, we're not changing what the advice process *does* but improving *how it does it*.

This brings me to the second key difference: the range of attendees will be broader. Given the advice process qualifiers, whoever convenes an advice forum will want to ensure that those attending represent the affected parties as well as those possessing relevant expertise. This means that attendees should include not only the relevant aligned architects but also at least one representative from each feature team (this is typically the lead, although business analysts, product owners, and QAs are frequently also present) as well as people from other programs of work: UX, product, data, operations, InfoSec, compliance/regulatory, risk management, and occasionally senior execs. If key affected party or expertise roles are not in attendance, it will be necessary for decision makers to engage them separately if the social contract obliges them to seek their advice.

The combination of these first two differences leads to the third and most important key difference: conversations happen in the open. The architecture advice process is great, but its conversations are usually one to one, with only the directly involved parties, decision takers and advice offerers, present. When conversations take place in an advice forum, there is an audience, so everyone can listen and many can learn. The amount of organizational, domain, legacy, and experiential information and architectural skill deployment shared at these sessions is unlike anything I have ever seen.

In my experience, advice forums are well attended and are the most proactive, engaging meeting of the week. Because of the nature of the traditional decision process they support, ADFs and ARBs tend to be dry, boring, and filled with rhetoric-fueled power struggles. Advice forums, on the other hand, encourage disagreement, but without the need to crown a winner. Advice forums can also celebrate failures or decision changes based on lessons learned and are consequently one of the most significant contributors to the quest for a learning organization. This all combines to broaden and deepen the general understanding of any architecture, greatly increasing the chances that it will end up in the running software.

Running an Architecture Advice Forum

Let's turn now to how a standard advice forum might run. In the following sections, I'll talk about what happens before, during, and after a forum. Later in this chapter, I'll devote a section to convening your first-ever forum. Throughout both these sections about setting up and running, I'll refer to the "convener of the advice forum." This is most likely the person (or people) who has decided that an advice forum might prove beneficial.

Before an Architecture Advice Forum

Prior to any advice forum, the session's agenda should be created and shared. Irrespective of where you are storing your ADRs, a great way to do this is to simply create a new wiki page.[1] The title of the page should state that it's an advice forum and the date it's happening, such as "Architecture Advice Forum, 27 November 2024." This is important because old advice forum agendas are a great resource if you ever need to piece together a holistic historical view.

Bring All Your Advice Forums Together Under a Single Parent Page

Curate this agenda collation with a parent "Architecture Advice Forums" page, and below that (as child pages), place all the historical agendas as well as the current one. It's really handy to put these record pages next door to your ADR library, which I described at the end of Chapter 6. That way, you not only have the immutable change log made up of your ADRs but also the records of the meetings that contributed to them. This grouping makes it easy to find things, and transparency builds trust.

Sharing the Agenda

Once the empty agenda page for your next advice forum has been created, you can share it with all invitees, ideally a few days in advance. Teams and individuals who have decisions they want to share at the advice forum can then link their ADR documents to the first agenda item. A "first come, first served" approach works as well for this. If anyone has any pertinent AOB (any other business), they can add it at the same time. To keep the meeting focused and on topic, AOB topics should be in tune with the primary goal of the advice forum: the timely offering of advice to efficiently

---

[1] If you're skilled, you can even make this a page template in your wiki tooling to make it really easy.

facilitate optimal architectural decisions. That means the convener of the advice forum meetings might decide to step in at some point if proposed topics are drifting off topic.

While this pregathering crowdsourcing is underway, the advice forum convener can have a look at ADRs that came up at previous forums and see if they need a check-in. Typically, this will happen when an ADR has the same status as before: either "Draft" or "Proposed." Those that do can have their ADRs linked to the second standing agenda item.

With this done, you're all set for your advice forum to run smoothly.

Welcome ADRs for Advice Seeking at Any Point in the Gathering

While it's great if your agenda is fully populated in advance of your architecture advice forum, that's rarely the case. I've lost track of the number of times I have had to refresh the agenda wiki page during an advice forum to show a "just added" ADR that a team wants to discuss. This is fine. The primary goal of the meeting is, after all, the timely seeking and offering of advice, leading to rapid decision transit. Saying "no, you're too late" achieves nothing beyond undermining faith in the process. If no one is putting their ADRs in before the advice forum convenes, conveners can model good behavior by ensuring that the ADRs they are involved in directly are listed and by doing a bit of judicious "chivvying up" of teams who are known to have an ADR to bring.

Opening an Architecture Advice Forum Session

With the agenda page in place and populated, an advice forum session is set up to run smoothly. At the start, it can be handy to pay attention to who has been able to make it and who hasn't. If people can't make it, their apologies can also be logged. It helps to know so that attendees don't get the impression that they have met the social contract of advice seeking purely because they took their ADR to the forum. For example, if Mimi, the SRE lead, wasn't in attendance, then her advice should still be sought afterward if required.

Once those who are going to attend have turned up, kick off the first agenda item by inviting those who have submitted ADRs for discussion to introduce them. ADRs are worked through one at a time. Top to bottom.

Introducing an ADR

Introducing an ADR for advice should be a simple affair. There is no need to read every part of the document out loud. Instead, the presenter of the ADR might highlight the standout points: something about why the decision was required, things that make it significant or noteworthy, surprising things that have been discovered so far, and aspects of the decision that folks are particularly keen to obtain advice on. They can then open up the session to those who feel inclined to offer advice.

It's important to realize that the way a particular ADR is presented will depend on the stage it's at, the nature of the decision at hand, and more. Even ADRs that have already fully been through the advice process, not requiring any further inputs and in the "Accepted" state, should be shared with the advice forum so that everyone gains awareness of the fact they've happened. At the other end of the scale are ADRs that are still in "Draft" and are looking for advice on all aspects, starting with the context. Both are valid inclusions in an agenda.

Offering and Receiving of Advice

After an individual ADR has been introduced, advice offering can take place. This is no different from one-to-one advice sessions, except now it can be one-to-many and there is an audience.

It is important to note that the convener of the advice forum doesn't need to step in to make sure the right people offer advice; that's up to those doing the deciding. It can help, though, to remind those present that silence is taken as the decision to not offer advice despite it being sought.

Advice Doesn't *Have* to Be Sought and Shared at an Advice Forum

The presence of an advice forum doesn't mean seeking, offering, and receiving advice *has* to happen during the forum itself. It is primarily a supporting practice to optimize the seeking and offering with some significantly beneficial side effects (boosted trust and group learning). Advice can be sought *before* an advice forum and offered in response before, during, or after the forum (some or all of these). Advice can also be sought *during* an advice forum and offered in response during or after the forum (or both). Or advice can be sought after the forum. Whenever and wherever it happens, advice for a decision must always be sought as per the social contract. It must also always be recorded.

Recording the Advice

As you might expect, the presence of an advice forum doesn't change how advice is recorded either. Advice offerers are still obliged to record their advice in the form of comments under the ADR in question, although this doesn't often happen in real time. Consequently, it can help to remind attendees to write notes concerning the advice they offer so that it all makes its way into the ADRs.

While it can't be expected that advice is recorded the instant an advice forum ends, it ought to be completed in a timely fashion. Therefore, it might be necessary in the early days of the adoption of the architecture advice process for the advice forum convener to remind folks that advice should be recorded, even going so far as to add placeholders in ADR documents in a way that sends out prompts and lets others know that the person in question had advice to offer. (For example, in many tools you can tag people in documents with an @ symbol followed by their name. This then alerts them via an email that directs them back to the document.)

Finally, a wee reminder: all advice should be recorded, whether the deciders welcome it or not, whether it's specific or meta. It's all useful. It can feel a little pedantic to keep reminding people of this at the early stages, but once teams and architects start returning to ADRs and the associated advice forum minutes for various reasons, they will be glad they were disciplined. Also remember it's a good practice to at least acknowledge advice in the ADR, even if it's not incorporated as a change. The dynamics of asynchronously received advice are different from advice received face to face, but the social contract of the advice process remains the same. Deciders hold all the power to decide. Let's look at these social dynamics in more detail now.

Social Dynamics at the Advice Forum

Let's consider how the architecture advice forum affects the wider sociotechnical dynamics, both in the resulting decisions (and subsequent software) and in individuals and their interactions.

When I first introduced the architecture advice process, I suggested that advice (as opposed to opinion) fundamentally changes dynamics within groups. Let's examine that further.

Recall that the social contract of the advice process allows anyone to decide, but in the process of doing so, deciders must seek advice from all affected parties and those with expertise in the matter. The best way to seek this advice is with targeted conversations that not only get at the advice but also the reasoning behind it.

Conversation is a key term. Conversations are interactions taking place between equals, and in the advice process, everyone is equal. This equality affords the opportunity for interactions within the advice process to seek out and take advantage of the reasoning. Because of their conversational nature, these interactions are generally a more open and healthy discourse, resulting in the sharing of knowledge and fueling co-creation. Adding an advice forum to this powerful mix offers the regular time and space for multiple interactions, one after the other, each of them happening with an audience.

But beware, the greatest strength of the architecture advice forum—these face-to-face, synchronous interactions—is also the greatest risk to the overall architecture advice process. It's a strength because, by providing the opportunity to seek and offer advice in a group setting, it is a superb opportunity to highlight the right kind of conversations that underpin the architecture advice process. When this happens, the quality of conversations is self-reinforcing, leading to more and more of the same. However, the group setting can also be a point of weakness. If an advice forum becomes a regularly recurring battleground for the wrong kind of behavior—confrontational argument and pulling of rank—then these dynamics threaten to undermine the whole endeavor of moving to a decentralized, conversational decision practice.

Architectural Interactions Are Adversarial and Hierarchical by Default

The adversarial, hierarchical interaction style persists because of an assumption that is embedded in many organizational cultures (one that is *particularly* focused in software architecture, sadly). The assumption is that decisions are best taken after a round of intellectual *argument* and that argument takes the form of an *oppositional interaction between distinct parties*, frequently never resolved until someone pulls rank or appeals to a higher power for arbitration. (You could substitute the word *debate* here for *argument*. The result is the same.)

Why is this a particular danger when an architecture advice forum is added to the mix? Because the nominal similarities between an advice forum and its close cousins, ADFs and ARBs, mean that when attendees first attend advice forums, their default interaction mode is frequently still adversarial and hierarchical. In many cases, it is the only way attendees know how to act at architecture decision meetings, meaning that these inclinations surface unbidden. It is how attendees expect things to work, and it is how they expect to interact with others.

These assumptions about the default interaction mode in software architecture sessions are so insidious that they will happen subconsciously, even when everyone understands and is signed up to practicing the architecture advice process. This is despite the fact that deciders have total freedom to decide in any way they see fit, *taking into consideration all the advice*, without the need for a "winning" argument to have triumphed and some form of consensus arrived at. You can spot these legacy assumptions in the language attendees will use, the positions they take, and their mode of engagement. One simple example was the architect who would conclude every ADR discussion at an advice forum with the words "So, do we all agree?" They knew this was wrong, and we'd spoken about it more than once, but it still kept slipping out.

All this means that without an explicit awareness of an alternative way to interact—one that replaces the default adversarial and hierarchical mode—interactions will head in the opposite direction from the one you are aiming for in an advice forum. Let's move now to consider this in depth and gain some clarity on the alternative positive system dynamic we want to learn and cultivate.

Coalescent Argumentation: An Alternative to Adversarial Argument

Because adversarial forms of argument are so ingrained, extensive study of this zero-sum mode of argument and its alternatives has given rise to a particularly useful new approach: argumentation. *Argumentation* is the *exchange* of arguments. It's a collective activity of producing and exchanging reasons to support claims or defend or challenge positions. Argumentation comes in many forms, the adversarial kind being the one we know best in our common, as opposed to philosophical, use of the term *argument*.

Argumentation consciously moves away from *argument* precisely because of the latter's confrontational, hierarchical baggage.[2] While retaining the coming together of individuals with diverse perspectives and experiences (a good thing for the moving forward of any discipline, not least software architecture), it distinguishes itself by the way in which people interact in these circumstances.

There is a nonadversarial form of argumentation well suited to the advice process, advice forums in particular. It is called *coalescent argumentation* and is cooperative rather than adversarial. The approach was identified and described by Michael A. Gilbert in the book of the same name (Routledge).

How does coalescent argumentation work? First, it is a method of inquiry. Conversations don't just seek sufficient information to find fault with others' arguments; they now aim to collectively get to the nubs of problems or challenges in ways that all parties understand. This adversarial antipattern should sound familiar.

Coalescent argumentation doesn't just seek more information. It also actively steps back from overly intellectual fault finding by focusing on a shared goal of understanding and making the best advice—suggested direction plus reasoning—understood by all.

This isn't to say that coalescent argumentation shies away from the tough stuff. The approach acknowledges that *views* (and therefore advice) can be in opposition, but importantly, this doesn't put the holders of those views in opposition too. It also points out the need to acknowledge the dependencies between decisions (frequently

---

2 A complementary approach used in some parts of the sociotechnical systems theory space (e.g., by Calvin Pava in the 1980s) is deliberations and discretionary coalitions (*https://oreil.ly/2Ly1T*).

the source of the opposition) and how one decision can affect others. Sounds like the "affected parties" we know and love, right?

Fostering a collectively coalescent mindset at an advice forum has two major consequences. First, greater room opens up for recognizing the middle ground among people who seem to disagree. Exploring this common territory also suggests ways in which alternative solutions may be developed.

Second, by acknowledging where we agree, we sharpen our focus on the areas where we do not, on these places where the real creative work of software architecture can be deployed. As Gilbert puts it, coalescent argumentation asks not "What can I disagree with?" but "What *must* I disagree with?"

Because of all this, a coalescent approach to decision making is collaborative, and the defeat of ideas or of others is not the goal. Instead, the goal is to find mutual ground and build shared ideas there. Think back to the goals of architecture practice: we are trying to build coherent and cohesive systems that are aligned to business value, and we are doing this within a social system, the assembly of individual teams who are trying to flow and learn. It's not a big leap from coalescent argumentation to software when you realize that our sociotechnical systems are basically collective ideas made manifest in code and organizational structures and culture.

Let's consolidate and map this approach to our core elements: the architecture advice process and ADRs. That will allow us to see how coalescent argumentation, if coaxed and nurtured, can happen in real time at an advice forum.

The Architecture Advice Process and ADRs as a Coalescent Approach to Deciding

The coalescent argumentation of the advice process can be most clearly observed in ADRs, so I'll use that as my focus in this subsection. When it is first drafted, the Context section is the place for the decider(s) to map out the decision landscape *as they see it*. The Consequences section (if they get this far on their own) can then articulate the perceived options for the decision and how they see each affecting this context space. It is their opportunity to lay out their perspective. You could see this in both of Chapter 4's example decisions.

In "Story 1: A Development Team Decides to Use Release Toggles" on page 78, you can imagine how the context would have taken a very dev-centric perspective—the goal being to remove long-lived branches. They then came up with only one option: boolean checks in code. Not unexpected given that the decision arose from developers, and code is what they have most control over.

In "Story 2: An Architect Decides to Unpick a Workflow Problem" on page 84, the context would have initially captured the problem as known to the architect: that this important shared service had evolved over time, resulting now in multiple hard-to-resolve defects arising. Because they knew their experience of the code was lacking, the architect didn't articulate any options. They went straight out and spoke to the affected parties, seeking their input and advice.

The Advice section then serves to (1) validate and firm up the shared territory of the middle ground and (2) isolate divergent positions via specific points of disagreement. In an ideal world, the former is incorporated back into the Context section, making it a clear statement of what is agreed on. The latter can also be incorporated into the Context, but it is far more likely that the development of alternative solutions will surface in the Consequences section. This clarity and focus on what is important can also allow less-tangible aspects—the urgency of a decision, for example, or the fact that there is a concern about available skills or spare time considering already full backlogs—to come to the fore. Because they are now explicitly stated, they can be considered and taken into account.

Again, you can see this advice-fueled clarity and focus in both of these example decisions. The advice for the release-toggles decision brought in the perspectives of other teams as well as QAs, infra, product management, and more. The context became broader but focused on the real needs. The multiple benefits of being able to release and unrelease became very clear. The fact that other teams coded against in-development features was captured, as were insights into how environment variables might be used. This in turn led to many more options as well as more nuanced understandings of the cross-collective impacts of each option. During this, some advisers weren't shy about signaling their issues. The QA would have more work to do, for instance. Such honesty made the decision better.

The advice for the workflow service did even more work. The coalescent approach meant that the focus was on understanding and getting to the real points of difficulty. This led directly to the problem being understood in far greater detail, allowing it to be split into multiple parts that could be progressed separately, bringing in specific advice for these as required. If the problem hadn't been treated in this way, it's easy to imagine the various teams, who used the service in their various ways, having competing ideas about how it should be refactored. That would have served no one.

These scenarios all demonstrate a key power of advice offering. The more focused and backed up with reasons a piece of advice is, the easier it is for the decider(s) to isolate and subsequently respond to in their design. The architecture advice process rewards the coalescent argumentation form of disagreement because those advisers who ask, "What *must* I disagree with?" and then make clear why they disagree in their advice are easier for the deciders to engage with. On the other hand, advisers who hold on to the old approach of thinking, "What *can* I disagree with?" and then refuse to clarify with a why, are more difficult. This coalescent dynamic of advice serves to positively reinforce the social contract based on transparency, honesty, and trust.[3]

When the socially disruptive urges of adversarial argument are replaced with the positive interaction dynamics of coalescent argumentation, an architecture advice process reinforced by an architecture advice forum can be a powerful thing indeed.

Advice Forums Catalyze Powerful Group Dynamics

Given that the coalescent nature of advice offers an alternative to hierarchical arguing, how might attendees experience advice forums? Some aspects will differ depending on the role you're playing at the time: as an advice offerer, an advice seeker, or even an observer, not participating but learning about how architecture is practiced. Other parts will be the same for everyone. I'll consider the differences for each of the three roles before discussing a key experience that everyone will share.

In each case, I'll take us back once again to Story 1 from Chapter 4. The team did a lot of research before they decided to speak to the "affected parties" (in their case, teams who depended on the feature that was about to be toggled off). In that previous non-advice-forum version of the story, the team making the decision had to identify those affected teams and approach them directly, individually, and serially. They had to do the same with those with expertise. Both this and the advice-forum version are shown in Figure 8-1, comparing the modes of interaction without an advice forum and with one. The version with an advice forum shows that advice conversations are less parallel, with the added bonus that they might have observers, too.

---

3 This coalescent dynamic of focusing on a design in progress and offering advice might seem familiar to those who practice pair programming. The criminally underappreciated XP Pair Programming Idioms (*https:// oreil.ly/TItpf*) contain four strategies: "Your baby is ugly," "That isn't what I said," "Let's try your idea first," and "None of the above." All of these are different strategies for getting your message across. (You might not want to use the exact phrases that the strategies contain, however…)

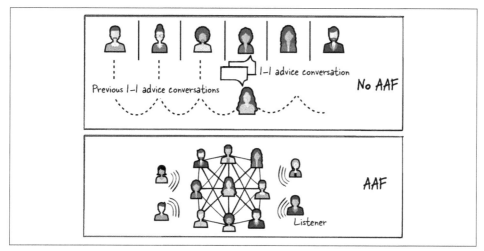

Figure 8-1. Comparing the interaction modes of the "no advice forum" approach (multiple, one-to-one serial interactions, one after another) with the "advice forum" alternative (multiple conversations, all in the same forum, with an audience of other advice offerers as well as nonadvising, learning observers)

Let's consider how the advice forum version will be different for each role in turn, with the two types of advice *offerers* first.

The Experience for Advice Offerers

With an advice forum in place, each "affected party" team is represented by default, so they can simply jump in. This reduces the risk of the decision-making team missing one of these affected teams, but it also lets any single affected team hear the advice of the others. This not only speeds up the process of advice offering but also deduplicates it (although teams are still able to voice support for advice offered by others). In the specific case of the feature-toggles decision, the problem of "toggled off" features effectively disappearing was raised by many teams. When this happens, it becomes easier to focus on that specific point of concern because of the number of teams who are liable to experience it negatively. This strengthens the coalescence, too.

It is not only the affected parties who would be present at the advice forum, though. Many of those falling under the "expertise" banner would be present, too. JB, the lead QA, definitely would be, as would Fiona, the systems architect, and Yinka, the infra engineer. It's quite possible that Monira, the product manager from another team, would be there, too. All could offer the same advice that they offered in the serial version of the advice-gathering process, but now they would have the added benefit of hearing the advice offered by the affected teams as well as the advice from one another and could give further advice accordingly. It is at this point that if inclusion is brought to the fore, the sharing of genuine experience and collaborative reasoning can be incredibly powerful. This is easier said than done, however, and I'll spend all of Chapter 15 talking about how to achieve it.

I am discussing a many-to-many conversation, instead of a series of one-to-one conversations, which is a key strength of an advice forum. This offers both an openness and a speed advantage, but most important, if psychological safety is high, it allows advice offerers to bounce off one another, clarify one another's points, ask further questions, and zoom in more on the decision at hand. Specifically in this instance, the problem points were sharpened by Yinka, the infra engineer, who offered more detail and experience on how this might be implemented. The option to toggle on and off based on an environment variable, for instance, might allow teams to set the switch to "on" for tests in their pipelines, mitigating the issue they had identified. These direct conversations between the engineer with expertise and the affected parties can be extremely powerful.

The Experience for Advice Seekers

Advice-*seekers* benefit greatly from advice forums, too. Remember, advice seekers are in no way obliged to incorporate the advice they are offered into their decisions. Combine this with the multiway conversation that the forum opens up, and the listening and coalescent practices can really kick in.

Those with relative expertise (and affected parties) can *only* offer advice. The decider (or the deciding team) retains the power to select an option and take the decision. No one else has any power to command the deciding team in this act. This can be concerning to advice offerers if a point of advice that they feel is really important seems to be ignored by the advice seekers.

The face-to-face, real-time, social nature of the advice conversation at the forum reinforces the social contract, acting as a counterbalance. It is harder to ignore or dismiss out of hand advice that an adviser feels is central when it is shared in a wider group. If this is the case, others will notice it and, if they agree with the advice, add their support to it. However, there is a near enemy here. It is not uncommon that those who are used to deciding or simply being listened to will enlist others, consciously or unconsciously, to back up their point by weight of numbers if they feel they are being ignored. The way to combat this is for advice seekers to zoom in on and coalesce around the specific aspects of disagreement at hand, working together to uncover the reasoning behind the advice to come to the best-fit solution possible. Again, the act of collaborative argumentation over divisive argument is preferred.

Because the deciding advice seekers retain the power to decide, they no longer need to think defensively. They are freed to really listen and listen deeply, asking clarifying questions and understanding the scope and nature of any issues. They are released to work collaboratively to come up with the best solution possible, given the circumstances. Discord (either open or implicit) can be replaced by collaboration and co-creation.[4] In my experience, the advice process does mitigate the worst case, but when this isn't possible, remember that the advice forum is only for advice seeking and offering, not for deciding. Decisions can be taken afterward, in safer private forums, taking into consideration all the advice, one-to-one and in front of many, written and verbal. The best architectures are based on trust and decentralized power, so don't be forced into feeling differently. (Chapters 12 and 15 go into the difficulties of deciding and how to combat power plays respectively.)

In the release-toggles example, this is the correlate of the conversation in the previous section. The advice-seeking team could also participate in this conversation, and even if they didn't but rather simply stood back and listened, their end design could definitely benefit as a result (perhaps even removing all the issues the advice offerers had raised with their proposal).

The Experience for Learning Observers

Tackling a challenging decision as a conversation has another benefit. Because the advice process means it need no longer be confrontational, practices of complex rhetoric and obfuscation lose their power. Brewing architectural "battles of wits" can be deescalated. Consequently, the co-creative, open, calm, inclusive conversations among equally valued participants that result are more instructive and easier to follow. All parties attending the advice forum, even if they have no remit to participate in a specific ADR-backed decision, can follow along and are therefore free to focus on all the relevant specifics of the decision, which are no longer obscured and obfuscated by power plays.

For bystanders, this makes the advice forum a place far more conducive to both awareness of the full sweep of in-flight decisions and to learning. If attendees feel the need, they are welcome to ask clarifying questions and make suggestions. Not only that, but they can also witness the practices of metacognition at play, observing the way in which others conduct themselves. That's powerful.

An example of this might arise in our release-toggles decision. Rita, a developer attending the advice forum for the first time, might ask for clarification about what everyone means by "toggle" and what precisely is meant by the term "release." Even if all the parties involved in the advice offering and seeking were clear on this (and it never fails to amaze me how often they aren't), Rita's question leads to a sharpening in understanding of the specific issue at hand and what exactly is meant by various terms in the remainder of the document. Besides helping Rita there and then, when written down, this strengthens the power of the ADR, both as a record and a future

---

4 Note here that I don't say "conflict." Conflict, when experienced in a safe environment, is generative. So how do you create and maintain a safe environment? Chapter 15 has what you need.

learning resource. Again, it takes both individual leadership and a degree of psychological safety for Rita to put her hand up. This is a safety everyone benefits from. Chapter 15 will help you foster and protect that safety, and Chapter 16 will help you understand how it can lead to individual acts of leadership.

There is one more benefit of the advice forum for learning observers. Directly exposing all attendees to the option-making part of the process supports those thinking about making their first, tentative steps into the world of architectural decisions. The mystery of this step, multiplied by the impression that decisions need to be argued over and defended against those with vastly more experience and organizational cachet, has made a step into even a small architectural decision seem like a step too far to many. When option making is seen in operation, it becomes clear that the social stakes around deciding are greatly lowered, which in turn allows far more time and energy to be devoted to the far more important technical aspects. Trust again has a chance to grow.

Shared Participation in Concrete Creativity

So far, the experiences of each of the three roles have been different. But there is one dynamic more than any other that makes the advice forum version of the architecture advice process so powerful, one that arises from the sense of psychological safety and trusting collaboration that makes it so hospitable for learning observers: the magic of creativity and completely new ideas.

The most impactful software decisions are frequently the ones that are the most creative. Creativity is not simply a matter of applying the same old patterns that everyone else has applied. Neither is creativity small incremental changes made around the edges. Creativity is something new, something risky, something that hasn't been tried before, and (let's be honest) something that stands a not-insignificant chance of failing. But if they do succeed, creative solutions can have big impacts for relatively small investments.

Creativity stands little chance of emerging when nonstandard, difficult-to-defend, easily dismissed ideas are not shared. Sadly, because of the adversarial nature of traditional architecture practices, this is precisely what often happens. In those circumstances, only a few at the top of hierarchies, safe in their ivory towers, feel safe and protected enough to take such leaps. What's more, when they do, they are only able to make gigantic steps, in circumstances stripped of the right-now, hands-on detail available to those running the software that is meeting the needs of users—detail that can mean the difference between a great idea that will work and an expensive and complexity-multiplying disaster.

On the other hand, in a psychologically safe, trusting, decentralized, deciding environment—one where collaboration, co-creation, and celebration of diverse outlooks and ideas are nurtured—the collective intelligence can be tapped and incorporated.

When the many are encouraged to float ideas, they can be collectively understood and worked on together. In this world, "lines of argument" can be "followed" instead of arrayed against one another adversarially, with someone "losing" at the end. The zero-sum game of adversarial deciding is replaced with something collaborative and generative.

The high-bandwidth advice forum is an ideal place to broach such ideas and to have them examined and really tested by a range of stakeholders from all over the socio-technical system. In doing so, it unlocks the magic of group creativity.

Architecture Advice Forums Foster Conceptual Integrity and Social Cohesion

I've just examined the benefits an advice forum brings to individuals and individual decisions, but there is more. An advice forum also brings together potentially disparate aspects in two complementary and connected areas: the distinct parts of distributed software systems and the independent teams that build them.

The goal of the former, commonly referred to as "conceptual integrity," is that the separate parts of the system look, feel, and act as if they are part of a whole. The goal of the latter, commonly referred to as "social cohesion," is that everyone working on the system trusts one another's ability to think and and feels comfortable enough to work well together.

Connecting them effectively is a highly sociotechnical intervention. In the following subsections, I'll explain the interaction between these technological and social aspects at the advice forum, paying particular attention to how they are interrelated.

I've taken my lead from key principles in Donald G. Reinertsen's book *The Principles of Product Development Flow* (Celeritas). He looked at the system dynamics of product development from a Lean perspective, distilling 175 principles from this. Many of them apply to the advice process approach to software architecture, and I'll return to them in Chapters 13 and 14, but some of them apply directly to how an advice forum operates, so I'll tackle them now.

Decentralizing Execution While Centralizing Coordination

It's not easy to achieve effective decentralized execution in product development. Whatever your approach, it must shun top-down micromanagement without sacrificing coordination. It can be achieved by following a number of principles, and the advice forum is an ideal place to apply them.

First, the advice forum offers face-to-face communication (Principle D22 in *The Principles of Product Development Flow*). This real-time, high-bandwidth communication is not only the most efficient format for collaboration, but it also makes coordination or the lack of/need for it very clear. Those playing an architecture role are responsible in great part for shepherding overall conceptual integrity, but they must do it *collaboratively*. They cannot simply tell teams what to do.

While ADRs make it possible to observe and provide advice on individual in-flight decisions, an advice forum affords architects (and everyone else) the opportunity to interrogate the mental models behind specific decisions with representatives of all teams. This in-between work is an excellent way to surface the state of the current shared architectural concepts in the context of concrete decisions. When mental models are aligned, then this will be clear, and when they are not, this will be equally clear. This is also an opportunity to take a temperature check on trust and safety levels.

This shared understanding of the state of the collective architectural view (for good or bad) is incredibly valuable: it gives everyone an early opportunity to see where conceptual integrity is under strain and, consequently, coordinate efforts to rectify matters. This can take place within the decision at hand or in a separate one.

In Chapter 4's Story 2, the workflow service component had, over time, become overly complex and a point of coupling between teams. Had an advice forum been in place where each of the individual decisions leading to the current state of affairs had been individually shared as ADRs, then the problems may have been spotted earlier. This might have resulted from those in an architecture role hearing about the addition of yet more responsibility (in the form of new architectural patterns) being heaped onto this service. It might equally have come from other teams asking clarifying questions about the component: what it could do, what it couldn't, and perhaps what it could be *made* to do. Other early warnings of strain on a system component might spring to your mind from some of your personal experiences.

However it comes to light, once a strain on conceptual integrity has been identified, how might it be remedied? The advice forum offers various opportunities.

In an ideal world, a directed, architect-led and -owned intervention would not be required. How so? Reinertsen makes it clear that direct face-to-face coordination between peers is preferable when all the required information is present in the teams that need to realign (Principle D13). The focus for such between-team realignment can arise wholly from within the teams themselves, or it can be prompted by deft advice questioning from an architect. (Architecture is far more about asking the right questions than getting the "right" answer.) These realizations can lead to decisions and actions to remedy the conceptual drift, with architects providing input in the form of expert advice as required.

When this realignment takes place at the advice forum, in whole or in part, it happens in front of everyone. By witnessing such coordination arising without the need to be initiated or driven by "outside forces" (those who in traditional mental models are assigned positions "higher up the organizational hierarchy"), the power of the collective is seen in operation, enhancing group cohesion.

What's more, when the realignment happens at the advice forum, those not directly involved in this team-to-team organizing still become aware of both the fact it is happening and the nature of this coordination. They can provide additional information or clarification if needed, and yet again, overall group cohesion is enhanced.

While team-to-team realignment can sometimes remedy strains on conceptual integrity, at other times something more significant is required. This is the need for a more focused centralized effort, which Reinertsen calls the "Principle of Virtual Centralization" (Principle D5). This principle states that it is desirable to be able to quickly reorganize decentralized resources (the prioritized time of a number of teams) to create centralized power when necessary. He uses the example of "tiger teams" (a team of specialists assembled to work on a specific goal or solve a particular problem) convened in some organizations when a program of work gets in unexpected and severe trouble.

We saw the need for such a team already in the way the Story 2 played out in Chapter 4. But how would it be brought together?

Under traditional approaches, a tiger team would be convened by hierarchical diktat, taking away the power from the very people who were experiencing the problem. The taking away of power negatively affects group cohesion and stands the risk of including the wrong individuals.

In an advice-forum-flavored version of this story, following initial conversations about the decision at the advice forum, an agreement could be made there and then to convene a virtual cross-team group that would work together with the relevant architect and other experts. This form of "virtually centralized" team is clearly emerging directly from across the affected teams, strengthening group cohesion as well as standing a far greater chance of incorporating all the right context, expertise, and affected teams from the outset, and therefore of success. I've seen the motivation of these teams be far stronger, too, driven by the deeper understanding of the problem to be solved but also cognizant of the blockages to flow it is almost inevitably causing multiple teams.

Deep Domain Expertise: When Centralization Works Best

What about decisions that require expertise these groups do not themselves contain? In those circumstances, the need to coordinate and the information to coordinate around arise from very specific advice-offering experts.

Let's consider some concrete examples that concern highly specialized sets of domain knowledge. I'm thinking here of areas such as information and data security, legal and regulatory compliance, and the audits that go with all of these. The people with this expertise will have titles like Information Security Officer and Regulatory Compliance Officer.

Knowledge in these areas is highly specialized. It also changes rapidly. These are skills that neither the teams nor the architecture roles could expect to have or maintain. That's precisely why there are people whose job is to solely focus on and keep up with their specific area of expertise. The application of this knowledge in the way an organization works and in the software it uses to support that is very important. Frequently, domain experts are also the person who would get fired, or perhaps even end up in court, if problems arise in their areas. These factors all combine to mean that we can't simply capture what they know as a series of CFRs (which I'll cover again in detail in Chapter 9) and leave them to go about their business.

Therefore, there is great need for these experts to be aware of all architectural decisions as they are being made to contribute their expertise as required prior to decisions being taken. These people need to be on hand to *interpret* proposed architectural decisions in light of the current state of the art in their domain, because they are the only people able to do this.

This is Reinertsen's Scale Principle (D2): "Centralize control for problems that are infrequent, large, or have significant economies of scale." An advice forum is again the place to achieve this.

By ensuring that representatives of key domain-expertise roles are present at advice forums, you are providing them with a timely opportunity to deploy their knowledge and experience, and teams and architects can incorporate the fruits of their decision-specific advice from the outset (although these experts ought to be sought for their advice irrespective of whether you have an advice forum or not). This gives an additional boost to the conceptual integrity of the wider system because the policies these experts interpret will likely apply in some way to all teams and all parts of the system.

This sharing also works in the opposite direction, as long as these experts feel able and comfortable to participate in such a highly technical gathering. When people in such roles do participate, I've often had feedback that the weekly advice forum is *incredibly* useful to them and a great use of their time. Without an advice forum, they find out about a decision after it has been taken, frequently after it has been developed, and in the worst-case scenarios, after it has gone to production and is serving users incorrectly or unsafely. This is precisely what these experts are looking for as they play their role in the organization.

Transparency for Social Cohesion and Trust

All of these examples illustrate how the advice forum is a place to deliver on the key goals of decentralized execution *and* centralized coordination, but it goes further. In providing a place for both to take place, the advice forum benefits all attendees with greatly increased transparency around the practice of architecture. That in turn leads to increasing trust and growing social cohesion. Let's dig into both now, highlighting further benefits of this transparency.

Transparency means anyone can influence the many small decisions

Let's take a step back and consider the broader timeline of events. How does conceptual integrity in our systems slip? The answer is: gradually. Step by step. One commit, one change set, one decision at a time. And how does social cohesion erode? The answer applies yet again: gradually, step by step, when teams are set against each other through no fault of their own.

I've seen massive programs of work go off course far more frequently due to the gradual (and almost imperceptible) accretion of small decision after small decision, almost in geological time. This is how good decisions incrementally become obsolete and blocking decisions. This is how a system that was fit for purpose one day keeps going for too long, despite the world around it changing, and slowly becomes a thorn in everyone's side. (I'll dig into the changing nature of decisions over time in greater detail in Chapter 14.)

A thread running throughout this book is the sociotechnical nature of software engineering. An important early warning signal of such conceptual slippage might arise as a consequence of the software delivered by a single team, working in a corner somewhere. An advice forum offers the opportunity for that team to offer advice based on what they have seen and learned, in just the same way and on the same level playing field as the CTO can. The architecture advice forum, as a face-to-face practice of the architecture advice process, allows *anyone* to influence these small decisions.[5]

Reinertsen sums this up deftly: "While big decisions are important…most companies have weak systems to ensure that the many small…decisions are made correctly. Collectively, these small decisions have enormous economic impact."[6]

The transparency around all significant architectural decisions can have an enormous impact on wider social cohesion, too. There's nothing like a massive, top-down, one-way decree to convince everyone that senior management understands little and cares even less about them than they originally feared.

5　That's not to say that people will automatically start giving the same weight and credence to a piece of advice from a junior developer in a marginal team when compared to the overall strategic direction shared by the CTO, but at least the opportunity to hear this information is present, in a strongly attended forum, and if people are putting their listening and coalescent argumentation skills into practice, that advice stands as good a chance as any of being heeded, understood, and incorporated.

6　Reinertsen, *The Principles of Product Development Flow* (Celeritas, 2009), 37.

The safest, most inclusive, highest-trust version of an advice forum is one where those in senior technical positions attend—enterprise architects maybe, or a senior vice president, or perhaps even someone at the executive level such as the CTO—sharing their advice alongside everyone else. As I mentioned earlier in this chapter, advice forums offer excellent forums for sharing or reinforcing key messages that keep the small decisions aligned.

Everyone gets exposure to in-flight decisions, their sequencing, and their coordination

Let's now consider the advice forum audience, because remember, advice forums don't just have a list of key invitees. It's important that they are open so that anyone in the organization can attend.

Again, this benefits system integrity and social cohesion. Because advice seeking and offering take place "in public," all attendees gain exposure to in-flight decisions: not only the thinking behind them but also their coordination (who needs to be involved, etc.).

Witnessing all this unfold allows nonparticipating attendees to note what is going on elsewhere and share it with their team: the adoption of a new technology or usage of a pattern, for example. This then allows them to react or respond accordingly, such as rescheduling a piece of work or refactoring.

Key in-flight-decision information sharing is very important. Reinertsen again: "For decentralized decisions, disseminate information widely" (Principle D17). A focus on team decoupling and internal cohesion does not mean that information should be collected in isolated local pools. Reinertsen gives a great example: the cost versus weight decision rule used on the Boeing 777. The maximum weight of the plane was calculated at the overall (system) level, as it needed to be. The total weight of the plane had to stay within a certain limit, and this total limit needed to be shared because it was a weight limit all teams were taking portions of.

Equivalents in software are not hard to find. As architects know, some aspects of the *overall* system are important, and this information should not be restricted to architects alone. Standard examples in software systems include end-to-end response times and error budgets. By sending delegates to advice meetings, teams gain an insight into the bigger-picture developments in these key aspects as much as the architects who are working with them day-to-day do.

This is also important because coupling between subsystems can be complicated and, when you broaden the scope to the surrounding sociotechnical system, unpredictable.[7] Not only that, but a force that affects one team from the "outside" might equally

---

7 Both Vlad Khononov (*https://oreil.ly/fXiJi*) and Kent Beck (*https://oreil.ly/SAHkK*) pointed out various forms of this in their talks at DDD Europe 2023 (*https://oreil.ly/DFLCL*).

affect one or more other teams. Knowing about the pressures on the entire sociotechnical system can help everyone within it sense—and collectively make sense of—far more of the available information than the building and running of their systems alone offers them.

Architecture advice forums actively foster trust

As a consequence of broader and more transparent involvement, advice forums foster trust among all attendees. This trust is not only built up between teams, but it also helps those who traditionally have held both decision power and decision accountability understand that others can be trusted to make balanced, well-informed decisions.

This ability to *see* decision power being deployed by others (with the support of advice) helps demonstrate that the required skills are present. Previously traditional architects—and, even more, senior technical stakeholders right up to CTO/CIO/chief scientist level—can watch others decide. They can witness the collaboration driving the architecture forward, in both the large and the small decisions. They can also see the learning. It is the combination of all this that leads those in these previously all-powerful positions to have greater trust themselves. The development of this trust is, more than anything else, the critical success factor for the architecture advice process.

For many reasons, this general raising of transparency pays dividends, including a general raising in the level of trust. Trust is built through experience (Principle D23). "What builds trust?" Reinertsen asks, continuing: "We trust someone when we feel we can predict their behavior under difficult conditions…Psychologists use the term *social expectancy theory* to refer to the ability to predict the behaviors of other members of our social group. They point out that we can work effectively with people when we can predict their behavior."

The advice forum offers this by letting the key parts of decisions—specifically, finding and working through specific points of contention *collaboratively*—happen out in the open, cognizant of and, hopefully, inoculated against the worst of organizational politics. (Part IV acknowledges that this can't be left to chance and describes ways to achieve this.) Not only can those involved in the specific decision *see* how their peers think and work, but so can everyone else. This exposure of the fundamentally hard work of making and taking significant architectural decisions *to potentially everyone* means that everyone can get inside others' heads and see how and why they are acting in the way they are.

Even the simple fact that advice forums are regular is beneficial. Reinertsen's "Principle of Cadenced Meetings" (Principle F19) states: "There is no need for a meeting announcement, and no need to coordinate schedules. Meetings that are synchronized to a regular and predictable cadence have very low set up costs. They contribute very little excess overhead." Short, predictable, frequent meetings offer ample opportunities for coordination and feedback (both of which we know we need with our decentralized approach), meaning decisions can't get very far off track. On the other hand, long, infrequent, and ad hoc meetings offer less of both as well as dampen the general sense of forward progress.[8]

But there is more to cadence than predictability, smart calendar management, shorter feedback loops, and respect for creative flow. The right kind of cadence, in the right ways for the right purpose, is a sociotechnical power move.

The Strengthening Ritual of Cadence

Because the advice forum is a regular meeting with the same people and the same shared goal taking place at the same time, week in and week out, it plays an incredibly important role with regard to social cohesion, trust, and conceptual integrity.

The benefits of a steady cadence can go very deep, and it all comes back to trust. This happens because there is a ritual element at play. Why "ritual"? Well, with rituals everyone participates actively, and trust is key for the magic to manifest.

Now, I realize if you're a hard-nosed, facts-driven, intellectual individual, the word *ritual* might send shivers down your spine. But remember, Agile has had "ceremonies" (stand-ups, demos, and the most important ceremony of all, retrospectives) for years. Why might *that* term be in broad use? It's because it was selected (consciously or unconsciously) to reflect the softer, more human, more social aspects of the team sport that is software delivery.

But let's be honest—these days, how frequently do we see these Agile ceremonies doing the job they were intended to do? I'd argue it's incredibly infrequent. For most of us, they have become just that, hollow ceremonies, with everyone simply going through the motions, unclear as to why they are being performed, probably led by some anointed high priest of Agile. The hollow ring of the word *ceremonies* might have been prescient.

For my taste, there is also just a little too much resonance here with the "high priests of architecture," resident in their lofty ivory tower.[9] I chose the word *ritual* carefully because, while it comes from a similar place, it's more personal but at the same time more participative. It's also something I hope no one can sell you a tool to help with.

---

8 Why is this so effective? To paraphrase Reinertsen, it is because a regular meeting, with a predictable, simple, focused, and valuable agenda, planned in advance and in everyone's calendars, balances the transaction cost of holding a meeting against the cost of delaying decisions. By reducing the transaction cost, we can cost-effectively hold meetings more frequently.

9 There's also a slightly more distant echo of the fact that the 17 signatories of the Agile Manifesto in February 2001 were all white, middle-aged men. Martin Fowler, one of the original signatories, called this issue out himself in his Agile Australia keynote in 2017 (transcript: "The State of Agile Software in 2018" (*https://oreil.ly/a1myI*)).

So what does ritual do that ceremonies don't? Remember, there is no predictability or control in today's complex, hyperconnected sociotechnical systems. As social individuals, this raises our anxiety levels. When we are aiming to increase trust, raising anxiety is the exact opposite of what we need. Ritual—the performance of it and the knowledge that it is there—reduces that anxiety.

Ritual also nurtures social cohesion. Although rituals can be performed personally,[10] group rituals are more powerful than individual ones. Collective ceremonies, with everyone participating in their own way, have been shown to make people more inclined to be cooperative and more generous to group members.[11]

A regular, focused, productive session—one with a common purpose that derives its value directly from many interpersonal connections—is rare. In the fast-moving world of today's software systems, we don't just benefit from this kind of thing—I'd argue that we *need* it.

Why? Every time we create something out of software, we are headed into the unknown because it's never entirely clear where we're going. Frequently, in fact, it's entirely *unclear*. Getting together specifically to tackle this uncertainty as a group turns it into a collective experience—one that fosters trust rather than undermining it. (The inevitability of uncertainty in software engineering is a big topic—one I'll come back to in Chapter 14 when I'll share other ways to embrace it.)

Many of the traditional approaches to the practice of architecture and more generally of software engineering (XP practices aside) moved us away from such interactions. They put in place structures and bureaucracies that, in attempting to manage and control, *separated* people from one another. Role splits such as "architect" and "developer" became more strictly defined, and traditional meetings such as ARBs served to strengthen those hierarchical distinctions. Group rituals like the advice forum, which bring everyone together as a collection of peers with a shared goal, are a dramatic means of *recollectivization*. They consequently help massively to unlock the magic of high-performing teams.

It is for all these reasons that an architecture advice forum is one of the most powerful supporting elements in any adoption of the architecture advice process, at least until the mechanics are understood, trust has been established and is growing, and

---

10 You could argue that test-driven development (TDD) has a strong ritual element. Think about the red-green-refactor cycle and the many patterns that aim to keep you on this path: "never go more than 10 minutes without running your tests" and so on. This certainly is intended to reduce anxiety: just read Kent Beck's preface to *Test-Driven Development: By Example* (Addison-Wesley) and see how much he talks about rituals. You might be surprised.

11 For a book-length academic treatise on this, see *Ritual: How Seemingly Senseless Acts Make Life Worth Living* by Dimitris Xygalatas (Little, Brown).

the new mindsets have been unlocked. I'll move on to that now as I turn to setting up your first advice forum and the part it can play in beginning this transition.

Kicking Off the Advice Process with an Advice Forum

If the architecture advice process and ADRs are the solid basis for your postrevolution practice, an advice forum is the perfect supporting practice from which to safely experiment with them. An advice forum is perfect because it is something that everyone can see in calendars, attend, and witness the new way to practice architecture unfold in front of them. It's also very simple—simple to run and simple to participate. The fact that an advice forum is scheduled builds trust across the organization once they know what it is and how it will operate. Finally, it can start small and be expanded easily. So how best to go about it?

Terms of Reference

You'll likely need to begin with a formal definition of what the advice forum does and how it works with the advice process. Some organizations like to have formal terms of reference (ToR), one-page documents describing the purpose and structures of meetings. These can be very useful when setting things up, bringing clarity for those who might need it. If you've not come across one before, a single-page ToR can be found on the GitHub repo that accompanies this book (*https://oreil.ly/pgyJU*). Even if you don't need one, it can help to have it simply to clarify the key aspects for yourself (and you can share it with people when they ask what the advice forum is for).

I've used ToRs when talking to both technical executives and the most senior architects. You'd be amazed how much even the existence of this one-pager can do to both clear the necessary ground for your new practice and build just enough trust with these key individuals to allow you free-enough reign to get your first advice forum set up and then establish a general cadence for both the forum and the practices it supports.

If You're Using the Advice Forum to Kick Off the Advice Process

If you are incorporating one, your first advice forum is a great place to announce the move to a new way of practicing architecture and explain to everyone what this means for them.

Your transition to the advice process needs to be gradual. You shouldn't set this up for all the teams in your organization all at the same time. A tightly scoped, experimental advice forum is a great place to kick off trying the advice process and ADRs. Begin with the basic approach I described here. Once that is established, you can try some further experiments with aspects of the forum itself to make it your own. More than anything, starting small like this allows trust within the first group to build. That in turn opens up the space and builds psychological safety and the ability to fail and learn.

Such an experiment also lays the foundation for other teams and architects to adopt the practice if they think it is appropriate. I've happily welcomed spectators (and occasional accidental participants) to advice forums. Coming from other parts of the organization where I had no mandate to operate, they could see the benefits of how we were approaching things nonetheless, and many subsequently returned to their areas of the organization to set up their own versions.

Who Convenes the First Advice Forum?

This leads to the key question: "who convenes your advice forum?" The answer, at least to begin with, is "you, dear reader." You are the person because you are aware of sufficient need to read this far in the book, and you have likely felt the pressures of the five revolutions significantly enough to consider acting on them. You will consequently have both the drive and the motivation.

Your scope will be appropriate, too. Only set up your advice process/advice forum experiment for the community that you have the power to affect. If you are part of a single team, just set it up for yourselves. You are the only ones who are adopting the architecture advice process practice, so all the other invitees can only be advice offerers.

If you are an architect, you can set up your advice forum for one or more teams that you work with. In these circumstances, both you and the teams can initiate decisions, and everyone else is an advice offerer.

As attendees see it in action, your experiment will likely attract more teams and individuals who want to be part of it. This is a good thing, but make sure to let your experiment run unchanged long enough to gain all the learnings from it. Once that has happened, then you can move to a permanent advice forum, potentially including others as decision makers if they want to participate.

How the First Advice Forum Will Differ from Subsequent Ones

While most advice forums require next to no preparation, the first one will be different. You'll need at least the following (unless you have already done these things in earlier experiments with the advice process):

- Get your ADR template in place and make sure it can be used by everyone to create their first ADRs.[12]
- Set up your ADR library—empty for now.

---

12 There may be reticence to do this. I've always found that helping teams write their first few ADRs unblocks. You don't need to catch all decisions, just enough so that everyone can see how the advice process works and the benefits of working within it.

- Get ready to explain your experiment to everyone. You'll need to cover what the architecture advice process is and how it works. You'll definitely need to cover what it does to accountability. You'll also need to make sure that everyone knows where to find the ADR template and the (currently empty) ADR library. Finally, let everyone know how long the experiment will be time-boxed for and how the outcomes will be assessed.

- You might need to do a little admin to fit comfortably into your organization's surrounding structures. I'd recommend providing the ToR for the advice forum and a FAQ that you can point people at (and update).

Once you've done this, you're all set. This inaugural session will open with a one-off agenda item explaining what the experiment is to everyone. Then, you just drop back to a standard advice forum format as I described earlier in this chapter. Subsequent advice forums simply keep this standard format.

You might be thinking, "Given what we covered in the book so far, there seems like an awful lot to remember when running an advice forum. How will I ever cope?"

Remember, like the other parts of the advice process–based approach, the advice forum is simple. I came across all these benefits in organization after organization, and I've heard reports of it happening in others where I've never been involved. All you need to do is *keep the focus on the work, and its value, its flow, and the feedback arising from it.* If you keep those at the front of your mind, protect the space and you won't go far wrong. And remember, it's an experiment, and experiments don't fail— they let you learn.

Alternative Advice Forum Flavors

What I've described is a vanilla advice forum. But it's not an advice forum at its most basic. I've described a standard starting point but not one to be deployed unthinkingly.

The fundamental nature of the advice forum is a regular, face-to-face meeting (or probably videoconference, if I'm being honest), attended by the advice-seeking and advice-offering collectives. It's a place where deciders seek and advisers offer advice *in real time.* Beyond and within that boundary, feel free to do whatever you like with the advice forum. There is a lot of space left for cultural differences to express themselves and for unique collective rituals to form.

It's also a great place to experiment explicitly, while you have everyone's attention. With the caveat that you stay aligned with the purpose of the gathering *and* you make sure that *everyone* attending cares about what you are adding, removing, or changing, what might be some experiments you can think of? I've collected some of mine in a separate article, "Alternative Advice Forum Flavors" (*https://oreil.ly/ikt5F*).

Conclusion

Despite the fact that an architecture advice forum is not an essential element for the architecture advice process, it still has a lot to offer. I showed how simply it can be run, allowing everyone present to focus on the various social dynamics it engenders. I discussed how it can lead to a new way of collaborating on architectural decisions, one focused on the specifics of problems and the areas of disagreement, and avoids the clashes of personality and ego that so frequently get in the way. I showed how this in turn can nurture trust and support the vitally important social contract, ending by considering how an advice forum may well be the ideal way to kick off your advice process journey.

In covering all this, I've been consciously avoiding spending too much time on the related questions of direction and destination. I've also underrepresented the topic of alignment. The reason for this is because sometimes these matters don't need to be handled explicitly. Sometimes, the mission of an organization is so explicit and ingrained in everyone and everything they do that there is no need to supplement it. Everything just "happens." But such circumstances are rare.

I'll begin in Chapter 9 with the next supporting element that considers means to keep everyone aligned: testable CFRs and actionable technology strategy.

Testable CFRs and Technology Strategy

This chapter will begin by weighing the importance of alignment with your organization's vision and goals. It will consider how that can be achieved in a decentralized, revolutionized, feedback-centric world with minimum restrictions placed on the decision space—restrictions that need to be understood and agreed to by everyone. To achieve this big-picture goal of alignment, you need a minimal viable level of agreement, covering both *what* you need and *how* you intend your systems to work together effectively.

With that laid out, you'll learn about a two-part supporting element. The first part gets very specific (but not very directive) about the "what" in the form of testable cross-functional requirements (CFRs). Indeed, because this isn't the first time CFRs have come up in this book, I'll spend quite a while on them.

The second part complements this, getting directive (but not very specific) about the "how" in the form of technology strategy. Unlike CFRs, I won't go into detail about how to create a strategy as it's outside the scope of this book. I will, however, give you the means to ensure that any strategy you have is suitable and sufficient.

The Importance of Organizational Alignment

Imagine you're in the lucky position of already taking all the right decisions with all the right people, in all the right places, at all the right times. Your architecture practice is not just efficient—it is *effective*. This magical state of effectiveness comes from organizational alignment, and it goes beyond what the architecture advice process and ADRs provide.

That's not to say the advice process is useless. It offers incredible efficiency for your architecture practice. It enables you both to maintain the overall conceptual integrity of your system architecture and to develop and sustain social cohesion, allowing trust to develop and thrive. It does this by enabling everyone—both teams and those playing an architecture role—to make efficient progress and build well-architected software in a revolutionized world.

But efficiency doesn't guarantee effectiveness. Misplaced efficiency is at best ineffective and at worst counterproductive. Therefore, in this section I'll lay out what effective alignment looks like, how to detect if you have insufficient alignment, the common levers for achieving alignment, and how to know how much you need to align on.

Alignment Doesn't Guarantee Effectiveness

Although alignment implies that everything is working together toward a shared goal, it's no guarantee of value. Say you're in a dragon boat race on a team with five other people. You're rowing in sync and moving at a swift pace. Sounds good, right? Well, maybe. Only if you're rowing toward the finish line. Otherwise, you can go as fast as you like, but that won't achieve your collective goal.

Let's look at a more technical example. Recall the point in Chapter 4's "Story 1: A Development Team Decides to Use Release Toggles" on page 78. Think about the point *before* the team sought advice. Their first attempt at a design wasn't bad, at least not for their needs. But as soon as they received advice, they found that it would have actually impeded others: specifically, teams that were relying on the APIs that the deciding team were going to expose.

A few pictures might help the more visually minded. Consider a collection of teams working without any architecture practice at all—not the architecture advice process nor one of the traditional alternatives; all teams are completely unaligned, as I've visualized abstractly in Figure 9-1.

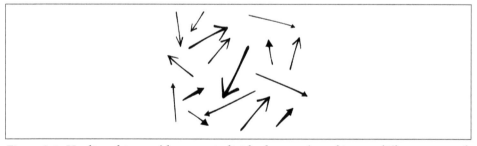

Figure 9-1. Unaligned teams (shown as individual arrows) working on different parts of a shared system, headed in different technical directions and canceling each other's efforts out[1]

---

1 This "arrows" figure and the others that follow in this chapter owe a lot to the similar figures in Chapter 11 of Peter M. Senge's *The Fifth Discipline: The Art and Practice of the Learning Organization* (Doubleday).

Despite the fact that each team (represented by individual arrows) is making progress, when you consider the overall system (all the arrows together) the sum of the parts is opposition and conflict.

This hints at one of the benefits of advice. Not only does one team gain assistance from others, resulting in a better decision, but they are also gently nudged into alignment with everyone else working collectively on the shared, overall system. Furthermore, because advice is offered in the open, everyone else can be aware of it too, aligning with it themselves. In the Story 1 example from Chapter 4, after receiving the advice, the team made their toggle setting configurable via an environmental parameter. This allowed other teams in multiple environments to set the toggle as *they* wanted, whenever they needed it. You can see this aligning effect of an architecture practice such as the advice process graphically in Figure 9-2.

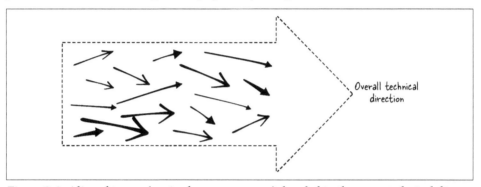

Figure 9-2. Aligned teams (again shown as arrows), headed in the same technical direction (as indicated by the dotted arrow that contains them all)

With such an aligning practice, teams are generally headed in the same technical direction rather than pulling in different directions as a consequence of their independent technical approaches. Now the progress of one team isn't impeding the progress of the others.

Such technical alignment is undoubtedly a good thing, but it's not good enough on its own because, powerful as it is, technical alignment says nothing about your collective destination or the agreed route(s) you'll take collectively to get there. With technical alignment alone, the place you get to is not one that you chose—it's just where you end up as a consequence of all of your individual decisions. Just like the dragon boat rowing team, you have no guarantee that you're headed toward the finish line.

A question to ask yourselves to find out if your alignment is merely technical is this: are you *effective* in moving toward your organization's goals? This is fundamentally important, and without it, all the technical alignment in the world won't help you.

Effectiveness is when your software systems deliver *impact* for your organization. This impact isn't simply the result of implementing the software features your organization asked for. Effectiveness is also deploying technology appropriately, realizing the value and benefits those features are intended to unlock, or failing fast when you learn that the value/benefit isn't there. Effectiveness is being able to move at a sustainable pace long-term and not get bogged down in technical debt resulting from feature request after feature request. Effectiveness is having a predictable and reasonable cost to run. Effectiveness is carrying an acceptable level of technical risk. Most of all, effectiveness is being able to react and respond to the needs of users so that the constraints of technology can be minimized and the opportunities it provides are realized.

You don't get this from technical alignment alone. You need a greater force to orient that alignment. You need organizational alignment.

Let's return to the representation of our teams as arrows, but let's zoom out a little farther. In Figure 9-2, you saw that all of the team arrows are pointing in the same general direction—toward the right. That's good, right? Well, not necessarily. If you zoom out, you might find (Figure 9-3, lefthand side) that the teams are headed in the opposite direction to the organization's vision and goals, represented by the larger dashed-line arrow. This broader misalignment means that your teams, while efficient, are not effective.

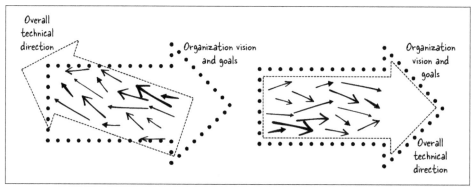

Figure 9-3. The lefthand diagram depicts multiple teams (yet again shown as arrows), aligned technically (shown as the smaller dotted-line arrow) but not with the vision and goals of the organization (shown as the bigger, dashed-line arrow), and the righthand diagram shows the same teams but now aligned to the vision and goals of the organization

Now, look at the righthand side of Figure 9-3. There, the team arrows, technical alignment, *and* larger organizational "vision and goals" arrows are all pointing in the same direction. Here, there is broader alignment, meaning the teams are effective.

You'll see that the difference between these two diagrams is now the alignment (or not) of the "team" arrows within a larger dotted arrow representing the organization with its vision and goals. The point is that, while it's beneficial that teams are aligned with one another, it's *more important* that they are aligned with the rest of the organization. Why does this broader type of alignment make them effective? Because an organization's vision and goals are what ultimately determine if a decision is appropriate or not.

Are we moving at a sustainable pace and incurring only manageable levels of debt? Again, the organizational vision and goals determine if something is appropriate. "Reasonable" run costs? Consult the organizational vision and goals. "Is this risk appropriate?" What do the organization's vision and goals say? Are we deploying technology in the best way, minimizing its constraints and maximizing the opportunities it offers, efficiently meeting the needs of our users? The organizational vision and goals have this covered.

I'll say it again: technical alignment among teams isn't sufficient for collective effectiveness. Everyone also needs to be aligned with the overall direction of the organization, as laid out in its vision and goals. Why? Because that tells us where the organization is headed and therefore where we should collectively be aiming for technically. *Effective* team alignment is a technical direction toward a destination, which is aligned with, and complementary to, the organization's overall direction and aspirational destination.

To be effective, you need to have an appropriately detailed and collective idea of this destination in advance as well as some shared bets regarding the route or routes you plan to take to get there. (Spoiler alert: this is where CFRs and a technology strategy come into play, but I'll get into both later in this chapter.)

Now that you understand the effect of organizational alignment, let's discuss how to detect when you don't have enough of it.

Detecting Insufficient Organizational Alignment

A major step in all of the decision processes I previously described was pulling together a set of decision options. In software, the *potential* number of these options is *huge* (hence the *soft* in *software*: *soft*ware is not only easier to change than *hard*ware, but its malleability also makes it capable of supporting both more options and subsequent changes). As such, it's easy for a decision process to go off the rails, proceed in an ineffective way, and lead to misalignment.

How then can you know if decisions are proceeding in a valuable, effective direction? Over the years, I've identified the following telltale signs that may signal misalignment.

The first signal is decisions that lead to duplication of nondifferentiating effort. This can be at any level of the stack and can come from any decider. For example, if services are all deployed to Cloud Provider A, but one team wants to take a decision to deploy their service to Cloud Provider B, then there will be a duplication of effort to set up and run the necessary infrastructure/platform-as-a-service components. Higher up the stack, there might be a need for a team to implement a small piece of simple workflow in a service, and there is an existing in-house workflow component that will work for them. Despite this, an architect proposes that they select the option that deviates, doing it their own way and bringing in a third-party library to meet their specific needs.

The second signal is deciders having debates with their advisers about the same fundamental points again and again. For example, there could be a debate about the interpretation of the concept of "tenant" on a multitenant software as a service (SaaS) system or of the suitability of the Command Query Responsibility Segregation (CQRS) architectural style for a new microservice. In these cases, the discussions likely spring from a clash between those who hold a cross-system perspective and those who see the complexities and benefits of working with an alternative (most likely locally different) approach.

The third signal is when decisions seem to be favoring the technical *at the expense of the functional*, either in the number of decisions (it's perfectly valid that some decisions will be about purely technical subjects) or in the balance of importance of the technical compared to the functional. For example, decision after decision focusing on the best cloud services, programming language, frameworks, and data persistence patterns might abound, without mention of a decision arising from functional needs; or discussions might revolve around the various pros and cons of different record serialization formats, getting very, very deep into arguments about submillisecond response times and resident memory sizes without stopping to consider if these aspects are even necessary.

I have been present at—and contributed to—discussions that flashed all of these signals. These discussions that signal organizational misalignment have one thing in common: they are always missing a key factor that would determine their validity, a factor that isn't either technical or architectural.

The option-preferring factor that is missing in all these discussions comes from the organization's vision and goals, and those differ from organization to organization. That's why what is right for one organization can be precisely wrong for the next.

What is "waste" for one organization is "investment" and "R&D" for another.[2] Clarity on what *your* organization values and privileges and conversely, what it devalues and ignores, is incredibly important when making options and taking decisions. An organization sets what it values and privileges in terms of its vision and goals. The problem is, this vision and associated goals aren't always explicit to those making and taking architectural decisions, but they need to be. What better way to make that alignment explicit than to capture it in the form of a shared agreement?

Four Means of Alignment

To achieve and sustain organizational alignment, your organization's visions and goals must be incorporated into decision processes. To do that, you need just enough collective agreement on where and how you are aligned.

The Open Group's Agile Architecture (O-AA) standard describes four "alignment mechanisms" of autonomous teams (*https://oreil.ly/gVZtz*). Aligned teams, it says, should have a "shared consciousness," feedback loops that "help to adjust behavior," "forcing functions (or guardrails)," and a "shared purpose."

Now, the goals of these four mechanisms are valuable, but the means don't all fit comfortably with an advice process approach because many are *imposed* from outside rather than *adopted* from within. The first two you have covered; the advice process and ADRs already provide the means to achieve a shared consciousness and feedback loops. And the other two? They are the focus of the remainder of Part II, but I'll distinguish them a little now because they work in different ways.

I'll address "shared purpose" in this chapter. It becomes an *actionable* technology strategy. "Forcing functions (or guardrails)" is split into three parts. The first and second parts, "commitments" and "guidelines," keep their names and will be covered respectively in Chapter 10 as a shared set of architectural principles and in Chapter 11 as a record of your collective experiences captured in a technology radar.

The third part, "restrictions and requirements," I'll rename as a set of *testable* cross-functional requirements. I mentioned CFRs briefly before, but I'll now explain how to use them to clarify the specific nonnegotiable forces that affect your design space.

These four means of agreement support organizational alignment by being more or less specific and more or less directive. Figure 9-4 lays them out, showing both the levels of direction they offer and their specificity.

---

2 The best explanation of this is in a sidebar in Eric Evans's *Domain-Driven Design* titled "Is Address a Value Object? Who's Asking?" (p. 98).

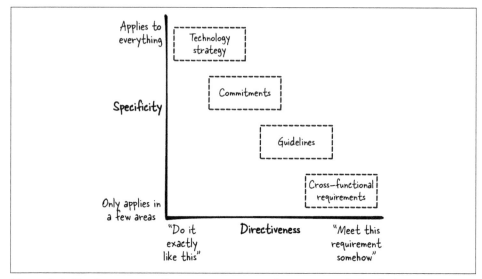

Figure 9-4. The four means of agreement, arranged to compare their relative directiveness and specificity

An appropriate combination of these approaches offers a clear way to factor your organization's mission and goals into your architecture practice. You achieve this by making clear what your organization values and what it doesn't as well as what your organization must do and what it must not. These approaches together offer everything you need to make both efficient and effective architectural decisions that are aligned to this mission and its goals.

So what does minimal viable agreement on these topics look like for you? I'll only touch on commitments and guidelines lightly here. I'll come back to them in Chapter 10 and 11.

You're Aligned When You're Not Surprised

Now that you are armed with a means to spot when you have insufficient organizational alignment, the next question that arises is "How do we know what's missing from our levels of agreement?" and the best way to do that is to apply the *principle of least surprise*.[3]

The principle of least surprise is useful because it's a probe right into the heart of your sociotechnical system. It states that, for anyone in a system, other parts of the system,

---

3 This is also known as the "principle of least astonishment," but I prefer *surprise* because experiencing surprise, even if it's not as extreme as astonishment, is still a valid data point when interacting with sociotechnical systems, and one I always try to be sensitive to.

including their colleagues, should act roughly as they expect them to. If you are all aligned in your agreements, then whenever you ask anyone working on the software what these things are for them, they'll reply with the same answer. If something or someone *doesn't* look or act how you would expect them to, then you will be surprised.

Let's have one example of each of the means to align in Figure 9-4. You'd expect there to be more alignment on the earlier elements because of their greater specificity, but don't take any level for granted.

First, consider a CFR specifying an overall response time. In Organization X, experiments and market analysis have both shown that users of a social media app will only tolerate a response time of less than 500 ms for any action performed. That's 500 ms total, so if everyone were aligned, you would expect to be able to ask anyone about this number and get the same response. Not only that, but you'd expect certain key individuals to know what their allocation of this time budget was and possibly what other teams' allocations were, too. While not everyone will be aware of all of this detail, you'd not expect (here's that surprise thing coming) differing ideas of the overall number. Everyone should always agree on 500 ms. If not, that's a big surprise, and an indicator of misalignment in a fundamental area.

Surprise at the CFR level is easy to test because of their specificity. I once worked with a client who had no explicit CFRs, something that initially sounded alarm bells for me. However, once I spent time with the teams, it became clear that there were CFRs, people knew them, and they were made manifest in the code. They just didn't need the intermediate step of writing them down in the form of requirements.

This client was also a great example of the other alignment mechanisms: commitments and guidelines. Despite the fact they ran a microservices architecture, all of their services were written in Python (guideline), using the same frameworks (guideline) and exposing similarly styled APIs (commitment). These agreements weren't written down anywhere; they had just come about because of the strong engineering culture and crusading nature of their vision.[4]

I'll talk more about means of agreement for guidelines and commitments in the next two chapters. For now, let's look at an example in the area of strategic technology direction, which they both depend on.

At Organization Y, all teams are working on domain-aligned services that are built in Kotlin, C#, or Go. The teams themselves are free to choose their implementation language, but the strategic runtime platform is Amazon's cloud. Therefore, all teams are

---

4 You might expect that in such an environment, where strong personalities abounded, the architecture advice process would have trouble operating. In fact, it was the opposite. The preexisting alignment at many levels meant that teams felt safe to decide for themselves, in great part *because* the options space was known and understood by everyone.

independently deploying to cloud components based on Amazon Web Services (AWS) that are prepackaged for them by an infrastructure platform/site reliability engineering (SRE) team. Then a new team comes along. They are building the organization's first data product. Their code is in Python, and they are targeting Google Cloud infrastructure, which they are managing and running themselves. This deviation could give rise to surprise; it would be natural to assume that all teams would be targeting the strategic cloud provider. Why not the new team, too?

That is, of course, unless the strategy needs some updating. There are clear differences between the purpose and architecture of the business-aligned services and their equivalents in the new services that underlie the data product. It might be the case that someone senior in the organization, the CTO perhaps, had looked at the relative merits of AWS versus Google Cloud support for data products and decided that the benefits of the latter were sufficient to add a new cloud provider to the mix. This should be reflected in the strategy, though. If not, you might eventually find that business service teams start deploying to Google Cloud infrastructure, too. That really *would* be a surprise, especially given the strategic investment in the infrastructure platform/SRE team packaging AWS services purely for their benefit.

The point here is that agreement needn't be monolithic at any level and is also subject to change. We'll see this again in the final example: an example of surprise around organizational goals and visionary objectives.

In this scenario, Organization Z has a SaaS product targeted at a specific slice of the insurance broker market: large brokerages that sell standard insurance products to thousands of customers, differentiated on price. This is in contrast to brokerages that might offer more bespoke insurance products to fewer customers, differentiating on the specifics of the coverage they offer. The consequence of this product strategy targeting the mass-market broker is that the core of the SaaS software is optimized for speed as opposed to flexibility; there are rarely requirements to change the logic that underpins collecting client information (e.g., location of property, value of property, etc. for home insurance), quoting, sales, and contractuals.

Given this, it would come as a fair surprise to discover that the line of business (LoB) module that defines the risk model behind a given type of insurance product was designed and implemented to be highly configurable on a customer-by-customer basis. Based on the business strategy, that requirement shouldn't arise, and consequently, this is unnecessary complexity and, more concerningly, a likely source of defects and performance issues.

As before, this *might* have come about because the executive (this time perhaps it was the Chief Product Officer) decided that there might be an opportunity to offer support in the SaaS to other types of brokerages—those selling fewer, more bespoke insurance products, for instance. Surprise still arose for two reasons. First, not everyone working in the SaaS codebase—at least not in the LoB module and its dependencies—knew this was being worked on. If they had, their surprise might have been lessened.[5] Second, the LoB module was now being designed to work in two different ways for two different purposes. It might have made far more sense to implement a new, "superconfigurable" LoB module that put less emphasis on performance *alongside* the existing one, integrating them both into the surrounding services separately. Then, the organization could have their existing products supported *and* experiment with additional offerings *without* adding confusion.

Therefore, at each of the means of agreement, one or multiple agreements about a certain aspect can be in place. Consider first the response-times CFR. I've worked with clients where they had one single, unbreakable response time in place, and had invested heavily in testing (at development, deployment, and runtime) to check that this never slipped. I've worked with other clients who had a standard "all response times must be" CFR *as well as* targeted CFRs for certain key actions. For example, the insurance broker SaaS product would have had two for the complicated step of quoting: one for the mass-market quoting service and another for the bespoke equivalent.

This doesn't only happen at the CFR level. The insurance broker SaaS example also showed that there might be multiple agreements about something at the business-vision level, and the strategic cloud example shows the same at the technology-strategy level.

From all these, it is clear that it's fine for there to be multiple agreements at any one level as long as there is a clear reason why each of them exists and what they apply to. This is important because these agreements are going to be used by teams and architects (and others in the business, in the case of the business vision) to make decisions, plan courses of action, allocate resources, and so on.

In summary, not all organizations need the same levels of agreement, they don't need to be about everything (just the things that are important to the organization), and they need not always be explicit. In all cases, what is important is that it's clear to everyone building and running the systems what agreements are in place, what they apply to, and that they all can ultimately be traced back to the organization's goals and visionary objectives.

Above all, it's most important that they aren't restricting the architecture practice space any more than necessary. Too much alignment is not only harder to agree on, but it's also unnecessarily restrictive on the design space you are carefully trying to protect. Given all this, how do you make sure you have the required levels and means of agreement but no more?

---

5 I mentioned in a previous footnote that I prefer *surprise* to *astonishment*. This is a great example of why.

Minimum Viable Agreement

A minimum viable agreement is in place when you are collectively building and evolving your software systems effectively and with little surprise. As the name suggests, *minimum viable agreements* make clear how to align with the organization's vision and goals—*and no more*. Too much agreement would impinge on the freedom of teams, which we are fighting so hard to protect.

So what might be the minimum level of agreement required in your organization? How might you find that minimum level? And once you find it, how do you make sure it is articulated in a format that helps *keep* everyone in agreement and aligned with the overall org direction? The answer lies in the complementary actions of CFRs and technology strategy, which were at opposite ends of Figure 9-4.

On the one hand, as you've just seen, CFRs provide a way for all teams to agree on just enough for their individual software components to work together coherently. CFRs do that by saying strongly *what* the collective system needs to do to achieve the organization's goals but not *how* it'll do it. That's why they are most specific but least directive.

And the "how"? That's the job of technology strategy, which is why it is by contrast very directive. But it's also the least specific because strategy is very high level, allowing lots of room for interpretation. That's why the other two means of agreement are there to fill in the commonly asked blanks in the form of guidelines and principles, again ensuring that everyone is collectively effective.

Taken together, technology strategy, commitments, guidelines, and CFRs—all derived from your organization's goals and visionary objectives—can define the minimal viable agreement that your organization needs to have in place to ensure that all of its separate parts are pulling in an effective direction. In the following sections, I'll step through how to use CFRs and what to look for in your technology strategy to make your minimum viable agreement explicit.

Cross-Functional Requirements

The most specific and least directive means of agreement is a shared set of testable CFRs. CFRs provide a way for all teams to do just enough for their individual software components to work together coherently.

CFRs are one of the key forces that shape a software architecture, which is why I mentioned them when I defined what makes for an architecturally significant decision. Requirements under the "cross-functional" heading are a diverse group, sharing little apart from the fact that they typically apply *across an architecture* (hence my preference for the term *cross-functional* as opposed to *nonfunctional* used by Michael Nygard and others).

These are the standard subtypes of CFRs:[6]

- Performance
- Capacity/scalability
- Availability/reliability
- Security
- Legal/regulatory
- Accessibility/usability
- Monitorability/observability
- Operability
- Cost
- Integrability/extensibility

Each subtype covers an area in which those interacting with the system will have assumptions. For example, everyone using a system will have an assumption about how quickly it will operate; they will also have assumptions about how it will respond when placed under increasing levels of load, how it will cope with failures, how much it will cost to run, and so on.

But assumptions are a bad basis on which to build and run a system. That's why specific, detailed, and testable CFRs should exist under the relevant subtypes for your system, so that the implicit assumptions of key stakeholders—those with the most skin in the game—can be turned into concrete expectations.

These concrete expectations can be specified as acceptance criteria and then turned into tests, either automated or manual. The tests can be executed in the build pipelines or on the running systems in production. They can even be referred to in teams' definitions of done.

Let's look at a few examples of testable CFRs. First the requirement format:

EXAMPLE
As a [ROLE]…**I want to** [ACTION]…**so that** [VALUE].

---

6 There are a *lot* if I start trying to be exhaustive. And being exhaustive is actually a trap. The key is to figure out what the important CFR areas for your domain are. For example, if you're writing software for a moon lander, maintainability might not be so important, but availability/resilience, on the other hand…

And then the acceptance criteria:

EXAMPLE

Given [CIRCUMSTANCES]...**when** [EVENT]...**then** [OUTCOME].

As I go through the examples, you'll see how CFRs help identify the minimum viable agreement of your organization and why an established format is useful.

CFR example 1: A testable access logging requirement

Let's get started with the first example. Here's the CFR:

EXAMPLE

As a DEVELOPMENT TEAM MEMBER

I want read access to and the ability to search ACCESS LOGS in the STANDARD LOG FORMAT using the STANDARD OBSERVABILITY TOOLSET

So that I can monitor the operation of my systems

And debug problems

You can see explicitly the stakeholder who cares about the requirement (the development team member, in this case), the requirement itself (writing access logs to a commonly agreed location in an agreed standard log format), and finally the value of having the requirement (logs will be available in a set of standard tooling, in a predictable format, alongside everyone else's).

I've picked this example to begin because both the need the requirement articulates and the benefits of having agreement in this area are clear. Having everyone's logs in the same format in the same place makes it easier for everyone to keep track of how the overall system is running. When combined with another CFR stating a similar requirement for error logs, they provide a reliable data source to help hunt down even those complicated bugs that pop up in the gaps between multiple teams' subsystems.

However, you might not have noticed what this CFR doesn't say. It says *nothing* about how anyone's code will write these logs. This is intentional. We might choose to do it manually, with print and if statements for levels, or we might choose to write our own logging library. Far more likely, we'll choose to use one of the many quality logging frameworks that handles all this for us. You can therefore see how, in not specifying this key detail, the CFR truly is a lowest level of agreement.

This is the first of three key aspects of a truly great CFR: it says *what* (we need logs that end up in an agreed place in an agreed format) you need to do but not *how* you need to do it (it doesn't say where the agreed place is nor what the agreed format is.).

However, this low level of CFR detail is not sufficient on its own. How do you know when you are *done* implementing a requirement, or enough of a requirement? It's all too easy to slip into overengineering CFR implementations if "enough" isn't clear, such as adding extension points "just in case" they're needed.

That's why the second aspect of a testable CFR is acceptance criteria that not only say when the requirement is met but also how to validate it. With acceptance criteria, you know when you are done, no matter what your route to implementation.

What are the acceptance criteria in our first CFR example? They look like this:

EXAMPLE

Given the system is running

When the system is accessed

Then a single log entry is written to STDOUT in the STANDARD LOG FORMAT

Given the system has been accessed

When the access log entry is written

Then that log entry is visible in the STANDARD OBSERVABILITY TOOLSET

And displays the correct access information

Given there are some access logs in the STANDARD OBSERVABILITY TOOLSET

When an AUTHORIZED USER conducts a search for those logs

Then those logs are found and displayed accurately

This level of detail is what makes a CFR "testable." These acceptance criteria can be turned into tests, either automated or manual, executed in the build pipelines or on the running systems in production. They can even be referred to in all teams' definitions of done.

Now, I'm not saying that the existence of these criteria will prevent overengineering, but when they are known, it makes it pretty hard to justify spending additional time on something beyond what is needed.

It's now time to explain something that might have been troubling you. Why are certain parts of the requirement and its acceptance criteria written in CAPITAL LETTERS? It's not because my caps lock key got stuck. These elements are the third and final aspect of a testable CFR. Testable CFRs always rely on clear and specific definitions of key concepts, which are unique to your organization's circumstances. Each of these is signified by the capitalized words and in the real world would link to a glossary, something like this:

EXAMPLE

DEVELOPMENT TEAM MEMBER
    A permanent member of one of the teams building and running one or more systems in production.

ACCESS LOG
    The record of a single server access request and its result.

STDOUT
    "Standard Out," one of the three standard streams of computer programming (the other two being STDIN and STDERR).

STANDARD LOG FORMAT
    The organization's standard log format. Ours is a JSON format with the following standard fields...

STANDARD OBSERVABILITY TOOLSET
    The organization's shared set of observability tooling. This is currently Splunk.

AUTHORIZED SYSTEM SUPPORT USER
    A member of a development team who has on-call responsibilities and requires access to the STANDARD OBSERVABILITY TOOLSET.

Having shared CFR definitions clearly articulated *in a single place* does more than simply cut down on your typing. It also makes clear that these are a shared view of what collectively defines your system. You can see, for example, that an organization-wide log format has been agreed on and that it's JSON-based. You can also see that there is a definition of the role that can access the standard observability toolset. You might also notice that one definition can rely on another: the standard system support user has access to the standard observability toolset.

First and foremost, this means testing can get really concrete. For example, tests can now ensure not only that the access log entries are written but also that they follow the correct format.

Second, as you can see in the definition of the observability toolset, having shared definitions is a safer place to articulate the current status of a "how." By keeping this definition out of the requirements and acceptance criteria of your CFRs, you protect your CFRs from becoming coupled with a specific point-in-time provider of this service. How do we know enough to say that, currently, it is Splunk? Park that thought for me for a few minutes. I'll come back to it before the end of this chapter.

The third benefit is slightly counterintuitive. By having these key elements of CFRs articulated once and stored in a single place, it becomes very clear when there cannot be a single CFR to define something, and that multiple CFRs, each more specifically focused, are required. For that, let's consider another example.

CFR example 2: Multiple testable performance requirements

Let's begin again with a cross-system CFR. Let's look at one about performance.

Requirement first:

EXAMPLE
As a member of the CLIENT SUPPORT TEAM
I want the system to RESPOND WITHIN 500 MS
So that I can meet BUSINESS KPI A

Then acceptance criteria (this isn't intended to be exhaustive):

EXAMPLE
Given the system is in NORMAL OPERATING MODE
And experiencing STANDARD REQUEST VOLUMES
When the system is accessed with a VALID ACTION
Then the system will RESPOND WITHIN 500 MS with a SUCCESS RESPONSE
Given the system is in NORMAL OPERATING MODE
And experiencing PEAK REQUEST VOLUMES
When the system is accessed with a VALID ACTION
Then the system will RESPOND WITHIN 500 MS with a "SYSTEM UNDER HEAVY LOAD" RESPONSE
And the system will RESPOND WITHIN 1,500 MS with a SUCCESS RESPONSE

Finally, the definitions:

CLIENT SUPPORT TEAM
A member of staff who handles standard support calls for users, such as password resets, locked accounts, etc.

NORMAL OPERATING MODE
The system is running as intended. All subsystems are in operation, and all third-party dependencies are available and responding accurately in a timely fashion.

BUSINESS KPI A
Reduced call-handling times leading to operational efficiencies and improved NPS.

STANDARD REQUEST VOLUMES
The overall system is experiencing a total of 1,500 requests per second.

PEAK REQUEST VOLUMES
The overall system is experiencing a total of 9,000 requests per second.

VALID ACTION
A request that the system do something it is designed to perform.

RESPOND WITHIN 500 MS
95% of all calls will take no longer than 500 ms to receive, process, and appropriately respond to a request; 99% of all requests will take no longer than 800 ms to receive, process, and appropriately respond to a request. All requests will be handled within 1,000 ms.

RESPOND WITHIN 1,500 MS
95% of all calls will take no longer than 1,500 ms to receive, process, and appropriately respond to a request; 99% of all requests will take no longer than 2,000 ms to receive, process, and appropriately respond to a request. All requests will be handled within 10,000 ms.

SUCCESS RESPONSE
A "200/OK" server response with an appropriate response body. The relevant elements of this will be reflected in the UI.

SYSTEM UNDER HEAVY LOAD" RESPONSE
A "503/Service Unavailable" server response with an appropriate response body. The relevant elements of this will be reflected in the UI.

This example is interesting because the CFR is making a big assumption. It's assuming that all requests to the system have to process a similar workload and can therefore have a hope of responding "within 500 ms."

Think again of the example insurance broker SaaS (Organization Z in "You're Aligned When You're Not Surprised" on page 216). Much of the processing that it offered their broker customers did fall into this standard "VALID ACTION" bucket, but not all of it, and their customers knew it.

Specifically in this subdomain, users were aware that running a quotation for a collection of insurance products was a complex and compute-intensive thing. Not only that, but they were aware of the fact that there are semipredictable events in the brokerage business, the main one being a surge in people looking to move their insurance after a well-known TV celebrity and money expert would have one of their intermittent shows and educate the public on matters financial. In these circumstances, the brokers knew they and their systems would be incredibly busy quoting customers for a period of 24–48 hours.

The distinct nature of this requirement targeted at a very specific area of functionality meant that it would be foolish to not capture *separate* CFRs to cover this area and these events. As you would expect for CFRs and requirements in general, they make clear what the system needs to do but not at all how it ought to do it.

Let's look at the additional requirement first (note the specific "QUOTE REQUESTS" action in the "I want" line):

EXAMPLE
As a member of the CLIENT SUPPORT TEAM   **I want** the system to RESPOND TO QUOTE REQUESTS WITHIN 10,000 MS   **So that** I can meet BUSINESS KPI B

Then acceptance criteria (this isn't intended to be exhaustive):

EXAMPLE
Given the system is in NORMAL OPERATING MODE   **And** experiencing STANDARD QUOTE REQUEST VOLUMES   **When** the system is accessed with a VALID QUOTATION REQUEST   **Then** the system will RESPOND TO QUOTE REQUESTS WITHIN 10,000 MS with a SUCCESSFUL QUOTATION RESPONSE

Given the system is in NORMAL OPERATING MODE

And experiencing PEAK QUOTE REQUEST VOLUMES

When the system is accessed with a VALID QUOTATION REQUEST

Then the system will RESPOND TO QUOTE REQUESTS WITHIN 500 MS with a "SYSTEM UNDER HEAVY LOAD" RESPONSE

And the system will RESPOND WITHIN 20,000 MS with a SUCCESSFUL QUOTATION RESPONSE

Given the system is in NORMAL OPERATING MODE

And experiencing PEAK QUOTE REQUEST VOLUMES

When the system is accessed with an INVALID QUOTATION REQUEST

Then the system will RESPOND TO QUOTE REQUESTS WITHIN 500 MS with an "INVALID QUOTE REQUEST" RESPONSE

And finally, the additional definitions:

EXAMPLE

BUSINESS KPI B
Generate 1,000 quotes for net-new customers within a 24-hour period.

STANDARD QUOTE REQUEST VOLUMES
The overall system is experiencing a total of 500 quotation requests per second or less.

PEAK QUOTE REQUEST VOLUMES
The overall system is experiencing a total of 5,000 quotation requests per second or less.

VALID QUOTATION REQUEST
A request that the system perform a quotation for an insurance product based on valid user information.

INVALID QUOTATION REQUEST
A quotation request that is unprocessable because of the contents of the user information provided. Standard "unprocessable" quote requests have one or more of the following features....

RESPOND TO QUOTE REQUESTS WITHIN 500 MS
>95% of all calls will take no longer than 500 ms to receive, process, and appropriately respond to a request; 99% of all requests will take no longer than 600 ms to receive, process, and appropriately respond to a request. All requests will be handled within 700 ms.

SUCCESSFUL QUOTATION RESPONSE
>A "200/OK" server response with an appropriate quotation response body. The relevant elements of this quotation will be reflected in the UI.

SYSTEM UNDER HEAVY LOAD" RESPONSE
>A "503/Service Unavailable" server response with an appropriate response body. The relevant elements of this will be reflected in the UI.

RESPOND TO QUOTE REQUESTS WITHIN 10,000 MS
>95% of all calls will take no longer than 10,000 ms to receive, process, and appropriately respond to a request; 99% of all requests will take no longer than 20,000 ms to receive, process, and appropriately respond to a request. All requests will be handled within 60,000 ms.

RESPOND TO QUOTE REQUESTS WITHIN 20,000 MS
>95% of all calls will take no longer than 20,00 ms to receive, process, and appropriately respond to a request; 99% of all requests will take no longer than 40,000 ms to receive, process, and appropriately respond to a request. All requests will be handled within 120,000 ms.

These additional definitions are a great way to pinpoint the requirements we've added because it's hard to see precisely in that sea of text wherever the word *QUOTE* is used. Let's look at some in a little more detail.

There are now additional CFRs focused specifically on insurance quotes. They follow the general convention, defining their more specific versions of the "STANDARD" and "PEAK" volumes, as well as a "VALID QUOTATION REQUEST." This allows us to specify expectations for how the overall system will respond to these specific interactions, which we know will be different from the general circumstances.

We also now have the definition of an "INVALID QUOTATION REQUEST." This is because it has been noted from past experience that bad requests, if not rejected rapidly, can cause big problems for processing at load. You can see this in the third acceptance criteria block. Overall, this allows us to continue having the benefit of clearly defined, and therefore testable, CFRs that are explicit in their scope.

The specification of testable CFRs is one great way of capturing agreement across the system while allowing for certain parts to be specified more explicitly when they differ from the norm (because "minimum" isn't the same as "least"). You've also seen that the clear definitions not only are a great way to reduce repetitive typing and keep your CFR specifications DRY but also make very clear the scope of where a given CFR's agreement lies. Does it apply to me, the system I'm working on, and the decision I'm taking? I'll check the definition and find out.

Most important, and it bears repeating, despite the fact that you can have additional, more specific CFRs when required, allowing for differences to be detailed where they arise, they still leave a lot of leeway for implementation. As I said earlier, they specify *what* the system must do, not *how* it should do it.

We've dealt with testable CFRs sufficiently to set you up for any further mentions of them in this book. There is a great deal more I could write about them, but this is not the time or place. We have the baseline means of clearly specifying a lowest level means of agreement, but there is space for more.

But agreement on CFRs alone doesn't equal zero surprise. CFRs let us be assured that the system will have a set of qualities, but not how those qualities will be achieved. CFRs explicitly leave open the possibility of everyone and all teams meeting them in their own way, even with the constraining force of the acceptance criteria and shared definitions.

Taken alone, CFRs as a mechanism could still lead to divergence for the sake of it. In fact, in my experience, it frequently does. But there is a corrective mechanism. Werner Vogels once quipped, "You build it, you run it." That's really a pithy way of saying: if you go your own way and choose to do something just for you, then it belongs to you, and you are responsible for looking after it all on your own.

That sounds like a lot of work. Doesn't it make sense, given that we know all the shared requirements in the form of CFRs, to meet some (even all) of them in the same way? The other three alignment mechanisms offer this in different ways. Of these three, technology strategy takes the lead, taking the organization's vision and goals and articulating them in a way that can shape our software.

Technology Strategy

A clear and explicit technology strategy is a second means of making your minimal viable agreement explicit. The absence of a clear technology strategy results in pains I already described: duplication of effort, endless debates on tech direction, or time and effort being spent on matters that don't contribute to the overall attaining of the goal, or the opposite, not enough time being spent on things that could help everyone move in a valuable direction.

Actionable technology strategy, on the other hand, offers a focused perspective on the organization's mission. Everyone knows who the customer is, what those individuals' needs are, and how the organization intends to serve them. When a technology strategy clearly and explicitly interprets an organization's vision and goals, then this "true north" can inform everything done in software.

Technology strategy then is—in simple terms—a statement to the organization as to how the technology parts of that organization will contribute to its mission.

You've seen glimpses of the fruit of this in the "so that" parts of CFRs and in the specifics of some shared definitions. These come from having translated the overall goal (e.g., supporting broker users in selling a certain type of insurance to a certain type of customer in a certain way) into some predictions about what this means in the day-to-day (e.g., the peak number of concurrent insurance quote requests that seems reasonable, given what is known about the market).

What technology strategy does

All good strategy, explicit or implicit, helps an organization focus its journey toward its vision and goals by prioritizing activities (and therefore preferencing decisions) best aligned with its needs and current level of maturity.

There are various flavors of strategy in any organization: product strategy, growth strategy, people strategy, and more. We are interested in the technology flavor, which states, in broad terms, how to best use everything at the disposal of the technical part of the organization. This will cover pure technology aspects such as intellectual property, people aspects (e.g., skills), partnership aspects (e.g., third-party suppliers), and cost aspects. Much of technology strategy directly applies to aspects we are focused on: in-house software and how it ought to be built, integrated, and run.

For those of us who are trying to make and take the best software architecture decisions for our specific circumstances, a technology strategy states what we've agreed we will do, what we won't do, and how we'll do the things we have in common. So what does this mean *in practice?*

How technology strategy works

CFRs are relatively straightforward because the way they are captured is very concrete. They state, very clearly and in detail, *what a system must do.*

Tech strategy is far from this. Strategy is about formalizing guesswork and placing bets. By its very nature, strategy tries to define *how an organization intends to move* from where it is now (probably somewhat known) to a vision of the future (largely unknown in its details) across a space and time period (not only unknown but also unknowable).

Despite being far less detailed, strategy needn't be without discipline. Holacracy (a method of decentralizing organizations) draws a nice distinction. To paraphrase Brian J. Robertson:[7] strategy is not prediction (foretelling, prophesying), it is projecting (throwing something forward).

The best strategies explicitly acknowledge this uncertainty, making the fundamental choices clear. The holacratic approach offers a way to do this where strategy is phrased in the form: "we emphasize X, even at the expense of Y." An alternative way of expressing strategic direction that captures the same concepts of choice and guesswork and is even more action/choice oriented is: "we bet that by doing [this], and not [this], we'll be able to achieve (organizational) outcome [X] despite [this] and [this] happening as a result."

Simon Wardley, another influential voice in the world of strategy, points out in his book *Wardley Maps* (PDF and other formats available on GitHub) (*https://oreil.ly/ Wt59D*) that "strategy is based on position and movement." Not only does strategy need to take into account where you are and where you want to go, but it ought to equally consider how you intend to get there as well as where you won't go. Wardley's point is that a strategy needs to indicate which of a number of possible routes you intend to take—not necessarily in detail but (again) in a way that meaningfully narrows the field of possibilities.

You can see this formulation in the holacratic phrasing, "We emphasize X, even at the expense of Y." We will do one thing, even if it means we don't do this other thing. Failing to do this can lead to near enemies of strategies. I was once advised that a strategy that doesn't say what you won't do is not a strategy. A product manager ex-colleague, Sheen Yap, has an even more memorable way of putting it: "If the opposite of your strategy seems absurd, then it's not a strategy."[8] It's a great test. I encourage you to try it. It's unlikely that what your organization calls its "technology strategy" will be phrased in exactly this way, but trying to articulate it using one or more of these framings will help you evaluate it.[9]

Let's now focus on effective decisions that are aligned with the organizational vision and goals. At the start of this chapter, I mentioned that the potential decision option space for architectural decisions is *massive*. We make this manageable by

---

[7] Brain J. Robertson, *Holacracy: The New Management System for a Rapidly Changing World* (Henry Holt and Company, 2015).

[8] I've since learned that Sheen was paraphrasing Roger L. Martin in his article "The First Question to Ask of Any Strategy" (*https://oreil.ly/KcHY4*). I like Sheen's phrasing better.

[9] There is a great deal you can read on strategy, technology, and otherwise if you are so inclined. I personally found the following very useful: *Enterprise Architecture as Strategy: Creating a Foundation for Business Execution* by Jeanne W. Ross, Peter Weill, and David Robertson (Harvard Business Review Press); Open Group Agile Architecture (*https://oreil.ly/vTbQn*); *Holacracy* by Brian J. Robertson; and *Good Strategy Bad Strategy: The Difference and Why It Matters* by Richard P. Rumelt (Profile Books).

---

appropriately narrowing this space through looking for suitable levels of agreement. There are four means of doing this. At the low-level, specific end, we capture CFRs, which (as the name suggests) "cross the system" and state *what* a system should do.

At the other end—the high-level, fuzzy one—we make clear our bets for *how* we will do it: both the routes we think we will take and the routes we won't take. When we have these in place, suddenly the decision process becomes far more focused, answers to certain key debates can be settled easily, and work can be directed in the right areas in the right amount, with the suitable level of duplication.

Strategy then is a set of answers to the key questions posed by the vision and goals of the organization. Technical strategy says, "Here are our default answers to these important questions." Now that we have clarity on what we should expect from a strategy, we can consider how extensive it needs to be to offer the minimum viable agreement you need.

Technology strategy is a form of agreement

Your organization's minimum viable agreement technology strategy needs to articulate to everyone practicing architecture both the extent and nature of the default answers to the important questions about your organization's vision and goals. Technology strategy ought to be clear whether it covers a lot or a little. It needs to also be clear if there is one way of answering something or if there are many (and in which circumstances each variation applies). Finally, it needs to be clear about how much effort will be put into codifying the strategic direction.

Let's look at how tech strategy is a form of agreement by returning to some of the examples from earlier in this chapter. I'll use these examples to explain the key aspects of tech strategy.

Strategy can answer a little or a lot. You'll recall that I shared the story earlier (in "You're Aligned When You're Not Surprised" on page 216) about Organization Y, which had "domain-aligned microservices written in Kotlin, C#, and Go." As clients go, that's actually pretty permissive. I mostly see clients who strategically mandate a single language (or set of languages—JavaScript always seems to make its way in somehow) and a single overarching framework. This is typically because investment has been made in hiring people with these specific skills and in supporting infrastructure to assist them in their work (binary artifact repositories, build pipelines, IDEs, etc.).

This isn't always the case. Think back to the client from "You're Aligned When You're Not Surprised" who hadn't mandated any specific language or framework, but everything had tended toward Python and Django anyway. What's important in this scenario isn't that the lack of strategy meant there had been alignment anyway but that the choice of language wasn't important to the organization's strategy. I was present in discussions with teams who were debating the selection of other languages for specific jobs. This was perfectly relevant to do. They knew that if they did select an additional language, they would need to learn it and make it work with the surrounding infrastructure.

You could also see this in the various mentions of cloud provider. I've seen clients whose strategy stops at the answer "use this cloud vendor, and no other." That's it—they don't extend into which cloud services teams can and can't use. On the other hand, I've seen clients where their strategy not only specifies what types of services but also in what regions of the world they must run and what default configurations they must have.

In all cases, there ought to be a justifiable reason for the extent of the strategic direction. Remember, we're looking for a minimum viable agreement here and no more.

Strategy can offer a single answer or multiple answers to a given question. A strategic direction can provide one answer, which it is hoped is the default answer for all circumstances. But there is another approach that is sometimes useful.

Organization Y (from "You're Aligned When You're Not Surprised" on page 216) had selected AWS as its cloud provider of choice, and that was where all its domain-aligned microservices were running. I described how a new data team had come along and was looking to use a different cloud provider—Google Cloud Platform (GCP), in this case. As I mentioned earlier, this didn't mean that the original strategic direction ("use AWS cloud services for all hosting") was wrong but that it needed more nuance. After a lot of due diligence to make sure that matters like the cost and complexities of multiple cloud providers weren't untenable and that the new data folks didn't just want to use GCP because they felt more comfortable with it, the strategy could be rewritten as follows: "use AWS cloud services for hosting business applications and use GCP cloud services for data applications."

Think back to the example of the insurance broker SaaS organization that had previously aimed for one type of customer, which had led it to focus its implementation of its lines of business support solely on the "predictable, industry-standard, run fast and reliably at massive scale" part of the market, to the exclusion of a "bespoke, configurable, smaller scale" implementation that would support a different type of client. This was derived directly from the vision and goals of the business, which had been focused in the same direction. But when the business decided to start expanding into different markets, it became clear that there was no longer one answer to this strategic direction and consequently, no longer a single answer to the technical strategy in this area. Again, the direction here would have been a shift from "support standard lines of business at scale" to "support standard lines of business at scale, and support moves into bespoke lines of business in niche markets." This makes it clear to deciders that there are two answers to a given question, so when they are making and taking decisions, it will pay to know which of the two they need to take into account.

Strategic investments codify strategic direction. This brings us to the last key aspect of an actionable technical strategy. You'd be forgiven for assuming that technology strategy is codified simply as words on a page (or on a slide), and that's it. The words are written, and the assumption is that the teams will follow them to the letter.

At the end of "Cross-Functional Requirements" on page 220, I said that the best CFRs described *what* a system should do but not *how* it should do it. I also borrowed Vogels's point that sometimes it makes sense to take advantage of the work of others rather than doing everything yourself.

When a technology strategy complements your CFRs, you can invest in more than words on a page. Instead, you can put real time, money, and people behind an agreement in the form of shared services.[10] Here are the levels of investment in these strategic services that I use:

Level 0: Words only
> For example: "Use AWS cloud services for all hosting, even though we could host a more appropriate version ourselves." This not only results in lots of different specific "implementations" of the thing (even if it's only in the form of cloud automation scripts or how-tos on team wiki pages) but also in no sharing of experiences. The same issues are encountered and subsequently solved each time.

Level 1: "Speak to this expert"
> There are one or more known experts in the organization who *at the very least* have experience setting this strategic thing up for themselves and can help others to do it, too. This results in lots of copies of the same thing all over the place, each probably a little different because of the lessons learned from doing the last one and the vagaries of the specific circumstances at hand.

Level 2: "On-request"
> There is one place to go to get the shared work done and a person, or group of people, whose job is, at least in part, to do this work. They are most likely relying on some repeatable artifacts they have produced to make this work simpler. They still need to be involved to do the work, however, even if they are running some automation or are using some templates that they created. There will most likely be a delay between the request being logged and the work being done.

---

10 As I write, this is currently called a *platform* looked after and managed by a platform team. Frankly, the term is now so widely used that it's beginning to lose all meaning, sometimes seeming as if *everyone* wants to build a platform instead of delivering value to an organization's end users.

Level 3: "Self-service"

Teams (and others) who need the work done can self-serve (by running a job, or filling in a template, or calling an API, or depending on a library). The service that is self-served is built and maintained by the expert group, and they will roll out upgrades, bug fixes, and so forth. The teams (and others) who depend on this don't need to think about any of that besides considering when to deploy the upgrades.

Investment Doesn't Automatically Make Something Strategic

Just because there is an investment in shared efforts doesn't mean that what they produce is strategic. I'll cover methods for providing feedback on current technology strategy in Chapters 10 and 11. There is also a separate article (*https://oreil.ly/0sXxN*) on the accompanying website that explicitly tackles the use of technology radars with regard to strategy.

It is important to acknowledge the tension inherent in these increasingly codified strategic services because they are, well, centralized. We'll also see in the next two chapters how the presence of such strategic services shouldn't in any way remove the decision rights of individuals. But does that mean that if you can't mandate that a shared service is used, investment in it will be a waste?

It's worth making clear that just because a service is shared, it needn't be low quality; it ought to be the opposite. The strongest argument for a central service should be that it takes away the grunt work of meeting CFRs and lowers the cognitive load of teams. A current example of this is infrastructure scripting languages in development teams. I've very rarely seen any who relish rolling up their sleeves to fix problems in the Terraform scripts when something goes wrong. Far better if the standard, shared pieces are maintained centrally in a way that can be self-served.

If we listen to Vogels, if we build it, then we *must* run it, so there is sense in investing in centralized strategic services. There is a benefit in *not* building something in that you don't then have to run it. Take, for example, the case of a new regulation appearing with regard to the encryption of data at rest and in transit. Even if an individual team no longer needs to keep any eye out themselves for these changes because of their access to system-wide deciding via an advice forum and open ADRs, if the infrastructure is all hand-rolled within the team, then the only people the team has recourse to when implementing any new requirement is themselves. That's a waste of their time as well as a hassle, distracting the team from their more important, more exciting work.

In summary, technology strategy can offer a great way to not only have a minimal viable agreement on the "how" of software but also lead you toward some actual shared code to back it up.

Working Toward Your Organization's Minimal Viable Agreement

So what does the combination of just enough testable CFRs and just enough technical strategy give you? The authors of *Enterprise Architecture as Strategy* call it a "foundation for execution." This foundation gives clarity on both the "what" (cross-functional requirements) and the "how" (technical strategy), both aligned with the overall organization's vision and goals. It's the solid base on which all our decisions can be made and taken, and consequently on which our systems can be built.

As discussed, when working toward your organization's minimum viable agreement, start with making sure your CFRs are testable, following the guidance in this chapter to do so. As for your technology strategy, developing one from scratch is outside of the scope of this book. However, if you have a go at articulating it in one of the formats I shared, such as "we emphasize X, even at the expense of Y" or even "we bet that by doing [this], and not [this], we'll be able to achieve (organizational) outcome [X] despite [this] and [this] happening as a result," then you'll have the means to engage those who do own it (typically "chief," "IT," or "enterprise" architects). I'm confident they'll welcome such an engagement with one of the primary tools in their kit bag.

Conclusion

The goal of this chapter was to help you to see the importance of organizational alignment because without that, your software is in great danger of failing to deliver value. I described the goal in this decentralized, feedback-centering world as being a minimal viable agreement. I also showed you how staying alert for surprises at the decisions of others is a great way to spot when this agreement is lacking.

I then described the second supporting element that offers a means of achieving this via CFRs, which answered the "what" questions, combined with an actionable technology strategy, which answered the "how." In doing so, I was able to go into more detail on CFRs because they are more specific to you and the software you build. Technology strategy, on the other hand, is less within your control. But there are two ways to make it more directly relevant and also feed the strategic investments. I'll cover both of these remaining two supporting elements in the final two chapters of Part II.

CHAPTER 10

Collectively Sourced
Architectural Principles

In the previous chapter, I argued that while a technology strategy is essential for effective alignment, it is rarely sufficiently specific to guide day-to-day architectural decision making, specifically when answering the question *"How* will we do this?" For that, a greater level of detail about the shared agreement is required.

This chapter introduces one way of achieving that detail: explicitly capturing architectural principles—which are key commitments, the third alignment mechanism—that make clear how you collectively intend to construct and run your software systems. I'll introduce you to what good architectural principles look like, how they fit into the advice process, how to source them from teams, and how they evolve as time passes.

Having architectural principles in place will mitigate the three warning signs of lacking essential agreement: decisions that lead to duplication of nondifferentiating efforts, repeated debates about the same fundamental points, and technical decisions taking precedence over functional ones.

Source Architectural Principles from Everyone Involved

Architectural principles are a means of capturing key agreements regarding *how* you collectively intend to design your software systems. They are a practical embodiment of your organization's tech strategy that help keep everyone's decisions aligned with the organization's overall direction. They are another means of articulating your minimum viable agreement described in Chapter 9.

A set of principles transforms the organization's abstract vision and goals into a form that can be used to direct software development and make concrete decisions. Targeted, explicit architectural principles are an incredibly powerful tool, but they are (in my experience, at least) rarely conceived and deployed effectively.

Failure to take advantage of architectural principles is problematic in any approach, but in a decentralized, feedback-centric world like ours, having effective principles becomes essential. This is because they are superb at aligning decisions effectively without the need for imposing any form of hierarchical or outside control. Poorly conceived principles don't just fail to offer this collective commitment to alignment but actually get in the way, undermining the ability of the advice process to build trust, enable learning, and deliver high-quality decentralized decisions at a pace that factors in feedback.

The best way to capture architectural principles and ensure that they align with your organization's goals and vision is to source them from a broad range of people, including all teams. By including the collective, you both sidestep the accusation that the principles are being imposed from elsewhere and get the benefit of having coverage of all aspects of the system from a far wider variety of perspectives. Better principles result—ones that actually assist in deciding and that everyone feels a stake in. Let's begin by spending a little time considering the nature of principles themselves.

Examples of Architectural Principles

At a minimum, *architectural principles* should consist of a title that describes the principle, a subtitle that is a call to action, the rationale as it pertains to your core domain or organizational mission, and the implications to the same. There are further elements that could be added, but I'll discuss those later in this chapter.

The following are two examples of good architectural principles. We can begin with one that I wrote based on the Team Topologies (*https://oreil.ly/EZqqQ*) "stream-aligned team" organization model:

EXAMPLE

Principle: Value independence of teams most highly.

Subtitle: Split solutions along team lines.

Rationale: The strength of our approach to building and running our suite of products relies fundamentally on the independence of our teams and the flexibility it gives them to address market opportunities. The downsides to this are acknowledged, but the upsides are felt to outweigh it, especially when the difficulty of predicting future needs is taken into consideration.

Implications:

- Duplication of both function and data will inevitably arise. Rather than fight this, we embrace it, acknowledging the need, in certain circumstances, for noticeable eventual consistency and data replication.

- The combined licensing, runtime, and support costs of multiple third-party solutions may be higher than the costs of a single, shared, cross-product-team solution.

- Solutions can be designed for the needs of the team that owns and runs them. They need not concern themselves with the needs of other teams.

- Both systems and the third-party services/solutions they are built on will tend to be smaller and more specifically task focused.

- Teams that go their own way need to self-support any third-party services/solutions that they adopt independently.

Some organizations share their principles publicly, such as the John Lewis Partnership, which inspired the second example (*https://oreil.ly/Wz7n4*):

EXAMPLE

Principle: "Cloud native" means our cloud.

Subtitle: Take advantage of the effort the Infrastructure Platform team puts into making the cloud consumable.

Rationale: Strategic investment to package our self-serve cloud native services helps us focus on building differentiators and supporting a rapid pace of change, while reducing operational complexity and managing overarching systems. This is particularly important where we run a larger set of distributed, smaller systems, which need to operate independently, for example, in the smaller divisions of the business.

Implications:

- Use the Infrastructure Platform as the runtime for business services, as it has been built specifically for our needs, and provides a curated set of tools and services to achieve this.

- Don't couple business services to the underlying cloud provider's offerings in any way.

- Only the Infra team can build bespoke extensions to their Infrastructure Platform. Instead, engage the Infrastructure Platform team to extend their offering for you.

- Build business services to take advantage of cloud features, and be tolerant of cloud failure scenarios. For example, consider variable network conditions and minimizing local state to support automatic scaling.

- Abstract compute, storage, and network resources from business services, isolating them from underlying infrastructure dependencies and therefore improving portability.

Let's see now how these principles might fit into the advice process and how you'll see this in the resulting ADRs.

Characteristics of Good Architectural Principles

So what makes a good architectural principle? For me, it's the following:

- It must explicitly link back to one or more of the organization's strategic goals.

- It should have a simple name that has a clear meaning and is easy for everyone to remember.

- It should indicate "how" something should be done.

- It must articulate the consequences/implications it necessarily contains within it (the results of applying the principle).

- It provides criteria with which to evaluate architectural decisions and therefore help you pick one option over another (which in practice means a principle must be "S.M.A.R.T"[1]).

S.M.A.R.T. Criteria for Evaluating Architectural Principles

Specific
They are not fuzzily or generically worded.

Measurable
They must be bounded.

Achievable
They must be possible to both design and implement using current technologies.

---

[1] The careful reader will have noticed that this is similar, but not the same as the *SMART* used to describe things like user stories or, more generally, goals in some walk of life (where *R* stands for "relevant" and *T* for "time-bound"). This articulation comes from *The Art of Scalability* (Addison Wesley Professional, 2015).

Realistic
> The collective and the organization must be capable of delivering them.

Testable
> The principle can be used in "testing" any potential architectural decision.

While these are the desirable characteristics of a principle taken on its own, a lone principle won't be sufficient to offer you the minimal viable agreement you require. Between 8 and 15 architectural principles is the sweet spot. A set of architectural principles should number neither too few to cover the key commitments that architectural principles articulate nor too many that teams cannot remember them all. This is important because you're looking for your principles to support decisions within the architecture advice process by articulating shared commitments. For them to work effectively it's essential that they make sense, fitting comfortably in the heads of everyone doing any deciding. Hence, the 8–15 principles.

By "fitting comfortably," I mean the principles shouldn't be in conflict or directly contradict one another, but it is entirely possible (desirable even) that they are in tension. The goal of a set of useful principles is to guide and nudge decisions so that they keep everything and everyone headed toward the overall organizational goal.

Consider the two example principles you just saw: "Value independence of teams most highly" and "'Cloud native' means our cloud." It is conceivable that the first principle could lead a team to consider rolling their own Kafka cluster on top of Amazon Elastic Kubernetes Service (EKS) as opposed to using Amazon Managed Streaming for Apache Kafka (MSK), which other teams are using. I've seen this happen when, to get the control they need or to manage costs effectively, teams take on the additional responsibility themselves.

The tension between these two is a healthy one. It ensures that during deciding, the compromises are only those that are necessary, and they are made clear to the teams or individuals making them. In this example, it is clear that additional responsibility is to be taken on by going it alone, which will mean that the team will be motivated to reduce the scope of this deviation as much as possible.

Characteristics of Poor Architectural Principles

And the near enemies? Poor architectural principles share one or more few key characteristics. They conflate principles with practice, or they are unrelated to architecture.

First, architectural principles are not practices. Principles describe how things in your architecture "happen or work." Practices tell you *how to make* those things. Some examples of practices are TDD, trunk-based delivery, and pair programming. These practices are ones I advocate for myself, but they're not *architectural* principles. If a principle doesn't provide you with the means to evaluate the various options in an ADR, then it's a waste of one of your 8–15 principle slots.

Principles can be unrelated to architecture as well. Think, for example, of the various principles you'll see around project planning (of which the 12 principles behind the Agile Manifesto (*https://oreil.ly/LDMiz*) are the best example) and software quality management ("shift security left").

Architectural principles are a means of stating your collectively agreed commitments regarding how you will design your systems. As such, they direct your architectural practice and evaluate your decision options. Architectural principles help pick among various approaches to implementing micro frontends (*https://oreil.ly/kdrux*), or help decide if it really makes sense to hand roll an OAuth 2.0 implementation,[2] or guide an evaluation of a self-hosted Lucene (*https://lucene.apache.org*) on AWS versus Amazon OpenSearch Service (*https://aws.amazon.com/elasticsearch-service*).

Principles Can Be Cross-Functional Requirements in Disguise

Principles can also sometimes be CFRs in disguise. How might you spot when this happens?

CFRs are about very specific matters. The example CFRs in the previous chapter covered topics such as exactly what will be logged how and where, expected response times down to the millisecond for either a part or the whole of your system, that you will encrypt data in transit to meet certain standards, and so on. Architectural principles are far more general: "value independence," for example.

This means that, while CFRs are nonnegotiable, principles are there to help, but it's not necessary to follow them blindly, especially when there are two principles in tension (in those cases, it is likely impossible to meet both, and that is perfectly fine).

Third, CFRs say "what" but not "how." Principles say "how," not "what." While CFRs are outside the implementation black box, telling you what they expect, architectural principles are inside the box giving you advice, saying, "This is the way we usually do it."

---

2 The answer is almost definitely "no," but perhaps you're that one organization where it would make sense. But, as Schneier's Law (*https://oreil.ly/9u5dX*) states: "Any person can invent a security system so clever that she or he can't think of how to break it."

Architectural Principles Complement an Advice Process and ADRs

Principles are shared commitments, nudging all decisions in the direction deemed appropriate for achieving the organization's vision and goals. This doesn't mean that all principles will apply to all decisions; they won't, and if this is your experience, then either the decision you are currently considering is *way* too large or your principles are not S.M.A.R.T. enough. I'll come back to how to make your decisions the right size in Chapter 13.

As a decider, whenever a new decision comes up, it pays to take a quick scan of your list of principle titles and see if any are applicable. If any are, it is likely you will already know what the principle is, and if not, you can read the description and the rationale, confirming if it is relevant to the decision at hand.

It also pays to reread the implications. This primes your mind to focus the options space. But this focusing need not simply be a narrowing. Sometimes, a principle will prompt a decider to think about something that they might not have considered because it isn't "the best option" for them. This is one of the key benefits of principles: they remind everyone making individual, point decisions of the broader commitments that keep the collective headed toward the organization's vision and goals.

As the deciding proceeds, the applicable principle(s) can also offer nudges as to consequences of various options (ideal for listing in your ADR's Consequences sections). Again, this is helpful because it helps you focus this aspect of the option making and then take steps in a direction that makes a positive difference to the organization.

Principles will also likely come up during advice seeking and offering. If a principle has been missed or misapplied, then it is likely this will be commented on (which is welcome).

I've frequently found it useful to add a section to the top of the ADR where applicable principles can be listed. It takes up very little space, and it primes the reader as to the broader context within which this decision sits. It's also handy to link the title of an applicable principle in an ADR to the principle details. This is not only beneficial to those who are unaware of the details of the principle, but it also means that if principles change in the future (which I'll get onto later in this chapter), you have a persistent, point-in-time link to the principles that applied at the time of the decision, greatly increasing the value of the ADR as a point in the historical record of your architecture.

More generally, deciders should feel free to link to principles in any of the other sections of an ADR that I outlined in Chapter 6.

Capturing Your Architectural Principles with a Principles Workshop

You're hopefully sufficiently interested to experiment with an explicit set of principles. How might you go about getting them in place? You may already have something called "architectural" or "engineering principles" in your organization, but you aren't satisfied with how they're working. I frequently encounter them as an architectural artifact, created by architects and consumed by architects but never really relied upon outside that group. This is usually the root cause of the problems.

The way to ensure that architectural principles work for all deciders is to get everyone working to build and run software capturing (and maintaining) them together. This approach also offers an opportunity for everyone to engage with the organizational vision and goals and the resulting technical strategy, to understand them and consider what they all mean for the practice of software architecture.

You can put an explicit set of architectural principles into place by holding a workshop, including both development teams and architects. This allows everyone to engage directly with your organization's vision, goals, and tech strategy, and consider what they mean for the practice of software architecture. In the spirit of decentralized deciding, this workshop could be convened and run by anyone, but it is most likely that the person kicking it off will be someone playing an architecture role.

To have a productive principles workshop, I suggest using an approach inspired by the *Art of Scalability* by Martin L. Abbot and Michael T. Fisher (Addison-Wesley). One key aspect of this approach is their argument that for any set of architectural principles to be successful, teams that deliver against them need to feel a sense of ownership.

Facilitating Creative Workshops

There are more facilitation notes and tips in the following subsections than anywhere else in this book. This is because they describe a large-scale, co-creation workshop that works best when split across multiple sessions. I've tried to provide enough detail for those new to such a role without getting in the way of the description of the workshop itself.

If you are already an experienced facilitator, then feel free to skim these facilitation notes. If you find them useful and want more, the short Thoughtworks article "Workshop Wisdom" (*https://oreil.ly/uW4xj*) has great ideas, as does a vast array of the contents of *Collaborative Software Design* by Evelyn van Kelle, Gien Verschatse, and Kenny Baas-Schwegler (Manning).

Preparing the Inputs for Your Principles Workshop

Before you run a principles workshop, you need sufficient information about your organization's goals and visionary objectives because they provide the means to validate every potential architectural principle as it arises. They also offer the ability to see that you are not biased in favor of one aspect of the organization's focus at the expense of others. Consequently, prior to your workshop, it is essential to have both your goals and your visionary objectives stated in such a way that they can inform your principle discovery.

Sourcing your organization's goals

Prepare by gathering info about your organization's goals. These can be pretty fuzzy in their natural state, in which case you will need to distill them into something significantly more concrete.

Start with whatever you can get your hands on that gives you an up-to-date view of your organization's overarching vision and goals. This can be a generally available presentation or a document that ideally sets out the current vision as well as one or more explicit goals, each with specific target metrics and dates against it. These might be things like "reduce operating costs by 20% of the current total by 31 December," for example, or "release [existing product X] in three more countries by the end of Q4," or even "complete the merger with [acquired company Y] by the end of next calendar year." The document you have might contain many of these or only a few. If you have this level of detail, then you're lucky. If it's not available (and I'm constantly surprised as to how frequently this kind of thing isn't available), then you'll have to do a little detective work and pull things together for yourself.

If you're engaging in detective mode, begin with some preliminary research. Look first at your organization's website. It will usually state—although at a high level— what its mission or goals are. If you are a public company, then you can also look at financial reports as there will usually be a set of statements as to how the leaders in the company see the future and what they are doing to prepare for it. You can also glean a wealth of detail from sessions like town halls, major announcements, and the like.

Informed by this, you can then talk to your exec in charge (typically, it's a CTO, but it can be a CIO or a COO, and you might also have someone called a "chief scientist" who will have opinions on the organization's priorities). Starting at the top of your part of the organization means you'll get the most senior person's views on the organization's priorities. Chief product officers, chief digital officers, and chief data officers may also have useful inputs.

When you have this "top of the tree" information, you can validate if you think it's necessary by asking those at the next level down from the C-suite in the hierarchy for their current perspectives on the topic. You will want those playing roles with titles like "enterprise architect" or "chief architect." Much of what they provide may already be articulated through a technical strategy lens, and you'll want to see if you can link this back up to the organizational vision and goals. This should be relatively simple, and if it's not, then it's a good opportunity to point this out or to fix it if you have the power to do that.

Extracting three themes

Whatever means you employ to get your organizational vision and goals, and assuming they are consistent (or you've managed to make them consistent), you are ready to start identifying themes. By *themes*, I mean a concept that recurs throughout something, and you are looking for three of them. It sounds like an arbitrary number, but in my experience, it's not only possible to settle on this number but also sensible. The goal is that your themes will be both collectively exhaustive and mutually exclusive. That is to say, taken together, your themes will encompass all the aspects of your vision and goals, while individually, each theme doesn't overlap with either of the other two.

Let's look at an example from my personal experience. The client was a scale-up that was in the process of transitioning from one business model (shrink-wrapped software) to another (SaaS). They were operating in a competitive environment and focused (at least for the time being) on a few countries, where their immediate growth was expected to come from migrating their old customers onto their new offering. They would offer a better-quality service than their customers were used to, with incremental additions of market-leading features to entice new customers and keep the existing ones satisfied and disinclined to move.

Luckily for us, the organizational and product goals were clear, and more important, no massaging was needed to elicit the themes, which were as follows:

- Operational excellence
- Customer responsiveness
- Product leadership

It's worth a few words on each to be clear on what they mean so that you can be assured they are both exhaustive and mutually exclusive:

Operational excellence

This meant "how systems are run." The client knew their customers had surrendered their local instances of the software for a SaaS service so expected it to be better run than when they ran things themselves.

Customer responsiveness

This meant how individual customers experienced the SaaS product. These customers were previously used to having their own copies of the software, which was set up and configured for them and their needs. They should continue to feel as if they were the only people using the new SaaS version, able to have significant control over certain aspects of the SaaS product suite—both the elements they chose to license and their ability to have full visibility of their usage of the platform and how much individual features were costing them.

Product leadership

This referred to the client's ability to deliver new and innovative features to their target customer segments, driving existing markets forward and potentially opening up new markets in the process.

Hopefully, these examples give you an impression of how you might take your organization's vision and goals and gather them into three separate but complementary themes. But what if you're not lucky enough to have such clarity? What if the strategy is either missing entirely or simply useless?

In that case, you need a little more help. Sara Taraporewalla's article "Creating an Integrated Business and Technology Strategy" (*https://oreil.ly/umIgG*) provides a structure you can use to interpret your organizational inputs, whatever form they come in, and from there distill your themes. I've simplified[3] the groupings she uses for the various types of strategy[4] as follows:

- Grow our impact
  - Expand to complementary products
  - Expand to new markets/regions
  - Expand customer segments
  - Inorganic growth

---

3 I've moved a few around, shortened a few of the titles, and removed others. The ones I dropped, while important to overall technology strategy, don't lead to architectural principles.

4 This gives a nice balance between "revenue growth" and "revenue protection." You can also think of it as "external value orientation" and "internal value orientation," which are terms the EDGE/Lean Value Tree approach uses. See *EDGE: Value-Driven Digital Transformation* by Jim Highsmith, Linda Luu, and David Robinson (Addison Wesley).

- Strengthen our foundations
  - Accelerate time to value
  - Increase customer satisfaction with improved quality
  - Reduce cost and minimize operational risk
  - Enhance organizational decision making
  - Internal and back-office systems

Each of these subbullets is a potential strategic direction that an organization can pursue, and your organization will very likely be pursuing multiple (either consciously or unconsciously).

Let's see how the SaaS example maps to this structure. Considering the strategies under the first heading, "grow our impact," my client had strategies to expand to complementary products as well as customer segments. They were not growing inorganically (acquiring other companies), nor were they intending to move into new markets or regions.

Considering the strategies under the second heading, "strengthen our foundations," the client was very keen to "increase customer satisfaction with improved quality" and "reduce cost and minimize operational risk." "Accelerate time to value" was particularly important for the client, but not in the standard way. Their move to a SaaS model was going to allow them to get customers up and running on their product faster (no more on-prem servers to procure and set up for each of their individual customers, and they were intending to invest in simplified data onboarding support). Their approach to SaaS was also intended to allow their customers to select which modules from their suite of offerings they wanted to have, which clients could self-serve by enabling or disabling themselves. For their customer base, this was the kind of responsivity they were looking for.

Taken together, this gives us three themes as follows:

- Grow through new products and new customer segments
- Increase customer satisfaction
- Reduce cost and minimize operational risk

If you look back to the themes from before, they're satisfyingly close.

Setting Up Your Principles Workshop

Once you have identified your three themes, you are ready to set up for your principles workshop. As the convener of the workshop, you'll also be the facilitator. This means you will be there at the start before everyone else and there at the end tidying up after everyone has left. More importantly, it means you will be responsible for

ensuring that the agenda is understood and followed and that everyone can participate and bring their expertise and experience to bear.

To convene the workshop, you'll need to:

- Identify who to invite
- Find a time block (or two) where everyone is available and send invites
- Prepare the space/online board for the workshop

Let's step through each of these in turn.

Identify invitees

An architectural principles workshop benefits from having a lot of people present
who represent a broad range of stakeholder groups. You should look to invite everyone from software development, infrastructure, operations, software/systems architecture, security, UI/UX, product, and (if it's of particular importance to your
company) regulatory and/or legal. Not everyone needs to come, especially if the
potential attendee list is massive, but you should rearrange if you can't get at least one
developer per team and at least one person representing each of the other roles. I've
run this with groups of more than a hundred attendees, but make sure numbers aren't
getting bigger than you are comfortable with.

You should also make sure that no group is over- or underrepresented. The point of
this session is to bring together various viewpoints and ensure that a broad consensus
is reached on the set of architectural principles. If some attendees walk away feeling
as if their views have been ignored, then the desired outcomes (a key set of widely
understood commitments that will align everyone to the organization's vision and
goals) will not be achieved.

Find a time for the workshop and book it

You will need three hours total to run the workshop, but it actually works best if you
split it into two sessions of one and a half hours each, with a night, or even a weekend, between the first and the second parts. This gives attendees time to mull over
what they heard in the first half of the workshop and bring anything they think of to
the second part. They don't even need to actively do this—things will just pop into
their heads.

Once you know where you will all convene, send out the invite with a link to the
agenda. The following is an example agenda for a two-part workshop; I'll talk about
each activity in a later section:

Session 1 (if you're splitting the workshop over two days)
- Kickoff: goal of the workshop, our organization's vision and goals, and key definitions.
- Split: group breakout to propose architectural principles.
- Reconvene: each group shares their initial principles.
- Split (again): modify principles as individual groups.

Session 2 (f you're splitting the workshop over two days)
- Re-reconvene: groups present again, and duplicate principles are identified.
- Dot-voting (round 1): everyone votes on the collated principles and the top 8–15 are selected.
- Black-hat session: consider implications.
- Dot-voting (round 2): The whole group debates the resulting principles. Another vote is held, and the principles are reranked.
- Commit to adoption and close: everyone commits to adopting the selected principles.

Prepare the workshop space

Your final act of preparation is to make sure you have the space set up in advance. You will need the following:

- A welcome area
- A definitions and criteria area
- The collaborative working area
- Working group breakout areas
- A parking lot to capture topics for future discussion

If the workshop is in person, you will need paper to write the various areas on, some sticky notes, and some markers.[5] It helps a lot to lay these areas out along the wall or virtual board in this order.

---

5 Sharpies, or some other strong-colored marker, show up the best when photographed. This is important if you intend to take pictures of the workshop notes for record.

The welcome area should have the agenda for the session(s) and the intended outcome. You can take the agenda from your invitation, and the intended outcome should be something along the lines of "Align on 8–15 S.M.A.R.T. architectural principles to help us deliver on the organization's three strategic themes."

The definitions and criteria area should have both the definition of an architectural principle (e.g., "a basic idea or rule that explains how the architecture works") and each of the S.M.A.R.T. principle's criteria. If you have existing architectural principles, capture one or two of them in the target format. (If you don't have these, then you can just use the examples from earlier). See the example in Figure 10-1.

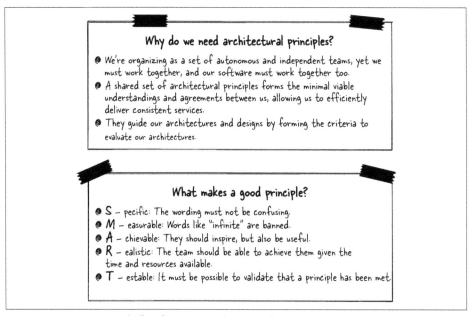

Figure 10-1. An example "Definitions and Criteria" area

The collaborative working area is where the shared view of principles will come together. At its center is a three-circle Venn diagram as shown in Figure 10-2. (If it's physical, this will be about three to four feet in height. It's going to end up with a lot of sticky notes on it at the end.)

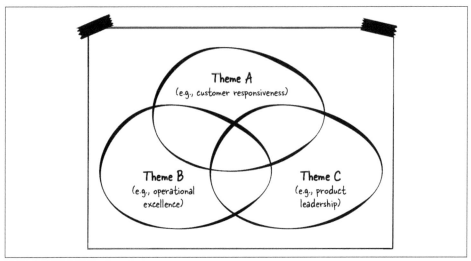

Figure 10-2. The "three strategic themes" layout for the principle workshop's collaboration area—note the three themes here will be different for your workshop

Each circle in this Venn diagram is one of the three themes you previously identified in your preparation. Why are the three themes set out like this Venn diagram? Because this will allow us to identify principles that align to one, two, or all three themes. While the themes themselves need to be "exhaustive and mutually exclusive" as I mentioned earlier, the principles that deliver them don't need to be. This layout allows everyone to see if a theme is under- or overrepresented by the principles being captured.

It also helps to have a key off to one side of this area that clarifies what is meant by each theme. See the previous explanations for these example themes for an idea of what to include. It should be easy to refer to these theme clarifiers as the workshop proceeds. An example of this is shown in Figure 10-3.

The group breakout areas are placed around this collaborative working area. In both a physical and virtual space, these will likely be to the right. In a physical space, this can be any surface where sticky notes will stick. A six-foot by four-foot area is sufficient for this. The key point to bear in mind is that at various points in the workshop, breakout groups will be moving their proposed principles into this shared area.

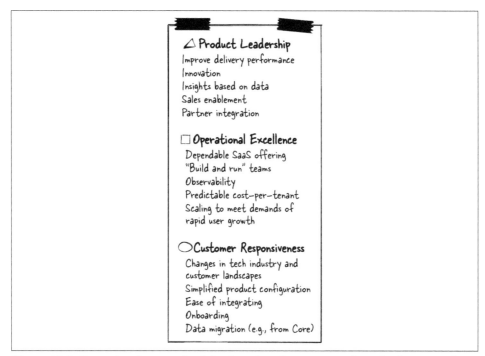

Figure 10-3. Extra details on each of the three key themes—note how this layout makes clear how the principles should directly contribute to the achievement of the goals

Finally, the parking lot is where the workshop facilitators can put topics that come up during the course of the workshop but that don't fit in the agenda. When they come up, someone writes whatever it is on a (virtual) sticky note and puts it in the parking lot. If there is time at the end of the workshop, then these items can be returned to. With all this ready, you are now ready for the workshop.

Running Your Principles Workshop

Whoever is facilitating should ensure that the agenda is understood and followed and that everyone can participate fully, bringing their expertise and experience to bear.

Kickoff: Goal of the workshop, goal of the organization, and key definitions (10 minutes)

Begin the session by sharing the goal of the workshop. Answer any questions and offer clarifications as required. Refer to the areas you have prepared, as people will want to read as well as hear the information and refer back to it during the course of proceedings.

Next, show attendees around the space you've prepared (virtual or physical). Start with a reminder of your organization's vision and goals. Then explain the themes that were distilled from this and the structure of the Venn diagram area. Clarify what an architectural principle is and explain the S.M.A.R.T. criteria for critiquing them. Mention that if anything comes up that is not on the agenda, it'll be captured and put into the parking lot for later discussion. Give attendees an opportunity to ask questions.

Close out the kickoff by organizing the attendees into working groups—the number will depend on the number of attendees. It's important to ensure broad representation of viewpoints in each team. The best way to do this is to ask everyone to group together based on their job role. (If you're meeting virtually, you can get them to write their names on virtual sticky notes and group them by role.) Teams should comprise one person per job role. If one job role is heavily represented (probably developers), then you can put two of each of these folks into each team. A nice way to achieve this is to make these division rules clear and allow everyone to self-organize.

Split: Groups break out to propose architectural principles (30 minutes)

Working groups then split up and capture as many architectural principles as they can think of. The goal at this point is to get as many as possible. The most efficient way to do this can be for everyone to work individually for a fixed period of time, writing each principle on a separate sticky note, and come back together to explain and deduplicate.

Principles should be captured at the title plus (ideally) the subtitle level. There is no need to write the rationale or implications; those come later. The primary goal here is breadth not depth, and a free flow of ideas is welcome. Encourage attendees—for now, at least—to disengage their critical minds, even forgetting about the S.M.A.R.T. criteria.

As this slot comes to an end, the team should collate their principles, deduplicate them, and select one of their members to present them when everyone reconvenes. This might involve a bit of discussion as individual principles are explained. If it is not clear if two principles really are duplicates, then simply place them next door to each other, ready to present both, one after the other. As facilitator, encourage everyone to apply the S.M.A.R.T. principles. They take a bit of getting used to, and you will very likely see well-meaning suggestions of general principles such as KISS ("Keep it simple, stupid!" a principle first noted in the US Navy in 1960) and DRY that, though laudable, don't meet the key S.M.A.R.T. criteria. You can see an example of this collation in Figure 10-4.

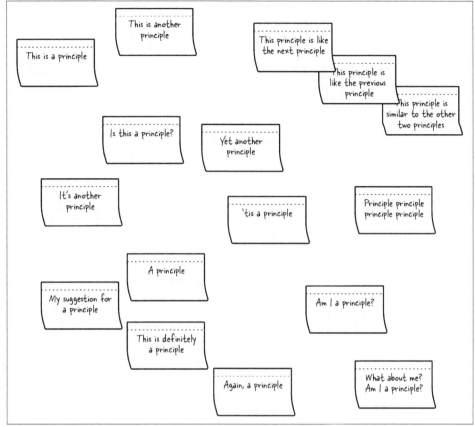

Figure 10-4. How a group's breakout area might look at the end of the first "split" slot, with principles spread around and some grouped if they seem to be the same

Reconvene: Each group shares their initial principles (20 minutes)

Once the time is up for the initial principle collection, bring everyone back together. Explain that each group will now present their principles to the collective. Make it clear that the goal is to understand what other teams have done in enough detail so that you can steal any principles that you hear about from others. You want your group to have *at least* eight principles at this stage that you think are suitable. It's not a competition. Such "copying others' homework" is encouraged.

Each group then presents their principles, in no particular order. They can make it clear if one of their principles is similar to those from another group but isn't a duplicate. Once all the teams have presented their principles, it's time to split up again.

Split: Modify principles as individual groups (30 minutes)

The teams split again. The idea this time is for each group to update their principles, based on how their viewpoints have changed after hearing everyone else's ideas.

This is also the first time when teams should think about where each of their principles sits on the "strategic themes" Venn diagram and capture any implications that arise. What teams are looking for is good coverage of all areas of the Venn diagram, without major bias toward or away from any one theme. Implications should also be captured uncritically at this point, again relying on the free flow of conversation and ideas to unlock everyone's creativity.

To map their principles locally to strategic themes, each team can simply ask, "Does this support the first theme?" If it does, then it should be tagged as going in that theme's circle. They then ask, "Does it support the second theme?" If it does, it should be tagged with that theme too, mapping to the part of the Venn diagram where the two theme circles overlap. Finally, they ask, "Does it support the third theme?" If it does, the principle is tagged with that strategic theme as well, again mapping to the relevant section in the themes' Venn diagram. This tagging can be achieved easily with three symbols, as shown in Figure 10-5.

Let's look at a few examples, given the following example principles from the start of this chapter and our three strategic themes for the company transitioning to a SaaS business model.

Principles:
- Value independence of teams most highly.
- "Cloud native" means our cloud

Themes:
- Customer responsiveness
- Operational excellence
- Product leadership

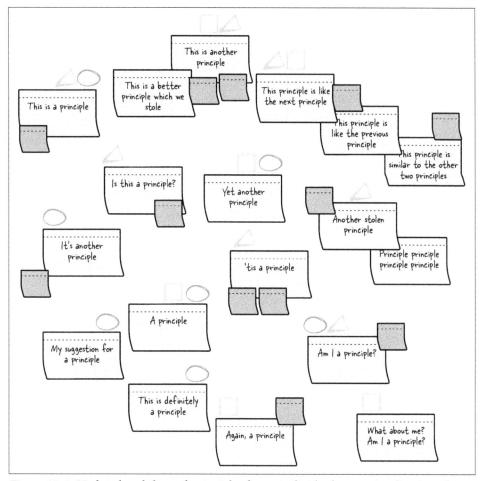

Figure 10-5. Updated and themed principles for an individual group: implications that came up in discussion are shown as the darker square stickies, and themes are signified by the small triangle, square, and circle symbols top left of the rectangular principle stickies

"Value independence of teams most highly" would go under "product leadership" because, if the organization is to continue to develop empathy for end users and innovate, teams need to have a direct relationship with them, as unmediated as possible by others. It has no direct impact, however, on how the systems might be operated or on the responsiveness to the customer as defined in the themes.

"'Cloud native' means our cloud" would map to all three themes: "customer responsiveness," "operational excellence," and "product leadership." This is because the cloud's flexibility allows for rapid response to clients' changing needs. It also enables economies of scale and infrastructure costs that are more closely related to compute usage. Finally, the on-demand nature of cloud compute and rapid support for new paradigms mean that product-development focus can be put on the smarts, and the "undifferentiated heavy lifting" can be left up to the cloud partner.

Looking at the coverage of these themes overall, "product leadership" has two themes mapped to it while "customer responsiveness" and "operational excellence" have only one each. As more themes are mapped, you'll want to keep an eye on this balance to make sure it doesn't tip over completely in favor of some areas at the expense of others.

If you are running this workshop in two halves, close the first day with a reminder of the agenda for day two. At the opening of day two, allow groups a five-minute revisit of what they had at the end of the previous session and allow them to make changes that have arisen overnight or during the weekend. Once everyone has made any further adjustments, it is time to come back together

Reconvene: Groups present again, and duplicate principles are identified (20 minutes)

Now is the time to really bring everyone and everything together. There has been no expectation prior to this point that any team has been thinking about the end result or a bigger picture beyond what their team has done. Now the emphasis is going to change.

Just as during the first time everyone came together, each team again presents their current principles. It will be faster this time, highlighting the ideas that were copied from others (and the reasons why they were copied) as well as implications that have been noted. As each principle is presented, it can be moved to the shared strategic themes Venn diagram. If a principle has arisen from multiple teams, put them hard next to each other so it is clear they are the same but have come from multiple sources. This might look like Figure 10-6.

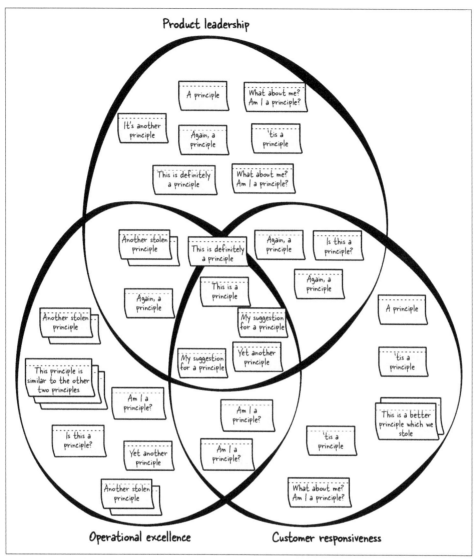

Figure 10-6. All of the groups' principles mapped to the strategic themes Venn diagram prior to dot-voting

When all the teams have presented and all the principles have been mapped, it is time to start selecting the shared set of 8–15 principles that will be taken forward.

Dot-voting (first round): Everyone votes and selects 8–15 of the top collated principles (5 minutes)

At this point the groups can disband, and everyone is back to working as an individual member of the collective. There will be two rounds of voting, with an intervening discussion. In both rounds, everyone gets eight votes to select the principles they think should be adopted.

Prior to voting, remind everyone once again what these architectural principles will be used for (commitments that help make strategically aligned decisions) and what your organization's vision, goals, and strategic themes are. If anyone has any questions, now is the time to answer them.

Everyone then votes for the principles of their choice with a colored dot. Everyone should use the same color. If there are a set of sticky notes that everyone has agreed represent the same principles (i.e., they are placed hard up against one another), then a vote for one is a vote for the entire set.

When the voting is complete, the votes for each principle should be counted and the number written clearly next to the principle (or principle set) for all to see. The 15 principles with the most votes are the ones provisionally selected. But we're not done yet. That was only the first round of voting.

Consider implications (20 minutes)

The first round of voting allows everyone to see the general direction that the collective is headed in. Prior to the second voting round, which is binding, it makes sense to take a step back and consider things from a "black hat" perspective.

"Black hat" thinking comes from the "six thinking hats" (*https://oreil.ly/fRyAr*) approach created by Edward de Bono. Each hat represents a different way of thinking, and when combined, they offer a rounded view on matters that avoids overemphasizing some aspects and completely missing others. For example, the green hat is "creativity" and encourages the generation of ideas and possibilities. Everyone effectively had green hats on when each group initially collected their proposed principles. Another is the red hat, which centers feelings: intuition, hunches, and gut instinct.

The black hat is "cautions," and it's what we need most here. This point, after the first voting round, is a great time to collectively wear it because everyone has just been through a process of selection and will have eliminated many of the possible principles they felt they didn't like for some reason. But we ought to consider the implications of all principles for all our future systems.

By wearing the black hat, we can welcome the sharing of these implications because we want to record them against the principles. (They will later be captured as per the template I shared earlier.) We want to know the downsides of adopting each principle, and if a principle has no perceived downsides, then that itself is a warning sign.

Either it's too general to be a useful principle (remember, we need them to help us select one decision option over another, narrowing our decision space), or we collectively have a massive blind spot that will inevitably lead to trouble in the future.

Therefore, after you have explained how black-hat thinking works, give everyone a new set of sticky notes of a color that's not been used yet, and encourage them to put on their cautious black hats and contribute implications that each principle has inherent within it. (Focus on the negative ones—the difficulties, weaknesses, and dangers that a principle brings—because the positive ones are less valuable.) The more we have, the merrier. Encourage everyone to focus on the highest dot-voted items in particular as it is likely these will be the ones ultimately chosen. If anyone is against any principle for solid reasons, then now is the time to make the reasons for that heard.

Once everyone has put down their implications, go round them all quickly, reading them out. Make sure that everyone knows what each implication means. Don't get into debates about the rights and wrongs of any of them, but do make sure everyone understands them all, and if this process brings even more concerns to the surface, capture those against the relevant principle, too.

Dot-voting (second round): Another round of voting, and the principles are reranked (5 minutes)

A second and final round of dot-voting can then take place, but now everyone should mark their votes with a different symbol. Everyone again gets eight votes. The first round of voting is not counted (that has served its purpose to focus minds with regard to implications).

Again, remind everyone that the idea is for the principles as a set to have a balanced coverage of the themes. After the voting is complete, total up the new votes for each proposed principle and record the figure beside it. Then highlight the 8–15 principles that received the most votes.

Commit to adoption and close (10 minutes)

The collective now has its selected principles—implications and all—and it is time to collectively commit.

Let everyone know that the next step will be to capture the selected 8–15 principles in a more permanent format ready for use in decisions. At this point, you should ask for everyone's explicit commitment to adopting them but make it clear that you still want to know if certain parties have issues.

To achieve this without ignoring any remaining dissenting voices is to "disagree and commit."[6] This means that those who still have drawbacks or concerns with the principles selected are encouraged to write their concerns on a sticky note as the meeting wraps up or directly afterward. They should place these "drawback/concern" stickies next to the principle (or principles) in question, thereby recording them in context.

As you announce this, make it clear that these disagreements will also be captured, as will all the principles collected, the ones ultimately selected and those that didn't make the cut.

Presenting Your Principles Ready for Use

With the workshop completed and the commitment gained, it is now time to begin the administrative task of taking the results of the workshop and turning them into a set of fully fleshed out architectural principles.

The best publishing platform for these principles is a wiki, ideally one that has a commenting facility. It makes most sense to put the principles in the same shared (i.e., commonly accessible and editable) part of the wiki as your ADR change log, one principle per wiki page, pulled together underneath a single hub page.

The Architectural Principles Hub page

The Architectural Principles Hub page is essentially a list of links to each of your individual principles, but it ought to also contain some key framing information: the same as what you already prepared for the workshop. The top half of the page, which needs no scrolling to access, should have links to pages for each of your currently committed principles.

Next, I place a Context section. First comes the current three key strategic themes, ideally with links to your organization's published vision and strategy to give context. There should be a few sentences or a short paragraph for each theme, not just the title. (Refer back to the examples in "Examples of Architectural Principles" on page 240 if you need to.) This not only serves to remind those present at the workshop of the framing of the principles, but it also offers this same information to new joiners and others who didn't attend the workshop, who come along after the fact and are more like consumers of the principles, at least initially, than shapers (though we'll get onto how principles ought to continually evolve later in this chapter).

Second, you will need a definition of an architectural principle and of the S.M.A.R.T. criteria. Again, you can take this from the examples earlier in this chapter.

---

6 Apparently, this phrase, which is now famously part of the leadership principles at Amazon, may have originated at my alma mater Sun Microsystems. It does seem familiar because I saw this kind of behavior a lot there as my professional life was beginning.

Third, I incorporate a representation of the principles mapped to their respective areas in the strategic themes Venn diagram. This reminds everyone of the importance of balanced support for the overall strategic direction of your organization. Typically, this is a photo of the Venn diagram at the end of the workshop or a screenshot of the same if your workshop was virtual.

Making up the remainder of the page is a Lineage section. When the page is first created, I populate this with the list of everyone who attended the workshop and, more important, the principles that were included in the dot-voting but didn't make the cut. I also ensure that the "drawback/concern" stickies information is recorded. This serves multiple purposes:

- Principle suggestions are not forgotten—they may have been ahead of their time.
- Those who proposed the principles are not forgotten.
- Those who continued to have reservations are not forgotten.

Taken all together, this page ought to serve as the beginning of a small cultural hub, one where a part of the shared minimal viable agreement necessary for effective software and systems can be nurtured.

Individual principle pages

Beneath the hub page in your wiki structure should come your individual principle pages.

I've already shared a basic format for a principle in this chapter, and that forms the majority of the content for a principles page. Let's just step through it again, talking about the process of populating this from the workshop outputs, during which I'll highlight a few essential additions that serve to embed the principle in its heritage and context:

EXAMPLE

Principle: Value independence of teams most highly.

Theme(s): Product Leadership

Subtitle: Split solutions along team lines.

Rationale: The strength of our approach to building and running our products relies fundamentally on the independence of our teams. The downsides to this are acknowledged, but the upsides are felt to outweigh it, especially when the difficulty of predicting future needs is taken into consideration.

Implications:

- Duplication of both function and data will inevitably arise. Rather then fight this, we embrace it, acknowledging the need, in certain circumstances, for noticeable eventual consistency and data replication.
- The combined licensing, runtime, and support costs of multiple third-party solutions may be higher than the costs of a single, shared cross-product-team solution.
- Solutions can be designed for the needs of the team that owns and runs them. They need not concern themselves with the needs of other teams.
- Both systems and the third-party services/solutions they are built on will tend to be smaller and more specifically task focused.
- Teams that go their own way need to self-support any third-party services/solutions that they adopt independently.

Background:
This principle was adopted at the Architectural Principles Workshop held on [DATE]. At the time of adoption, the following concerns were raised:

- [DRAWBACK/CONCERN] raised by [NAME]/[anonymous]

The Theme(s) section is an addition. This is where you record the strategic themes that the principle supports, either one, two, or all three of them. The Rationale section should state the benefits of the principle with regard to the themes. The Background section is the other addition. This is where the drawbacks and concerns are recorded in raw form; write down the exact contents of the sticky note, and if the person who raised it is happy to be named, then this can be recorded, too. Otherwise, they can be attributed to "anonymous." You might be wondering about duplication with the Implications section. It's a matter of trust building. Showing the raw feedback allows people to be heard and their contributions valued. The duplication is a small price to pay to make sure their voices are recorded in context.

Sharing the new principles hub with everyone

Once I've typed up all the principles in this way, I share the hub with all attendees of the workshop and ask them to validate that I have captured everyone's understanding correctly. You can invite everyone to comment on the principles and suggest additions. It's best to have a deadline for this after-the-fact commenting so that it doesn't run on forever. A week is usually sufficient. This is where it's handy if your wiki (or however you host things) has a rich commenting feature that shows comments in context and allows people to reply. Conversation about the finer details is welcome, especially if, when converting from sticky notes to electronic form, you lost some nuance or simply misinterpreted something.

Once the week allowed for commenting is up, final changes can be made to the principles, and then they are ready for use. Announcing this to everyone by email is a celebratory way to mark the adoption of the principles by the collective.

Recording the adoption of the principles as an ADR

Although it's not essential, it's well worth capturing the adoption of these initial principles as an ADR. This will be very lightweight (don't fall into the trap of repeating the principle itself) and offers a great opportunity to articulate why this principle is important. The result is that you have a clear point in the timeline for your organization's architectural decisions where these principles were adopted.

It can also help to use more ADRs when your principles inevitably change, either by the addition or removal of a principle or by a change to the nature of an existing principle. In this latter case, you will have to exercise some discretion. Only significant changes to an existing principle warrant an ADR. Clearly, a spelling correction is too small a change, while the addition of a new implication or significant change in the rationale might warrant it. In fact, now is a great time to think about how your principles might change as a result of being used.

Keeping Principles Useful

It's important to ensure that your team-sourced architectural principles are serving their intended purpose as a shared set of commitments aligning everyone and their decisions with the overall aspirational direction of the organization. That means there will be times when your set of principles will need to evolve to keep up with your organization's changing goals.

Not only that, but decisions and principles have a two-way relationship. Principles can affect decisions, of course, but decisions can affect principles as well. Feedback from decisions arising in the current technology landscape can cause updates to existing principles, the addition of new ones, or the removal of others. Furthermore, feedback from decisions could even affect your organization's technical strategy.

Feedback from Decisions Should Affect Architectural Principles

Architectural principles complement an advice process and ADRs. As such, decisions should typically comply with one or more principles, with those principles actively helping in the shaping and selection of the best-fit option. But what happens when one or more principles are actually making a decision harder? You may be surprised to learn that this is not necessarily a bad thing. Remember, we are always trying to decentralize and learn from feedback, and this can be another of those circumstances.

A single decision conflicts with a single principle

The most common encounter between decisions and principles is where the two are in conflict. I've seen circumstances when a team needs to deliver a feature that relies on a feature not offered by Heroku, their cloud provider of choice. Their identified options were to build the additional functionality themselves, which they didn't recommend, or to temporarily take advantage of a different cloud provider for this specific service, which they preferred. In doing so, they were directly going contrary to an agreed principle of "only target Heroku."

In such a situation, the first thing to do is to make this conflict explicit in the ADR, highlighting it to advisers. The Rationale and the Implications sections of the relevant principles are incredibly useful when writing up the pros and cons of each option as they help focus precisely on the areas of tension.

It's then a great point to engage the advice process and the power of the collective at the architecture advice forum to really get all the best minds and varied perspectives on the problem, recording all this in the ADR as usual. This focus offered by the conflict will facilitate the process of argumentation that I covered in Chapter 8, and it will allow collective experiences and advice to be effectively brought to bear. Whichever way the decision goes, the options and their consequences as well as the decision that is eventually taken will be well served by this. Let's consider now the circumstances when this happens more than once.

Repeated conflicts between multiple decisions and a principle are a signal to change

Individual decisions going against one or more principles isn't really a cause for concern. Given the evolutionary nature of software architecture and the wicked nature of decisions, it's inevitable and doesn't signal that something is wrong or needs to be updated in your principles. But as the heading of this section says, feedback from decisions should affect architectural principles. How can you tell when a principle should change?

Changes to individual principles can be either *incremental* (updates that necessitate an extension or clarification) or *fundamental* (updates that lead to invalidation or replacement). Incremental changes happen most frequently; an additional implication might be added, or the rationale be made more explicit. Such updates can occur after only a single decision calls them into question.

Fundamental updates happen far less frequently and have a more profound impact. Usually, an existing principle is retired and replaced with a new one. This is not a bad thing. Principles are, after all, a shared agreement and commitment *at a certain point in time*. If a previous agreement is frequently challenged by specific circumstances, then it's time to see if a new, more appropriate principle can be brought to bear. Creating this replacement principle should not be difficult. It should be evident in the decisions that have led to it, either in the decisions themselves or in the advice that surrounded them. I'll discuss how in a minute.

Spot missing principles and those that should be retired

There is another circumstance where the set of principles will need to be changed: when decisions keep coming up where no applicable principle exists. You will be most aware of this when one of the antipatterns of decision making from "Detecting Insufficient Organizational Alignment" on page 213 keeps arising: the repeated debate, decision after decision, about a key point of design. If an applicable principle were available, then these recurring debates wouldn't happen. It's as clear a signal as any that you have a gap. Again, identifying the principle that is missing should be a relatively simple matter, given that it will take the place of the debate that keeps coming up.

There is one final circumstance that ought to give rise to changes in your set of principles, and that is discovering that one (or more) is not required. It's not unusual that, when you are first creating your set of 8–15 principles, everyone works to make sure there is really good coverage and that all possibilities have been thought of. This is a good thing. However, in the actual application of principles to decision making, it can turn out some of them are never applicable. If this is the case, it's good practice to retire them.

How might you know if a principle can be retired? If you record applicable principles in ADRs, then you can very easily look to see if some of them are never referred to.

As you can see, there are several reasons why and ways that principles will evolve over time. Principles should then be maintained and updated to reflect the organization's shared experience, which is the topic of the next section.

Updating and Maintaining Principles

As discussed in the previous subsection, there are instances where you may need to update, add, or retire principles. Here's how you would go about that.

Use ADRs with a more rigorous adoption process to update your principles set

When a principle is replaced, a completely new one is added, or a redundant one is retired, an ADR should be created to ensure that the process is open and transparent. In the first two circumstances, the contents of this ADR will likely be driven directly by the advice on the ADRs that heralded the need for the update. In the latter, it is enough to point to the fact that the principle has not proven useful in any recent decisions.

However the change arises, the transparency and inclusive nature of an ADR provide an appropriate counterbalance to the desire to change. It's not unusual if the creation and socialization of such an ADR drive the proposed principle change in a better direction. For example, a proposal to retire a principle might instead result in it being updated to make it relevant again.

This ADR should go through the standard decision process, with advice being sought and offered up to the point of adoption. The adoption needs to go through a far more rigorous agreement process as the retirement or replacement of a principle is something everyone needs to commit to. Consequently, I use either the democratic or the consent decision process (described in Chapter 3) at this stage. Finally remember, if this principle replaces an existing one, link this new ADR to the ADR that heralded the adoption of its predecessor.

I should point out that these principle-changing ADRs can come from anyone in the collective. Typically (at least initially), it will be those playing overall architecture roles who initiate these, but that's just because their perspective affords them a cross-everything view. The fact that anyone can take on this responsibility allows everyone to keep collectively learning and share the responsibility of custodianship of the overall system.

New CFRs Can Also Arise from the Advice Process

New or updated principles are not the only thing that can arise from the advice process. New CFRs can also sometimes appear.

The best example I have seen of this was with a developer who had just had a nightmare debugging a particularly heinous issue. They had concluded after one very late night that a shared trace ID should be included in all service-to-service requests and in the morning wrote an ADR. (Standards such as OpenTracing (*https://oreil.ly/OZrqn*) rely on the concept of trace IDs to achieve exactly this.)

The ADR was a good one and proposed a suitable way for all teams—no matter what their tech stack—to add it, but it had a CFR hidden inside it. That CFR, when we extracted it, went as follows:

- **As an** on-call developer
- **I want to** be able to associate individual service-to-service calls with one another and the client call that originally triggered it
- **So that** I can more easily debug defects that arise as a result of the interaction between disparate parts of our distributed system.

Once this was captured and added to the CFR backlog, the ADR could refer to it and focus on the how without having to worry about the why.

Maintain your set of principles

Whenever your set of principles changes, for whatever reason, it's important to reflect this in a way that ensures the active principles continue to perform their function while not leaving gaps in previous decision histories. This means two things in practice:

- Historical ADRs continue to link to the relevant version of a principle.
- The hub page is up to date, both with regard to active principles and the Legacy section.

For the first point, it can be sufficient to update the title of a retired principle to include the flag [RETIRED] if that's what has happened to it. If a principle has been changed and the changes are incremental, then there is no need to take any action (the wiki history will be able to show its state at any point in the past). If the changes are more significant, the best way is to create a new principles page, based on the old one, and to link it back to the original. Then the original can be retitled to include the flag [OUT-OF-DATE].

For the second point, the title flags from the individual pages will hopefully be showing. This will allow you to move the [RETIRED] and [OUT-OF-DATE] pages down to the Legacy section, adding commentary and links to the relevant ADRs as appropriate. Then, any new members of the principles set can be added to the main list.

Feedback from Decisions Might Affect Technical Strategy

Just as a series of individual decisions can combine into a signal strong enough to create a change in the shared principles, a version of this force ought to be able to drive a change in the overarching technical strategy of the organization, perhaps even in its vision and goals.

Remember, strategy is the collectively agreed means of getting to a shared destination. The traditional Chinese saying "crossing the river by feeling the stones" describes the steady exploration of new things. If you think about crossing a river barefoot, this is exactly what you do. You have an idea of your ultimate destination—a specific spot on the far bank where you will be able to climb onto dry land—but you might not make your way there in a straight line. You might in fact, given your feeling of individual stones, take a very circuitous route, and you might even change your destination if you stray too far off your original line.

This is the same thing that can happen with individual technical decisions (feeling stones for the next step) leading to changes in principles (updating your route) and, sometimes, to changes in strategy or organization vision and goals (changing the point on the far bank that you are aiming for). Although creating a tech strategy is outside of the scope of this book, it's important to acknowledge that things as small as technical decisions can and ought to have an influence on it. In this revolutionized world, it's critical that organizations as a collective listen to such feedback and allow it to inform their way forward. When they do so, they can realize significant advantages.

Architectural Principles and Their Relation to ADRs, Advice, and CFRs

The capture, use, and evolution of architectural principles can lead to interesting interactions with other elements of decentralized practice that give you feedback on how useful they are to your decentralized practice. Take advantage of this feedback to make sure your principles work best for you. For example, implicit principles might be hiding in ADRs and advice. Additionally, it can be beneficial to encode the adoption of new principles by the collective in an ADR. Further discussion on both topics can be found in a separate article on architectural principles and their relation to ADRs, advice, and CFRs (*https://oreil.ly/6xVIR*).

Conclusion

Good architectural principles capture key agreements regarding how you collectively intend to construct and run your software systems. In this chapter, I showed how to source such principles from a broad range of stakeholder groups in a facilitated principles workshop, ensuring that everyone is aligned with your organization's goals in the process.

Because these principles are sourced from and used by the entire collective in decisions made every day, they are constantly tested for their ability to support that deciding. This constant exposure to the reality of teams and the overall system architecture keeps them useful.

But although architectural principles act as guiding lights, they don't capture everything that is essential about the environments in which architectural decisions are made. How do you also take note of the surrounding and rapidly changing technical landscape and climate? Enter the final supporting element: your own technology radar.

CHAPTER 11

Using a Technology Radar

Being aware of the technical landscape and climate that surround you is important for an effective decision process. Decisions benefit from being informed by your colleagues' and your wider organization's collective past experiences and future intentions. But such a wealth of technical information can seem difficult both to capture and to manage.

In this chapter, I'll discuss how the collective intelligence can be distilled into a set of regularly updated guidelines—the fourth alignment mechanism—and used to inform everyone's future decisions via a fourth supporting element to the advice process: a technology radar that provides a snapshot of the technologies and techniques used in your organization right now.

I'll start introducing you to the technology radar by giving you a real-life example of how it's used in Thoughtworks before going on to describe how a technology radar fits into the advice process. I'll close by discussing how feedback from using the technology radar in deciding can—and ought to—lead to updates in the radar itself.

Sense Tech Trends and Capture Guidelines

There is always a wealth of knowledge and experience in your organization about your technical landscape and climate. Sociotechnical systems are terribly complex, so it can be valuable to uncover and maintain a distilled set of guidelines that record what has been tried, what has failed, what might be worth investigating, and what has been learned across your software engineering organization.

This isn't a trivial task. Seeking out this information can open up an ocean of inputs and opinions. Capturing and presenting the collective experience of the technical landscape needs to be done in a clean and accessible way. If not, it's easy to drown in the sea of raw information.

Technology Radars Continually Collect and Share Guidance

A technology radar captures a snapshot of the technologies and techniques used in your organization as well as your collective experience with them. First created by Thoughtworks, and structured like the radars you imagine air traffic controllers sitting in front of, the technology radar is an "opinionated" view of technology trends (both current and receding) in software languages and frameworks, tools, platforms, and techniques. Its biggest strength lies in how it uses the radar metaphor to visually represent these important aspects of the current technology landscape and the climatic movements of various technological "blips" across it.

The Thoughtworks Technology Radar, as I write, is shown in Figure 11-1.

Tracking these tech-trend "blips" as aircraft would be tracked (albeit a lot slower moving), the radar allows viewers to rapidly see, for example, what is up and coming in the world of frontend frameworks (Astro, apparently), what's the current flavor of the month (I'm reliably informed it's Svelte at the time of writing), and what's beginning to fade. (Did anyone actually enjoy using AngularJS?)[1]

The beam of the Thoughtworks Radar sweeps the global tech landscape on a six-month basis. These sweeps crowdsource experiences of Thoughtworkers on client-delivery projects, and the blips that represent these projects are positioned based on how they are being used. For a blip to appear on the radar, it has to have been used in delivery on at least one client project. To be centered, a blip has to have become a Thoughtworks "sensible default," meaning it's their go-to unless specific circumstances suggest an alternative is preferable. Taken together, the collection of blips and their respective positions is a powerful summation of the organization's collective experiences and perceptions across all clients.

A technology radar is therefore a great tool for sharing guidelines about a significant number of technology trends, in a compact and consumable form, and all sourced from a vast collective.

---

1 By the time you read this, my next/current/old-news picks will be laughably out of date. That's the point. Things change fast in the world of tech, and no more so than in the world of web frameworks, apart from perhaps large language models.

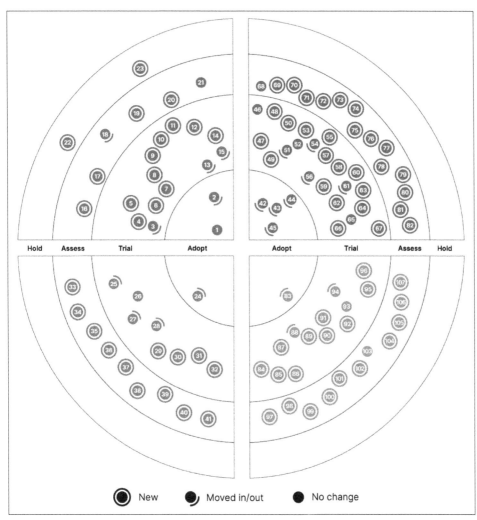

Figure 11-1. *The main overview of the Thoughtworks Technology Radar (Volume 29, published September 2023)*

How the Thoughtworks Technology Radar Works

Let's take a closer look at how the Thoughtworks Technology Radar works. You can see and interact with the latest version on the Thoughtworks website (*https://oreil.ly/ Qg1ob*).

Figure 11-1 shows the September 2023 Thoughtworks Technology Radar overview. The radar consists of blips, which are then categorized into quadrants and rings. The quadrants represent:

- Techniques
- Tools
- Platforms
- Languages and frameworks

The Thoughtworks radar is interactive. Clicking on the Tools quadrant opens a zoomed-in view, with the names of each blip now listed and the names of the rings more evident. See Figure 11-2.

Each blip on the radar represents a technology or technique that plays a role in software. Their position in a given ring on the radar represents Thoughtworks's confidence in recommending that technology to their clients.

What are the rings? Starting at the outside and moving in, you have:

Hold
Proceed with caution.

Assess
Worth exploring with the goal of understanding how it will affect your enterprise.

Trial
Worth pursuing. It's important to understand how to build up this capability. Enterprises can try this technology on a project that can handle the risk.

Adopt
Thoughtworks strongly feels that the industry should be adopting these items *where applicable*. Thoughtworks uses them *when it's appropriate* in their projects.

A blip combined with its ring position therefore clearly and succinctly captures Thoughtworks's current opinion on a topic.

As on a regular radar, blips are in motion. Their positions on the Thoughtworks Technology Radar change to represent Thoughtworks's increasing (or decreasing) confidence in recommending them as they move through the rings over time.

For example, the Mermaid blip is represented as a circle with a quarter ring around it, indicating it has been on previous radars and has moved in this particular edition. If you look really closely, you can see that on the Mermaid blip, the quarter ring is on the side closest to the center of the radar, which means its move was inward; Thoughtworks is increasingly confident in recommending it to clients.

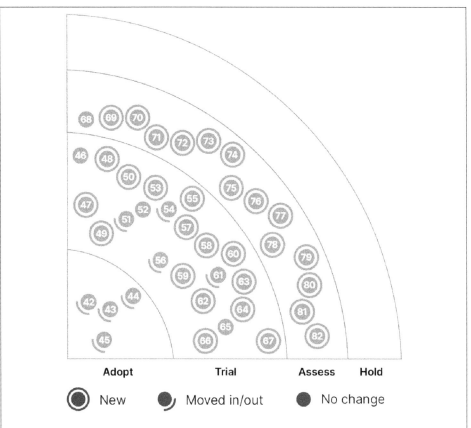

43. Mermaid

Adopt

Mermaid lets you generate diagrams from a Markdown-like markup language. Since we last featured it in the Radar, Mermaid has added support for many more diagrams and integrations with source code repositories, IDEs and knowledge management tools. Notably, it's supported natively in popular source code repositories such as GitHub and GitLab, enabling the embedding of and easy updates to Mermaid diagrams in the middle of Markdown documentation. Many of our teams gravitate toward Mermaid as their diagram-as-code tool due to its ease of use, multitude of integrations and wide variety of supported diagram types that keep growing.

Figure 11-2. The tools quadrant of the Thoughtworks Technology Radar with the details of the Mermaid blip expanded (Volume 29, published September 2023)

Each blip is accompanied by a short piece of text that is special to each version of the radar. You can also view the blip's history to see how it has changed, or moved throughout the radar, over time. The history of Mermaid is shown in Figure 11-3.

Adopt ⓔ

Mermaid ↗ lets you generate diagrams from a Markdown-like markup language. Since we last featured it in the Radar, Mermaid has added support for many more diagrams and integrations ↗ with source code repositories, IDEs and knowledge management tools. Notably, it's supported natively in popular source code repositories such as GitHub and GitLab, enabling the embedding of and easy updates to Mermaid diagrams in the middle of Markdown documentation. Many of our teams gravitate toward Mermaid as their diagram-as-code tool due to its ease of use, multitude of integrations and wide variety of supported diagram types that keep growing.

Trial ⓔ

Mermaid ↗ lets you generate diagrams from a markdown-like markup language. Born out of need to simplify documentation, Mermaid has grown into a larger ecosystem with plugins for Confluence ↗, Visual Studio Code ↗ and Jekyll ↗ to name a few. To see how it works, you can use the Live Editor ↗ on GitHub. Mermaid also has a convenient command line interface that lets you generate SVG, PNG and PDF files as output from definition files. We've been using Mermaid in many projects and we like the simplicity of describing graphs and flowcharts with markdown and checking in the definition files with the code repository.

Figure 11-3. The full history of the Mermaid blip on the Thoughtworks Technology Radar

At the top of Mermaid's history page is the blip's current status ("Adopt") and when it moved to this status (September 2023). The text on the right gives Thoughtworks's current thinking on Mermaid as a tool and why the collective feels it deserves its place in the "Adopt" circle.

Complementing the blip's current position are its previous entries on the radar. For Mermaid, there is only one of these, from way back in November 2018 when it entered the radar in "Trial." You can see from that text what everyone thought about it then. This text is unedited from 2018.

Other blips have more entries because their progress (or otherwise) across the radar has been far more noteworthy and eventful. The OpenTelemetry blip (*https://oreil.ly/7QaiE*) is interesting. It has collected four entries since its first appearance in March 2017 but has never managed to move out of "Trial" status.

Other blips also have a long history, but their movement is not always toward the center. The AWS blip (*https://oreil.ly/_sUdT*) is illustrative here; it first appeared in July 2011 at "Adopt" status, with this ring position being reiterated in March 2012. However, in its third and final appearance on the radar in November 2018, AWS moved out to "Trial" because there were by then solid competitors in the market in the form of Microsoft Azure and GCP.

The AWS blip illustrates one final important point. While a blip might stay on the radar, it is not always represented visually. This is solely to preserve screen estate, highlighting what Thoughtworks thinks is most important at the time of the current version. All blips, current and future, can always be searched for.

It's Not Just Technologies that Belong on the Radar

Thoughtworks includes both patterns arising and antipatterns in the "Techniques" quadrant. These are a valuable place to share lessons and guidance that don't relate directly to a specific technology. I am always on the lookout for "ESBs in API Gateway's clothing" (*https://oreil.ly/ifs4p*), for instance.

Hopefully, you can see how rich a tool for capturing and sharing guidelines *over time* a technology radar is. Not only does it capture and organize a fantastic amount of information, but it also shows trends over time and (most important for our purposes) the tribal knowledge associated with historical movements and current positions of blips.

Your Internal Technology Radar Will Be Structured Differently

Although your technology radar will look and work similarly to Thoughtworks' Technology Radar,[2] your organization will make use of it slightly differently, both in terms of its content and its structure.

First, while Thoughtworks doesn't list any in-house tooling that their clients might have created (it's the clients' intellectual property, not that of Thoughtworks, after all), your internal radar is under no such restriction. Locating internal solutions in all quadrants, strategic or de facto, along with honest assessments of their applicability and current state as blips is a very powerful way to make it easy for everyone to know what's available to them in the form of invested-in strategic defaults. (I'll return to this in more detail in a later section of this chapter where I'll explain just how powerful this can be and how to harness it.)

Second, while your radar and the Thoughtworks version both capture and present guidelines about the adoption of current and past technology trends, *your context and focus will be very different*. The Thoughtworks radar is broadly focused: externally, across the entire technology sector. Your radar, on the other hand, will fit into a very specific niche: your decision processes and their encompassing sociotechnical system. While the Thoughtworks radar exists to help their clients make good decisions and avoid bad ones, your radar will focus on supporting distributed decision making within your specific internal landscape and climate.

---

2 The biggest differences are that the backing site isn't included (I'll show how to make your own), and blip icons don't change to indicate movement between volumes.

What this typically means for the structure is that the quadrants stay the same (Techniques, Tools, Platforms, and Languages and Frameworks) but the rings reflect the transit of technologies through your organization (becoming "trial," "adopt," "hold," and finally "retire").

You're not bound to using these, but they are the ones I've repeatedly found most useful, and for the remainder of this chapter, they are the ones I'll use for examples.

Your Radar's Place in an Advice Process

How can an internal radar interact with your decision process? As with architectural principles, you can start by adding a section in your ADR template for Relevant Radar Blips as per the following example. Deciders can then list the pertinent blips in the ADR—both their position and detailed notes—which brings them explicitly into individual decisions.

EXAMPLE

ADR00X – [TITLE]

Date
Dec 22, 2022

Status
[DRAFT]/[PROPOSED]/[ACCEPTED]/[ADOPTED]/[SUPERSEDED]/
[EXPIRED]

Decision
[A summary of your decision in a few lines.]

Relevant radar blips
[List here all blips that are directly relevant to this decision, whether the chosen option follows their guidance or takes another route. This can help create and focus both your options and their consequences.]

Context
[The context of your decision—the surrounding environment in which it was taken (including any constraints), the relevant steps which took you to this point, and the forces which made it necessary.]

A blip and its ring convey a lot on their own, but don't forget the explanatory text. This is a rich resource, especially if a blip history is also available. (I'll talk about how to capture blip history in "Updating Your Blips" on page 294.) For example, before trying something new—a tool, library, platform service, or technique—a team can see if anyone else in the organization has looked at it already, without having to ask.

Deciders can see highlights of what others learned from the experience and more by referring to the blip's description text. If you choose to capture it in ADRs, this description can flag which teams the experience comes from, which can point advice seekers in the right direction.

Consequently, the radar allows deciders to rapidly scan the range of pretried solution options at a glance. Furthermore, the ring position of blips illustrates clearly not only the current suggestions and associated guidance (relevant blips in "adopt") but also the investigated futures (relevant blips in "trial)" and remaining legacy (blips in "hold" and "retire"). Incorporating such guidance can improve your decisions significantly, embedding them more explicitly in your organization's current context.

The presence of relevant blips and their positions can feed directly into a decision ADR's options and their consequential pros and cons. If a blip is widely adopted, then making a decision that agrees with its position and description becomes moot. (This is a solid indication that you're not in the process of taking a "significant" decision.) However, as with architectural principles, a decision that looks like it is going to deviate from the current blip landscape—either by treating a blip as if it is in a different ring or by adding a new blip—must flag this fact explicitly in an ADR, explicitly addressing it in the text of the Context, Options, and Consequences sections. Even in these cases, the "default" (i.e., blip-aligned) options ought to be listed in the ADR, if only to articulate why they aren't preferred.

Highlighting relevant blips calls out any tension between an in-progress decision and the current collectively agreed technical guidelines as represented in the radar. This clarity is excellent grist for advice offering, whether it takes place in an architecture advice forum conversation or not. Any discussion, argumentation, and advice arising will likely focus on two key areas:

- Why does this decision need to take a different path?
- What is unsuitable about the defaults that are in existence?

Advice focused in this way is incredibly valuable. It can call in other blips, historical and up and coming, resulting in a rich and productive conversation. The resulting laser-targeted advice can then be recorded in the ADR and rolled into the decision.

However you use your radar to navigate your technical landscape, bear in mind that the radar's guidance (compared to principles) is advisory in nature rather than a reflection of a shared commitment. The radar is fundamentally a reflection of a current state and its past as well as the guidance arising from that. Radar blips give an idea of what, if anything, is the current de facto solution in a problem space: what's been done in the past and what teams might be experimenting with. Forging a new path when it comes to decisions that relate to blips is a lot less likely to raise eyebrows, but such a deviation should be specifically and concretely addressed in an ADR.

While the majority of radar-decision interactions flow from blips to decisions, this is not a one-way relationship. As I've just shown, decisions and the ADRs that result from them can exert a force in the opposite direction, updating the radar. There are two main circumstances when this feedback could take place. I'll cover them in more detail later in the chapter, but I'll mention them now as they arise from the interaction between decisions and the radar.

First, while many deciders will flag their adherence to the current radar guidance by saying, "Our decision aligns to these blips," others will be saying, "Our decision contradicts the current blips and their position." Perhaps it's the spiking of an entirely new framework or a decision that moves a specific practice from "trial" to "adopt." In these cases, the radar may be due for an update.

For example, if a decision is taken to try out a new language, then a blip should be added in the "Languages and Frameworks" quadrant's "trial" ring. Or if a decision is taken to migrate a number of Kubernetes Pods from a previously standard home-grown kOps cluster running on AWS Elastic Container Service (ECS) instances onto Amazon EKS, then the EKS blip might move from "trial" to "adopt" while the kOps and ECS blips might move to "hold."

You could make updating the radar explicit via a process, though in my experience, this happens anyway without anyone having to push it explicitly. Remember, your goals here are the broadest engagement with your evolving architecture as possible, as well as a growing architectural mindset across all team members. I'll discuss how and when I go about this in "Updating Your Blips" on page 294.

Second, considering the longer-term blip lifecycle is useful for those wondering where to place strategic investments. Perhaps the time has come for the delivery platform team to make a self-serve template for a certain shape of Rust microservice, or on the other hand, time and effort perhaps ought to be put into the intentional removal of that last Bull mainframe running that old customer database. (I consider this in more detail in the "Consciously Managing Strategic iInterventions" section of a supplementary article on the book website (*https://oreil.ly/4ZO8j*).)

Creating Your Technology Radar

Let's now use the open source Thoughtworks "build your own radar" (BYOR) tool to build an interactive version of your radar. (You can find the example spreadsheet with links to the published radar here (*https://oreil.ly/CAJf2*).) With that, you can visually map out the technology trends affecting your organization, past, present, and future. Importantly, alongside each of them you can capture the guidance that everyone wants to share about their relevant experiences.

To use the BYOR tool, go to the Build Your Own Radar page (*https://oreil.ly/zzJTD*) and follow the instructions to create a new spreadsheet for recording your blips.

You're then ready to start with what can be the most fun part: collecting the blips. This is the equivalent of sweeping a radar beam around a full 360 degrees, sensing what technologies and techniques are in each of your four quadrants.

After gathering the raw blip data from the experiences of your entire technology organization, you'll then go through the "sense-making" steps of sorting and validation, focusing, positioning, documenting, and finally publishing. All of these steps will happen in the spreadsheet. At any point in the process, you can pass the spreadsheet data to the BYOR tool to render it in the format I showed you in Figure 11-1.

Blip Gathering

In this step, the goal is to gather the raw, unfiltered suggestions for blips from all relevant parties. The task of gathering radar inputs and turning them into something that offers guidance to everyone is not a one-person job. Just as architectural principles should come from the collective, so should radar blips. Unlike architectural principles, however, blip gathering is best done asynchronously.

Your First Radar Sweep Takes the Longest

Your first sweep of your radar will take the longest because it is starting from nothing and capturing the most blips–everything you have now in your organization. It's establishing a baseline.

It's essential that you offer everyone the opportunity to be involved so that you get the most accurate and detailed overview of your current landscape and the prevailing climate. When you capture that, your radar stands the best chance of being useful in its task of offering guidance and aligning everyone.

To run a sweep, you first need to decide how much of your software engineering organization your sweep will cover. It works best to set this scope around one or more (or all) products *along their entire lifecycle*. Sweeps bounded by departmental, organizational, or role lines tend to miss important blips, such as testing tools or rollback techniques that will affect those same products.

This means you will be including disciplines like operations, UX, product, QA, security data, and delivery. Organization-supporting functions like people teams (aka human resources), finance, and legal are likely to fall outside your net, but you should give serious consideration to including teams like regulatory and others that, in other circumstances, are sources of CFRs. If you are in doubt, in my experience it's better to leave them out this time and include them in a future sweep or add their blips one at a time afterward.

Once you have your list of people, you can begin. The easiest way to do this is with a spreadsheet that has your columns and valid fields preset. Figure 11-4 shows what a Google spreadsheet doing this might look like. (All the following spreadsheet images are linked to online versions.)

name	ring	quadrant	description	source
Kotlin 1.8	adopt ▼	languages... ▼	Our team is experimenting with Kotlin 1.8. Heavy use is being made of the Lombok @Builder support which is cutting down significantly on boiler plate code. Migrating Android codebase from Kotlin 1.7 was very simple. We've not touched any backend services compnents tho. (We love the improved <a href="https://kotlinlang.org/docs/whatsnew18.html#improved-objective-c-swift-interoperability">Swift interop</a>)	Mark Copeland
Our ADR template	adopt ▼	tools ▼	Our ADR template, based in ADO, is embedded in how we decide. We're still using the default, though we have experimented with a few extra fields.	Andrew Harmel-Law
Architecture Advice Process	adopt ▼	techniques ▼	Having experimented with a single team, and then on a small programme of work, the Architecture Advice Process is now used for all significant architectural decisions (and many regular ones too).	Andrew Harmel-Law
AKS (Azure Kubernetes Service)	adopt ▼	platforms ▼	All our microservices run in Azure Kubernetes Service (AKS) pods. It works great with Azure DevOps and allows teams to focus on the work of building and running systems. Infra teams have found it easy to configure, leaving us to focus on the value-added work.	Isha Soni

Figure 11-4. A Google spreadsheet used to gather blips containing some example data in each of the fields ("isNew" column hidden) (https://oreil.ly/DG_VG)

Notice that on the right, there is an extra column not in the Thoughtworks spreadsheet: *source*. I'd advise against adding fields apart from this one. As you create and start to use the radar, it helps to know who submitted a blip, whether an individual or a team. This allows everyone to go back to the submitter if something about the blip is unclear. And it has benefits when the radar is in use, but I'll get to those later.

When you share the blip collection sheet with everyone, make it clear what your intentions are by including a cover sheet that describes the technology radar concept, explains the process you are asking everyone to follow, and links to the Thoughtworks Technology Radar and explainer videos, so contributors have a good idea of what they are doing. It also makes sense to state clearly how this will fit into your decision process.

How you drive the collection will depend on your organization's engineering culture. I've worked with clients who've announced the call for blip submissions at an all-hands meeting and then shared the empty spreadsheet with everyone with a deadline for completion; everything else just self-organizes. I've also had clients who began similar announcements but then hosted a series of facilitated sessions, moving team by team and collecting blips that way. Most organizations sit somewhere between these two.

The description is the most valuable field to capture at this stage. Encourage contributors to dump raw information in here. If there is disagreement about a blip, capture that too, and if different teams have different thoughts on the same blip, suggest that they log their versions separately. You're very much not looking for agreement here, simply awareness. Commenting on the descriptions of blips that others added should be encouraged. If disagreement exists, then surface it.

Letting teams and other groups self-organize works well, but be aware of the specifics of your culture because you want to be confident that the blips gathered will be broadly representative and of a solid enough quality to take to the next stage. By this, I mean:

- For each blip, all columns need to be filled in.

- This is an initial scan: you want *everything*, future, current, and legacy. If it's affecting your organization right now, capture it.

- It's not just technology—remember techniques. Don't restrict yourself to industry-standard approaches either. Capture how *you* do it, pattern or antipattern.

- Don't worry about duplicates—the "focusing and positioning" stage resolves that.

- Capture all the major versions of all the things you use. If you have Java Runtime Environments (JREs) from version 1.1 all the way to version 21, then add blips for each one. If you have several versions of a library, list them all out, too.[3]

- Capture all the variety of the things. If you mix home-developed Kubernetes clones, kOps, EKS, and a million other flavors, list them all out.

- Think about the entire software delivery lifecycle, from ideation to sunset.

- Think about the entire tech landscape, from Internet of Things (IoT) to offline cold storage in a permafrosted Icelandic bunker.

- Don't forget standards: open, closed, and de facto internal.

Lock Then Copy the Sheet After Every Step Is Completed

Before moving on to each subsequent step in radar creation, lock your blip-gathering sheet ("protect" is what Google Sheets calls it), then take a snapshot copy to work on. This means the data won't continue to change underneath you as latecomers try to add their last few blips, but it will mean they are disappointed. To avoid this, set a deadline for the current stage.

---

3 This is advice, not a rule. Not everyone follows semantic-versioning principles, especially when marketing gets involved. The goal is that you get enough details of blips that are significantly different enough to be treated separately.

Blip Sorting and Validation

At this point, you will have a lot of blips in their raw form, as shown in Figure 11-5. If you rendered your radar right now, it'd be unfocused and not very usable. More important, it stands little chance of representing a *balanced and nuanced* view of your technology landscape and climate. To make sense of this raw data, the collective will need to be involved a second time to focus and position the collected blips. For that activity to be a success, whoever is running the radar-creation process will need to do some prep to first sort and validate the blips. That is the goal of this step.

name	ring	quadrant	description	source
Kotlin 1.5	adopt ▼	languages... ▼	First version of Kotlin at NuOrg. Used for a few experiments which went well, ending up in prod. Some backend services. None mission critical.	
Kotlin 1.8.10	trial ▼	languages... ▼	We've started playing with kotlin again in our team.	Seema Satish
Swift 4	adopt ▼	languages... ▼	First version of Swift that we used. Adopted completely after we dropped ObjectiveC. (Hiring Swift developers was easier.)	Mark Copeland
Azure Functions	trial ▼	platforms ▼	We used them to build the entire Customer Onboarding microsite. This is a great use case as it runs infrequently, and when it does it is fundamentally a complicated, async data ingestion pipeline.	Isha Soni
kotlin 1.7	adopt ▼	languages... ▼	Kotlin version our Android app currently targets.	Mark Copeland
Kotlin 1.8	▼	▼	Our team is experimenting with Kotlin 1.8. Heavy use is being made of the Lombok @Builder support which is cutting down significantly on boiler plate code. Migrating Android codebase from Kotlin 1.7 was very simple. We've not touched any backend services compnents tho. (We love the improved <a href="https://kotlinlang.org/docs/whatsnew18.html#improved-objective-c-swift-interoperability">Swift interop</a>)	Mark Copeland
Our ADR template	adopt ▼	tools ▼	Our ADR template, based in ADO, is embedded in how we decide. We're still using the default, though we have experimented with a few extra fields.	Andrew Harmel-Law
Architecture Advice Process	adopt ▼	techniques ▼	Having experimented with a single team, and then on a small programme of work, the Architecture Advice Process is now used for all significant architectural decisions (and many regular ones too).	Andrew Harmel-Law

Figure 11-5. Selection of raw, unsorted blip data after gathering but before sorting and filtering, focusing, and positioning ("isNew" column hidden) (https://oreil.ly/uCrjg)

This preparation involves tidying up the blips in a way that respects the raw data you have at the moment.[4] Your radar should reflect what is going on in your organization *right now*, not where the organization hopes to be. Bear this in mind as you sort and validate each blip in turn, undertaking the following tasks in the following order:

---

4 A bit like tidying your child's bedroom. Is that a random pile making its way glacially toward the bin or is it a carefully thought-through and optimized filing system? Best to leave it for now and check with them first…

1. Ensure that all the blips have isNew set to "true."

2. Correct omissions (i.e., put things in quadrants or rings if these were not set).

3. Clarify with the author if a blip is not clear.

4. Group rows that are the same.

5. Group rows that are related.

6. Group rows by quadrant.

7. Group rows by proposed ring.

Postsorting and postfiltering, you should have something like the sample in Figure 11-6. Every blip is set now to "isNew=true" as this is the first radar, the source has been validated, and the ring and quadrant have been guessed for Kotlin 1.8, which is now next to the blip for Kotlin 1.8.10. The teams of the blip submitters have also been added for clarity.

name	ring	quadrant	isNew	description	source
Kotlin 1.5	adopt ▾	languages... ▾	TRUE ▾	First version of Kotlin at NuOrg. Used for a few experiments which went well, ending up in prod. Some backend services. None mission critical.	Paul Fitzsimons (Payments Back End)
Kotlin 1.7	adopt ▾	languages... ▾	TRUE ▾	Kotlin version our Android app currently targets.	Mark Copeland (Mobile)
Kotlin 1.8	adopt ▾	languages... ▾	TRUE ▾	Mobile team is experimenting with Kotlin 1.8. Heavy use is being made of the Lombok @Builder support which is cutting down significantly on boiler plate code. Migrating Android codebase from Kotlin 1.7 was very simple. We've not touched any backend services compnents tho. (We love the improved <a href="https://kotlinlang.org/docs/whatsnew18.html#improved-objective-c-swift-interoperability">Swift interop</a>)	Mark Copeland (Mobile)
Kotlin 1.8.10	trial ▾	languages... ▾	TRUE ▾	We've started playing with kotlin again in our team.	Seema Satish (Infra)
Swift 4	adopt ▾	languages... ▾	TRUE ▾	First version of Swift that we used. Adopted completely after we dropped ObjectiveC. (Hiring Swift developers was easier.)	Mark Copeland (Mobile)
Azure Functions	trial ▾	platforms ▾	TRUE ▾	We used them to build the entire Customer Onboarding microsite. This is a great use case as it runs infrequently, and when it does it is fundamentally a complicated, async data ingestion pipeline.	Isha Soni (Cards Back End)
AKS (Azure Kubernetes Service)	adopt ▾	platforms ▾	TRUE ▾	All our microservices run in Azure Kubernetes Service (AKS) pods. It works great with Azure DevOps and allows teams to focus on the work of building and running systems. Infra teams have found it easy to configure, leaving us to focus on the value-added work.	Isha Soni (Cards Back End)
Architecture Advice Process	adopt ▾	techniques ▾	TRUE ▾	Having experimented with a single team, and then on a small programme of work, the Architecture Advice Process is now used for all significant architectural decisions (and many regular ones too).	Andrew Harmel-Law (Architecture)

Figure 11-6. Selection of sorted and filtered blip data, ready for focusing and positioning (https://oreil.ly/mxkkO)

Respect the Submitted Raw Blip Data

It's very important to respect the inputs that have been provided so far.[5] By all means, correct spelling mistakes in the data entry and group them to make the upcoming focusing session efficient, but don't stray beyond this list—by deduplicating, for example. Just because you think it's a double or disagree with it doesn't mean you can change it. That kind of activity comes next.

Blip Focusing

After sorting and validating the blip information, it's time to involve the collective again to further focus them. In this step, the goal is to check that the blips are valid, verify the blips' description text, and decide which quadrant the blips belong in. Unlike the gathering step, the focusing step should be done synchronously in a workshop. These workshops can often take up to four hours.

The attendees for this blip-focusing session will ideally be the same group who were asked to contribute the raw blips in the first place. However, if this is an unmanageable number of people to have tied up in long working sessions, ask each group to send one or more delegates whom everyone in the group empowers to act on their behalf. By *group*, I mean a development team or one of the disciplines (e.g., UX, product, infra, InfoSec, etc.).

Even with reduced numbers, blip focusing is still one of those "expensive" workshops if you multiply the number of attendees by the number of hours it takes, which is why the sorting and validation step is so important, as you want to be able to move through similar blips rapidly.

Don't Scrimp on the Focusing Time

If you're sweeping your radar cross-organization, then gathering the number of invitees for a four-hour session might simply be impractical. Splitting the session into two 2-hour pieces or even four slots of one hour each is fine. It's also workable to run sessions for different products. For example, gather the teams working on a cloud-based SaaS solution (not just the development teams—don't forget the platform and supporting functions) for one session, and then separately the teams working on the mobile app or some on-prem, thick-client systems.

---

5 This is the "Monira Rhaimi method." Monira would never move sticky notes that had been placed by others if they weren't present. The notes represented their authors' conception of something, which should be treated with respect if we expect them to trust us.

Despite all these warnings, blip focusing can be great fun. There are very few opportunities for everyone to get together and discuss the technology trends that are affecting your organization right now.

During the session (or sessions, if you split them up), work through every blip gathered, one after another. This is why it helps to have everything sorted in advance. If there are a lot of rows that cover the same thing, then treat them all together.

For each blip, check if it is valid, clarifying the text in all cells as appropriate. If it is a duplicate, then discuss and merge, taking care not to lose any of the valuable description data and sources in each of the individual blips. If someone remembers something that everyone forgot, then add it to an existing blip or a new one.

Individual Blips for Major Versions of the Same Technology Trend

If you are running multiple major versions of something, be that a framework or library, a language, or even a platform, represent each version on the radar. This allows you to show where the collective thinks everyone should be moving as a default and where all your legacy is. This is one area where your organization's radar will differ from the Thoughtworks one.

It is also important to agree in which ring a blip sits. It will be self-evident in most circumstances, but when it's not, you can refer to the ring definitions and if you need to, split a blip in two so that it can sit in both places. If this happens, make sure that the names and descriptions of the new blips refer to the reason they are in that specific ring. (Doing this often clarifies each of the blips and fits them to their ring homes.) For example, you might have "Azure Functions for infrequent workloads" in "adopt" and "Azure Functions for flexible workloads" in "trial."

As the discussion progresses, make sure you (or another nominee) capture all the commentary that surfaces. Disagreement is fine; you're not looking for consensus. If there are two ways to do things, show it. Two conflicting opinions as to the best way to do or use something? Make both clear.

You will likely find that the "techniques" quadrant starts off relatively empty compared to the others, but watch out as discussion continues for things that could go in here. This is a place where tribal memory and lessons learned can be captured. The Thoughtworks radar has some great examples of this, such as "tracking health over debt" (*https://oreil.ly/enmVB*), "bounded buy" (*https://oreil.ly/2NHhI*), "Lambda pinball" (*https://oreil.ly/1KeXz*), "team cognitive load" (*https://oreil.ly/TrOOM*), "miscellaneous platform teams" (*https://oreil.ly/UIAQz*), and "ESBs in API Gateway's clothing" (*https://oreil.ly/VKtt-*). (As you can see, this is an opportunity to get creative with names. This isn't just for fun. If a name is memorable, then a technique stands a better chance of being adopted or avoided if it's a bad smell.)

Once you're done, you should have a selection of blips, something like the sample in Figure 11-7. Note that Kotlin 1.8.10 has been merged into the Kotlin 1.8 blip. Also, some more detail on other teams' use of Azure Functions has been added.

name	ring	quadrant	description	source
Kotlin 1.5	adopt ▾	languages... ▾	First version of Kotlin at NuOrg. Used for a few experiments which went well, ending up in prod. Some backend services. None mission critical.	Paul Fitzsimons (Payments Back End)
Kotlin 1.7	adopt ▾	languages... ▾	Kotlin version our Android app currently targets.	Mark Copeland (Mobile)
Kotlin 1.8	adopt ▾	languages... ▾	Mobile team is experimenting with Kotlin 1.8. Heavy use is being made of the Lombok @Builder support which is cutting down significantly on boiler plate code. Migrating Android codebase from Kotlin 1.7 was very simple. We've not touched any backend services compnents tho. (We love the improved \<a href="https://kotlinlang.org/docs/whatsnew18.html#improved-objective-c-swift-interoperability">Swift interop\</a>) We've started playing with Kotlin again in our team (Infra Team)	Mark Copeland (Mobile), Seema Satish (Infra)
Swift 4	adopt ▾	languages... ▾	First version of Swift that we used. Adopted completely after we dropped ObjectiveC. (Hiring Swift developers was easier.)	Mark Copeland (Mobile)
Azure Functions	trial ▾	platforms ▾	A few teams have experimented with Azure Functions. All but one have used them for back-end housekeeping. Cards team used them to build the entire Customer Onboarding microsite. This is a great use case as it runs infrequently, and when it does it is fundamentally a complicated, async data ingestion pipeline.	Isha Soni (Cards Back End), Seema Satish (Infra)
AKS (Azure Kubernetes Service)	adopt ▾	platforms ▾	All our microservices run in Azure Kubernetes Service (AKS) pods. It works great with Azure DevOps and allows teams to focus on the work of building and running systems. Infra teams have found it easy to configure, leaving us to focus on the value-added work.	Isha Soni (Cards Back End)
Architecture Advice Process	adopt ▾	techniques ▾	Having experimented with a single team, and then on a small programme of work, the Architecture Advice Process is now used for all significant architectural decisions (and many regular ones too).	Andrew Harmel-Law (Architecture)

Figure 11-7. Selection of focused blips ("isNew" column hidden) (https://oreil.ly/Bof_O)

Blip Positioning

Once you have all your blips deduped and allocated to the right quadrants, you can collectively position them, assigning each blip to the appropriate ring. If you are keeping the defaults, these will be trial, adopt, hold, or retire. Unlike focusing, this can be done offline and asynchronously, which also allows everyone in the greater blip-providing community to contribute. Invite everyone who could have submitted a blip, whether they chose to or not.

Prepare for positioning by taking a copy of the sheet with the focused blips on it and making a new column for each person who will vote. Each cell in these new columns should only allow each of the rings and "not voted" as values. Open the voting by sharing the blip-positioning sheet with everyone who is enfranchised. Each voter then votes for the ring they think each blip should be placed in.

Voting Might Flush Out More Comments—Welcome This!

There's nothing like a radar that is about to make its way into the open to flush out final comments on the blips. To capture these, encourage everyone who is voting to add these closing thoughts in the form of comments on the relevant blip's description cell. That way, voices can still be heard, and the last bit of context juice can be squeezed from everyone.

As with blip gathering, set a time window for this voting (a week is generally good, though if engagement is high, then one to three days can work, too) and remind people when the voting window is about to close. Once the voting window closes, protect the sheet so that no more voting can take place. The position of each blip is the ring with the majority of votes. Crunch the results and set the ring position for each blip accordingly, as shown in Figure 11-8. You can see that while they are not always unanimous, the votes all have clear winners. Some blips have shifted position: Kotlin 1.5 has moved to "retire," and Kotlin 1.8 has moved to "trial."

name	ring	isNew	Votes: Paul	Votes: Seema	Votes: Mark	Votes: Isha	Votes: Andrew
Kotlin 1.5	retire ▾	TRUE ▾	retire ▾	hold ▾	retire ▾	retire ▾	retire ▾
Kotlin 1.7	adopt ▾	TRUE ▾	adopt ▾	adopt ▾	adopt ▾	adopt ▾	adopt ▾
Kotlin 1.8	trial ▾	TRUE ▾	trial ▾	adopt ▾	adopt ▾	trial ▾	trial ▾
Swift 4	adopt ▾	TRUE ▾	adopt ▾	adopt ▾	adopt ▾	adopt ▾	adopt ▾
Azure Functions	trial ▾	TRUE ▾	trial ▾	adopt ▾	trial ▾	trial ▾	trial ▾
AKS (Azure Kubernetes Service)	adopt ▾	TRUE ▾	adopt ▾	adopt ▾	adopt ▾	hold ▾	adopt ▾
Architecture Advice Process	adopt ▾	TRUE ▾	adopt ▾	adopt ▾	adopt ▾	adopt ▾	adopt ▾
Swift 5	trial ▾	TRUE ▾	trial ▾	trial ▾	trial ▾	trial ▾	trial ▾
iOS 12 to 14	retire ▾	TRUE ▾	retire ▾	retire ▾	retire ▾	retire ▾	retire ▾

Figure 11-8. Selection of blips and their votes ("description," "quadrant," and "source" columns hidden) (https://oreil.ly/tmGUg)

You are now ready to move to the final stage of preparation prior to publishing.

Blip Documenting

At this point, you have all the raw information required to create your first technology radar, but it's not yet in a digestible form. The goal of this step is to take all the raw information from the descriptions, as well as any further comments that arose during the focusing and positioning steps, and turn that into a short paragraph or two of useful prose for each blip that would support the organization's decision process.

While refining the documentation for each blip, it is important to retain all the information gathered from the previous steps. Capture the points of tension or conflict as well, as every bit of information is useful. You may also want to refer (and link) to other blips or to other architecture documentation, such as your tech strategy, high-level architecture, ADRs, and more.

At Thoughtworks, a few individuals take on this job, but each blip description is shared internally for everyone's comment and feedback via a universal, editable Google document. This allows everyone to see and comment on the proposed text for each blip. This text should capture how the blip is viewed by the collective, any points of tension or conflict that have been identified during the latest sweep, and any other information that may assist someone when making a decision that pertains to the blip.

Again, this commenting/feedback phase has a time box placed on it, after which the finalized text will be copied back into the spreadsheet ready for publishing, which is the final step.

Radar Publishing

Once the blip descriptions have been written and reviewed, you are ready to publish the first edition of your radar.

When you use the BYOR tool, there are a number of ways to host the result. The simplest, which involves no infrastructure on your end, is to use the free Thoughtworks hosting service. This has a few restrictions. You have to use a Google spreadsheet as your data source, and unless you choose to protect it, your radar effectively becomes public. If you are using this approach, you just need to provide it with a link to your private or public Google spreadsheet of blips. (Don't forget to protect it so no one can edit it.) This will then render the contents of your spreadsheet just like the Thoughtworks one, allowing everyone to interact with it in the same way.

If this hosting method or the associated Thoughtworks terms of use (*https://oreil.ly/3qTm5*) contradict your organization's InfoSec and data security policies, you can still use it, but you will need to find a different place to run it; it's just a JavaScript npm service reading from URL-accessible files, and a Dockerized version is available. Alternatively, there is a plug-in for Spotify's Backstage developer portal (*https://oreil.ly/3KvNG*), and other alternatives might be available by the time you read this.

However you host your technology radar, when it is published, it will look like the Thoughtworks one. Figure 11-9 shows our example radar published with the Kotlin 1.8 blip highlighted and the tidied-up description on the right. Note that all the blips will display as "new" as this is the first edition of your radar.

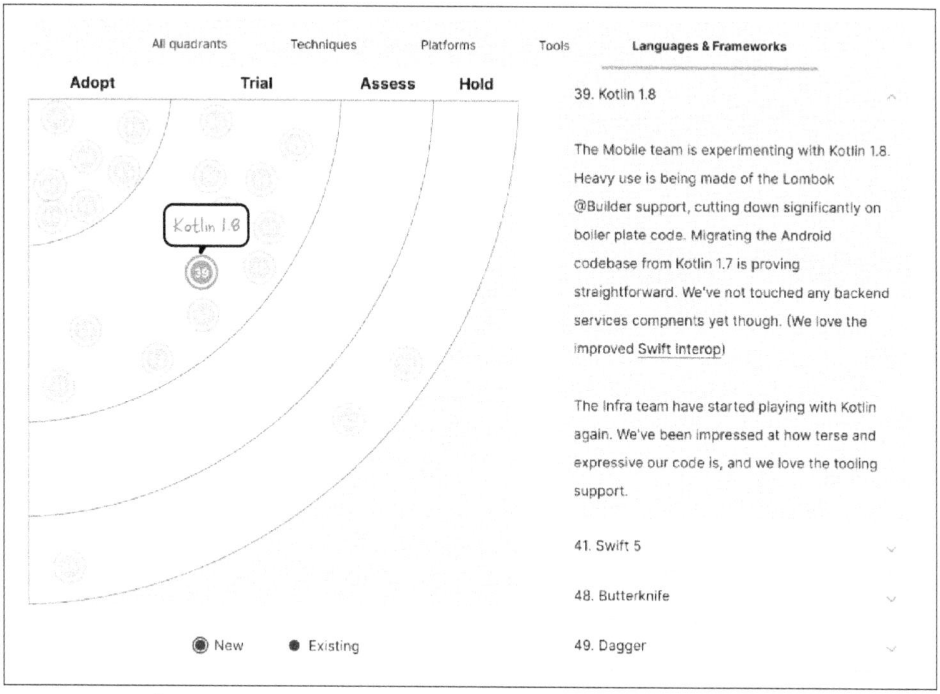
All quadrants
Techniques
Platforms
Tools
Languages & Frameworks
Adopt
Trial
Assess
Hold
Kotlin 1.8
New
Existing
39. Kotlin 1.8
The Mobile team is experimenting with Kotlin 1.8. Heavy use is being made of the Lombok @Builder support, cutting down significantly on boiler plate code. Migrating the Android codebase from Kotlin 1.7 is proving straightforward. We've not touched any backend services compnents yet though. (We love the improved Swift Interop)
The Infra team have started playing with Kotlin again. We've been impressed at how terse and expressive our code is, and we love the tooling support.
41. Swift 5
48. Butterknife
49. Dagger

Figure 11-9. The published internal radar, showing the details of the Kotlin 1.8 blip

Once your technology radar is published, you can send out an announcement email with a link to your interactive radar so that everyone can start using it in their decisions. You'll also want to remind everyone through any other communication channels where architecture decisions are discussed, such as an architecture advice forum. Make it clear that while your radar is in the same format as the Thoughtworks one, it serves a different purpose: to capture the collective guidance in a format that can support decentralized deciding.

Don't forget to take advantage of the fact that you can generate a PDF of your radar. This is a great alternative for folks who prefer to consume their information in a static format. You can also use it as a snapshot of the current state of the radar that can be archived.

However you choose to publish the radar (on the Thoughtworks hosting service or on your own), or however your people choose to consume the information (as an interactive radar, a text-only document, or a PDF), the goal is to socialize your radar so that it becomes another useful tool supporting organizational alignment and your decision process as you collectively practice software architecture.

Updating Your Blips

One tech-radar sweep isn't enough. A traditional radar used to track aircraft sweeps regularly and continuously, capturing updated views of the surrounding airspace. Similarly, a technology radar should periodically sweep the current tech landscape and organizational climate, turning them into updated guidelines.

The frequency of these sweeps depends mainly on how rapidly these environmental factors are changing. I've seen quarterly cadences work, and half-yearly, too. The key is to pay attention to how the radar is being consumed (or not) at the advice forum and elsewhere. That should give you a good idea for when it's worth investing in a refresh.

Periodic Resweeps

Always plan for periodic resweeps, whether or not you capture ad hoc updates arising from individual decisions. These follow a very similar set of steps as the initial creation of the radar, but with a set of preexisting blips. The second and subsequent gatherings will go much more quickly because they harvest far fewer blips.

Prepare for a resweep by copying the published blip data into a new sheet and setting all the previous blips' "isNew" values to "false" (Figure 11-10). You can then encourage the blip submitters to contribute to this new sheet, once again setting a deadline for blip submissions. (Remember to set the previously published radar spreadsheet to read only and label it clearly.)

Make it clear to contributors that for the existing blips, this is not the time to suggest changes in ring position, but additional information in the description cells is welcome. This should be appended to what is already there, flagging who contributed it. This might be as simple as recording that more teams have adopted a blip or that they have moved away from it.

name	ring	quadrant	isNew	description
Kotlin 1.5	adopt ▾	languages... ▾	TRUE ▾	First version of Kotlin at NuOrg. Used for a few experiments which went well, ending up in prod. Some backend services. None mission critical.
Kotlin 1.7	adopt ▾	languages... ▾	TRUE	Kotlin version our Android app currently targets.
Kotlin 1.8	adopt ▾	languages... ▾	TRUE FALSE	experimenting with Kotlin 1.8. Heavy use is the Lombok @Builder support which is cutting ntly on boiler plate code. Migrating Android Kotlin 1.7 was very simple. We've not touched ervices compnents tho. (We love the improved href="https://kotlinlang.org/docs/whatsnew18.html#improved-objective-c-swift-interoperability">Swift interop</a>) We've started playing with Kotlin again in our team (Infra Team)
Swift 4	adopt ▾	languages... ▾	TRUE ▾	First version of Swift that we used. Adopted completely after we dropped ObjectiveC. (Hiring Swift developers was easier.)
Azure Functions	trial ▾	platforms ▾	TRUE ▾	A few teams have experimented with Azure Functions. All but one have used them for back-end housekeeping. Cards team used them to build the entire Customer Onboarding microsite. This is a great use case as it runs infrequently, and when it does it is fundamentally a complicated, async data ingestion pipeline.
AKS (Azure Kubernetes Service)	adopt ▾	platforms ▾	TRUE ▾	All our microservices run in Azure Kubernetes Service (AKS) pods. It works great with Azure DevOps and allows teams to focus on the work of building and running systems. Infra teams have found it easy to configure, leaving us to focus on the value-added work.
Architecture Advice Process	adopt ▾	techniques ▾	TRUE ▾	Having experimented with a single team, and then on a small programme of work, the Architecture Advice Process is now used for all significant architectural decisions (and many regular ones too).

Figure 11-10. Setting the blips from the last edition of your radar to "isNew=false" ("source" column hidden) (https://oreil.ly/1Hxco)

Newly submitted blips will most likely appear first in the "trial" ring. It is also likely that a greater number of techniques will be submitted for this quadrant than when the first scan took place. This seems to happen because the concept of this quadrant tends to sink in only after the initial collection, but this section really blossoms as organizational learning kicks in. Blips in the "techniques" quadrant are an excellent place to make guidance born of experience actionable. Blips can reaffirm what has been learned, making it available to those who have yet to join or have yet to take on the responsibility of deciding. Some classic examples of this from the Thoughtworks radar include: "SAFe™" (https://oreil.ly/sDP7L), the aforementioned "ESBs in API Gateway's clothing" (https://oreil.ly/LMXNv), and "Cloud lift and shift" (https://oreil.ly/MhDGu).

Wherever new blips land, you will again have to perform the same tidying-up activities as in "Blip Sorting and Validation" on page 286 to prepare for the next collaborative stages. The process of sorting and validating the new and updated blips is exactly the same as the original process.

The subsequent stages also proceed in a similar fashion to the first pass, but less time needs to be allocated. Sorting and validation and focusing need take place only for new blips, but the former is still best achieved in a workshop, which will take significantly less time than the first time around. Two hours is usually appropriate, but you will know how long you need based on your experience from the first workshop.

(Re)positioning applies to all the blips and should again be done by opening up the sheet to all in the blip-providing community. Not every blip needs to move, however; your radar should reflect reality, and if nothing has changed, then there is no need to update anything.

After (re)positioning is complete, documentation needs to reconsider all blips, too (though not all preexisting blips may need an update if they've not moved rings). This is a great time to discuss and provide updated guideline notes for all blips that stay on the radar, even if this text is largely based on the version from the previous edition's blip. Calling out that something about a blip hasn't changed can also be useful for the reader. Remember that the goal is to make your collective wisdom and experience explicit, whatever that is. On the other hand, if a blip has moved, then it's a great opportunity to explain why in the text. If increased—or decreased—numbers of teams are using it, then this should be reflected. Finally, if a blip is no longer applicable, then it should be removed completely. (I'll discuss strategic divestment and retiring legacy technologies in the final section of this chapter.)

Resweeps update your radar, but they have another benefit. By retaining the history of blips, they provide a valuable learning resource and reference library. But wholescale resweeps aren't the only way to capture blip updates.

Ad Hoc Updates Based on Shared Experience

While periodic resweeps keep your radar entirely up to date, they're not the only source of changes. Blip additions, movements, and clarifications should also emerge from the advice process and architectural decisions.

Recall that a decision that effectively adds a new blip (either because there are currently no blips that apply in that circumstance or because all those that do apply aren't sufficient or satisfactory for some reason) or a decision that advocates for a blip to be treated as if it were in a different ring is a solid indication that a decision is "significant." This fact should be highlighted in the ADR and advice sought. But what happens after the decision is taken and the ADR adopted? This should (at least) flag the blip as a candidate for an ad hoc update of the technology radar.

Decision-driven blip additions or updates are best moved forward via another ADR. If it's an entirely new blip, then this ADR should be raised by the team or individual who took the initial decision. If it's a blip update, then this responsibility will likely fall to someone with a cross-system (probably architecture, but possibly a platform team) role.

ADRs are a great format for such changes, and they can be very lightweight. Unlike with updating the set of principles, it is sufficient to add or update the principle in reference to the ADR that prompted the change, sharing the proposed new ring, the new text, and the reason for the addition or move.

If you choose not to update the radar at this time, don't worry. You can always catch the blip and update it when your next sweep comes around, and you have your explicit flagging of the deviation in the ADR. Whenever I postpone a radar update, I keep a list of these potential ADRs, which I can use to prompt everyone when the next sweep takes place to ensure that nothing gets missed. These can also be checked when another decision comes along that looks like it's proposing that the same blip be moved. (It needn't be the same type of change—remember, ADRs are great for transparent technical discussions. When combined with an advice process, they have a high tolerance for a diversity of voices and advice.)

Capturing Previous Blips and Their History

However you update blips, it can be valuable to keep track of how they have changed over time. If you choose to do this, you can create something that works similarly to the history pages of the Thoughtworks Technology Radar.

To create blip histories, it's best to have a wiki-type environment where each blip gets its own page. This can also help when you retire blips from the main radar but want to preserve the fact that they were once blipped.

For each blip in the original radar, move it to your wiki, one blip per page. Group these pages together based on the quadrants if you like. (It makes browsing easier.) When you create a new page, follow the structure and layout of the Thoughtworks Technology Radar. When a blip makes it to a subsequent edition of the radar, put the new ring and details at the top of the page.

Link the blips in the current radar to their history wiki pages by adding a hyperlink to the blip description in the spreadsheet. This allows viewers of the radar to click through to these history pages. Having this guidance at your fingertips helps greatly when making new decisions.

> ## Further Uses for a Technology Radar
>
> As a technology radar becomes embedded within your advice process and wider soci-otechnical ecosystem, you may realize that it offers extra opportunities. I've collected the opportunities I see most frequently into a separate article (*https://oreil.ly/_dbUu*) that covers additional blip information you may want to capture as well as how to use your radar to consciously manage the higher levels of strategic interventions that I introduced in Chapter 9, both investments and divestments.

Conclusion

This chapter described a fourth supporting element: your own technology radar. I considered how it offers a fun way to both sense for and make sense of the more subtle signals in your sociotechnical ecosystem and offer contextualized advice on them. I showed how important the end result is as a support for the advice process generally as well as a source of potential strategic investments and a way to manage strategic divestments.

The technology radar takes the last place in my go-to mechanisms for supporting and promoting decentralized and feedback-oriented practices of software architecture. There might be alternatives—especially the supporting elements—and I encourage you to experiment with them all, making sure you keep the goals of your approach in mind.

As you probe, you will learn a lot more about the practice of decision making and its place in both software development and sociotechnical systems. Part III focuses on both topics from multiple angles, with the goal of enabling everyone who decides to practice decentralized architecture for flow and feedback.

Finding Your Way Through the Decision Landscape

By now, you are now well prepared with elements—both core and supporting—to reinforce decentralized deciding. But deciding is still hard. Part III offers support for everyone who participates in this core architectural practice so that they are aware of the complex dynamics of decisions in sociotechnical systems. You will learn how decisions *actually work*.

Chapter 12 focuses on the softer, more personal, human aspects of deciding. It looks in particular at how *framing, creativity, bias, and fear* all play a far bigger role than we like to admit in software decisions. It introduces ways of thinking, approaches, checklists, and more than a dash of cognitive science so that you might become more aware of your human frailties and not fall prey to them as you practice architecture.

Chapter 13 broadens the scope beyond the individual, considering how best to approach decisions to tackle *architectural variability*, or what is more colloquially known as "unknown unknowns," and the unpredictability and power of software that arise from them. It looks in depth at the pain that variability can cause architectural practice if it is not addressed before moving on to a series of proven principles and strategies for working with variability and using it to unlock the full power of software.

Chapter 14 threads both of these aspects together, looking at how variability plays into the *interconnectedness of decisions*, from both a technical and a sociological perspective. It offers four distinct but complementary perspectives on this interconnectedness. In each case, it shows how the use of extreme programming spikes can cut through to the essential learning, feeding directly into ADRs as a consequence.

By the end of Part III, you will have an appropriate mental model and set of techniques to collectively tackle the practice of decentralized deciding with a focus on feedback and find your way through the complex decision landscape.

CHAPTER 12

The Art of Deciding

The practice of deciding is more than determining that a decision is needed, identifying options, seeking advice, and ultimately selecting a decision. Deciding also involves working with the tender aspects of human nature, such as emotions, feelings, and creativity. These softer aspects aren't easily defined or predicted.

This chapter focuses on this softer side, revealing how human aspects—both personal and interpersonal—affect our decisions and considering how framing, creativity, bias, and fear, all play important roles in the art of deciding. Within the context of the ADR-supported decision process, I'll explore how these human aspects affect the context first, then the options and consequences, and finally the taking of decisions, while not forgetting their role in advice seeking throughout all of this.

The Importance of the Softer Side

As software professionals, we tell ourselves that the act of deciding is a purely intellectual one. The architectural practice of deciding *does* include a great deal of facts and thinking. But it also—if you listen to others—is an incredibly social and creative act. This listening doesn't come as easily to many of us.

I know from experience that holding diverse ideas in our minds at the same time can feel incongruous, uncomfortable, or even impossible. However, the advice process and ADRs are a great help. The process helps us conceptually limit the scope through framing and improve our ability to engage others' thinking.

Framing the Context

The Context section of an ADR is your setting-off point, both for decisions and for this exploration of the human aspects of deciding. It is in your Context where you make clear (to yourself and future readers) why a decision is required. Architectural decisions always have a context because it's essential to know what the decision depends on: the circumstances that led to the decision being necessary. The Context section is the place where you state those circumstances clearly, and hence it is the embarkation point from where all decision journeys set out.

Excluding Is as Important as Including

Sometimes, the most difficult part of a decision is getting everyone to understand that there is a problem. How you present contextual information helps shape people's perceptions—yours and others'—and ultimately helps everyone understand what you are trying to achieve.

For example, consider two maps representing the same world differently. The first map has a scale of 1:1. This map, and the country it represents, are the same size and share the same level of detail.[1] Picture that for a second: *everything* in the world is represented life-size. Nothing is more important than anything else. Not very useful.

The second map is at 1:1000 scale. Not only is it smaller, but it is also opinionated about what it frames. *Your* home country is in the center, taking up most of the surface area. Surrounding it, but decidedly smaller, are perfunctory representations of the other countries that border yours.[2]

Neither map is *wrong per se*, but the second one is vastly more useful, despite its far lower levels of detail and accuracy. This is because the purpose of a map is to *simplify and abstract the key information about an area* so that you can *interpret* and *act* on that information. Maps orient us and help us figure out how to get from here to where we want to be. Maps help us make decisions.

The first map fails in that respect. Because it abstracts nothing, it doesn't help us focus, nor does it remove extraneous detail. It does nothing to narrow the decision space. The second map emphasizes what's most important to us (our immediate area) and gives us sufficient contextual information about the remaining surroundings.

These two maps demonstrate the importance of framing when deciding. I've described two, but there are nearly infinite ways to map the same space, depending

---

1 This paraphrases the famous one-paragraph short story by Jorge Luis Borges, "On Exactitude in Science." (Or "On Rigor in Science." The original title in Spanish is "Del rigor en la ciencia.")

2 This refers to the 18th-century Chinese map that opens the first chapter of Eric Evans's *Domain-Driven Design*.

on the decision you want to support. By placing a frame around the boundaries of a decision space, you focus on what is relevant to the decision at hand. This isn't to say that you should ignore reality beyond the frame, but the act of framing highlights what things you should pay attention to *for this decision*.

Crafting the Context section of an ADR requires framing our challenges or needs in a way that highlights how they affect the decision at hand. The Context section tells us what we should be concerned about and excludes everything else. Framing describes both the circumstances and why the decision matters now.

Framing the circumstances

By removing distracting and irrelevant details and being definite about scope, framing can reveal that two opposing elements cannot both be true. Framing directs everyone's attention to whatever is incongruent or blocking, setting the stage for productive discussions.

Framing time

Framing includes the time frame of a decision. How far away from where we are now will this decision extend? All decisions have a finite lifespan, even if that's not explicitly stated. Nothing lasts forever, so describe the impact of time in the Context section part of an ADR.

Decisions "expire" naturally as things change, not always on a fixed date. Expiry can happen when a stage of a service's evolution has been reached. (Chapter 14 will consider the impact of time on decisions in far more depth.) The (probably apocryphal) story I've heard is that Google designs their systems to grow to 10 times the predicted scale. Beyond 10x, they can't predict what other factors will affect the design. Taking architectural decisions now about something that might have a vastly different context by the time it comes to pass is a futile activity. Far better to acknowledge that at some point in time, the decision will need to be revisited.

Time plays another important role in decisions: it limits how long you have to implement the decision outcome. Given infinite time, the decider might deeply consider the many different options available. But there is never infinite time to decide. All decisions are framed by the time by which a solution has to be delivered. Finite time frequently drives decisions in very different directions.

Using framing to describe only the key circumstances and important timescales adds clarity to your decisions and your decision process, distilling a decision down to its truly important elements. The context tells you exactly what is within and without the decision frame. During the context-writing part of the ADR-supported decision process, you may not know exactly how some elements will affect the ultimate decision, but you will know which elements aren't in the frame.

Gathering advice during the context-writing process helps framing. Hearing someone articulate the challenge in their own words or give their perspective can clarify the decision's context. Advice is not confined to your options and consequences. Seek advice to sharpen your context, too.

Questions That Improve Judgment Around Framing

You can take a methodical approach to capturing the context by working through a series of prompts. Professor Joseph L. Badaracco of Harvard Business School offered five questions to improve judgment around deciding.[3] The first three directly assist in understanding the context, asking:

1. What are my core obligations?
2. What will work in the world as it is?
3. Who are we?

"What are my core obligations?" This question ensures that you have identified the right stakeholders and the obligations you have to them in this context. The question "What are our duties to others?" works as well, calling to mind the social contract and culture of trust we're nurturing and protecting as part of the architecture advice process. Take time as you craft your context to make sure you have the right people in mind, both inside and outside your organization (I'll talk more about involving the right stakeholders in the next section).

"What will work in the world as is?" This question is a reality check. Is the decision, its options, and its consequences based on the *actual state of our world*? This question makes us aware of immovable or unchangeable things, no matter how inconvenient they are, because it removes our blinders. It is too easy to talk about how things would work in a perfect world and ignore our complicated and messy reality.

For example, a client I worked with was designing a system that operates in multiple countries around the world. The problem was making the services highly available, with no lag, everywhere. In a perfect world, the solution would be a cloud-based system. Problem solved!

In reality, the service had to be available in Turkey and China. Both countries were deemed to be strategically important. Turkey and China legally require that both the software and data reside locally in their territories. We couldn't just implement a cloud-based solution. When we included reality in the context, the problem became more complex.

---

3 Joseph L. Badaracco, "How to Tackle Your Toughest Decisions" (*https://oreil.ly/1r37G*), *Harvard Business Review*, September 2016.

"Who are we?" This question reminds you that your context needs to reflect your organization's values. When setting the context, this is the most important of Badaracco's questions. Forgetting to consider how a decision aligns with your organization's values inherently generates incongruity in the system.

Taken together, these questions provide a powerful set of thinking prompts that support efficient and effective decision framing.

Involve the Right Stakeholders

Badaracco's first three questions help you identify people who will be affected by your decision and others who are well placed to offer expertise. Go on and include them.[4]

However, a stakeholder list that is unnecessarily long signals two problems. First, it signals that your context is too broad, probably because you are trying to bite off a larger decision than necessary. Ask yourself, "Is my decision too big? Do I need to further define and sharpen my problem area? Can I tackle this decision in multiple parts? Do I need to pull back on the aspirations of what I am deciding on?" (Think back to "Story 2: An Architect Decides to Unpick a Workflow Problem" in Chapter 4 for an example of this happening.) I'll go into more detailed techniques for breaking down a decision that is too big in Chapters 13 and 14.

Second, when your list is too long, you may be including stakeholders out of perceived social obligation. The social contract in this process is to seek advice from those affected and those with expertise. Go back to Badaracco's first and second questions and check that each person is directly affected or has relevant expertise in the current reality.

People might feel they should be included in a decision simply because of their place in the hierarchy. Use the context to clarify who will be sought for their advice and why—and equally who won't be included and why not.

One of the first systems I worked on was a portal to find information about individuals making their way through the English and Welsh legal system. Thirteen agencies were involved, each with some interest in the treatment of these people. There were a lot of stakeholder needs to be balanced. We realized that by displaying information to a smaller set of users and use cases (ideally one), decisions could be reached much more rapidly. For example, one screen displayed information for the prisons service, and another provided details if the individual was a minor. By framing relevant information on the second screen, youth justice teams, police, and social workers could act

---

4 Thoughtworks has produced a "Responsible Tech Playbook" (*https://oreil.ly/Re2Q4*), which brings together many tools and practices (some from Thoughtworks, some from elsewhere) to help you think about the potential hidden stakeholders of decisions you might take.

on that information appropriately. Other stakeholders who had no interest in it didn't need to ever look at it.

With the frame set around your context, you can step *into* the frame and start making and weighing up options. As you consider the options and their consequences, you'll discover if the frame is too limiting.

Discerning Options and Their Consequences

The Options and Consequences sections of an ADR are where you discover and describe future possibilities. The context frames your pending decision so that you can step through it into a delineated open space of options. This is the space where design of the decision options happens,[5] where you come up with the potential arrangements of elements that can meet your challenges or needs. This space is also where you consider each option's consequences, both positive and negative.

Don't Let the Frame Limit Your Creativity

The context gave you a coherent idea of your boundaries and the constraints of your decision frame. It also made explicit the elements you might need to position within it. But it went no further. The creation of options is a decidedly creative act, one that improves significantly with practice.

When you are option making, don't let the context *overly* constrain you. Pay particular attention to whether you are slipping into a single-solution ideal. Allow your creativity to roam freely, finding all the viable options.

Don't worry that this free thinking will be a waste of time or lead you down a blind alley. Your context helps you quickly evaluate the suitability of any options you consider. Considering options improves your understanding of your frame, and the frame can help you discover new options. This process is highly creative, helping you avoid grabbing a familiar, locally optimal solution and freeing you up to truly consider the entire framed landscape.

In *The Playlist*, Netflix's drama series about the rise of Spotify, engineers were wrestling with a key contextual constraint (one that carries a great deal of dramatic weight in the narrative): an audio stream *must* start playing in 200 ms or less. Anything above this would put users off adopting the service. Unfortunately, TCP/IP, the only protocol option, doesn't allow streams to start playing this fast.

---

5 If this makes you think of the space where design happens from Chapter 7 then congratulations, it is the same. The frame is helping you focus on the right part of that wider, whole-system space for the decision in front of you.

In a dramatic moment, someone suggests dropping the nonlossy aspect of TCP/IP initially. They will lose data, but the loss will have an imperceptible impact on users. The 200-ms target led to a new creative option, which is (in the drama, at least) to break the seemingly unbreakable rules of TCP/IP at the start of streams.[6]

This decision did have consequences, ones that the episode went on to discuss. Quality loss at the start of plays was acknowledged, understood, and judged acceptable (in the series, at least).

To avoid overfocusing on available options and their consequences and open yourself up to increased creativity, you can ask yourself two questions:

1. Am I considering only the seemingly obvious options? I have options A, B, and C, but am I dismissing a fourth option, D? Questioning your perceived consequences can help you uncover options you might have ruled out.

2. Am I unpacking my options sufficiently? It is not uncommon to think of an option A but not consider it in sufficient detail to realize that it actually contains within it multiple variants. Option A can become options A1, A2, and A3.

These variants can sometimes be powerful when they either extend an existing option or combine the best of both worlds,[7] but they are only beneficial if they don't magnify each option's downsides or if they don't add complexity when something simpler would suffice.

When discerning decision options, don't exclude things because of their consequences. One idea can lead to another, and an option's consequences can lead you to think of an even better option.

Seek Inspiration

Uncovering all of these alternate options and their consequences can sometimes be easy. Other times, you need to work a little to get there. However they arise, being aware of your personal mindset and ways of thinking is incredibly important. There's no secret formula for this. Self-reflection is your tool here. Learning from others is also deeply rewarding. Let's consider both of these sources of inspiration.

---

6 There are other interesting insights in the series into technical decisions being made—admittedly not very inclusively and with a great deal of emotion (almost inevitably amplified by the show's creators). *Halt and Catch Fire* (AMC, 2014–17) is another drama series where key software creative decisions, particularly the uncovering of a game-changing option and its subsequent implementation, are dramatized relatively faithfully.

7 If you think back to Chapter 6, there was a hybrid option in the first ADR example: "Option 5: combination of building name and generated ID."

Some individuals I have worked with undertake this entire option-making process internally. They will "think through" various scenarios, mentally listing the options and consequences. Such internal inspiration comes from your own knowledge, buried within your own brain. As such, you need ways to draw out that knowledge by writing it out in a tidy list, scribbling it on a sticky note, making quick sketches, or what have you.

Personally, I find that such sketching of ideas (I wouldn't bless them with the title of "diagrams" at this point) helps me think. Sketches of this kind are useful to me for all flavors of significant architectural decisions,[8] but they particularly help with structural, interface, and dependency decisions. Trying to draw everything out ensures that I think about the challenge from all the relevant angles. The physical nature of the act and its output also allow me to think about alternatives: "What if that line went from there to there, instead of from there to there?" and "What if this system (box) didn't know about this box—how would that change matters?" I can really think about them "in the round."

At this point, even though I am still working on my own, that doesn't mean I don't seek external inspiration too by doing some research. Such research can be in house in the form of other ADRs, but it also looks beyond the organization.

Such inspiration can be found in pattern books (those I listed in the Chapter 2 sidebar "Design Patterns" on page 41 and more). Consult them to see if any have a problem discussion and a problem summary section (if they follow the Alexandrian pattern style as Eric Evans's *Domain-Driven Design* does) or a motivation section (if they follow the style of the Gang of Four design patterns) that resonate with the challenge you are facing.

But don't be restricted to purely technical sources when browsing for inspiration. For example, I found a great deal to think about in Masanobu Fukuoka's ground-breaking book on agriculture, *The One-Straw Revolution* (Other India Press, 2009). In the book, he consistently challenged accepted wisdom, from "doing less and leaving things alone" to "embracing and working with emergent ecosystem effects rather than fighting them" to "letting the learnings from a regular harvest fertilize the next generation" to "cultivating difference and co-existence."[9]

All these are great ways to embrace and extend your personal creativity for option making, but I've intentionally held off on the most obvious source of assistance in this

---

8 Cast your mind back to Chapter 2 and the five types of significant decision: structure, cross-functional, dependencies, interfaces, and construction techniques.

9 My first ever conference talk, "The Five Whys," looked at seemingly counterintuitive decisions that trend-setting companies at the time had publicly taken, framed in the form of a set of questions (the "whys" in the title).

area: the advice of others in your organization. Let's turn there now, moving away from the wholly personal aspects to the interpersonal, which can be a source of both great value and great difficulty.

Sharpen Context and Options with Advice

Part II of this book showed how to nurture a culture that optimizes for decentralized deciding, with just enough supporting elements and no more. While the taking of decisions in an advice process lies in the personal realm, the social contract obliges deciders to move through an interpersonal stage to get there: that of advice seeking.

This social inclusion is no mere formality; it's a means of arriving at better decisions. In fact, advice seeking provides a formal means to answer Badaracco's final two questions. "What are the net, net consequences of all my options?" is Badaracco's first remaining question, by which he means "What will each of my options lead to?" "What can we live with?" is his final question—another way of saying, "How comfortable do we feel living with this option in the future?" In both cases, who better to ask than those affected by the decision and those with expertise? And what better time to change course on a decision than at the point of deciding, rather than when construction has started?

Decisions that acknowledge and incorporate advice are far more likely to be a better fit for both your current and future challenge and context. However, a lot of potential nuance, tension, and even conflict can emerge when others are involved. Let's begin by examining the circumstances when everything in your architectural practice is working transparently and positively—that is, when trust (and safety) is high, agreement is sufficient, and surprise is low. In such circumstances, advice seeking can be an exhilarating experience.

Advice in these circumstances can sharpen your context as well as unveil and focus both consequences and options. This happens because the advice process taps into the intuition and differing perspectives of the advice offerers.

Psychiatrist Carl Jung said in a 1959 interview (*https://oreil.ly/Ugj9A*), "The intuitive person can see round corners." I'm sure you've come across such people in software: colleagues and coworkers who seemed able to see into the future far better than others could. Asking these people for advice about what they foresee, even though they might turn out to be wrong sometimes, can help you shift and tune the balance between options to your specific circumstances.

Differing perspectives, on the other hand, are easier to rationalize. More than anything, differing perspectives serve to counter personal blind spots. These blind spots are your "unknown unknowns" and your biases, and they arise in both your understanding of the current context and the options you have created from it. Someone's advice might reveal a consequential flaw that is obscured or hidden to you but glaringly obvious to them. Or it might highlight the opportunity of an option that seems self-evident to them but that you are completely unaware of. In the wicked sociotechnical world of architectural decisions, the fact that an advice process obliges the decision taker to expose themselves to both these inputs is phenomenal because their blind spots can be largely or even wholly removed.

Chip Heath and Dan Heath's *Decisive: How to Make Better Decisions in Life and Work* (Crown Currency, 2013) lays out the WRAP framework for making better decisions. Although it was developed for personal decisions, it works just as well for group decisions. It's particularly interesting to see how advice maps to this framework.

WRAP stands for:

- Widen your options
- Reality-test your assumptions
- Attain distance before deciding
- Prepare to be wrong

In the context of the architecture advice process, "widen your options" refers to making sure that you capture decision options beyond the ones that immediately spring from your own mind. It means seeking internal and external inspiration, as discussed earlier in this chapter. External inspiration includes seeking input from advice givers.

"Reality-test your assumptions" relates to both the context and consequences, asking, for instance, "Is the decider overconstraining themselves by a false assumption?" and "Has the decider assumed that an affected group or party would be against something prior to asking them, thereby cutting off options?" On the flip side, it seeks challenges: "Has the decider presumed something would be possible, missing something that says otherwise?" Advice allows the gathered collective to surface and discuss both of these.

Sharpen Your Options with Advice

As you incorporate advice, take the opportunity to sharpen the edges of your options. Making one distinct frequently makes the others more distinct as well because of the contrasts and delineations you are forced to draw. However, don't drown in tit-for-tat, pro-and-con pairings ("this is a pro for this option, and so it's a con for all the others"). When this happens, consider the following: first, which is the strongest point, the pro (the benefit) or the con (the drawback)? It is likely that the strongest point will be the deal-breaker and is what makes that option distinct, for either favorable or unfavorable reasons. This is the one to record.

"Attain distance before deciding" and "prepare to be wrong" are both more emotional than intellectual. They prepare you for the possibility of emotional damage as a result of exposing yourself to criticism. Both rely on metacognition skills.

Develop Your Metacognition

Metacognition is the awareness and understanding of your own thought processes. Whether you are entirely new to making and taking architectural decisions or you have this experience but have never engaged others to seek or offer advice, it pays to cultivate these skills. By being cognizant of why you think the way you do, you will ask better questions and give better advice. You will consequently be more open to advice and better placed to take what is valuable from it. When everyone learns these skills (organizational learning, again), the collective will have better conversations that are more productive, informative, educational, and fulfilling. The architectures will be better, too.

Metacognitive skills can be hard to learn for some, while others appear to have these abilities naturally. In fact, everyone needs to practice. The following are some simple exercises to help you, and others, improve in this area.[10]

Exercise 1: Share Your Reasons

A relatively easy way to upscale both your advice offering and decision taking is to acknowledge and then explicitly articulate the reasons that convinced you of an idea or theory. To do this, you need to be aware of why, and in many cases, you will discover that the reasons are not as intellectually or factually based as you first thought. (Remember, opinions are the near enemy of advice.) Perhaps you have a tendency to prefer things you personally have hands-on experience with, or perhaps you like something because you respect the person who suggested it more than others. This is not to say that any of these reasons are *bad*, but being aware of them, and being able to share this fact in either your advice giving or deciding, will again contribute greatly to a culture of transparency and trust.

Exercise 2: Are You Reacting or Responding?

Irrespective of whether you are seeking or offering advice, examine your thought processes and separate when you are reacting—acting on thoughts that arise—from when you are responding—paying attention to those feelings and taking time to decide how you want to act.

---

10 If these prove useful, and I'm confident they will, check out Diana Montalion's book *Learning Systems Thinking* (O'Reilly), which goes into them in far greater detail.

By doing so, you will become increasingly aware of your actions and learn to put aside your fears and biases (more on that later in this chapter and again in Chapter 15). For example, you will notice whether you treat people differently based on what you perceive as their identity. You may offer different advice depending on if you like the person or not. You may also be more open to listening to advice from someone you like. Understanding your reactions and responses will lead to better decisions, and it positively reinforces the move in your culture toward open and honest communication and weighing of options based on their individual merits irrespective of who shared them. That's not to say that you won't still experience reactions, both in yourselves and others. It's only natural—you're human. But being aware of your reactions, and being able to separate them from the advice and your proper responses to it, is a special kind of magic.

Yet another benefit of advice processes is that you can take your time. Once advice is gathered, you have as long as you need to undertake this winnowing process, separating yourself (your reactions) from the advice and taking the advice at face value.

This does take practice: to spot when you are upset by something or not thinking clearly, to acknowledge it, and to work with it. Give yourself the time to allow these skills to build. Enlist the help of others to get their third-party perspectives. Also recognize that this is natural, and that different individuals and specific circumstances will give rise to responses in you that others won't. It's simply human psychology at work, and you have the power to work with it and change it.

Remember, advice seekers are not obliged to take advice from such people out of a feeling of deference or of guilt. Remember, too, that advice is advice, wherever it comes from, and as the decider you are only obliged to listen to and understand it but *not* to follow it.

Exercise 3: Intentionally Seek Advice That Challenges You

In Chapter 5 (the section "Seek advice from those with conflicting views" on page 108), I suggested that you consciously engage people who you believe will disagree with you as a way to strengthen your decision. The *A* and *P* of WRAP make it clear why this is beneficial: you *attain distance* by sourcing it from the advice of others, and by engaging specifically with these alternative perspectives, you help yourself *prepare to be wrong*. As a direct consequence of this, you will be exposed to new options and consequences that (initially at least) you are likely to disagree with. The same goes for advice regarding the context.

Even if you think an option arising from advice is terrible, treat it as you would any other, even if you end up dismissing it. Use it to attain distance from your preferred option and practice preparing to be wrong. Perhaps your initial reaction was correct and the advice is wholly terrible. But perhaps you're only half right and it contains something valuable. Or perhaps you're entirely wrong and it is the piece of advice that completely changes your perspective. (This is why "Exercise 1: Share Your Reasons" on page 311 is so critical. *Why* is this a terrible idea? *How* did you reach your conclusion? You want others to follow your thinking path so that they can see where theirs diverge.) By trying to take all these positions explicitly, you will develop a better understanding of why it's really a bad or a good option and, inversely, what makes an alternative a better option.

As you challenge yourself to treat all advice equally, use the experience to develop your metacognition skills. Become more aware of your own thinking processes. Ask yourself, "Did I react rather than respond, dismissing this advice out of hand before attaining distance and preparing to be wrong?" If you are unsure, ask yourself, "Was I comfortable engaging this person?" which might make you aware of interpersonal issues blocking you. This is important because in the transparent, high-trust environment you're looking to build, if someone has the ability to share knowledge and insight with you that you need, why would you not speak to them? And yet you may have felt reticent. It's good to know why, even if the reason is that they're simply not very nice people.

The reasons for your reticence may surprise you. Perhaps you are less certain of your decision making, and you are worried that they will point out the flaws you are yourself half aware of. Perhaps they will give rise to feelings of lack of ability on your part. Once you are aware of these emotions, you can interrogate them a little. Are they based on factual reality? Perhaps you are less skilled in a certain area, which is why this person is fulfilling the "expertise" role in the process, or equally, perhaps not.

Now, I've focused heavily on advice seekers here as they are the more active parties in the advice process. It's not just advice seekers who can benefit from attaining distance and preparing to be wrong. Advice offerers can also become aware of and attain distance from their preferred options and perceived consequences. They can also prepare to be wrong. Witnessing advice seekers not following your advice can be an equally interesting experience. Analyzing how it felt to offer your advice can help you change both the advice you offer and the way in which you offer it. You can step back from arguing and pushing, and step into offering and discussing. I'll share a story about how I personally felt about such an experience at the end of this chapter.

Coping with Uncooperative Individuals

So far, I've articulated the subtle, semiconscious reasons why advice seeking might be difficult. However, things might not be that hidden. You might be very aware of the reasons you're not seeking a certain individual's advice.

Sadly, power hierarchies—formal and informal—play far too significant a role in software engineering. These hierarchies, either explicit or implicit, structural or cultural, can lead some to assume that their advice should always carry more weight than the advice of others. It can also result in some individuals feeling less obliged to share reasoning and experiences—those who perceive themselves to be higher up one or more of these hierarchies. This is because software development is knowledge work, and knowledge, as the adage goes, is power.

I've written elsewhere (*https://oreil.ly/FN9wN*) about how unevenly distributed knowledge can protect power bases in software systems and also about how software and systems make it very easy to make that knowledge opaque or even hidden. The architecture advice process offers an appropriate way to break into those power bases, making that hoarded knowledge both transparent and accessible, and letting it flow where it is needed. But to those whose perceived value to the organization or sense of worth in an organization relies entirely on the uneven distribution of knowledge, it is a threat. Being asked to not only offer advice but also to be open about the reasoning and emotions behind it can be intensely threatening for some. It makes them feel challenged, undermined, and less secure. It exposes them to the accusation that they made mistakes.

When you believe you have encountered such individuals, try these approaches: attempt to follow the process and deploy all the techniques I've shared so far. In many cases, this will work.[11] Use metacognition to be aware of your thoughts and feelings, and acknowledge that you are uncomfortable. Remember that being a source of advice and wisdom as well as a wealth of historical knowledge and past (probably undocumented) decisions is seen by many as a position of responsibility. In many cases, there is a reason for that person being party to that knowledge. Perhaps they've simply been around longer. Making it clear that the sense of worth gained from contributing to a group effort can trump any solo effort might be enough to entice that person into the circle of trust.

If these approaches fail, someone else who has a positive or neutral relationship with the adviser can be sent in to seek advice from the troublesome person in question. It is not unknown for two individuals to have a personality clash that brings out the worst in both of them, and intermediaries can help provide the necessary distance to get out of argument and into argumentation. Alternatively, you can swap your comms from synchronous and face to face to async and via chat or through the comments on an ADR. I've frequently seen situations arise where different thinking styles and speeds result in clashes that seem to be about the content of a decision but in fact aren't.

But what if, after everything, the individual still refuses to participate? Or worse, they are actively undermining the advice process? For starters, you have in your ADR's advice section a record of their failure to cooperate. You might also have the person

---

11 Another description of such an individual is in the article "The Rise and Fall of the Dungeon Master" (*https://oreil.ly/6_bTT*), wherein Alberto Brandolini does a superb job of laying out the emotional and intellectual challenges of being such an individual.

or persons who brought in the advice process to appeal to—likely those architects who gave away their decision power to the collective. At this point, it makes sense to escalate, engaging them and asking for their assistance, which might proceed in the following order of directness:

1. Remind the recalcitrant individual of the advice process and how it works. The person you escalated to ought to also highlight the new role of everyone in the process and the benefits that result. Perhaps there has been a misunderstanding. Assumption of good intent can again help here.
2. Make the social contract clear and how it holds all parties to account.
3. Highlight the existence of the ADRs and how they make accountability clear, both of the decision taken and of the advice offered and whether it was incorporated or not.

Above all, remember that under the advice process, the advice seeker is also the decision taker. If after everything, you still feel the decision ought to go in a direction contrary to the gathered advice, then decide that. If you do, make sure that you have captured all the advice fully and faithfully.

However it plays out, and if you can bear it, it's worth spending some time subjecting yourself and your reactions, responses, and feelings to a little analysis. I'm not suggesting that you locate the root of all problems within yourself, but I am encouraging you to engage in some postmortem metacognition. These difficult encounters are ideal testing grounds for the metacognition skills you and your colleagues are learning. If you can strengthen them in this environment, even a little, then you can be proud of your development.[12]

What I've covered here is a point instance, occurring between (most likely) two individuals. But problems can go wider and deeper. The same individual might be repeatedly problematic, or a team might make a series of decisions that go against a significant amount of advice. If hierarchical thinking is culturally embedded, causing either quiet acquiescence or secret revolt, then broader interventions are needed. I'll go into these broader dynamics and how to tackle them as a collective in Part IV.

Whether your advice-seeking experience is wholly enjoyable or hard work, it has a job to do. But it's not an end in itself: you must ultimately take the decision. This too

---

12 I once took a meditation class. I revealed to the teacher that I had a *deep* fear of flying, which was no fun as my job meant I had to fly twice a week. (Thankfully, those days are long gone.) They pointed out that to some, this would be a blessing. Semiweekly, I didn't need to do any work to bring to mind my fear; it was laid out before me, on a plate (or more accurately, on a plane). I could engage with it and slowly build up an awareness of how it felt to be scared: naming it, sitting with it, and accepting it. It didn't particularly make me enjoy flying any more—I'm still no fan of turbulence—but it did help develop my metacognition skills when working with it.

can be a struggle because there is rarely (never?) a clearly evident "best option" for architectural decisions, at least not for significant ones.

Deciding takes place amid uncertainties. Despite doing your best to frame the context, then consider all the relevant options and their important consequences, you still have no guarantee that the desired consequences will follow. Let's move on and tackle this seemingly instantaneous yet also frequently difficult step of "decision taking" next.

Selecting a Decision Option

Choosing can be incredibly hard. For every "I choose you" there is one or more "I do not choose yous." By taking their pick, a decider selects a hoped-for future, cutting off, possibly irretrievably, a selection of alternative futures. Preparing options and considering consequences can either assist in this or make it more complicated. That preparation work will provide clear support for one option over others, or it will have highlighted the multiple options, each with potential benefits and drawbacks. But none of it removes the need for the decision taker to take this leap into the unknown. Considered in this way, it's no wonder that many find this step in deciding the hardest. Paths are being chosen, but doors are also being closed.

Delaying a decision offers no refuge. Pushing a decision into the future might offer the delusion that you have more control over a decision than you really do. I previously alluded to the Agile concept of "last responsible moment," but too little time is spent thinking about *when* that moment is. It is far better to consciously decide not to act than to put off even the idea of a decision until it is almost too late. By deciding, no matter what option you select, you maintain control. By consciously deciding *not* to act, you are exercising power rather than handing it away.

One significant reason why decisions are put off is their perceived irreversibility.[13] When a decision is perceived as irreversible, it is easier to put it off because it represents potential mistakes that cannot be corrected. *Irreversible* means that I offer myself a reason to avoid selecting an option until I am 100% certain it is the right one.

---

13 It has become a cliché to talk about Amazon's distinction between one-way and two-way decisions. (Jeff Bezos wrote about these in the 2015 Amazon Shareholder Letter (*https://oreil.ly/A1xd2*), in the section "Invention Machine.") Two-way decisions are reversible while one-way decisions aren't. While classifying the decision in front of you as one-way makes you feel important, the truth is, very few architectural decisions are one-way. In fact, while the reversing of an architectural decision might turn out to be costly with regard to time and other resources, that does not alone mean it is a one-way decision. Indeed, while writing about a definition of software architecture in a 2003 article (*https://oreil.ly/quEb1*), Martin Fowler spent time considering "things that people consider hard to change" as a candidate before concluding that "one of an architect's most important tasks is to remove architecture by finding ways to eliminate irreversibility in software designs." It could be argued that one of the pressures behind each of the five revolutions was precisely this.

In reality, most decisions are reversible.[14]

When taking decisions, you need to become aware of, and overcome, feelings of fear and potential bias. Both can lead to delaying a decision or choosing an option for the wrong reason. To be aware of them and use that awareness to take the best choice on offer is also part of the art of decision taking. Let's consider fear and personal bias in turn.

Overcoming Fear

Fear is a big part of deciding—so big, in fact, that in Joseph Bikart's *The Art of Decision Making* (Watkins Media), it is divided into its constituent parts: fear about the choices we take[15] and fear about the consequences of those choices.

In fear of the choices we take, there are two aspects to consider: fear of rejecting a better option and fear of choosing the wrong option. In the world of architectural decisions, we have a term for how this manifests: *analysis paralysis*, when you continue to investigate and polish your options and their consequences way beyond what is necessary.

I don't mean the analysis paralysis that you frequently see when groups have no clear decision process and no clear decision taker. It's a close cousin but not the decision-taking-freezing kind. "Fear of the choice" analysis paralysis (where you continue to investigate and polish your options and consequences as a way to avoid taking the decision) is a psychological means of delaying the inevitable: your taking of a decision that is clearly yours to take and one that you know is needed.

In doing so, you are very likely straying outside your decision's contextual frame and worrying about things external to it, despite the conscious effort you put into defining it. You tell yourself, "If I do a little more work on the context framing and consequent option making, one clear option will rise to the surface, and all others would fade into irrelevance." But this never happens because that's not how wicked architectural problems work. Far better to trust in the already-tapped advice process, your ADR-supported deciding, and the wisdom and support of the collective.

Trust what you have and who you have collected it from, and take your choice.

---

14 That is not to say that irreversible decisions don't exist in software architecture. A decision to open source a codebase under a certain license cannot be backtracked, for instance. Once it's out there, it can be forked, and then it's out of your control. Another example is when you make a change to a publicly available API.

15 Bikart actually terms it "the choices we *make*," but I've chosen to refer to it as "the choices we *take*." Recall from Chapter 3 that I described the act of deciding as having separate option-making and decision-taking steps. My language reflects that here.

Fears about the consequences of our choices roam far more widely. In *The Art of Decision Making*, Bikart identifies five different fearful consequences. Although he discussed them in regard to personal decisions, they still apply to decisions made as a collective:

Fear of failure
> What if the option I selected, which everyone agreed *was* the best option, turned out to be a failure because of events outside my control?

Fear of heights
> What if I selected the *right* option, and everything goes really well, and we end up victims of our own success?

Fear of identification
> What if I become associated with this decision, for good or bad or even both, and people only ever see me in light of it? ("There goes that person who decided we would move from AWS to Azure.")

Fear of lack of recognition
> This is the flip side of the third fear. What if I get no credit for this decision? What if everyone regards it as "made by the collective"?

Fear of selfishness
> Specifically, the fear of being perceived to have acted in a selfish manner. This is different from acting in a selfish manner but not wanting to take the social responsibility that results. What if I take a tough decision but everyone simply thinks it was solely for my benefit?

All of these fears are not rational. You can't reason with them. All you can do is feel them, acknowledge them, and take action anyway. The advice process helps with this in all cases, by giving you further distance from the decision or offering alternate perspectives, or both. If you notice you are experiencing one or more of these fears, simply returning to the advice you have captured on your ADR can be enough to allay it.

Overcoming Bias

Bias is an inclination in favor of or against something that might be considered unfounded. Once you are aware of your biases, overcoming them is easier than overcoming your fears. There are *many* different biases, but I'll share the ones that, in my experience, offer the greatest challenges to architectural practice and organizational learning. They are listed in Table 12-1.

Table 12-1. Common biases and their impact on technical decisions

Bias	Impact on technical decisions
Nonlinear probability weight	Small probabilities are overweighed, and large probabilities are underweighed.
Reference dependence	Outcomes are evaluated relative to our own arbitrary reference point. I "gain" if something is better than my reference point and "lose" if it is worse.
The asymmetry of gain and loss	Losing something produces more pain than gaining the same thing.
Sense of knowledge	Why better-informed people find it difficult to think about problems from the perspectives of lesser-informed people.
Cheerleader	People see others (and their ideas) as more attractive when they are part of the same group.
Sunk-cost fallacy	The tendency to continue a strategy or course of action simply because we have invested heavily in it, even when it is clear that abandonment would be more beneficial.
Loss aversion	People are more sensitive to perceived losses than to equivalent perceived gains.[a]

[a] In their article "Prospect Theory: An Analysis of Decision under Risk" (*https://oreil.ly/rWjNl*), Daniel Kahneman and Amos Tversky suggested that losses can be twice as powerful psychologically in biasing decisions.

This list is not exhaustive. There are many others. (The Cognitive Bias Codex visualization (*https://oreil.ly/O_t3f*) created by John Manoogian III will get you started.) However, it pays to look out for all of them, particularly in yourself, when deciding. Even a practice as simple as checking this list before you decide can be helpful.

Wherever you look to find out more about biases that might affect decisions, I encourage you to think about how the architecture advice process—as well as organizational learning and the nurturing and supporting of the shared culture that it engenders—might ameliorate some or all of these.

Taking the Decision

Selecting an option in your head is one thing, but when you make it public—when you write it in the ADR and share it with others—that can also be a difficult moment. In the advice process, there are multiple parties who can experience strong feelings at this decision-sharing point: those taking the decision and those who might have taken the decision in a traditional approach, such as an architect. Let's consider each in turn.

When You Are Taking the Decision

First let's put ourselves in the shoes of the person (or team) taking a decision. I suggested in Chapter 6 that you "try the decision on for size" by updating your ADR to reflect your decision *but keeping it private*. Trying the decision privately allows you one last opportunity to gain distance from the decision and perhaps even shift your perspective on it a little. Seeing something in its nearly final written form can be revealing and can give you some last-minute comfort. It's like reading over an email before you hit send.

You can optimize the final step before taking a decision and changing your ADR status to "accepted" by allowing yourself one or more of the following "optimum conditions" as you do it:

- Find a quiet time
- Find a quiet place
- Sleep on it

Finding a quiet time and place affords you the mental space to sit with your decision without interruption to see if anything else springs to mind. This isn't an active pursuit. I just read over the ADR one more time and make sure I've understood everything and taken everything into account. I'm not going back through the deciding, and I'm making sure I'm not letting fears and biases get the better of me again, but I am "checking my working." I'm also giving myself the time and space to focus on this decision alone. Perhaps this isn't long, but it is something you explicitly carve out of the background noise of everything else.

The third condition is the most powerful because it's actually a supercharged combination and extension of the first two conditions. In my experience, I wake after a night sleeping on a decision with a quiet confidence that what I have selected consciously the day before is the best I can do given the circumstances. Sometimes, you don't have the luxury of this approach, but I bet in the vast majority of cases you do. As you get more and more comfortable with deciding, I encourage you to try saying to yourself, "I'm going to sleep on this," and then pick it up again the following day and see how you feel about the decision. You'll probably be surprised how well it works.[16]

When Others Are Taking the Decision

What about those who previously did the deciding but are now providing advice and observing? In my experience, while deciding is hard, watching others take decisions that you used to be responsible and accountable for is harder. Here's an example of why.

Pete Hunter was the engineering director at one of the first clients where the architecture advice process was deployed. When we retrospected on how it had gone, Pete described how he personally had experienced fear and anxiety as the teams initially

---

16 The power of sleep when learning is described in detail in Barbara A. Oakley's *A Mind For Numbers: How to Excel at Math and Science (Even if You Flunked Algebra)* (Penguin).

began to understand the advice process, tentatively assuming the responsibility of seeking advice and taking decisions. He had been concerned that there would be a free-for-all of deciding, but this hadn't happened. He also shared how he had been scared that those now doing the deciding wouldn't have the skills or the experience to make good decisions, and he had been scared they would be selfish.

But Pete's introspection went deeper.[17] He was aware that underneath these rational concerns, more emotional, irrational elements were exerting their influence. It became clear, for instance, that when we preferred an ADR option, our advice offered was not just our experience talking but also our bias, and beneath that a need for control. We were advising teams with the assumption that they would simply select our preferred option. It's far easier to hand over your power to decide, Pete suggested, when you assume everyone will decide the same as you would.

For example, one of the teams was working on client list onboarding services for the business-to-business SaaS product we were building. They were looking at different ways to approach this, and one of their proposed options was to use Lambda (Amazon's function as a service (*https://oreil.ly/myTtD*) offering at the time). The team did everything they ought to under the advice process,[18] including seeking advice from Pete and me. To say we weren't convinced would be an understatement. We offered our advice: there were no other Lambda-based services in the architecture. Lambdas were renowned (in our experience at least) for having slow startup times, and they weren't very friendly to higher-level languages like Java and C#. They could lead to overly splintered architectures. How would they monitor them? How would they deploy them? How would they test them?

The team listened to all this and took it on board. They tightened their scope and did some research, but when it came to it, they announced that they had decided to stick with their preferred option. Lambdas were about to enter the organization's ecosystem.

After this announcement, I felt hurt and a little scared that they had gone contrary to our suggestions. I thought we'd made it pretty clear that we thought what they were planning to do was *a really bad idea*. And yet, I felt like they'd ignored us. I felt undermined and exposed.

So I suggested to Pete that we overrule them, taking the decision power back into our hands.

---

17 It's from these open and honest conversations with Pete that I learned to see to a far greater extent the impact and power of the advice process. Many of these learnings are infused throughout this book.

18 They actually went even further, but that's the topic of the next two chapters.

Pete, however, had understood the social contract better than I had. "We can't over-rule them," he counseled.[19] If we did, then *we* weren't following the advice process. If he and/or I intervened even once, it wouldn't be seen as a one-off thing by the collective. It would immediately push us back to the traditional approaches. "We need to let go and support them," he suggested, "and we need to help everyone learn from the experience, whatever happens, wherever it happens, and whenever it happens."

And Pete was right.

I'm sharing this because I want you to know that I remember how it feels to be an architect used to the traditional mode of operation who is now watching others take decisions instead. But you need to remember why we're all embarking on this ride. As I laid out at the very beginning, the systems you build and the world you live in need us to practice architecture differently. No one said it was going to be easy to begin with, but once you learn to enjoy the ride, it's fast and exhilarating. You'll experience feelings you're not proud of, or even entirely aware of. The job of an architect *does* change when you adopt the advice process, but it doesn't go away—while you are letting go of the decisions themselves, you're now stewarding the ever-learning, socio-technical system surrounding them. You're now in charge of making sure that deciding is happening in a lot more places, with a lot more people, a lot more frequently. You're doing architecture the Ruth Malan way, by ensuring that conversations that need to be happening are happening.

As an architect letting go, here are the key points to remember so that others can decide:

Let go of deciding and grab hold of conversations
   Help the learning spread. Teach everyone what you know. Let your knowledge and experience flow.

Get better and better at giving great advice
   Learn to share the reasons for your thinking. Don't just offer opinions.

Stop trying to be part of every decision
   This is your habit or need for control coming out. The more the advice process works, the less you will be able to take part in everything. Scale by removing yourself as the bottleneck.

Get comfortable seeing decisions not work out and help everyone learn from them
   Be honest with yourself: have all your decisions worked out as you hoped? Don't expect the decisions of others to always work out either. Be patient and help everyone learn.

---

19 I am aware of the irony of this. To say I learned a lot working with Pete is an understatement. The reason you are reading this book is, in large part, because of him.

Help people write great ADRs
Writing is a skill that takes a lot of practice, so help everyone cultivate it.

Focus on building and protecting trust
A highly performing, trusting software engineering organization is the most satisfying thing to build. It doesn't happen on its own.

Coach everyone so they can engage with the advice process
Remind everyone that there is no need to agree but that there is a need for trust.

Help with argumentation
Identify the healthy tensions and work with others to separate those from the unhealthy ones.

Check your bias and share your privilege
Learn to listen to all voices and support those who are being ignored. (I'll go a lot deeper into this in Part IV.)

Pay attention to how you feel
Acknowledge it and learn from it.

None of these points makes it any less of a challenge to let go of decision power, but they will help direct your softer, emotional energy to the right place. That'll free up energy for the more solid, intellectual stuff.

Conclusion

This chapter offered you a perspective on the softer but probably more influential side of deciding—the parts of deciding that can't be analyzed or reduced to an algorithm. In this chapter, I showed how these soft parts affect your deciding, from understanding and consciously working with the context of decisions to using creativity and inspiration to gather and elaborate options and their consequences. I also looked at how an awareness of your experience of the softer parts can help you seek and offer the best advice, and even to take the hardest step: selecting the option to move forward with. I trust that this has given you not only a name for things you might be half-aware of and techniques to make them more explicit and part of your deciding, but also (and most importantly) permission to take these para-intellectual aspects of this key act and learn collectively to be better at them.

Given all this, you're now prepared to tackle the next chapter, which discusses how to lean on the harder, nonhuman parts of decisions to optimize for flow and feedback and tackle variability. All of which turn out to make the softer parts easier, too.

CHAPTER 13

Tackling Architectural Variability

In software, you never build the same system twice. In fact, software engineering could be considered the art of effectively and efficiently making something more or less new every time.

Because of this constant newness, every significant step you take in software development is a step into some unknown. Every significant decision you take is a selection of one hoped-for future at the expense of all other possible futures.[1] And you only find out if that hope is valid when it's turned into code and tested, ideally by real users in production.

Acknowledging that you're always making a new system is another way of saying that there are many unknowns in software development that need to be addressed—unknowns that are present *throughout* a system's cycle of evolution. Product managers and other planners call this *variability,* and it encompasses both the fact that no one can ever predict *exactly* what they're building and they can never know precisely how long it will take them to build it. In such a world, consistent flow and feedback are the best they can hope for.

Phrased like that, you can see why product managers would care about variability: they want some form of predictability in a world of unknowns—a predictability that can only come from flow. You should care, too, because the practice of software architecture and its results have an arguably greater impact on variability than anything else—both positively (when done well) and negatively (when done badly).

---

1 I concede that there are repeatable stages in the delivery lifecycle, most notably exemplified by the ideal that is continuous deployment, but those stages take place from the point that we consider all forms of design (right down to the level of code) to be complete—the point after which everything ought to be completely predictable.

To address the unknowns, decisions need to happen: architecturally significant decisions. This act of architectural deciding has a double impact on variability. The first hit comes from decisions taking place as work moves from an idea on a product backlog or feature list all the way down to production. The second hit comes later, when a single decision today has a direct impact on the flow of work in the future.

This chapter will describe how variability manifests in the practice of software. It will then show you how to work with it, both within your delivery flow and to optimize for that flow. I'll close the chapter by describing how enlisting variability can not only tackle risks but also unlock value.

The Effect of Variability on the Practice of Architecture

Variability represents the unknowns to be addressed in your software systems as you build, run, and evolve them. Many of these unknowns are likely to affect the structure, cross-functional characteristics, dependencies, interfaces, or construction techniques used within our flow of software development. That means these unknowns will be acknowledged and addressed with architecturally significant decisions.

While architectural practice offers the means to engage with variability, it doesn't remove it. Can you tell how many architectural decisions will need to be taken for a given system before you start? No. Are you able to know when and where decisions will need to be taken in advance? No. Can you know the outcomes of those decisions before you take them? No. Can you tell how long it will take to make a decision? No. Do you know if the selected option will work as intended? No. Most importantly, can you guarantee that your current decision won't give rise to further decisions? No.

The paradox of software architecture practice is that it both confronts and causes variability. Decisions resolve unknowns, but they also give rise to further unknowns because they open up new possibilities.

Both sides of this paradox are important to understand, and the best way to do this is by considering how you experience variability day to day. I'll begin with the difficulties variability introduces before considering the benefits.

Variability Makes Developing Systems Difficult

Variability makes developing systems difficult because it adds unwanted complexity. That's undeniable. In fact, architectural variability presents us with four identifiable types of difficulties:

- Variability is hard to work with.
- Variability comes from unpredictable places at unpredictable times.

- Variability produces cognitive load.
- Variability produces communication and synchronization load.

Variability is hard to work with

Working with architectural variability in our decisions and the decisions of others is just plain hard.

In the absence of variability, everything is as you expect it to be. In this idealized state, everything is at your fingertips. This is not to say that you are not solving problems—you are, but the elements you need to solve those problems are at hand. Things are predictable, and you can act on those accurate predictions.

It's far too easy to dream about this idealized, impossible state. Planners and executives fantasize about "software development factories" with everything they need prepared for them in advance and at their fingertips. In this utopia, all variability has been foreseen and removed, and all that's left is for us to type up the design that someone else has prepared in advance.

Architectural variability disrupts this utopia. APIs *don't* work like you thought they would. That subsystem *can't* scale like you hoped it would. That problem you thought would be solved by a singleton pattern was actually *an entirely different problem*. Or the solution you had in mind *didn't actually solve anything*. Or you actually had *multiple problems*. Or that other team that you need to integrate with hasn't decided on their integration style yet, so you can't code against their stub and instead have to mock what you guess it will look like. Or the solution to one problem actually caused problems with my other solutions. Or…

This is all architectural variability, and you have to address it. You're confronting not just one possibility but many, which multiplies the work. And on top of that, you may not know what to consider until it happens. All of this makes your practice of architecture harder.

Variability comes from unpredictable places at unpredictable times

All this architectural variability comes from unpredictable places and at unpredictable times—both social (human and interhuman) and technical. No matter how hard you try to think about all eventualities, the actual variability will surprise you more often than not. In fact, this is one of the contributors to the emergence that I described back in Chapter 1 (in "Architectures Should Allow for Emergence" on page 24).

At that time, I'd failed to foresee the effect of certain scaling patterns on the reclaiming of "reserved" ID numbers from a fixed-size pool, resulting in them ultimately running out. Remember, I'd done a bunch of thinking, and I'd covered a lot of scenarios, but it still hadn't prepared me for the scaling bottleneck problem.

Such periods of design flow, uninterrupted by variability, when you think you've accounted for all eventualities, can give you the false confidence that you have foreseen all circumstances and managed all possible outcomes. I thought I had achieved the ideal state.[2]

In actuality, it is impossible to predict even a fraction of the variability that arises from our running software, let alone that which comes from other team members, other teams, and beyond. You might be able to avoid some difficulties by knowing things better, but nowhere near all of them. The world around us and our systems are not just hard to predict; they're impossible.

That means, whether you like it or not, you can potentially experience architectural variability anywhere and at any time.

Variability produces cognitive load

Working with all this architectural variability breaks us out of flow at a personal and a team level, increasing our cognitive load.[3] Dealing with unpredictable variability means there is simply more to think about. You need to think about all the potential possibilities, of which there could be an infinite number. To make this number manageable, you might assess each for the likelihood they will happen. For those that remain, you then need to consider if the potential impact outweighs the cost and effort to mitigate them.

Even after all this, you're still not guaranteed to have thought of everything important because there will be things you're simply not aware of. Recall the tracking-IDs case again. I can tell you it was a significant effort trying to weigh up all the various permutations of operation, success, and failure before we released. And we still didn't foresee everything, the unused blocks of tracking IDs being the example I described.

Variability produces communication and synchronization load

Architectural variability doesn't just have these first-order cognitive load effects; it has second-order effects, too. Variability additionally means time away from the architectural work of designing, shipping, and evolving software systems because all that

---

2 Even comically small variabilities can be impactful. One of the best developers I know lost a day's work to a change in the way Java dates printed. JDK 17 used a standard space between the time and the "p.m." while JDK 21 used a narrow, nonbreaking space. (Google it if you like. I had to.) Sure, changing a Java version is likely to lead to some problems. But ones like this? I'd bet you have stories of your own from your personal experience.

3 I'm thinking about all three kinds of load here: intrinsic, extraneous, and germane. *Team Topologies: Organizing Business and Topology Teams for Fast Flow* by Matthew Skelton and Manuel Pais (IT Revolution Press) has a good introduction to the topic, with specific focus on software delivery.

---

change and unpredictability inevitably require additional communication:[4] between individuals in a team, between teams, between teams in different organizations, and between organizations, stakeholders, and users. The effects ripple out. You can't escape them.

There is also inevitably effort that must be put into keeping everyone, their systems, and their plans synchronized. My team's unpredictability has caused unpredictability for you and your team, which in turn will likely knock on to other teams. The work of delivering the overall value-delivering system needs to be resynchronized.

My experience with leaking tracking IDs is again illustrative. We were given our tracking ID batches by another team, who managed them with a system of their own, pushing the data into many backend systems. When we started asking for more IDs more frequently, we had to synchronize with their work practices and release cycles.

All of this variability is inevitable: you can't remove it simply by planning more or by thinking harder at the design stage, and wishing it weren't there only makes things worse.

Variability Is the Lifeblood of Software Development

Given all these downsides, why does anyone in software development put up with all this variability? Why don't we simply act with more discipline to prevent it?

In manufacturing, that's exactly what happens. Variability, even at the micro, individual-part level, is viewed as a bug in the system. If a thousand widgets are delivered from stage one of a process to stage two, then the expectation is that they are all of suitable quality. That they are all the same. It is the assumption that everything will be just as it should be: predictable. When it's not, action is taken. Major aspects of Lean manufacturing help to ensure this.

But this *can't* work in software systems because variability in software engineering is the opposite of what it is in manufacturing. In software engineering, variability is a feature—the most important one.

Variability is a feature because of software's primary characteristic. Software's power means it can do virtually anything we can imagine. And it can deliver that value incredibly quickly. A decision can be taken, the required change implemented, and the result shipped to millions of users within a matter of days, hours, or even minutes. Everyone downstream of that decision either reaps the benefits or the terrible consequences. Most likely, some (unpredictable) mix of the two.[5]

---

4 Yup, I mean meetings.

5 As I write, the CrowdStrike incident (*https://oreil.ly/RDqft*) is the most significant example of this effect.

Variability is the inevitable manifestation of this. Not only can I make my software do anything I want, at any time, but everyone else also has the same power at their fingertips. Not only is it hard to predict the impact of my code, but it is impossible to predict what everyone else's software might do. Variability arises from this everywhere: from the work being done, the challenges being encountered and met, the software making contact with other teams and with the outside world, and the decisions being made in anticipation of and because of all of these.

Consequently, variability is the lifeblood of software. Variability is the signature of the power of software being unleashed. The variability of software offers an incredible number of ways for us to do anything.

Architectural decisions are at the heart of this, for good or ill. Decisions are where you make the step from a set of possibilities to the selection of a hoped-for outcome. These decisions include those taken by you and by others.

This is precisely why any practice of architecture must not only stop trying to hold back the forces of chaos but also allow for and embrace emergence. That's why it's so important that we learn to work with architectural variability effectively.

Working Effectively with Architectural Variability

Variability in software development is both inescapable and important. To minimize the negative effects and boost the benefits, you need to factor variability into both how you practice architecture and the decisions you make. This means looking at how variability affects the broader development and delivery flow of software development.

I'll begin by locating the architectural practice of deciding within the broader development and delivery flow of individual teams. I'm thinking here of decisions that arise because of a team playing a user story that implements a thin slice of a larger feature from their backlog.

A user story—a single, independent slice of feature functionality that meets a user need—is a perfect vehicle for architectural decisions precisely because it is an embodiment of such functional context. Importantly, user stories are also team-sized and iteration-sized, and they flow all the way from a placeholder for a conversation (about a specific need) down to code running in production.[6]

---

6 Martin Fowler (as usual) has a pithy summary of what a user story is (*https://oreil.ly/9yxGq*) on his bliki. He also has a few words to say on the topic in a separate post about why use cases and user stories are different (*https://oreil.ly/TVhvY*). My main source for how to use user stories is Mike Cohn's *User Stories Applied for Agile Software Development* (Addison-Wesley), but I have also found myself returning again and again to Jeff Patton's *User Story Mapping* (O'Reilly).

We previously considered the decision-process flow of teams using the advice process. Let's zoom out and look at the broader development and delivery flow of those teams. I've shown this in Figure 13-1. You can now see upstream the user stories/features that the teams hope will offer their users the service they need, and downstream you can see those features implemented (incorporating the necessary decisions taken), running in production and generating feedback.

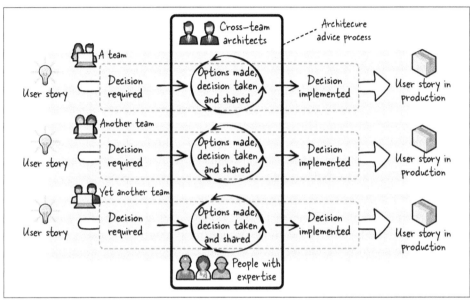

Figure 13-1. The full development/delivery flow of a user story, from conception all the way to its deployment to production, ready to generate feedback

Keep this broader picture in mind as you read the rest of this section, as it'll help you understand how to work with variability within architectural practices in the full development/delivery flow.

Tackle Variability by Taking and Testing Decisions Rapidly

Architectural decisions are only validated when they are tested. It is when a decision is implemented—running in production and generating the feedback that tells us how it is actually working out[7]—that the unknowns it tackles are removed and we have taken our step into the future, making it our present.

---

7 I used to work with a product manager who, every time I made a bold statement about the benefits of some decision I'd made, would ask, "How do you know?" That continues to give me pause for thought. Knowing is important. Being in production and in front of users is important. Otherwise, you're just guessing (and hoping).

Just like user stories and features, until this validation point is reached, any given decision's suitability or unsuitability is unknown. Prior to the validation point, you are working in the dark, hoping that the implementation, integration, and contact with live traffic doesn't invalidate your hoped-for outcomes.

Decisions that sit within the work flowing through teams are ideally placed to do this. In fact, that's the whole point of product flow: to get to the feedback as soon as possible. That feedback is as useful (I'd argue *more* useful) for architectural decisions as it is for features of a system given that decisions have a broader field of influence.

Test Decisions Deeply Using Their Functional Context

Validation of a decision doesn't simply ask, "Does this work?" That's too general and won't confront the specific sources of variability that *your* delivery is subject to. You need to remove the variability of *your* unknowns. Validation of a decision must specifically ask, "Does this work *for us*?" Therefore, the only way to amply test an architectural decision and get suitable feedback is alongside "just enough" of your system's functionality as well as alongside the architectural decisions that have already been implemented.

Viewing architectural decisions as fundamentally associated with the features that they underpin and enable is powerful. Without those features, architectural decisions not only have no purpose, but they also lack any means of being meaningfully tested. You are delaying tackling variability until those features *are* implemented. This is precisely why user stories, with their slices of functionality that meet a user need, are ideal partners.

Associating architectural decisions directly with functionality has another strength. User stories, by their very nature, are end-to-end slices of value, and they are only "done" when they are running. We can't know if a user story is valuable until it has completed this journey. (This is why user stories have a "so that" element as well as acceptance criteria. Both capture *why* the work is being done and the code being written in the first place.) The same stands for architecture decisions, which is why stories are such great vehicles for flowing decisions through the teams in their functional context. They can both be "done" at the same time.

If you look back at Figure 13-1, you can see user stories taking this journey toward "done," with their accompanying decisions. As each story makes its way from left to right, a number of activities are performed, many requiring architectural decisions on their way through.

Some of these architectural decisions will not be what I classified previously as "architecturally significant," but others will be, and every time some of this architectural design work comes up in the form of architectural decisions that have to pass through

---

an advice process. (Figure 13-1 shows the flow of the story that has decisions that must pass through the advice process once on its way to production.)

A Decision's Significance Doesn't Affect the Flow of Work

How do you know in advance if a decision is architecturally significant or not? Especially with all these unknowns and variability? It turns out that treating all decisions as if they *are* significant and following the process is usually the most efficient way to ensure that all decisions are treated appropriately. Nonsignificant decisions simply pass through the process a lot faster.

Use Walking Skeletons to Test Your Earliest Decisions in Their Functional Context

When you are up and running with delivery, the flow of decisions in their functional context is easy to imagine. Indeed, such in-flight decisions have been the bread and butter of the examples in this book so far. These decisions are brought on because of the next feature in front of a team or brought about by the challenges of system evolution that one or more teams are facing.

But what about the first decisions tackling the variability inherent in a *new* system? These are decisions arising when there is little but a blank sheet of paper or a blank whiteboard in front of you and when variability is at its peak. These decisions can easily feel as if they have no functional context that we can use to validate them.

Address this with a *walking skeleton*[8] that combines the central architectural decisions with just enough core functionality to test them. Walking skeletons, as described by Steve Freeman and Nat Pryce, are "an implementation of the thinnest possible slice of real functionality that we can automatically build, deploy, and test end-to-end."[9] Furthermore, walking skeletons "should include just enough of the automation, the major components, and communication mechanisms to allow us to start working on the first feature." It's that first feature (captured as a group of initial stories) that drives these conversations. (Finding these initial stories isn't easy, but Jeff Patton's *User Story Mapping* has your back.)

Getting your initial architecture decisions running as soon as possible using user stories around a walking architectural skeleton[10] is incredibly well suited to tackling

---

8 The concept and term was originated by Alastair Cockburn. I've also heard similar concepts referred to as a "steel thread," "tracer bullets," and an "aspirin use case."

9 Steve Freeman and Nat Pryce, *Growing Object-Oriented Software, Guided by Tests* (Addison-Wesley, 2009). Interestingly, the header in the book is called "First, *test* a walking skeleton" (italics mine).

10 A large part of Freeman and Pryce's entire book.

early-stage architectural variability. The riskiest decisions can be tackled early, and if they fail, they place less accumulated investment in jeopardy. In other words, it is far cheaper to uncover a bad decision by testing it on your walking skeleton architecture at the start of development than it is to trip over it at the end. (I'll come back to this in more detail in the next chapter when I consider the relationship between decisions.)

Freeman and Pryce list four of our five categories of significant decisions in their description: "automation" recalls our construction techniques; "major components" is another way of saying structure; and "communication mechanisms" (when broken into their constituent parts) are our "dependencies" and "interfaces."

And our last category: cross-functional characteristics? They are equally important, and "just enough" of those should be considered in a walking skeleton, too.

Consider, for example, a key security cross-functional characteristic captured in a testable CFR: you need to support OAuth 2 (*https://oreil.ly/MLcXo*) for user access delegation. It is far better to incorporate decisions around this into your walking skeleton than to try and add them at the end, only to find that OAuth doesn't work how you thought it did with your functionality. I'll pick inclusion in the walking skeleton, thanks.

Working in this way, tackling key architectural decisions early and often, you incrementally sense and respond to the arising variability from the outset. You can identify and work through the architectural decisions you need as you need them. This has the side benefit of keeping your architecture work strongly aligned with your functional work, meaning it can be planned in with everything else that is being built rather than as gigantic refactorings.

Tackle Variability with Smaller Decisions

Big decisions can be difficult at any point in development because of the increased pressure they put on deciders. By "big," I don't mean decisions of great impact. Nor do I mean only "significant" decisions. I simply mean decisions with a broad scope and therefore with many moving parts to consider.

The pressure these monsters impose comes from all their interdependencies (internal and external), the resulting knock-on effects, and all the other unknowns of variability that are brought in. There are more of all of these precisely because of their scope.

Decisions with too broad a scope are usually easy to spot. Not only will they be affecting a number of teams, but they will also be threatening to do so in a way that removes a great deal of the teams' autonomy. For example, you might be faced with the decision at the beginning of a new product: "Which of a cloud provider's service offerings will we use for all our systems up front?" You saw another broad-scoped decision in "Story 2: An Architect Decides to Unpick a Workflow Problem" on page 84, which dealt with the decision to refactor the workflow service. It ended up as three smaller decisions:

- Refactor the workflow service to firm up usage patterns
- Reimplement shared business logic as a Kotlin library
- Remove state from the performance-optimizing workflows

I'll use this example throughout the rest of this chapter. For brevity, I'll refer to it as Story 2.

User stories, the vehicle for architectural decisions, are embedded in the world of "just enough," too. Patton has a great way of defining the two key aspects of a user story:

- A right-sized story from a development team's perspective is one that takes just a few days to build and test.
- A right-sized story from a business perspective is one that helps a business achieve a valuable business outcome.

In other words, user stories should be small and valuable, and that ties in nicely with Donald G. Reinertsen's use of the concept in *The Principles of Product Development Flow*: "Many small experiments produce less variation than one big one" (Principle V7). Small user stories are valuable not only because they offer value to the user. They are *also* valuable because they address variability.

Taken together, this is a significant volume of experiential evidence pointing us toward the benefits of small decisions associated with equally small and valuable slices of functionality that are implemented and tested together.

Benefits of reducing decision size

Reducing decision size has three benefits: it makes tackling variability easier; it reduces overhead; and because it encourages faster feedback, it reduces risk.

Variability is tackled earlier. The first benefit of smaller decisions is that they have a smaller gap between "decision needed" and "decision taken." That tackles variability head-on and earlier in your workflow. Intuitively, this seems correct, but Reinertsen conducted statistical analysis and showed that smaller units of work spend shorter times in teams' work queues (i.e., backlogs) *by an order of magnitude* (Principle B1).

Let's consider the route *not* taken in the second example of the advice process, Story 2 from Chapter 4. In that example, the original big decision was broken down into three smaller decisions. But what if it had not been? Tackling the problem this way, all at once, would have meant a lot of work would need to be completed in a lot of places, across multiple teams, before all the separate pieces could be deployed together and the result of the decision (success, partial success, or even failure) could be declared. The variability inherent in this approach would be significant. (If that is beginning to sound like one of those "eternally 80% done" refactoring stories you've had haunting you on backlogs, this is likely why...)

Now, reconsider the path that *was* taken in the scenario: the three smaller decisions also involve work across teams, but each decision is less work on its own, and each individual decision spanned fewer teams. The opportunity for variability to creep in is reduced. Delivery will of course have knock-on effects between teams, causing some unpredictability and delay, even some rework, but that's a lot easier to manage. For example, consider that none of the teams had ever used Kotlin Multiplatform before. They underestimated the subtleties of getting their automated builds and binary artifact repositories reconfigured to make everything work. This caused variability, but only on the work for that decision. The other two streams of work from the other decisions were unaffected. The fact that the decisions are split also means that there is less work in delivering each of them individually, so they generate validating feedback sooner.

This perspective offers significant insight to those responsible for the overall architecture of a system. To get all of the teams involved starting work at the same time, given all their other priorities, would have been a massive effort. In fact, it's well-nigh impossible (hence Reinertsen's "order of magnitude").

When big decisions are broken down into a set of smaller decisions, the variability becomes more benign because it can be tackled earlier.

Overhead is reduced.   Reduced decision sizes also have a positively reinforcing effect on everything about development flow and the resulting feedback that addresses variability. They do this by reducing the human-processing overhead associated with deciding and implementing those decisions.

This is Reinertsen's Principle B5 that reducing batch size reduces overhead: "This is unexpected as most devs think that small batches raise overheads." Because this benefit may seem counterintuitive, let's break it down. A common assumption is that larger numbers of smaller decisions increase the transaction cost of individual decisions. What are the transaction costs of an individual decision? Well, in the architecture advice process, the cost is writing an ADR and seeking, understanding, and incorporating the advice. More decisions equal more of all three of these.

But that framing misses some important facts.

First, smaller decisions have smaller scopes, which frequently means that less advice needs to be sought, especially on the "affected parties" front. This is a win, but it's not the most significant one.

Second, a smaller decision scope means there are fewer interdependencies to worry about within the decision, which means that the sheer effort of wrangling all the advice and applying it to the decision at hand is reduced. Although there will likely be some degree of implementation ordering required, the fact that a big decision has been split into smaller decisions means that each has value independent of the others. Forward progress is made, decisions are validated incrementally, and variation is removed step by step as opposed to in one big jump. There are simply fewer factors to take into account, and that's very welcome for anyone practicing architecture, especially those with less experience.

Finally, when a decision is small, it gets planned, delivered, and deployed more easily, where it can generate that essential feedback. I mentioned earlier how larger decisions are harder to begin work on and harder to keep on top of and track when they are being implemented. I also mentioned how this work typically takes a lot longer. All this creates yet more work—that of monitoring and reporting.

It's easier on the people involved.   Larger decisions also bring about knock-on effects, including psychological ones, that cause things to get even worse. To summarize Reinertsen again, large decisions lower motivation and urgency by delaying feedback (Principle B7), large decisions cause exponential cost and schedule growth (Principle B8), and large decisions lead to even larger decisions (Principle B9). On the other hand, smaller decisions prioritize feedback, increasing the engagement and motivation of everyone involved.

Consider again if Story 2 from Chapter 4 were tackled as one big decision. First, the work planned would be of significant size. Everyone would know that it will take a significant amount of time to implement in all its aspects and that a lot needs to be done before things will be ready for testing. As this realization dawns, the focus would subtly and almost imperceptibly move to "not being the team that is the blocker." No one needs to be the fastest; they just don't want to be the slowest. Because estimates are so large and based on so many unknowns, the sense of urgency in all teams becomes diluted. Everyone is secretly happy when they have excuses to delay. The end date drifts out gradually. Delivery management eventually gets concerned that this drift is becoming permanent and starts trying to get involved to fix it. This is a significant piece of work with high visibility to senior leadership, so a "big push" is put in place to turn things around. But all that really happens is that the motivation and urgency drop further, the cost and schedule grow even more, and everyone starts looking for the next, even more senior intervention.

Reducing the size of your decisions avoids all this. Glorious.

Feedback is accelerated and risk reduced.   Yet the benefits of smaller decisions with regard to tackling variability reach even farther. Implementing smaller decisions is easier because there's simply less to do. When you combine this benefit with all the others I have listed, you get perhaps the most powerful benefit: smaller decisions most effectively reduce the risk of variability causing something unpredicted to happen, and *that* allows you to access the power of variability.

Software systems can't avoid the forces of chaos, and as we saw, the unpredictability of software is the source of its power. To access this, your architectural practice should actively embrace uncertainty. (This is paraphrasing Reinertsen: "The optimum failure rate in product development is much higher than in that of manufacturing" from Principle B3.) Accepting that some decisions won't work out allows for others that might bring *deep* benefits. If you try to be too predictable, you don't consider that new library or service, or see what happens when you refactor that legacy batch processing service to run on Lambda. That misses out on the full power of software.

Reduced decision sizes allow you to more safely embrace the increased uncertainty of riskier decisions because they offer faster access to feedback, without which you cannot know if your decision is good or bad. And while bad decisions are a risk, it is a bigger risk to have potentially good decisions blocked or affected by a bad decision and not know it.

Not only that, when one bad decision can have a significant impact on future decisions, wouldn't you want to know as soon as possible whether that decision was a good one? I would. Large decisions can hide within them the possibility of many poor subdecisions, or to paraphrase Reinertsen again, "An entire decision is limited by its worst element" (Principle B10).

When a decision is large, the small part that holds everything back (the "worst element") will affect everything else in the decision for a myriad of reasons. You can try to discern in advance what this might be and thereby minimize its effect, but as you saw in my experiences with the leaking tracking IDs in Chapter 1, it's impossible to guess them all. The only way to be sure is to decide, implement it, and capture the feedback.

Small decisions reduce this problem of decisions being sunk by their worst element. A large decision is far more likely to have within it a really gnarly problem. The same decision broken down into a set of smaller decisions will still have that large challenge, but now that large challenge is affecting only one or, at worst, a subset of all your decisions. Other decisions will no longer be tied to it and can be taken and implemented independently. You have increased your ability to flow.

As a result of all this, everyone's conception of decisions can change. Understanding that large decisions are nonmonolithic and that breaking them up means variability can be addressed sooner offers a new way to view the practice of architecture. That in turn makes it easier to convince people that a splitting approach is valuable.

It means that a journey from A to B can be turned into a series of more predictable milestones: the first step of "we'll relocate everything from on-prem to Azure" becomes "let's move our most recent microservice from being hosted on-prem to being hosted in the cloud." The first milestone of "let's transform this app from a RESTful one to an event-driven one" becomes "let's refactor this single interaction between these two services from RESTful to event-driven." The initial investigations of "let's make this application multitenant" become "let's make this service multitenant."

These smaller decisions seem pretty good, and they are. They're definitely an improvement on the gigantic leaps I initially shared. But they might still be bigger than they could be. They could possibly be broken down further.

But how?

Splitting large decisions into multiple smaller ones

Once you've identified that you have a decision with too broad a scope, you need to figure out how to split it into smaller ones. For some decisions, that could be pretty straightforward. For example, "What architectural approach should we use for our microservices?" could be broken down by asking, "What are the different types of workloads our microservices tackle?" Other decisions may be more difficult to split. The following are heuristics that I've learned. You can combine them to keep splitting decisions until you get to the point where you can split no further.

Understand the problem context and solution options with an ADR. The clarity offered by writing an ADR is frequently sufficient to realize that there are multiple decisions in front of you. For example, say that you're writing the Context section and you realize that there are three problems that happen to be taking place in the same area in the code. Or say that you're writing the Options section and you have captured various alternatives that address very different parts of the problem.

In both cases, these would be great prompts to break the decision up and consider each part in separate ADRs. It is frequently the case that when the context and then the options are considered, fracture planes appear, and ways to break matters down become evident. More on fracture planes shortly.

Watch out for the "similar" trap and focus on what makes things different. As you look for places to split, beware of a predisposition among both developers and architects to assume that if situations *seem similar,* then they must be the *same*. Over and over, I observe gigantic decisions not being split solely because of some small shared element.

This predisposition arises, in my experience, from our love of abstraction, and I've been as guilty of it as anyone. We tend to hear a word like *config* or *customer* or even something in the business/problem domain[11] and assume that everything relating to those words goes together. But *similar* doesn't mean *the same*. For example, customers

---

11 I discovered this the hard way working in criminal justice. A significant part of my conference talk with Gayathri Thiyagarajan, "Combatting the Near Enemies of DDD" (*https://oreil.ly/E5Ime*), focused on this problem.

may have a set of separate representations in your system, and configs may configure a collection of vastly different things.

Learn to focus on what makes these potentially shared elements *different*, rather than what makes them similar. Doing so will make things that truly are the same pop out. Look into what different types of config there are or what the different varieties of authentication need, or (and this is the power move) dig deeper into the business domain to understand the subtle nuances in user needs that always surface when you look for them.

Identify fracture planes.   Once you have sniffed out some areas of difference, investigate them further to find out exactly where the splits, or fracture planes, might live. You can find these fracture planes occurring in a few different places:

Functional fracture planes
> The practice of architecture is, in many ways, the act of taking a big problem or challenge and breaking it into smaller problems or challenges while not losing sight of the big picture. We can't build everything at once, so part of architecture is discerning smaller elements to tackle without compromising the big picture. As such, in the practice of architecture, we look for functional fracture planes.

> A technique for identifying functional fracture planes is to ask, "What must this thing (component, service, subsystem, subdomain) *do*?"[12] Figuring out usage patterns and differentiating them is a classic trick, one that was deployed in Story 2 from Chapter 4. In that case, the investigation focused very specifically on what the workflow service would do *and how it would do it*. Stateful was out. Stateless was in. The difference between these brought to the surface the different usage patterns. If there are multiple usage patterns required, then it is perfectly valid to tackle them in separate decisions.

> This isn't to say that they won't end up being delivered by the same component, but the two won't get conflated into the same decision as you are evaluating your options. The old microservice adage "do one thing and do it well" springs to mind here. It applies well beyond that specific architectural style.

Delivery-timing fracture planes
> Sometimes, the inclination to split a decision based purely on usage isn't strong enough. In those circumstances, it can help to consider delivery timing. Do all of these challenges need to be taken on all together? Frequently, it is the case that one or more parts of a challenge can be tackled now while other aspects can be

---

12 I ask myself this even when I'm working alone. I've learned to use this to avoid the "same data means it must be the same thing" trap. Thinking about the jobs something performs lets you see how much it has on its plate. "Do one thing and do it well" then flows easily.

tackled later. While this is a weaker cleaving force than "there are different usages by function," it can be very helpful. For example, in Story 2 of Chapter 4, the third decision was something that was less urgent than the first two, so it was decided to address that one later.

Codebase-location fracture planes

If timing isn't a strong enough cleaving force to split a large decision, then you might consider location. Specifically, where in the codebase does your decision apply? If that's multiple places, then you can split down those seams, too.

This time recall Story 1 in Chapter 4, where a development team decided to use release toggles. In that case, the decision was already localized—a single team wanting to scratch their own itch. But imagine if the same challenge had come from an architect who might have tried to tackle the decision across all teams, all at the same time. That would have been a mistake. The elements in code that this ended up needing were either in specific teams' codebases or in the preexisting environment config support from the infrastructure. Another way of saying this is "if teams don't need to be coupled, don't decide in a way that means they have to be." (In fact, deciding in a way that decouples teams is such a powerful act that I'll cover it separately later when I consider how decisions can affect future flow.)

Unblocking flow of work fracture planes

You can also split large decisions by seeking out the smallest decision (or decisions) that are needed for delivery work to start. This means splitting decisions into those that are shared among teams first and proceeding to the single-team-focused decisions afterward. For example, split out the decisions about an API between two teams from decisions about the internal implementation of that API. This approach unblocks work and allows teams to work independently. It also reduces the scope of the team-internal decisions and provides them with a concrete context within which to play.

This might not be popular with all concerned. Some teams and individuals aren't comfortable beginning work without knowing all the details of what is going to happen at both ends of an integration implementation. In those circumstances, you will need to make sure that the required level of detail is captured in the decisions or ADRs that define the shared elements, such as in the API contract. The context ought to be laid out in a way that accommodates everyone's needs. The various options need to be clearly understood and well balanced. Shared contract tests and other continuous integration validation between teams offer a relatively simple way for teams to get an early warning if a breaking change is required.

The heightened focus on the shared elements is important because these central, shared decisions will be relied upon again and again as subsequent decisions are taken.[13] They have to bear the weight of all of all decisions that will follow. As a consequence, these decisions can take longer. Again, having a place to craft a mutually beneficial statement in the form of an ADR is a boon.

An example of such a discussion might happen in the design of an API consumed by more than one team. If it's a multiconsumer discussion, then more formal consumer-driven contract approaches can help greatly. Such an approach allows different consumers to make their individual expectations explicit. Tools such as Pact (*https://docs.pact.io*) can offer a level of support to decisions, making it clear when the provided API might not be able to meet the aggregate expectations of all consumers.

The "shared decision that unlocks everything else" fracture plane

My final useful fracture plane is a question: "What are the decisions we need to take to be able to take this decision?" A close relative of the "codebase-location fracture planes" approach, this splits a decision into the parts that can be implemented first or quickly and those that have to wait a while. Sometimes, you won't be aware of the parts that can be implemented first, and this can be a good prompt to think about that.

This question can have a very powerful effect. I've seen discussions about the best way to implement a multitenant solution becoming blocked because no one had noticed that the decision around who a "tenant" was hadn't been taken. Identifying the issue, rewinding, and considering that decision alone, then returning to the previously deadlocked decision, has always had an unlocking effect. (I'll consider the most powerful time to tackle these decisions in more detail in Chapter 14.)

No matter how you arrive at them, smaller decisions improve delivery flow. Continually applying a flow mindset also helps drive out the right decision breakdowns. As the implementations start flowing, all the benefits I've listed are unleashed. This is because your decisions get into production faster and generate the feedback that tackles variability. But variability can also be tackled with decisions that affect future flow. In essence, these are decisions that make future deciding easier, and that's where we'll turn now.

---

13 I once had an interesting conversation with Luciano Rahmalo, author of *Fluent Python* (O'Reilly, 2022), about when he'd use optional types. As a leading Pythonista, he was disinclined to use them without good cause. Where it would benefit, he thought, was in the liminal spaces in codebases where teams met. There, the explicit nature of types would serve to make the expectations clear, reinforced by the Python interpreter.

The Impact of Architectural Decisions on Future Flow

At the beginning of this chapter, I said that architectural decisions have a double impact on variability: first, on decisions that occur during the development and delivery flow, and second, on future flows of work. The chapter up to this point has addressed the former. Let's turn now to the latter.

Good Technical Infrastructure Enables Small Decisions

Many of the five software revolutions achieved their impact because good technical infrastructure enables small decisions. Cloud computing, for example, allows me to rent Google's CPU cycles rather than having to purchase my own servers and house them in my own data center. With a cloud computing account, I can have an idea, and within hours if not minutes, I can put that idea in front of customers and see if my decision holds water.

Good technical infrastructure reduces transaction costs. The transaction cost of spinning up systems in the cloud is *significantly* lower than in the days of "big iron" when I started my career. In those days, you needed to purchase whole servers, wait for them to be manufactured, delivered, racked, and cabled in and an operating system to be installed before you could even think of beginning to use them.

Automated testing reduces transaction costs, too, as does the separation of (continuous) deployment from product release. All of these reduce the obstacles and human frailties inherent in the journey from having an idea, deciding to implement it in one or other ways, and then seeing the idea out in the wild and gathering feedback.

But the five revolutions didn't just reduce manual labor and the potential for human error. They also allowed many separate decisions to be in flight at any one time, at various stages of the idea, decision, implementation, deployment, and feedback cycle. Product experimentation and approaches like A/B testing leverage this to not only test multiple ideas at once but also compare them alongside one another. Independent teams that have control over their own flow (the fifth revolution) are currently the ultimate manifestation of this decoupling of flows. The ability to tackle variation is available everywhere and to everyone.

The advances of the five software revolutions, when combined with a decentralized approach to deciding—where only the necessary people need to be brought into any given decision—mean that teams have everything they need to enable small decisions, tackle variability, gather that essential variability-removing feedback, and flow.[14]

---

14 Especially when you remember the inclusion of the construction techniques aspect of significant decisions. Decisions can now be taken in many of the areas that the five revolutions unlocked, too.

Good Sociotechnical Infrastructure Enables Small Decisions Too

Knowing that variability can cause you problems motivates you to reduce or remove it. A revolutionized, feedback-centric environment where teams *expect* to be predictably flowing is ideally suited to spreading this motivation to reduce variability.

The advice process delivers the ability and permission to tackle this variability because it allows whoever is deciding to craft a decision that is as small as needed while ensuring the required involvement from others. Smaller decision sizes and the fact that they can arise from anywhere in the sociotechnical system as needed mean many more decisions can be at various stages of completion, all independent of one another. When combined with the support of whatever aligning minimal viable agreements are in place, the sociotechnical system can really flow. As with all efficient sociotechnical systems, when teams realize how they can use the advice process to their advantage, they are able to optimize for it.

Use the Advice Process to Decouple Decisions for Flow

After reading the previous section, you may be wondering, "If you succeed in splitting a decision but all the parts are still highly coupled, wouldn't the benefits of the splitting be reduced or even completely erased because the teams still have to collaborate and synchronize?"

You're right.

The way to solve this issue is to decouple decision parts in exactly the same way we would in software. Loose coupling between subsystems—both technical and social—enables small decisions. This is Reinertsen's Principle B15: "Working with small batches requires that we reduce the dependency between batches."

In traditional architectural approaches, architects are responsible for managing and minimizing such coupling because of their cross-system viewpoint. It's one of the main reasons they become a bottleneck. But with the advice process, *everyone* can keep a constant eye out for unnecessary links with others, triggered by their experience of flow.

With the advice process, teams can take action to reduce or even remove such coupling whenever it arises by identifying its source(s) and collaborating in the open to resolve it. Perhaps this means that functionality is moved from one team to another, or perhaps shared APIs are refactored to hide internal information more effectively. Or perhaps the team comes up with another solution of its own creation. The point is, the power and means to do this are directly in the affected team's hands, allowing them to shrink the time gap between "a decision is needed" and "a decision has been taken." As Reinertsen says, "Once a product developer realizes small batches are desirable, they will adapt a product architecture that allows them to flow in small, decomposed batches."[15]

The benefits of small decisions are reinforced when teams look to split large decisions along fracture planes to improve the smooth running of the advice process. Specifically, when you break a large decision into smaller decision parts, it is beneficial to aim to minimize the number of decisions where the number of parties sought for advice is large. The scope of the remaining decisions then means that the number of affected parties whose input must be sought is smaller.

This all naturally leads (especially if it is encouraged) to the gradual discovery and reinforcement of a stable set of interteam interfaces that promotes more explicit knowledge management, enabling parallel flows of work on interrelated subsystems. Because the teams have had greater input into this, they understand it better, and resulting implementations are cleaner and code is generally higher quality. Most importantly it increases confidence that everything will integrate well at a system level because the appropriate level of attention has been paid by the teams to the appropriate integrations, whether they are via explicit APIs or something less formal.

Enlisting Variability to Combat Risk and Uncover Value

So far, I have focused on the consideration of optimizing architectural decisions for flow and feedback with the goal of reducing the four pains of variability. But variability isn't all bad. It's the source of software's power, too. But it's a power that brings with it great risk, and it's into this final area that I will now carefully tread.

The true value of architecture practice is unlocked when you harness architectural decisions to both combat risk *and* uncover value. How might you take what you have learned so far and use that to achieve and maintain the right balance between the risk and value? What do you need to prioritize? What do you need to watch out for? This closing section will consider all of these questions. While this discussion is primarily aimed at those with an overall-architecture perspective, there is no reason why those with a more team-local viewpoint shouldn't be aware of these principles, too.

I'll begin by dealing with the topic that many feel is the most controversial.

Fast and Wrong Is Better Than Slow and Correct

"Fast and wrong is better than slow and correct" triggers many who use traditional software architecture practices,[16] but in product management circles, this is how many decisions are made. Wrong being better than correct seems unnatural, but not

---

15 *Principles of Product Development Flow*, 127.

16 It did when I shared the phrase on LinkedIn as I initially drafted this chapter.

if you remember that this phrase comes from a system optimized for *learning*. Architecture practice that works with variability needs to adopt this perspective, too.

How can a decision that fails, a bad decision, be preferable to a decision that succeeds? It can be preferable when we don't know if a decision will work because "not knowing" is a form of variability. Even if a decision turns out to be so bad that schedules need to be reestimated, and many teams need to dump or refactor their work, and perhaps even penalties need to be paid, it's *always* better to know that sooner rather than later.

Remember, it's *only* when you test a decision by receiving the feedback from trying to get it into production that you remove the variability from that decision and know whether it's a successful decision or not. When you *know* whether a decision is a success, then you can move on: either fixing it or building on top of it. Both can be done with increased confidence. If you don't know, you can't act. You are placing yourself at the mercy of variability and relying on hope.

I sometimes hear, "But (product/senior) management hates for things to fail," as a challenge to the "fast and wrong is better than slow and correct" approach, but that ignores a significant portion of the overall picture. Of course, management would *love* for everything to proceed completely as everyone predicted: on time, on budget, with perfect quality, and without surprises. But anyone who has worked anywhere near software for any meaningful length of time knows that the power of software and the variability that accompanies it make this impossible. So they welcome the next best thing: knowing as soon as possible when things have gone off track with the assurance that the lessons have been learned and the steps are already underway to remediate matters.

There is a side benefit to this, which again bolsters trust and cements the ability of teams to self-organize and self-manage. When everyone sees that work is proceeding stepwise and backed up by frequent and regular feedback, they trust more and leave the team more space. People feel less inclined to step in and interfere. This is again good for everyone. Management has visible progress, and the teams have space and trust.

Therefore, favor faster, potentially poorer decisions than slower, indeterminably perfect ones. Because variability will get you if you don't.

Watch the Outliers

Those are the steps to take when you have a clear-cut situation on your hands. A decision was taken, implemented, and proved to be a failure. But what about decisions that are still on this journey? What about decisions that take a long time to be decided or a long time to get implemented? It pays to afford them special attention.

You've most likely heard about high work in progress (WIP) being a "bad thing," and it is. This idea comes from Lean manufacturing, and it is bad in those environments because high WIP means there is too much inventory in play (raw materials that have been or are being converted into products but have not yet been sold). In software, there are additional problems from high WIP. It also means there is likely too much context switching going on, which makes everything slow down in such knowledge-intensive work as software development. When architectural decisions have a high WIP, there is another likely cause that is worth investigating: some decisions are likely stuck in their decision process.

To reduce decision WIP, focus on the decisions that have been in flight for the longest time (Reinertsen's Principle W15, "Watch the outliers"). If you have an advice forum, that's a great place to do this—just add the topic to the AOB section and move it to a standing agenda item if the "slow decisions" problem persists. How long is too long for a decision to be in flight? Simply start with the decision that has been in flight the longest. Lean calls this *aging analysis* (e.g., engineering jobs stuck in a WIP pool a long time are likely to be experiencing unexpected problems).

For each decision, examine why it hasn't moved at the speed of the others. Recall earlier when I discussed the "worst part" of a decision; frequently, your analysis will highlight that aspect. "Worst" can come from many sources. It might turn out to be a dependency that is not yet ready and so can't be fed into this decision, or a topic that is not very well known, or (most frequently in my experience) a decision that is simply too large. If the decision has been taken but implementation is taking a long time, this might then call into question the decision itself. And if the decision is good, is supporting architectural work required to remove blockers to the implementation of this (and most likely other) pieces of work?

A word of warning: investigations may well reveal that a decision is not as important as originally thought, and in such cases, it is perfectly acceptable to deprioritize or even shelve it, starting again from scratch later. On the flip side, don't use the analysis to artificially prioritize certain decisions over others, "fast-tracking" them, as it were. This raises the question: how might you know what the priority of architectural decisions ought to be?

Sequence the Most Valuable Decisions First

The greatest benefit of moving to smaller architectural decisions is that it gives you more control over which decisions you sequence when. With large decisions, this isn't possible, but with smaller decisions, it is. This is a step beyond *having* to sequence a set of decisions in a certain order and figuring out what that order is. This is taking advantage of the possibility to sequence for a certain gain.

Reinertsen has a pithy turn of phrase that can help you choose the order: "sequence first that which adds value most cheaply."[17] In architecture, the value is typically reducing risk and removing unknowns because without knowing if our systems are feasible, then all other prioritized value is built on sand.

The most valuable example of such sequencing is one I already introduced. Walking skeletons target key decisions in a system's architecture, ones that many subsequent decisions will depend on. But there are others. These days, systems evolve constantly, and architectural work on them is never complete. Product management will always make a strong case for some value-adding piece of work requiring a decision, but remember the risk-reduction "value," too. Story 2 from Chapter 4 is yet again a good example of this. Although it didn't add value by way of new features, it removed the risk of reputational damage.

Learning is also valuable. As Reinertsen reminds us, "A small, early investment to buy information is common in venture capital-based investment."[18] While the hope behind walking skeletons is that we will find a set of design decisions that will work, we can also prioritize decisions that will teach us something—clarifying a set of possible future options, for instance.[19]

Some great examples of this are buy-versus-build decisions or strategic decisions to invest in a shared component or service. For such decisions, it is valuable to know early, before lots of bespoke work takes place, if the components will integrate with and deliver value to the teams and their systems.

However you deploy the flexibility of small decisions, remember that by constantly striving to right-size your decisions and order them sensibly, you can not only tackle the worst effects of variability, but you can also make variability work for you.

Conclusion

The sum of all this means that you should double down on everything in this book. Always look to make decisions as small as meaningfully possible. Constantly work to get those decisions coded up, deployed, and gathering feedback. Treat failure as learning, celebrate it, be open about it, and factor it back into future decisions. If you do all this, you can tackle variability head on, minimizing its downsides and maximizing its benefits. The more you do that, the more predictably everyone can flow. Everyone practicing architecture, working to foster a culture of transparency and learning, plays a significant role in this, both by modeling this mindset and by encouraging it in others.

---

17 *Principles of Product Development Flow*, 131.

18 *Principles of Product Development Flow*, 108.

19 See Gregor Hohpe's "Selling Options" (*https://oreil.ly/EZH2_*) for an enterprise architecture take on the same.

Even without any of the other elements in this book in place, small decisions would be something I would focus on. You won't have to wait long to see the benefits. By adopting smaller and smaller decisions, you will see their transition to code and their impact manifest there.

But there is one further tactic you can use to manage variability and make predictable forward progress. I'll cover that in the next chapter, the last one in Part III.

CHAPTER 14

Variability and the Interconnectedness of Decisions

People who practice architecture are confronted with decision after decision. These decisions come in all shapes and sizes, and in a sociotechnical system, decisions are affected not only by technical challenges but also by sociological ones.

When deciding, the challenges go beyond knowing which option suits you best right now. You also need to know how your decision will affect other decisions and if there are other decisions that affect yours. Other people's decisions can affect your confidence in deciding or sometimes lead to an out-of-control feeling if the decision is in someone else's hands.

In this chapter, I'll examine four ways that decisions can be interrelated. And I'll introduce you to a tool for understanding the relationships that connect decisions, boosting your decision pathfinding skills and helping you navigate through the tangled sociotechnical jungle.

Finding a Path Through Variability

We don't decide in a vacuum. Decisions are inevitably interconnected. Not only that, but the act of deciding is frequently hindered by emotion and ego. Interconnectedness and emotionality add variability. Unfortunately, variability arising from these two sources is usually the most expensive kind.

Expensive *technical* variability arises from not knowing which option will yield the best outcome given your context—or even if it will work at all—until you take it all the way to production.

Expensive *sociological* variability arises from the biases of those involved, including participants feeling a loss of control when the power to decide is shared.

Variability is expensive when technical and social factors make finding—and subsequently, navigating—the path through the inherent variability take longer. This is time you don't want to take because what you really want is to identify, take, and implement decisions and learn from the feedback as rapidly as possible.

To navigate your way through this universe of decisions, you need to look for patterns: patterns in structures, context, time, relationships between decisions, and your own thinking. By being aware of these patterns, you can make more informed decisions more rapidly and get the resulting architectures into production.

Although ADRs are a great way to support the decision process, they may not help you uncover variability and these patterns fast enough. ADRs are also not the best tool to focus people on facts rather than on inventing more options, which may crop up when you ask for advice.

What you need is a tool that quickly and safely probes for decision paths through the complex sociotechnical world, slicing through both technical and emotional decision coupling. A simple tool that everyone can use, that supplements ADRs, and that tackles variability in a way everyone can relate to. A tool that fits with the decentralized, evolutionary, feedback-based approach to architecture.

Extreme programming's spikes are that tool. Spikes are ideal for finding patterns and framing fact-based conversations. Spikes move the variability of decisions to the point in the decision process where it is cheapest—at the start—and help you understand the interconnectedness of your decisions. Let's see how.

Introducing Spikes

Spikes are investigations where you research, make observations, and test out options. They are time-boxed investigations of a single question or the search for the resolution of a single problem. A standard XP practice, spikes predominantly involve writing code to reach a concrete understanding of the problem. The aim of a spike is to gather concrete information *in the current context*, helping the team to learn about the question or problem at hand *as it relates to them*.

Spikes don't result in shippable product. Neither do they take decisions. Spikes do, however, help teams uncover a way forward for decisions, architectural or otherwise. For example, you might use a functional spike to investigate how a user might interact with a developed system. Architectural spikes investigate architecturally significant decisions—for example, the options to meet a CFR or a technology or pattern selection.

The goal of a spike isn't to draw conclusions; its goal is to gather information. These findings can feed directly into an ADR and the ultimate decision.

Spikes are represented on a team's backlog as tickets because they are work that a team plans and undertakes, but they aren't given a points estimate. Instead, they have a time box that states how long the team will spend investigating things. This serves to keep them on track delivery-wise.

Spikes embrace experimentation, and they factor in context, exactly like the Context sections of ADRs. In this section, I'll show how spikes fit into the advice process. Later sections will detail how spikes can help you address architectural variability and how they can be used to better understand the relationships between decisions.

Spikes Can Tackle Architectural Variability More Cheaply

Spikes are a perfect complement to a decentralized, postrevolutionary approach to architecture. Not only do they embrace architectural uncertainty head on by giving *concrete feedback* but they also can investigate their subject *in context*. The goal of a spike is to *learn from it*. Best of all, spikes do this without having to select one of your options and start it on its way to production.

Even practiced well, the advice process can involve a large number of people and a significant amount of time. Spikes substitute cheap variability for this expensive variability (Reinertsen's Principle V14). Spikes do this by offering *contextualized* feedback from throwaway code without having to follow the advice process or implement the resulting decision and push it to production (Principle FF8).

Architectural spike code is written with the express goal of learning that allows early and meaningful contact with a problem and replaces opinion and conjecture with facts (Principle D16). Or, as an ex-colleague liked to point out when option debates shifted from heated to deadlocked, "Code settles arguments."

If in Doubt, Spike That Decision

If you have any hesitation about whether a spike will help you deal with decision variability, try it. At the very worst, you will understand your question or problem better. The downsides of *not* doing a spike and then wishing you did later are worse. (You'll see exactly why later in this chapter).

So where do spikes fit into our bigger advice process picture?

Where Do Spikes Sit in a Decision Process?

Spikes sit right at the start of a decision process, touching the steps when the decision that is required is being defined as well as the option making that follows, as shown in Figure 14-1.

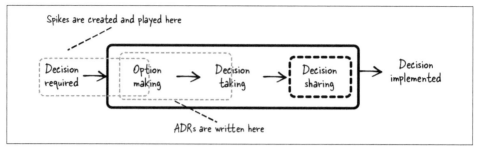

Figure 14-1. Spikes fit into an overall decision process at the start, somewhere around "decision required" and "option making"

The reason spikes start in the "decision required" step is because this is when the question or problem that the decision will resolve is first formulated. A spike then goes on to uncover and validate a set of options, testing one or more of them. Along the way, various pros and cons will surface. This covers the same territory as standard option making. It doesn't, however, go as far as weighing up those options and presenting them ready for decision taking. As such, spikes precede and then overlap with writing ADRs.

Spiking ADRs

When you investigate a potential decision, also known as "spiking an ADR,"[1] you gather feedback based on the actual writing and running of code before going through the full advice process or delivery flow down to prod. A spike can be initiated before or during the early stages of writing an ADR, when the context and options are being investigated. The observations you make during a spike can then inform your subsequent decision and ADR write-up. Cards describing spikes correspond closely with the major sections of an ADR.

Writing a spike

A spike can be initiated by anyone, but because spikes usually involve writing code, they will usually be played by a development team (see the sidebar "Who Plays Spikes?" on page 357). The work of a spike needs to be treated and captured like any other piece of work on a team's backlog. Writing a spike is similar to writing an ADR. In fact, the sections of a spike can directly feed into your subsequent ADR. Spikes and ADRs also both get updated as work proceeds.

---

1 Much of this section is based on my ex-colleague Cat Morris's Medium post, "How to Use Spikes as a Foundation for ADRs" (*https://oreil.ly/c8Z6H*).

The standard sections of a spike are as follows:

- ID
- Title
- Time Box

- Context
- Options Considered
- Consequences

Before adding a spike to a team's backlog, fill out the first three sections: ID, Title, and Time Box. Draft the Context and maybe jot some initial notes in the Options Considered section. You will fill out the Consequences section during and after the spike.

Let's take a closer look at each section with examples. The spike has a unique ID. Most backlog management tools will autogenerate one for you. The spike's title states the question or problem under investigation. I recommend writing the spike's title in the form of a question that the future ADR title will answer. The ADR from Chapter 6 with the title "ADR-002—Shorten Inventory IDs with Nano ID" might have been preceded by a spike titled as follows:

EXAMPLE

SPIKE-001—Can we have shorter, human-readable inventory IDs?

Explicitly state the time box (i.e., the specific amount of time set aside) that you intend to allocate to the work on this spike, such as:

EXAMPLE

Time Box:

One developer pair for three days

Combined, the Title and Time Box give focus to the spike from the outset.

The spike's next section, the Context, answers the following further questions:

- What is the value of answering this question?
- Why do you need an answer now?
- Who is affected by or interested in the answer?
- What are the constraints?

In our example (*https://oreil.ly/vKy7O*), the Context section might look like this:

EXAMPLE

Context:

Our current inventory IDs across the company for buildings, spaces, and providers are generated from UUIDs. Sometimes, humans have to read, share, or even manually enter these IDs, and it's painful due to their length and characters.

We want to investigate whether it's feasible to move to shorter, human-readable inventory IDs.

The Options Considered section contains the various ways that the spike's stated problem might be solved. Most of the detail here will arise and develop as you run the spike. After all, the point of playing the spike is to discover and test your valid options. But when you are first writing it, prior to putting it on the backlog you can capture the options that spring immediately to mind. For example, the draft Options Considered section for our SPIKE-001 example might look like the following:

EXAMPLE

Options Considered:

Random generated letters and numbers (some tool or library?)

Automatically generated sequence ID? (e.g., 1234, 1235, 1236, etc.)

Having an initial idea of your options also allows you to validate your proposed time box for the spike.

The Consequences section is written as you play the spike and after the spike has been completed. Let's talk about that next.

Playing a spike

Once written, the spike can then be *played,* which is just a fancy way of saying that the spike is being "worked on."[2]

---

2 I think it means "play" like "play a record," and I also like the implication that you're free to "play" without fear of failure. Spikes never fail because they're not meant to give you a pass/fail outcome. Their sole purpose is to help you learn.

Who Plays Spikes?

If the authors of a spike are a development team looking to decide for themselves (such as a team adopting a trunk-based delivery approach that needs a way to release toggles; see Story 1 in Chapter 4), then that team simply puts their spike on their own backlog and plays it as appropriate. But what about spikes that arise from those with a cross-system, cross-team viewpoint, such as people playing system architecture roles (which happened, for example, in Story 2 in Chapter 4)? Their spikes still go on a single team's backlog.[3] Typically, the host team will be the one most affected by the decision, though other teams will likely be closely involved (perhaps even running complementary spikes or loaning team members to the primary spiking team). The individual who initiates the spike will be part of this work, regardless of which backlog it is in. This provides an essential link back to the code and the current environment in which the spike investigation and resulting decision will live.

As spikes step across a team's board, pay attention to the time box set for the work. A spike that takes forever to complete can be as problematic as a decision that does the same (or even more so, given that you're hoping to use them to make faster, cheaper contact with a decision).

Playing the spike means concrete research is done and code is likely being written. Your problem or question is investigated in a way that provides data as feedback, something advice gathering can't do. This provides information to flesh out the Options Considered and Consequences sections. It limits the amount of guesswork in your ADR.

As you investigate, the following questions will guide your spike's focus, but they are not exhaustive:

- Which teams will have systems that will be affected?
- Will any downstream teams be affected?
- Will InfoSec be concerned?
- Will this cost any extra? Will this cost be one-off, annual, or per transaction?
- Will this affect system performance?

---

3 It's the standard Agile tenet—"Make all work visible"—but it's also basic manners. Product owners and business analysts don't take kindly to people with "architect" in their email signature asking teammates to do work on the side. The whole team decides on what work it does and when, and secret side projects go against that.

Our example might have the following Options Considered section at the end of the spike after the findings are recorded. You can see how investigations uncovered more option ideas:

> **EXAMPLE**
>
> **Options Considered:**
>
> Random generated letters and numbers with Nano ID or UUID 4
>
> Automatically generated sequence ID (e.g., 1234, 1235, 1236, etc.) from code or from a data store
>
> Manually generated
>
> Human-readable generated

And the Consequences section after the spike's investigations might look something like this:

> **EXAMPLE**
>
> **Consequences:**
>
> *Nano ID*
> JavaScript native, no new infra needed, works with serverless, lower chance of ID collision than UUID (link to code example).
>
> *UUID*
> Same benefits as Nano ID, but higher chance of UUID collision (link to code example).
>
> *Autogenerated sequence ID in code*
> Impossible to ensure uniqueness in a serverless environment without adding extra infrastructure.
>
> *Autogenerated sequence ID from data store*
> We don't currently have data stores that would support this.
>
> *Manually generated*
> Too much manual intervention (link to quick sums showing how often this would happen).
>
> *Human-readable generated*
> No library found. Too much effort to build ourselves.

Once the spike has been played, its learnings can be fed into an ADR.

Helping Play Spikes Is a Great Way to Be a "Hands-on Architect"

As Eric Evans points out in *Domain-Driven Design* (p. 60), if you don't stay acquainted with the code of systems and how it is solving problems, then you lose sensitivity to details that might not be available to you in any other way. These details include both the current state of the code with its inherent architecture and supporting technologies as well as the details of the potential options for new decisions on further system evolutions.

If you're a developer, spending time with the code is inevitable; you can't avoid such details. But if you are playing an architecture role, it can be easy to drift away from the details. Working with a team on a spike is a great way to get into that detail and short-circuit the feedback on designs by roughly implementing them. Spiking architectural questions without the teams who know the details misses out on much of what matters.

Feeding a spike's outcomes into an ADR

Once a spike has been completed, its findings will have a direct impact on the decision at hand. Here's how you can feed the spike's findings into your ADR.

First, turn the spike's question title into the statement of the ADR title. For example, the spike investigates the question "Can we have shorter, human-readable inventory IDs?" and the subsequent ADR decision states the intent to "Shorten Inventory IDs with Nano ID." If you started an ADR before stepping back to play a spike, then it can still be worth updating the ADR title if the investigation sharpened your question.

The Context of the spike can be copied directly into the Context of the ADR, supplemented with any further details that may have resulted from playing the spike. For example, did investigations uncover further constraints? How about further interested parties? The spike can also highlight who will be affected by and interested in the answer to the spike's question. Remember to put these people on your ADR's adviser list.

The Options Considered and Consequences sections of the spike can also feed directly into their ADR namesakes. In moving from spike to ADR, you have the opportunity to sharpen the Options and Consequences, turning whiteboard sketches from the spike work into diagrams highlighting the key learnings for future ADR readers. Remember to use the ordering and phrasing I shared to make this suitably explicit: "selected because/despite…" and "rejected despite/because…".

If you feel the learnings from the spike are conclusive, you can draft your ADR's Decision section. This step should be easier given everything you've learned from your spike's concrete implementations. You still need to follow the advice process, so put your ADR in a "proposed" state as it goes out for advice seeking.

Spiked ADRs Still Follow the Advice Process

Spiked or not, all ADRs still follow the advice process as normal. However, spiked ADRs tend to move relatively faster because of the additional detail and concrete feedback. Advisers may well have been aware of, or even involved in, the playing of the spike, and even if they weren't, the information articulated in the spike's outcomes and consequences provides them a far greater degree of detail that their advice can then complement. The concrete learnings from the spike's code focus any remaining argumentation.

Highlight Planned and In-Flight Spikes at Advice Forums

When spikes become part of your decision process, add an advice forum agenda item where teams can share spikes they are planning or that are in play. The social contract of the advice process doesn't count at this point. No decision is being taken. However, sharing work that is planned or is taking place allows others to offer useful input. You may receive additional options to consider or difficulties to watch out for. Sharing the spike's intention also helps teams avoid wasting time respiking things (which can occur when team independence is high).

Examining the Interconnectedness of Decisions

Because of the complex, ever-shifting nature of our systems, there is no "one right way" to think about decision interconnectedness. Not only do you have to think about the relationships between current decisions and their surrounding context, but you also have to think about how current decisions relate to decisions that came before them and decisions that might follow.

Spikes can effectively and efficiently uncover how interconnected a set of decisions really are. In doing this, they reveal the true nature of that coupling in your systems as they are right now.

Spikes act like scalpels. By writing code, you can carefully cut along the delicate, semi-hidden fracture planes between decisions, uncovering whether it is possible to separate decisions into smaller parts. Spikes are also a magnifying glass, allowing close and careful examination of your specific variability and its inherent coupling.

Over the course of your code-based investigations, you might discover that two decisions aren't separable at all because they share a fundamental aspect. Or you might discover that an apparently intractably large decision can actually be safely pried apart. As a result, spikes are the best way to effectively and efficiently find a path through the variability interconnected decisions present.

In this section, I'll introduce four different ways to view and understand these relationships between decisions. Decisions are:

- A series
- An inverted hierarchy
- Atomic
- A two-way conversation

In each case, I'll describe how to use spikes to gain clarity on that aspect of decision relationships.

Decisions Are a Series

Software architecture is the sum total of the decisions that have been taken during development: your decisions and the decisions of others.

To understand this relationship, you might model a decision series as a timeline with frequent decision points, as shown in Figure 14-2.[4] The paths from one decision room to the next represent the work of implementing decisions. The need for a new decision is represented by a room with doors at the end of the implementation line. The doors leading out of each decision room represent the options created or uncovered by the deciders. When an option is selected, the door is opened, and the path continues horizontally until another decision is needed. The model as a whole shows a series of decisions, joined by the implementation of selected options.

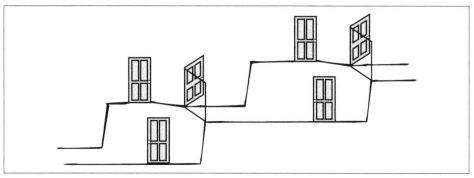

Figure 14-2. The thread through a series of decisions

---

4 Bikart in *The Art of Decision Making* has an entire chapter titled "Decision Flow" where he takes a step back from individual decisions to look at the overall flow of the journey from decision to decision.

As you take decisions, selecting options one after another, you are traversing time and space, specifically the design space where you practice software architecture—the thread of successfully taken decisions behind you is the path you took. The decision points with their option forks represent the paths (in the form of nonselected options) not taken.

When you use ADRs to support your decision process, the conceptual thread of implementation becomes more explicit. Your ADR history reflects the details of each decision point: its context and the available options along with their perceived consequences. Past ADRs are a rich resource, informing everyone's understanding of the overall thread of your software and systems architecture. Your timeline answers the question "How did we *get* here?"

Your ADR history also allows you to revisit all the decisions that make up your thread of implementation. With the benefit of hindsight, you can reevaluate the options you did (and didn't) create and select. This can generate powerful insights. The urgency and most of the emotion will have passed; you can learn equally from the successes and the failures.

Comparing spiked and nonspiked decisions

To better see how spikes can help you learn more safely,[5] let's zoom in on a single decision point and consider it with and without a spike (Figure 14-3).

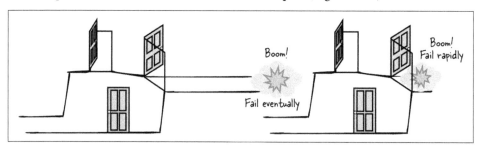

Figure 14-3. A single decision point, tackled without a spike (left) and then with a spike (right); the thread does not continue when an option fails as the decider backtracks and selects another option

Figure 14-3 illustrates a single decision point with three possible options. The illustration on the left represents what would happen if you had decided on an option, implemented it, and deployed it. The selected option turned out to be unfavorable, but you couldn't have known it without these implementation and deployment steps, so you spent a significant amount of time working toward an unfavorable outcome.

---

5 The "safety" here is both technical and psychological, as you will see.

You failed slowly because you had to go a long way down the wrong decision thread before you had the feedback to learn from.

Now, let's consider the right side of the figure, which represents the same decision point but being examined beforehand with a spike. With a spike, you can *investigate* an option and likely discover that it leads to an unfavorable outcome far sooner, without having to actually decide and commit work to implementation and deployment. In other words, you failed fast and avoided wasting time proceeding a long way down the wrong decision thread. Not only that, but because work done during a spike does not lead to production, no harm is done, and there is nothing to back out. This all means you are free much sooner to investigate another option. If this sounds familiar, this circumstance is the precise reason I stated that "fast and wrong is better than slow and correct."

Comparing the two diagrams, you can see that the amount of time (as represented by the length of the path) prior to the discovery that the selected option won't work is shorter when a spike is used. With ADRs alone, the decision goes through the advice process with an ADR and is taken, the user story to do the work then goes on a team's backlog, the code is implemented to production standard, it goes down the pipeline to production, and only then does it transpire that something doesn't work as hoped or intended.

With the spike, the options are thought up and the most promising option or options spiked first. This implementation shows far more rapidly that the option won't work as hoped and an alternative should be tried.

With both approaches, code is still written and run, and information is gathered. But with a spike-investigation mindset, code is written *to be thrown away* and run *on a trial or exploratory basis*. "Successful" and "unsuccessful" decision options are treated equally because there is no need to be "right." No decisions are taken. Nothing ends up in production, so nothing needs to be removed. We fail faster and in far more safety, so we can shift attention to other options or even other decisions. This all helps uncover variability and tackle it more cheaply.

Knowing quickly that an individual decision option will lead you away from the best decision thread—the one without the failures that leads to the next decision point—is a valuable perspective for an individual taking a series of decisions. It is orders of magnitude more important when the deciding plays such a huge part in a decentralized approach to architecture. Spikes offer a safe and rapid way for anyone to find out if one or more options at a given decision point will take the overall system architecture farther away from or closer to the overall thread. This is safe because no code is written that goes into production, but the key learnings can still be obtained. It is rapid because these learnings come *before* the advice process (at least before it is completed).

Spikes are an underused way to fail safely at decision points

The safety that spikes offer to fail at a decision point and learn from that experience is significantly undervalued in software architecture. We rarely stop, let alone back up, but using spikes in your architectural practice makes that far easier. Variability will always be present in software development, introducing risks and unlocking value. To get the most value from your architecture you want to take risks, trying things that might fail. Such risk-acknowledging practices—finding the best thread through a series of decisions, understanding that sometimes you'll get it wrong and then backtracking—is something there ought to be a lot more of. If we did use spikes in this way—tackling architectural variability and backtracking when we discover we are on the wrong path—we would be able to avoid much of the worst form of technical debt: design debt.

Design debt is the result of inappropriate decision after inappropriate decision, all piled on top of one another.[6] You know, the kind of debt that leads to estimates of six months to move a button from one side of a screen to the other.[7] Design debt arises in great part because our relentless forward movement forces us to stick with architectural decision after decision, even the ones we know have failed. Why don't we stop and fix them? Because the longer and more hard fought a decision was, the less comfortable everyone will be in reversing and revisiting it. This more expensive variability, even if we are a living embodiment of the downsides, puts us off. It's this that leads us to think so many architectural decisions are one-way. Very few are, but the longer we leave any one of them in our systems, and the more subsequent decisions we layer on top of each of them, the harder any one is to change.

Keep this idea of decision "layers" in mind because it's the next useful perspective on decision interconnectedness.

Decisions Are an Inverted Hierarchy

While viewing decisions as a series can be useful, it has limitations, especially when deciding collectively and in many places at once. After Michael Nygard pointed out in his post about ADRs (*https://oreil.ly/Xk0Mu*) that "the consequences of one ADR are very likely to become the context for subsequent ADRs," he felt the need to qualify his statement, aware that this could give an overly simplified, linear view. He continued: "This is also similar to [Christopher] Alexander's idea of a pattern language: the large-scale responses create spaces for the smaller scale to fit into."

---

6 This isn't to say that a decision was inappropriate at the time it was taken. Circumstances change, as you'll see later in this chapter.

7 True story. The button was in an old Visual Basic 6 codebase. It was accidentally being clicked by users, so it seemed like a good (and simple) thing to do to move it. But years of design debt had effectively backed it into a corner—specifically, the corner it occupied in this old UI.

Nygard's qualification points to the second perspective on the relationship between decisions: a decision's consequences set the context *for all subsequent decisions that fit within it*. This means that the *full extent* of your current decision's context is not always evident, especially if you consider only the consequences of the decision that came immediately before in the decision sequence. Consequences of decisions *way earlier in time* could *also* be contributing important aspects to your context, and the earliest, broadest decisions have consequences that set the context for many decisions to come.

Therefore, it is useful to regard the decisions in a program of work as being in an inverted hierarchy, with higher decisions sitting on top of, and within, the consequences of the lower, earlier decisions that "contain" them. In this view, the lower the layer a decision sits at, the greater its potential contextual influence on the decisions that sit on top of and within it. Note that the context for the very first layer is special—what sets *its* context?—but I'll get to that shortly. If you were to view the inverted decision hierarchy obliquely from above, it would look like Figure 14-4—decisions sitting on top of and within previous decisions.

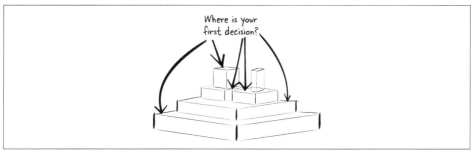

Figure 14-4. Top-down oblique view of the inverted decision hierarchy

The subsections that follow focus on those most important decisions that make up the lowest layers of any inverted decision hierarchy. I'll start by describing the characteristics of these lowest three decision layers. Then I'll share a way to find and represent the decisions that have already been taken in your circumstances: the ones that set the starting context for your first decisions. I'll close by discussing how spikes can be used to help with all this, no matter what layer you are deciding at.

The lowest three layers of the inverted decision hierarchy

You and your colleagues are here to architect, then build, run, and evolve real-world systems, but you never start with an entirely blank canvas for architecture work. You benefit from knowing all the relevant details about any context you start deciding within. To achieve this, you need to be aware of all the key underlying decisions that are already in play, decisions whose consequences will continue to have an impact on your architecture practice now and into the future.

Inspired by *A Pattern Language* by Christopher Alexander, Sara Ishikawa, and Murray Silverstein (Oxford University Press), I rely on a set of explicit characteristics that can help you identify the lowest three layers of decisions because they are so fundamental. Let's look at the distinct characteristics of each of these layers in detail, with examples of decisions so that you can see where *you* are starting to decide.

Decision layer 1: Independent products or programs of work.   Layer 1 decisions tackle the broadest aspects that organizations decide to influence: the focus of and delineation between independent products or programs of work. Layer 1 decisions articulate business models, set budgets, locate milestones and deadlines, and decide aspirational outcomes. They very much call on elements in the organizational vision and goals and actionable technology strategy. Consequently, layer 1 decisions are not directly technical decisions, but they do relate to technical concerns because technology dictates what is and what isn't possible.

That's why, unlike the higher layers, the context for decisions on the very first layer isn't based on previous decision consequences. The context for decisions in the first decision layer comes from factors that are out of an organization's hands: the users' needs and the broader commercial and technical environment.[8]

Some argue that layer 1 decisions should solely be taken by product management, or your organization's executive, but that's a mistake. Wherever layer 1 decisions arise from, technologists need to be involved in them because, at the very least, they can provide feedback on the feasibility of various options. Ideally, the software engineering department should be an active partner, shaping options and their consequences just like in any other decision. The role typically representing software engineering in this is an enterprise architect.[9]

For example, consider a layer 1 strategic decision to pivot a company's main product from a shrink-wrapped client-hosted product to a hosted (SaaS) offering. Additional layer 1 decisions identify the market opportunity and set the budget, so we know there will be two separate programs of work: the new hosted system and the continuation of the legacy products for existing customers. Further layer 1 decisions about the business model for this service decide that the new product will offer services to a previously unserved user community, but to do so, it will integrate with existing in-house operational systems for some capabilities (financial, CRM, etc.).

---

8 The equivalent of this first layer in Alexander et al.'s *A Pattern Language* is pattern number 1, "Independent Regions."

9 In Gregor Hohpe's *The Software Architect Elevator* (O'Reilly), he identifies patterns of higher-level architectural practice that fit well with the Alexandrian patterns at this and the next level: gardener, tour guide, and catalyst/superglue. All set the scene and offer attractor and repeller forces to guide things in a certain direction and away from others.

These decisions mean the company will need to rewrite many of their systems from scratch, both custom-facing and internal systems. Those rewrite efforts will be "greenfield," with the teams taking the advantage to go back to the basic customer needs and current surrounding commercial climate. The other part of the effort will be "brownfield" work, keeping the old product alive and viable so that it can continue to deliver value to existing customers.

Further layer 1 decisions in this example decide on the goals of the legacy and the new systems, and whether those efforts will be split. All this effort might be treated as a single program of work, and within that, a separation of the old product from the new. Or it might be treated as two separate programs. The selection of one or the other of these options is a layer 1 decision.

Given the consequences of such layer 1 decisions, what are the characteristics of the layer 2 decisions that sit above and within these?

Decision layer 2: Protect and mark limits. Layer 2 decisions provide clarity and essential detail to what was previously only fuzzily defined at a strategic and financial planning level.[10] They do this by defining the technical edges of the products and programs decided on in layer 1, protecting and marking their limits.

Layer 2 decisions are where those playing systems architecture roles likely become involved alongside their enterprise architecture colleagues. Layer 2 decisions primarily define the capabilities that live within new systems. But layer 2 decisions also decide on the capabilities that will come from elsewhere—from other systems or programs of work, either in house or third party—and identify key shared constraints that arise from all these other decisions. Such decisions all sit together at layer 2 because knowing "what function lives where" and "what data is mastered where" is essential if you are to avoid unnecessary complexity. Layer 2 decisions that "protect and mark limits" provide that clarity.

The concept of user identity in the new SaaS product is a key example of this. A layer 2 decision will define how and where the concept of SaaS "customer" is handled. If the organization makes a layer 1 decision to offer a business-to-business SaaS, then customers will be companies. If the organization wants to be a business-to-consumer SaaS, then customers will be end users or perhaps something like a family. Such "customer" decisions depend on the business model that came from the layer 1 decisions. Given the clarity on "customer," deciders can determine where these identities will live: will the identity management business capability live in the new systems? Or will it live in an existing system? If "customer" lives in one place, will updates need to be

---

10 The equivalents to this second layer in Alexander et al.'s *A Pattern Language* are the following patterns: (2) "the distribution of towns," (3) "city country fingers," (4) "agricultural valleys," (5) "lace of country streets," (6) "country towns," and (7) "the countryside."

cascaded down to or synced with systems that offer other business capabilities (e.g., billing)? These decisions then give the technical constraints. For example, the SaaS system will need to have the appropriate idea of a "tenant"[11] so that one customer doesn't see another customer's data.

Those are the interrelated collection of layer 2 decisions for the new SaaS systems. But what about those working on the legacy systems in the parallel program of work? Those teams might be deciding to offload some business capabilities, ones that had in a much older layer 2 decision been implemented in house but now can be superseded by a new layer 2 decision to move them to a third-party SaaS. Old constraints can be challenged, too, and decisions about these superseded.

Given the addition of the consequences from these layer 2 decisions, what are the characteristics of the layer 3 decisions that sit above and within these?

Decision layer 3: Self-governing, connected communities. Decisions at layer 3 take up the contexts offered by the consequences of layer 1 and 2 decisions and start dividing work up so that it can be tackled by multiple teams. Therefore, decisions at layer 3 have a strong social and structural focus. Layer 3 decisions identify the major subsystems and the teams that will own them. Layer 3 decisions also define the key connectivity between those subsystems and how owning teams interact.[12]

If your role requires a software/solution architecture perspective or an engineer in a team, you will likely first become involved here at level 3, either in the deciding itself or directly after it as teams are staffed. Techniques such as walking skeletons are useful here, as are collaborative modeling techniques.

Think once again of the SaaS and legacy programs of work example. Layer 2 decisions defined the locations of all the business capabilities: in the new systems, in the legacy systems, in the core systems, and moved to third parties.

Collaborative discovery and modeling techniques such as Event Storming (*https://oreil.ly/qKHF0*) can then be applied to identify and inform the layer 3 decisions. Such techniques identify distinct functional subdomains and group the identified business capabilities meaningfully. Layer 3 decisions codify these identified splits, define subsystem boundaries, and map them to teams. This manages cognitive load and ensures that coupling is low enough between teams so that everyone can flow unimpeded.

---

11 Amazon defines a *tenant* as "the most fundamental construct of a SaaS environment…Any customer that you sign up to use your SaaS environment is one of the tenants of your system" (from the AWS "Well-Architected SaaS Lens" documentation (*https://oreil.ly/FRk7_*)).

12 The equivalents of this second layer in Alexander et al.'s *A Pattern Language* are the pattern groupings 12–15 ("self-governing communities"), 16–20 ("connect[ed] communities"), 21–27 ("polic[ies] to control the character of the local neighborhood"), and 28–34 ("local centers").

Big-picture, domain-discovering approaches to layer 3 decisions don't just work for greenfield programs—they work for brownfield situations, too. The only difference is that in brownfield, there might be greater numbers of legacy systems in play. However, layer 3 decisions still need to be taken, defining what those systems will do, who owns them, how they are expected to integrate with everything else, and (importantly) whether they will be maintained, upgraded, refactored, or migrated into something new.

Layer 3 decisions make up the last largely predictable layer of the inverted hierarchy of decisions. Above layer 3, decisions become deeply tied to both the specifics of your domain and the current trends in software engineering. At these higher levels, architecture work will be trying as hard as possible to reduce coupling and keep up with technology. Layer 3 decisions offer the final set of wide-ranging and underlying consequences that subsequent decisions must likely take into consideration.

Some general points about decisions in layers 1–3. There are a few general points worth noting about these important underlying layers. Table 14-1 summarizes the key facts split by layer.

Table 14-1. The three underlying decision layers and the key questions they answer

Name	Purpose	Key questions answered
Layer 1: independent products or programs of work	Set the focus of and delineation between independent products or programs of work.	• Articulate business models • Set program budgets • Locate initial milestones and overall deadlines • Decide aspirational outcomes
Layer 2: protect and mark limits	Give clarity and detail to what was only fuzzily defined in layer 1.	• Define the capabilities that live within new systems and the capabilities that come from elsewhere (e.g., other systems/programs of work, either in house or third party) • Identify key shared constraints
Layer 3: self-governing and connected communities	Define what teams work on what and how those teams will interrelate.	• Identify the major subsystems and the teams that own them • Define the key connectivity between those subsystems and how owning teams interact

First, not all layer 1–3 decisions are made consciously. As with all other decisions, it's perfectly possible for some to see certain steps as "the only logical option" and therefore make decisions by accident. Irrespective of how they are taken, these are still decisions.

Second, layer 1–3 decisions aren't always made once. Like all decisions, they can be superseded. But when that happens, all too often no one thinks to bring in the full context from the original decision. A classic example of this is the long trail of authentication, authorization, and identity solutions that many of my clients seem to have. These always pop up because a decision is made to swap to a new solution but insufficient work is put into decommissioning the legacy solution (or solutions). It gets sticky because halfway into the work, someone uncovers a constraint that an old system can cope with but the new replacement can't. Now you have one and a half identity solutions as well as a problem of how to keep them all in sync.

Third, don't assume that the key stakeholders such as product management or various members of the executive team will agree with layer 1–3 decisions, especially the ones that haven't been made consciously and the ones that supersede previous decisions. Again and again, I've seen organizations struggling because different parts of an organization are committing time, resources, and effort to work that is in conflict. Conscious or not, intentional or unintentional, this always makes life for delivery of systems, and especially the practice of architecture, incredibly difficult.

It's for all these reasons, but especially the last one, that it pays to know in as much detail as possible your starting context for any architecture work you might engage in. The best way to do this is with a picture.

Identify your starting context

It can help to represent the context for your earliest decisions with a picture. This picture should be simple enough for everyone to understand, showing all the important layer 1–3 decisions that have already been taken: the conscious and the unconscious ones, the legacy ones and those that superseded them, the ones that everyone agrees on, and the ones that are openly or secretly disagreed with.

This picture will delineate the boundary of the system or systems you are working on. Inside this boundary sits the design space where you can take decisions and practice architecture as well as the capabilities that you own. Outside are all the other consequences of the decisions that have been taken already.

Such a representation has been important in software for decades. Given this, you will likely not be surprised to hear that there is a type of diagram that exists solely for this purpose. My personal favorite flavor is the system context diagram. Simon Brown's C4 notation (*https://c4model.com*) has the system context diagram as the first "C."

A system context diagram is very basic, which adds to its appeal (that's probably why I love it so); see Figure 14-5 for an example. At its center is a single square representing the system or systems we are about to embark on building. Surrounding that square are all the systems, actors, and other key dependencies that are outside our sphere of influence but that we depend on or have a relationship with.

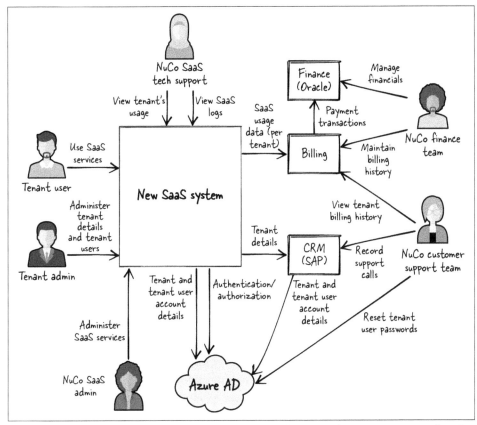

Figure 14-5. A system context diagram representing the example SaaS program of work described in previous subsections

The best thing about this diagram is that it doesn't matter what goes *inside* the box. In a system context diagram, the center box is left blank. You figure that part out later. The diagram's entire raison d'être is to show what is important *outside* the box, and therefore outside of your focus of work and ability to directly influence, before you start to decide.

Both the UML and C4 flavors of system context diagram do as their name suggests. They make explicit the underlying context *for all subsequent decisions*. This is why it's a perfect diagram to represent the consequences arising from the underlying decisions that have been taken before you start your architecture work, and therefore the context that you are starting with.

To do this, work through each of the layers in turn and consider its purpose (see Table 14-1), starting with layer 1. Ask the questions that the decisions at these layers answer, and if there are answers, note them down. For example, find out what the business model and aspirational outcomes for your program of work are (layer 1) and the capabilities the systems are intended to provide (layer 2). If there are ADRs or similar documents for these decisions, then that's brilliant, but it's not guaranteed. It can help to approach what you learn about such early decisions as if they were ADRs. I've worked with clients who have *retrospectively* documented key layer 1–3 decisions so the consequences were clear to everyone when they joined the program of work. Once you have what feels like a solid set of answers at a level, you can move on to the next one up and ask again.

As you get the answers, pay attention to the general points I made about underlying decisions. While decisions must have been made to start the work you are engaged on, they might not have happened explicitly, or perhaps not explicitly enough to move forward to the next layer. Also, there might be a catalog of legacy decisions, all still partially in existence. Knowing about these gives clarity, too. Finally, there are decisions that are in doubt or in conflict. It's unlikely to be your job to resolve such tensions, but by representing them, you can call out the fact that there might be problems ahead. Ideally, these blanks or conflicts will be filled in, at least by clear and explicit assumptions.

As you receive your answers regarding these underlying decisions, start representing them on the diagram. Elements that come from layer 1 and layer 2 decisions will sit outside your "systems" box. You ideally want to represent both stakeholders and other systems. You can represent whether both are inside or outside of your organization. Most important, you can represent the nature and directions of the dependencies. Are they dependent on you, or are you dependent on them? What resource or action are they dependent on?

Unlike layer 1 and 2 decisions, layer 3 decisions might be within your control. If they aren't, then represent them outside the box. For capabilities that are within your control, it can help greatly to place them temporarily inside the system context box, validating the relationships and adding detail to the elements outside. Once you have this extra clarity on the elements you don't control, empty your box again to keep the diagram focused.[13]

With all this in mind, review Figure 14-5. It shows the system context diagram for the example SaaS system I presented throughout this subsection.

That's how to figure out and represent your initial context, but sometimes, things can be a little messier. How do all these underlying decisions and their consequences interrelate? Have you uncovered all that you need to know to start your deciding? That's when spikes can help once again.

---

13 Don't lose this capability information when you empty the system context diagram box. Transfer the capabilities to another diagram, such as a business capability map or C4 container diagram.

Spikes uncover key underlying decision consequences

Sometimes, uncovering all those underlying decisions and the full nature of their consequences isn't as simple as asking a lot of questions. That's when spikes come into play—in these circumstances enabling you to discover and validate your underlying decision layers incrementally, by rapid-fire trial and error and learning.

Spikes achieve this because they confront you with your assumptions about the context you are deciding in. Because they focus on something *working in code,* they force you to make contact with the underlying decisions *for your context.* If you know about such decisions, then spikes validate what you know. If you don't know about such decisions or some specific detail about a decision, then a spike will trip over that and allow you to find out why it didn't work. Either way, making spiked contact with your underlying decisions helps to cement your understanding of your overall context.

Remember, spikes require you to write out the context in just the same way as ADRs do. This exercise alone gives you a way to very rapidly get to the point of context and locate it. Spikes allow you to test this point of context rapidly, too, validating (or invalidating) the apparent decision that led to it, *by writing code.* For example, if you are spiking a key aspect of a data regulation CFR and need to prove that PII (personally identifiable information, or anything that can be used to identify someone in real life) isn't shared between customers, knowing what a "customer" is is important. If this question can't be answered sufficiently to write a meaningful spike, you have uncovered a missing layer 2 decision.

Decisions Are Atomic

You could be excused for assuming that all decisions can be split again and again, ad infinitum, until all you are left with are tiny fragments spread out along your decision threads. But that's not the case. All decisions ultimately consist of a set of indivisible elements that cannot be separated any further, and it is important to know when you've reached the point of atomicity.

Isolating atomic decisions is important because a decision is *atomic* when you can't meaningfully make it any smaller: it has been pared to its fundamental elements— when there is nothing more that can be removed from the decision without making it irrelevant or meaningless without another still-to-be-taken decision.

How might you know what these core, indivisible aspects of a decision are? For some decisions, it's quite intuitive. For example, a decision about an API affects only the owners and consumers of that API. Or a decision about a design pattern is used to structure a specific and decoupled subsystem. Spikes will validate this scoping if your intuition is wrong. But for decisions that address *aspects* that exist across your system, it is not so simple. For those, you can use CFRs as your guide to find the atomic elements.

CFR interactions reveal atomic decisions

CFRs specify the cross-system attributes you expect of your systems—for example, how secure or how scalable it should be. By their very nature, CFRs specify characteristics that are shared across various elements of your system rather than located in one specific place.

Walking skeletons build just enough structure and functionality to test if those CFRs can be met and, most importantly, met in combination. It's when you combine CFRs with functionality that you discover how they interact, and in these interactions, you can discover your core atomic decisions. To illustrate how CFRs can help you identify these atomic decisions, let's look at three example CFRs that all apply to the same system and the direct consequences of each CFR individually:

The system must be elastically scalable
> This will have a strong influence on how session state is dealt with because an instance that processes my first request cannot be guaranteed to process my next request.

The system is expected to be cost-effective to run
> This will have a strong influence on the extent of the system's functionality as well as how much is built in house and how much is provided by third parties.

A certain part of the system ought to have a 95th percentile of its response times lower than 50 ms
> This will have a strong influence on what we design certain parts of the system to do and how we design them to do it.

It's easy to assume that the architectural decisions that realize these CFRs can be treated independently, but that might not be possible. If the same piece of functionality or structural element of the system is expected to manifest all of the CFR expectations—for example, being elastically scalable, cost-effective to run, *and* responsive—then any decisions taken with regard to one CFR will very likely have an impact on the decisions regarding the other two. That is to say, decisions on these CFRs, in this piece of structure or functionality, aren't independent.

This is why identifying the smallest parts of structural or functional elements of a system that have a role to play in delivering CFRs is key to identifying a decision's atomicity. When the structural or functional aspects that manifest CFRs are shared, the decisions that relate to them cannot be meaningfully split apart. Zooming in on only the relevant aspects of functionality or structure while ignoring the rest enables you to see if such decisions can truly be split or if they are needfully intertwined.

This "zooming in" on only the required parts of structure or functionality turns what might otherwise be a problem—one of having too-large, many-CFR-meeting decisions—into a solution. Software architecture allows us to decide on not only how we will meet our CFRs but also how our systems will be structured. Consciously design-ing system structures so that future decisions can be met as independently as possible is a valid goal—one that you actively want to pursue.

Spiking the architectures that you hope will deliver CFRs is a great way to discern precisely what structure or functionality might underpin them and therefore whether two decisions are separable. Not only that, but it is another signal as to the cohesive elements of any system: the ones that cannot be taken apart. Understanding such clusters is deeply informative, offering a way to keep not only the architecture but also teams and future decisions decoupled.[14] And the best time to find all this out is as early in delivery as possible.

Spiking atomic decisions is essential early on

While the importance of understanding decision scope and relationships persists throughout the lifetime of all systems (in later stages, it is likely that a decision com-promises the ability to fulfill a CFR), it is most important at the beginning. Resolving conflicts between decisions is far easier when our ideas are still flexible, especially when there is less code and fewer humans working on it.

Spikes give an extra edge to the approach of walking skeletons and a new impetus to use them early in the lives of systems. It's natural that the more intense design efforts at the early stages of your systems will involve a considerable number of shuffling ele-ments in the skeletons precisely in order to find a structure that can make delivery of the CFRs as independent as possible.

Spikes make the creation of walking skeletons more efficient, especially when deciding at layer 3 in the inverted hierarchy. Spikes help not only with discovering your system's independent parts but also with finding those parts that cannot (and should not) be separated. Most important, they make finding and testing the links between these inde-pendent elements and how they combine to deliver the CFRs evident, too.[15] This initial work is not easy, especially when attempted at pace.[16] It helps that spikes offer the safety

---

14 In *Notes on the Synthesis of Form* (Harvard University Press, 1971), Christopher Alexander takes a decidedly cross-functional view: "If we can find sets of [CFRs] in which there are especially dense interactions, we may assume, in those cases, that the density of the interaction resides in a particularly strong identifiable [struc-tural/functional] aspect of the problem" (pp. 121–122).

15 "The later in the process conflicting diagrams have to be integrated, the more difficult the integration is…Since the conflicts have to be resolved sooner or later, we should meet them as early in the process of realization as we can, while our ideas are still flexible. From this point of view, the fewer links there are between the major subsets of decomposition the better" (*Notes on the Synthesis of Form*, 123–124). If this sounds like the goal of the old unified-process "inception" phase, congratulations—you get a special "history of software architecture" merit badge.

16 Alexander is very clear in his writing that trying to find these seams at pace is hard. He calls it the "self-conscious design process" and compares it to design processes attempted gradually and over far longer (even cross-genera-tional) timescales.

to fail and learn, which can give teams the confidence and freedom to map out the broad aspects of future decisions.

This is important because of how rapidly decisions layer on top of one another when we move at postrevolutionary speeds. While the great majority of decisions in software *are* reversible, this reversibility reduces as we layer more and more decisions and the subsequent implementations on top of those. As you can probably guess, decisions at the lowest three decision layers are the most expensive and hardest to reverse. Using spikes to determine not only what is independent and should be kept so but also what is inextricably linked and will always remain so is incredibly important.

In *Domain-Driven Design*, Eric Evans talks about how finding elements that are inseparable and identifying how and where they are joined is essential to systems architecture. He calls this "supple design." Finding this design and the decisions that it contains is essential because they set the scene for everything that follows. It's impossible to get a design right the first time, and even if it were, technology keeps moving. Some decisions *will be superseded*—sometimes very fundamental decisions. The fourth and last perspective offers a way to think about this.

Decisions Are Two-Way Conversations

So far, we've focused entirely on the upward forces of decisions. For example, I showed that the lower a decision is in the inverted hierarchy, the more influence its consequences have on the decisions that come after it. I also highlighted how some decisions can be especially indivisible in complex and nonintuitive ways.

Not only that, few of the layer 1–3 decisions are directly "designed" or are "built" directly in code—not the decision on the specifics of a program of work, nor the location of a business capability in a system, nor the team that is going to build and operate those systems. None of them result directly in a push to trunk and a build being triggered. But they are all influential because all such decisions set the context for later codeable decisions.

As we build our systems on top of lower-layer decisions, increasing numbers of subsequent decisions fill in the blank parts of the architecture design space. This is how the initial software architecture in all its detail emerges, matures, and becomes more robust. For example, let's say that it's been decided at layer 2 that we'll constrain ourselves and use domain events to communicate between certain key parts of our system. Subsequent decisions then focus on the explicit nature of those domain events and who exactly can consume them. As you'd expect, this is the force of the earlier underpinning decisions working upward, stating very clearly the contexts for the contained decisions that follow.

But this upward *differentiating and detail-adding* process of deciding is not the only process that forms our overall designs. Later higher-level decisions—essentially every decision beyond those taken in the first release, minimum viable product, or even minimum viable experience—exert *downward evolutionary* forces on the decisions that underpin them. Because of this, decisions are actually engaged in two-way conversations, with current decisions interrogating and even challenging the right-now consequences of the decisions that preceded them.

A decision's consequences continue to emerge after they are taken

Although decisions are immutable, their consequences continue to emerge after they are taken. A great example of this is the arrival of cloud native apps. When I started my career in software, the cloud wasn't a thing, so cloud native wasn't either.

Then AWS was launched. Suddenly, not only did we want to be able to deploy our infrastructure using the command line, but also the desire to deploy and redeploy a new version of our Java EE app from the command line was suggested.

There were clear benefits—more deployments, smaller changes, lower risk, faster feedback—so we made small decisions to move toward this. But we rapidly hit a problem because consequences from earlier, lower-layer decisions were getting in our way.

The most memorable consequence concerned how we managed state. State was not something that gave us much cause for sleepless nights, but now we started to look at it in a different light. State was making more frequent deployments harder. State made load balancing across horizontally scaled instances harder, too. So we gradually took repairing decisions that removed state from our systems. Other decisions led us to incrementally realign to domain-aligned microservices, adopt the idea of cattle not pets[17] for our instances, treat logs as event streams, consider all environments as immutable, and so on.

All these "here and now" decisions were located high up the inverted hierarchy, but they were questioning the lower underlying decisions, putting pressure on them. Some new systems and services that were being built fresh at the time didn't have the legacy decisions to wrestle with, but those systems and services that were already in existence were forced into repair/evolution mode, and this exerted a downward pressure on decisions.

This downward pressure from later decisions on the earlier, underlying decisions is the fourth representation of decision relationships. Such later decisions offer a collection of quieter replies directed downward toward the underlying decisions, setting up a two-way conversation and pushing back on the louder, forward narratives of the three previous representations. This quieter half of this two-way conversation drives

---

17 Where you don't assume that the server instance running your code that was there yesterday will be there again tomorrow. It's believed this phrase was first used by Randy Bias (*https://oreil.ly/UR17I*) in 2012.

both repairs and evolution of the system(s) that sprang from the original decisions. This happens at a slower pace, *but it is happening.*

The constant evolutionary pressure of supply and demand competition

The other reason why current decisions exert downward pressure on previous decisions is because our software systems are all subject to another force of constant evolutionary pressure: that of supply and demand competition.

An approach to technical strategy called Wardley Mapping (*https://oreil.ly/1rQ0v*) does a good job of illustrating this. In Wardley Mapping, all capabilities an organization offers and consumes are plotted on a canvas. The x-axis represents the stages of evolution or maturity of a capability. The y-axis represents the visibility to a user.

Wardley Mapping proposes (*https://oreil.ly/iKNo2*) that all technology capabilities are pulled, either rapidly or slowly, along this axis on a journey from genesis (when the technology is unique, rare, constantly changing, or newly discovered), to custom (uncommon, frequently changing, requires artisanal skill, and no two are ever the same), then product/rental (increasingly common, more defined, and better understood), and finally to commodity/utility (scale and volume operations of production, highly standardized, defined, fixed, and undifferentiated).

This evolution means that decisions are all sitting on a slow but constantly moving conveyor belt. This movement brings changes in context, specifically increasing commoditization. The decisions that this change in context affect most dramatically are the ones that were taken the longest time ago and that underpin everything: generally, for decisions you had to take because something didn't exist, or it existed but not in a form that was useful to you or fit to your needs, it now looks like you would take them differently. The idea of state in the earlier scenario where J2EE meets the cloud is a classic example of this. *State* wasn't always as dirty a word as it is now. As I used to say in a talk, "What used to be expensive, slow, and hard has now become cheap, fast, and easy."[18]

Our architectures and the decisions they represent face this pressure. Even if your organization isn't a commercial enterprise, there always might be better (faster, cheaper, easier, lower friction) ways to do things. Under such circumstances, new decisions will be taken and old ones revisited to either evolve or repair your aging architectural implementation. In doing so, these decisions again apply downward pressure on the decisions that came before them.

In more traditional approaches to architecture, this two-way conversation between current and previous decisions frequently caused conflicts where there was barely

---

18 It's the talk that helped me understand there might be an appetite for this book: "A Commune in the Ivory Tower (*https://oreil.ly/XPGfu*)."

even a forum for this upward pressure to be exerted (instead, developers took to making memes and grumbling about architects on Reddit and Hacker News). But with an advice process, this pressure has not only a forum but also a means to execute. And it will need to execute. There have been five revolutions, but there will be more because the march of technology will continue.

Spikes investigate options to supersede previous underlying decisions

Spikes are perfect for investigating whether the resulting contexts of prior decisions have changed because decision consequences and contexts changing over time are yet another source of variability. As always, knowing rapidly if and how the perceived context has changed is invaluable for further decisions.

Spikes also allow for rapid experimentation with options to supersede previous underlying decisions. The classic example is when moving a system to the cloud or moving it from one cloud offering to another. Evolution might have caught up with you, meaning that your homegrown Kubernetes cluster running on Amazon Elastic Compute Cloud (EC2) instances ought now to be replaced by EKS. This *should* be a simple swap of runtime platforms, right? But a spike or set of spikes will tell you for sure in what context your extensive set of Pod-hosted microservices need to run. Spikes can do this because the code they result in is written and sits in your decision context *right now*, not in the decision context of the past.

Let's close by recapping, highlighting both the technical and social benefits of spikes in this world.

Interrelated Decisions Are Socially Complicated

Throughout this chapter, we've seen how spikes offer a way to tackle variability and make sense of the interconnectedness of decisions. Despite seeming simple, spikes have an outsized impact on collective trust and the social contract. When you start using spikes, you rapidly realize how intertwined the social and the technical really are when it comes to decisions and why deciding in such an environment feels so complicated.

While many of the difficulties deciders face are technical, it's a mistake to dismiss the social aspects. It's especially important for us because it happens a lot more with an advice process. These difficulties could best be summarized as stemming from a sense (a fear, even) of a lack of control.

It's likely that everyone and anyone following the advice process will experience this feeling at some point. Those in an architect role will likely feel it because they can no longer simply tell everyone what to do. Teams will likely feel it when they believe they cannot rely on their peers in other teams doing what the cross-team architects have decided will be the course of action.

While predictability in the world of software architecture is impossible, ignoring or denying the deep emotional need for a *sense of control* leads to a different kind of expensive type of decision: the one that means individuals will be scared to decouple decisions in case they lose their power and influence over outcomes.

The costs of emotional decision coupling are twofold. First, emotional decisions simply take longer to go through the decision process because, even if everything remains civil and constructive, there will be more conversations and more careful deliberations.

Second, if advice conversations become fractious in any way, a toll is taken on the trust and social contract that underpin the advice process. This cost has a knock-on to many other decisions, including ones that ought not to be expensive in any way. The increasing lack of trust will lead to increasing variability in decisions.

All of this social complexity further affects the technically interconnected world of decisions. It all adds greater variability, and as I described at the start of this chapter, this is variability of the most expensive kind. Yet again, spikes can help.

By using spikes to gather feedback on decision options rapidly, everyone has the opportunity to match their expectations (hopes, desires) against reality. Potential alternatives can truly be investigated and evaluated. Code is written and run quickly. This can be a very concrete way to build trust and tackle disagreements between affected parties head on. Spikes do this because they pacify the human desire for control and predictability, and they focus that need into an alternative, productive activity: writing code. A "spike ADRs first" mindset also helps to defuse arguments by offering a way for disagreeing parties to see and admit they were wrong, or see that their fears were unfounded, or see that they had underestimated the complexity or overestimated the potential of something.

Spikes are therefore the ideal tool for navigating this incredibly complex, ever-changing sociotechnical world of systems and decisions. They make the unknown known as quickly as possible and in such a way that everyone can learn and trust is protected.

Conclusion

This chapter laid out the sources of the most expensive forms of variability: the technical and social relationships between decisions. I showed you how to use spikes to investigate your decisions and tackle variability where it is the cheapest.

A big part of tackling variability is understanding the technical relationships between decisions. I shared the four ways you can look at these interconnections. First, you can view decisions as part of a series. By locating your current decision on the longer thread of decisions, you can better understand its immediate context. Second, you can view decisions as being part of an inverted hierarchy, where the consequences of the lower layers of decisions can still influence the context of decisions that follow them. Third, you can view decisions as being atomic. By looking at CFR interactions between decisions, you can focus decisions until they are at their smallest. Finally, you can view decisions as having two-way conversations with each other. Decisions of the past can affect those of the present, of course, but later decisions can affect the decisions of the past by superseding them. This allows you to keep up with the evolving technical landscape.

To close the chapter, I touched on the fuzzier but equally important social aspects that affect decision relationships. In all cases, I highlighted how different aspects of spikes can help to navigate these tricky waters as cheaply as possible. My hope is that after reading this chapter and the others in Part III, you'll have a more developed understanding of and intuition about the nature of decisions in the practice of architecture.

Centering the "Social" in Your Practice of Architecture

The fact that Part III ended with spikes—a purely technical, focused practice but one that offers wider group-level and social benefits—was not unintentional. With the advice process, the dynamics of the collective are of utmost importance. If you've gone to the effort of changing your practices so that *everyone can decide*, you'll want to collectively ensure that *anyone could decide*.

Part IV examines this social aspect from three angles, offering perspectives, strategies, and approaches to ensure that your "sociotechnical" system doesn't become "antisocial" for some. When you get it right, and you collectively nurture an open, generative, creative culture, then the results can be powerful.

Chapter 15 tackles the *social aspects of the transition of power and accountability* that the architecture advice process brings about. It considers transition first from the perspective of those who are gaining power, discussing in depth how psychological safety can be nurtured and protected. It then considers transition from the perspective of those whose power has been distributed, considering how this feels and (sadly) how acts of sabotage can be countered.

Chapter 16 moves on to the *importance of leadership* in the transition to the new way of practicing architecture and beyond. It busts myths around leadership and considers the good and bad aspects of common hierarchical approaches to leadership. It then explains how leadership can, and should, come from anywhere, describes the challenges of transitioning to such a form of leadership, and closes with the reasons it is of even greater importance when teams are independent, self-managing, self-organizing, and self-sustaining.

We close out with Chapter 17, which considers this new approach to decentralized architecture practice *within the context of the wider organization*: an organization that will now look and think very differently from those who are within your growing architecture advice process bubble. It considers the expectations of the wider organization on those practicing the advice process and introduces ways to meet those expectations without compromising on your practice and your decentralized culture of trust and learning. The chapter closes by answering the question "But does it scale?" with "Yes, but not how you think."

By the end of the book, you will have been introduced to everything I've ever needed to unlock an approach to architecture practice most suited to the revolutionized world of today's software systems—an approach that, more than any other, brings the broadest skills and creativity available to all of us to bear.

CHAPTER 15

The Transition of Power and Accountability

The architecture advice process sets in motion a series of personal and collective social challenges. Part IV, starting with this chapter, will help you understand those challenges. It will look more broadly at the sociotechnical system you've set in motion and help you avoid building yet another factory, just like the one you are trying to tear down.

In this chapter, I'll give attention to the "social" aspects, specifically the shift in power and accountability from a named group to the entire collective. I'll discuss the key obstacles and forces you will collectively encounter as you transition from a traditional to a decentralized, inclusive practice of software architecture. By being aware of these obstacles, you can ensure things don't become either "*anti*social" or "decentralization theater." If you're putting in all this effort to ensure that *anyone* can decide only to find that it's the "same old people"[1] making the same decisions in the same way—just like it always was—then it might feel like a gargantuan waste of effort. It's also a shame because not only will you fail to obtain the efficiency gains, but more important, you will also miss out on the many benefits that a more diverse, trusted, and self-managing collective of deciders has to offer.

Power Transitions Are Never Straightforward

Challenging established, traditional hierarchical power dynamics is a tricky thing to do. It requires individuals to break out of their standard sociotechnical roles, look at matters from a different perspective, and think with different mental models.

---

1 You could also insert "straight, white, and male" here. According to "Software Developer Gender Distribution Worldwide as of 2022" (*https://oreil.ly/XKTB_*), 91.88% of software engineers worldwide are men, and they are predominantly white, straight, American or European men under the age of 40.

There are different techniques to challenge people to think outside of their established sociotechnical roles. Edward de Bono's "six thinking hats" approach (introduced in Chapter 10) is a powerful technique that gives everyone permission to temporarily "play a different character" and look at things differently for a short period of time. Because it's so innocuous, you can use the technique for a single part of a workshop without worrying too much about how the exercise will be received.

Other techniques offer access to alternative perspectives by directly challenging the established, traditional hierarchical group power dynamics,[2] but they can actually misfire, heightening emotions and strengthening rather than disrupting hierarchy. More importantly, they do not seek to facilitate long-term change nor to remove a hierarchy. In fact, they all supplement the traditional hierarchical way of organizing by tackling its weak points. What we need is something slower and more long term that permanently challenges tradition and builds new, sustainable, and most important, appropriate practices.

Perhaps by raising the specter of power in hierarchies and the difficulties of finding workable alternatives, I'm finally giving voice to a concern that might have been lurking in your head since the beginning: "The advice process is all very well for those other organizations, but it'll never work here." I disagree, but I know where that concern comes from. It arises from the fact that software engineering teams don't exist in isolation, and neither do those playing architecture roles.

Everyone working on software systems is subject to the systemic pressures around them. These pressures don't come just from their positions and roles in their organizations. They also arise from their personal lives: their careers, their families, their social circles, all the way out to wider social dynamics.

Pretending that none of these external pressures have an impact on the practice of software delivery is naive. Ignoring the impact these pressures have on deciding is negligent. The starkest way I've had this explained to me was when a client responded to my proposal to adopt the advice process with: "This anarchy is all very well, but outside of the bubble of building and running systems, some of these people have influence over the salary or review outcomes of the others."

To adopt the practices that are better suited for today's decentralized world, we need to face the task of transitioning power in a way that makes sense. We need to confront the wider social dynamics that are directly engaged by the transition to the advice

---

2 For example, positive deviance (*https://oreil.ly/-Xq-M*) makes use of the ability of some to step outside or feel less constrained by the power dynamics of traditional hierarchies to enable them to be more creative and identify blind spots. Ritual dissent (*https://oreil.ly/7m3nj*) is another workshop approach that challenges proposals in a way that feels like a game, making the criticism less personal. Red teaming (*https://oreil.ly/5zFXl*) is a practice of rigorously challenging plans, policies, systems, and assumptions. The red team's role is to think like an enemy or saboteur, uncovering blind spots and weaknesses.

process. Let's consider this first from the perspective of those who gain power, then from the perspective of those who "lose" it. In both cases, I'll directly confront the legacy and external power structures that will likely get in your way. As we proceed, you'll see that there is emotional as well as intellectual labor at play here, and the burden of that labor will not be equally distributed.

The Transition for Those Who Gain Power

Although the concept of the architecture advice process is simple—it's only one rule, two advice-offering groups, and one social contract, after all—it brings about huge systemic changes. Transition isn't as easy as rolling out the advice process and watching decision power and accountability fall into place.

It's possible to fumble the transfer of the power to decide by not clarifying the changes in the social contract. Worse, it's possible that the power isn't transferred successfully because the collective lacks the feeling of safety to understand it and take it on fully.

This section discusses the transition of power as experienced by those who are gaining it. I'll confront the long-term effects of traditional, hierarchical power distributions and how apprehension about doing new things can be challenging. I'll go over what happens if those receiving power don't understand what they are now accountable for. I'll discuss why people might not want to exercise their newfound power. And finally, I'll talk about the source of these challenges: the feeling of safety—both how to understand it and nurture it.

Does Everyone Believe They Have the Power to Decide?

When rolling out the advice process, it is critical to communicate the process and how the transfer of decision authority comes hand in hand with the transfer of accountability. This is a *very different way to practice architecture,* and a degree of learning will be required from everyone.

Even then, it's possible that some may not act on their newly gained decision power.

Does everyone believe they were given the decision power?

Many with newly given decision power may struggle to believe that they were actually offered it. They are too used to decisions happening above them in the hierarchy or by certain roles.

This happens because preexisting social and cultural expectations and pressures are still in place. It's quite possible that, if you are in a role that has the power to decide on architectures and you suddenly just "give that power away," people won't believe it. Many will continue to see deciding as an architect's job. Why would anyone give their source of power away when they had spent so much of their career trying to earn it? To make matters worse, people can be reluctant to voice their disbelief from fear of appearing naive or misinformed.

These problems may manifest as teams heavily involving the traditional deciders when first adopting the advice process. You may also notice decisions teetering on the edge of being taken for a long time or decisions that everyone wants to keep reopening. This happens not because of a lack of expertise but because of caution. It's a combination of the team not believing that they actually have the power to decide (are they overstepping the architect's traditional role as a decider?) and their apprehension about doing something new.

Was the transfer of decision power properly communicated?

Those newly given the power to decide may have difficulty with the advice process because it was poorly communicated. This can manifest in two ways.

First, new deciders may not fully understand the advice process: either the social contract, with its redistribution of power and accountability, or the mechanics of ADRs, or both. This misunderstanding can result in teams disregarding the advice process and continuing to work as they always have.

Second, new deciders may receive mixed signals from those who previously held all of the deciding power. These signals may cause new deciders to have doubts about whether the power really was transferred, resulting in the hesitancy.

When they describe the new advice process approach, traditional power holders will communicate (both verbally and nonverbally) their *true* feelings about the advice process. If the traditional power holders aren't all in on the transfer, that will show. For example, their tone of voice may imply that there are some types of decisions that are excluded from this power transfer. Or an off-the-cuff joke may give the impression that some types of decisions are really scary and it's best to leave those to a special group who can handle the added pressure of being accountable. As with all communication, clarity and honesty are key, in both verbal and nonverbal areas, if everyone is to reach the same understanding as to where power to decide and accountability are shifting.

Transfer power openly and learn together

So what do you do when everyone doesn't believe they have the power to decide? To avoid all these confusions, address the problem at the source: with those who previously held the power to decide. Once the traditional power holders are comfortable sharing power, then their comfort and confidence will be reflected in their verbal and nonverbal communication. This in turn will make those who now have the power to decide feel more comfortable with deciding.

Perhaps this comfort isn't immediate, in which case, those having problems can be explicit about their discomfort with the advice process. This is new to everyone, and trust is a two-way street. Traditional power holders can show this vulnerability, be clear about exactly what they are concerned about, and be open about how they will need to learn to trust, too. This then allows the collective to help them allay these fears, allowing for a collective sense of camaraderie as everyone learns new skills together.

While honesty in communication is important, fundamentally, traditional deciders need to stop doing the work of deciding for teams. As long as they keep deciding, they are in danger of sending the signal that some decisions are best left to them. If that is you, try to turn off your instinct to initiate and drive decisions, and turn on your facilitation skills to help others identify and decide instead.

If You Have Experience, Facilitate Decisions Rather than Deciding Yourself

If you are someone who will be giving power away, take a look at "Source Advice from the Right People" on page 106, "Ask the Right People and Find Out 'Why?'" on page 108, and "Sharpen Context and Options with Advice" on page 309. All of these offer prompts that facilitate better deciding rather than doing the deciding directly. Also take another look at the section "The Architecture Advice Process and ADRs as a Coalescent Approach to Deciding" in Chapter 8 and see how you can assist everyone with learning to practice their coalescent argumentation skills.

Does Everyone Understand Their Accountabilities?

Another challenge that new deciders might face is understanding the transferred decision accountability. It's a big shift, one that new deciders will not be used to. Now, their name is on decisions. There is nowhere else to move the blame.

Clarifying the extent of accountability is important. It's quite possible the full extent of this won't be clear all at once to those new to deciding. There are aspects that affect architecture practice that might be unfamiliar, covering areas wider than decisions directly about software—decisions about product direction and relative priorities, for instance. Architecture's role in all of these will need to be learned.

Accountability is all the way to "done"

New deciders may not realize the extent of their accountability. Deciders are accountable for everything that happens from the point that a decision is needed to the point when the decision is implemented or considered "done."

I frequently see those new to deciding, especially those who are less versed in seeing the interconnectedness of systems, drafting ADRs without realizing the extent of what they mean. Most commonly, new deciders frequently fail to understand the extent to which the new accountability extends. (That's why I laid the standard decision process out for you in Figure 3-2 in Chapter 3, all the way up to "decision implemented," or "done," as Agile circles have it.)

This extension is the accountability for completion. I frequently see those new to deciding drafting ADRs, going through the advice process, perhaps even taking the decision and marking their ADR as "adopted," but then not actually updating the ADR to reflect the decision or prioritizing its implementation. This leads to expectation drift. Everyone following the decision will naturally assume that it has got into production, when in fact it hasn't.

You may therefore find it necessary to track the progress of decisions after they've been taken to remind everyone concerned that they aren't deciding for deciding's sake—reminding deciders that a decision is a promise to the collective up to the point it is implemented. Its ultimate purpose is to move forward the general state and capability of the shared software system, but that's unfulfilled until it is running in prod.

Everyone won't understand everything in the same way, at the same time

When you first roll out the advice process, the participants will be bombarded with a wave of new information that follows the transfer of deciding power and accountability. It's important to remember that not everyone will absorb all this information right away. Not everyone learns in the same way or at the same speed.

To ease the learning process, consider that not everyone processes information conveyed verbally as well as they do when it is written down, so putting the information in writing can help. You might also try conveying the information in yet other ways if the advice process still doesn't seem to be commonly understood. Diagrams or simple examples can work wonders.

Make the implicit (roles and responsibilities/accountabilities) explicit

To help everyone understand their newfound powers and responsibilities, you can provide them with a reference for the roles and accountabilities in the collective. The traditional way to do this is via a hierarchical "org chart" or organogram, but those come with too many problems. Not only are they inherently hierarchical, but they also permanently assign roles to specific individuals. With the advice process meaning that anyone can be a decider or an adviser, who fulfills specific roles is really unclear. Is everyone suddenly an architect? Or a developer-architect? It's better to represent these roles and accountabilities without tying them to specific people.

One such way is to use the "circles and roles" approach.[3] Circles and roles group accountabilities under named roles. When a single role has too many accountabilities, it becomes a circle that contains multiple roles. This division process continues until you have an inverted hierarchy of nested circles. Everyone is a member of the outer circle, playing its basic role. But folks might *also* play roles in some of the subcircles.

Recall first that all the accountabilities that were present in a traditional approach are still present under the advice process; however, they aren't concentrated permanently in specific people. Instead, they are spread across roles that can be played by anyone or by a flexible number of individuals, as decided by the group.

In a power-centralizing configuration, accountabilities are held permanently by a named few. Under a decentralized architecture approach, these are all made available to everyone in the collective to self-organize around. The prerequisite for this remapping to happen is for the collective's accountabilities to be made clear.

Let's take a look at a circles and roles view for the advice process, shown in Figure 15-1, to firm it up in your mind.

---

3 This again is stolen from holacracy, an approach to running trust organizations, which I first mentioned in "How technology strategy works" on page 231. There have been mixed reports from organizations adopting the approach in its entirety, but I've found that individual elements can be lifted from it easily and used on their own. See, for example, the *Harvard Business Review* article "Beyond the Holacracy Hype" (*https://oreil.ly/byY2K*).

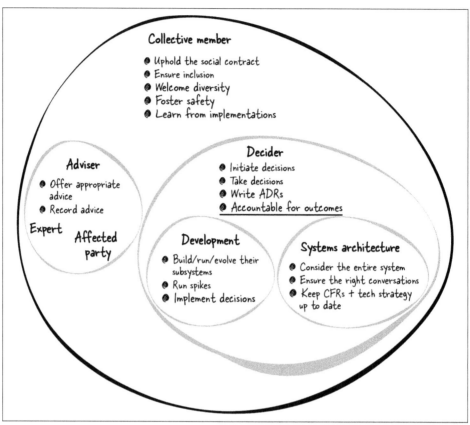

Figure 15-1. A circles and roles view of the advice process that shows the accountabilities inherent in the advice process, how they map to various roles, and how those roles interrelate

First, consider the basic accountabilities of those deciding: to both initiate and then take timely architectural decisions, to record them as ADRs, and to be accountable for the outcomes. All of these accountabilities used to be held by architects. Now they are held by anyone who needs to decide something. All of this is contained in the Decider circle.

Next, consider the accountability to implement those decisions, which includes playing spikes. This still clearly belongs within software development, so this is all contained within the Development subcircle. Those in the development role have the accountability to build, run, and evolve the subsystems that the team owns.

Development teams have one focus, but I also spend a lot of time talking about the importance of considering the overall system that sits outside the remit of the individual teams. That is also an accountability, which ensures that the right architectural conversations are taking place and that the technology strategy and CFRs keeping all this headed toward the organization's vision and goals remain up to date. That's not something that sits in any individual team. Instead, it belongs to the Systems Architecture role that is alongside Development.

Both the Systems Architecture and Development roles are specializations of the Decider role, sitting within its circle. But what about advisers? That is a separate role from decider, so it sits alongside the Decider circle with its two accountabilities to offer appropriate advice and record it. This again is a circle, as it contains two distinct roles within it: Expert and Affected Party advisers.

Remember, one individual can play multiple roles. They might develop, be a decider, and offer advice on others' decisions. Irrespective of what other roles they may play, everyone is a collective member. Each of these roles brings with it the associated accountabilities whenever the role is being played.

So far, all accountabilities have gone to specific roles within the collective. But where does the accountability to learn from feedback (from production and elsewhere) sit? This is actually something that everyone in the collective is accountable for.

Further collective accountabilities that everyone shares include upholding the social contract, ensuring inclusion, welcoming diversity, and fostering safety. These accountabilities go in the outermost circle, the one everyone sits within irrespective of the other roles they might play from time to time.

During the transition to the advice process, those who traditionally held power will probably do most of the initial work to facilitate learning from feedback. As I've discussed in this chapter, this is because they are in the best position to do so at the beginning of the transition. As more and more individuals take part in the advice process, you will start to see the accountability to learn from feedback spread out.

As you can see, a circles and roles structure makes the implicit role distributions of the advice process explicit. You have made it clear what all the roles are and their associated accountabilities. By using a circles and roles structure, you can also free yourself from the constraints of hierarchy and fixed job roles. Everyone can see that an individual can hold one or more roles and knows what to expect of them when they do. (I'll cover how this fits within the broader context of your organization in Chapter 17.)

Why Aren't People Taking the Power Available to Them?

The ultimate goal of the entire advice process approach is to remove blockers, freeing up the creativity latent in sociotechnical systems and allowing everyone to create, sustain, and evolve the best software systems that they are collectively capable of conceiving.

To do that, you've removed the most significant blocker of this happening: the centralized blocking of architectural decision flow. You've then set everything up so that the teams have the capability and ability to take decisions as independently as possible in pursuit of the outcomes they are focused on. Yet time and again, teams don't take advantage of the chance to decide. Why might this be?

The long shadow of hierarchical mental models

Sweeping away old mental models is hard. They have a habit of sticking around, hidden in plain sight: outside of, around, underneath, and interlaced throughout everything we see and do in our lives and work. Embedded into the patterns, trends, and supporting structures in everything we think and do. The particular mental model you are trying to challenge is how we think organizations—in fact, any large group in society—should organize to achieve their missions.

It's easy to forget how much we expect all organizations to work in the same centralized, hierarchical way.[4] Organizations also continue to suffer from the issue that they all adopt the same fixed hierarchy that plays a role in command, control, communication, and recognition of value.

Hidden underneath all of this are unspoken or unconscious assumptions about how organizations ought to be structured and run: hierarchically. We constantly look for and expect hierarchies, and we assume that a higher level on this hierarchy equals greater power and therefore deference. It's a hard habit to break. It's not by accident, for example, that when taking decisions at Amazon, the most senior attendees tend to speak last, to avoid influencing others.[5] This springs from an understanding that the default assumption of most people in the room will be to do what the person seemingly highest up the hierarchy says to do.

Entertaining alternative mental models of organizing

The idea of a self-managing, self-organizing, self-sustaining team has no natural place in both our hierarchical mental models and our organizational structures. Such teams are their antithesis. Therefore, a new mental model needs to be made from the patterns and structural elements I've described.

To allow this to happen, it is important to offer collectives a safe way to experiment with such mental-model refactoring—to try it on for size, if you will. The thinking hats exercise I mentioned earlier is one of those ways.

---

4 It could be argued that one of the reasons Agile "failed" is because lots of near-enemy forms appeared, such as SAFe (*https://scaledagileframework.com*). It didn't, but the term definitely lost all of its meaning. See also *platform, DevOps, cloud, AI*…I could go on.

5 Colin Bryar and Bill Carr, *Working Backwards: Insights, Stories and Secrets from Inside Amazon* (St. Martin's Press, 2021).

Thinking hats is intentionally playful.[6] Play feels safe because it is fun but also because everything about it is temporary. Everyone understands that the traditional order will be restored when the clock strikes midnight and the game is over. The thinking hats game allows everyone participating to free their thinking. It gives a temporary break from the traditional hierarchies and assumptions about who does what.

Other organizational thinking techniques go farther, acknowledging hierarchical models but explicitly inverting them.[7] But to practice the advice process, you don't want to be in a permanent state of shedding or inverting hierarchy. What is needed is a permanent change in your engineering culture, one that replaces the ossified power hierarchy with something that can ebb and flow as the software system and those building and running it require it. For that to happen, everyone needs to feel safe.

The Importance of Safety

Psychological safety is feeling safe from the arbitrary exercise of power that otherwise prevents you from contributing in the way you might be inclined. It is also feeling safe from the belief that you might be punished or humiliated for speaking up with ideas, questions, and concerns. It is even feeling safe to make mistakes and learn from the result.

"Play" or a time-boxed ritual or workshop can offer such safety for a short period of time—the duration of a specific workshop, for instance—but to get the full benefit that a decentralized, advice-based approach has to offer, you need something longer-lived.

Safe is a loaded word these days, so let's phrase it as "safe to learn." Learning requires inclusion ("this is for me"), participation ("I can contribute to this"), and challenge ("I don't always need to agree with everyone else, nor do I always need to succeed"). For a culture of decentralized deciding to emerge, there needs to be constant learning at every level. If there is insufficient safety to feel included, try things, possibly fail at them, and learn, then the whole enterprise is (at best) disadvantaged from the outset.

This safety is beneficial for everyone, not only in the obvious way: it also unlocks the widest possible set of collaborators. In a fixed hierarchical power dynamic, everyone is trapped in playing the "role" they feel has been assigned to them. Those higher up have to be "always right," "directive," and "in the know" about anything and everything. They are perceived as being more skilled and more experienced. These things

---

6 It's not by accident that the "hats" in many representations are ones made from paper, like children might create. It is the same motivation behind various rituals that share an idea of "the world turned upside down" as well as the medieval idea of a court jester or fool.

7 Which really is "the world turned upside down." I'm referring here to techniques and workshops like positive deviance, ritualized dissent, and red teaming.

can't possibly always be true, especially in the fast-paced world of software systems. The advice process unlocks the greatest amount of creativity and contributions from everyone involved.

Destigmatizing failure

Destigmatizing failure sends a message that safety is the overall goal. The best way to achieve this is for those who used to be at the top of the now-replaced traditional hierarchy to destigmatize failure by publicly demonstrating their personal fallibility, celebrating it, and involving everyone in helping them learn from it.

The best example of this can be heard in the *Land of the Giants* podcast. Season 2 covers Netflix,[8] and the first episode of that series introduces what Netflix calls "sunshining."

There is an example of sunshining in the first episode. Netflix's founder, chairman, and ex-CEO Reed Hastings describes how he decided that Netflix would split their service in two, coupled with a 60% price increase during a recession, and then doubled down with a famous "nonapology video" (*https://oreil.ly/RAyiq*). After this happened, Hastings "sunshined" his failure, which involved taking full responsibility and sharing with the company his comprehensive assessment of what went wrong and what he learned from it. Hastings described this in his book about Netflix:

> When you sunshine your failed bets, everyone wins. You win because people learn they can trust you to tell the truth and to take responsibility for your actions. The team wins because it learns from the lessons that came out of the project. And the company wins because everyone sees clearly that failed bets are an inherent part of an innovative success wheel.[9]

Sunshining is a big ask. It exposes those who are not traditionally used to demonstrating such vulnerability (the ones occupying positions higher up or at the top of the hierarchy) to experiences and feelings they are not used to or that they thought were far behind them. Yet that alone is beneficial. It potentially brings to the surface for them personally all the elements that are required for true collective safety. Being aware of all this affords the opportunity to establish empathy for everyone who will be participating in this, which is a key first step.

Fostering the levels of safety

Given how important psychological safety is to the success of the advice process, how can you foster it? First, everyone needs to know what is required for everyone else to

---

8 Yes, them again. I can't help it if not only are they a poster child for this kind of approach, but they also tackled it *at scale* and publicly talked about what they did and how they did it.

9 Reed Hastings and Erin Meyer, *No Rules Rules: Netflix and the Culture of Reinvention* (Penguin, 2020), 157.

feel safe. Such an understanding is *most* important for those who probably already feel safe because they will be taking a lot for granted.

What specifically are the "already safe" not aware of? Safety to learn can be broken down into three levels:

- Feeling included
- Feeling safe enough to contribute
- Feeling safe enough to challenge

As with all models, levels of safety also have their problems[10]—the implicit assumption that individuals move linearly up and down this scale, for example. The model also ignores the dynamics of teams. Indeed, it has been noted by others that if a team has different members at different stages of this journey, then the dynamics can be off (because checking that everyone feels equally part of both their team and the overall collective is the place to start).

Why doesn't this model explicitly mention "feeling safe to learn"? Other models, such as the one discussed in Jitske Kramer's *Jam Cultures* (Management Impact Publishing), do include this. In my experience, you learn both by contributing and by challenging, and so safety to learn (including to learn from failure) arises from the combination of safety to contribute and safety to challenge.

Let's work through each level one at a time before stepping back to consider learning, including learning from failure.

Feeling included.   Inclusion isn't merely a seat at the table, nor is it just being allowed to speak. It's being listened to, being understood, and having the power to act.[11] True inclusion means being able to say "I am…" and to be heard and valued for it.

Technically, the advice process offers the power to act to everyone, but is everyone automatically listened to and understood? The advice process thrives on the breadth of viewpoints available. Given that, how might you promote inclusivity to ensure that all three factors are present?

There have been *many* studies showing that truly diverse teams have significant benefits. Diverse teams are "smarter,"[12] they build better (and more ethical) products

---

10 As domain-driven design nerds like me love to say, "All models are wrong, but some are useful," which is generally attributed to the statistician George E. P. Box.

11 You will come across various flavors of this statement. I've iterated on this one over the years as it suits the purposes of the advice process perfectly.

12 David Rock and Heidi Grant, "Why Diverse Teams Are Smarter" (*https://oreil.ly/e4_8d*), *Harvard Business Review*, November 4, 2016.

because they are more creative and better at problem solving,[13] and they generally make better decisions.[14] Most importantly, truly diverse teams that really understand these benefits are most inclined to be even more inclusive because they can see the positive impact of listening to and understanding everyone.

It all comes back to decisions.

The book *EDGE* lists the prerequisites for good group decisions.[15] Alongside the clear need to include individuals with sufficient knowledge (in our case, advisers), the authors list five criteria that define these "truly diverse teams":

- Diverse social perspectives
- Trust and respect among the participants
- Participants being open to others' ideas
- Facilitators who are adept at encouraging wide participation
- Participants who are willing to participate

What a place to work! But it's pretty much the diametric opposite of "stick a bunch of people in a team/collective/organization and hope they get on with it" that we tolerate daily.

Such inclusion is hard but by no means impossible. And the benefits—not only in the form of better decisions but more generally of a profitable, creative, inclusive, learning workspace—are there for everyone to enjoy and benefit from.

Adopting the advice process unlocks the hardest part: it gives everyone the power to decide to decide. But this alone doesn't magically mean that the rest of the criteria will manifest.

It remains to collectively ensure that everyone, each with their unique views and experiences, is included. *EDGE* calls for "trust and respect among the participants" and "participants being open to others' ideas." While it opens the door, the architecture advice process is no guarantee of this occurring.

The next step on this path toward great group decisions is to ensure that everyone is included and to value the differences this offers: those "diverse social perspectives." This isn't straightforward. Acknowledging the differences that inevitably arise from true inclusion also acknowledges contradictory thoughts and needs. For some, even that feels like too much.

---

13 "9 Powerful Benefits of Diversity in Team Collaboration" (*https://oreil.ly/ks7Eb*), VirtualSpace, July 19, 2023.

14 From the Cloverpop whitepaper "Hacking Diversity with Inclusive Decision Making" (*https://oreil.ly/iU5wN*).

15 Jim Highsmith, Linda Luu, and Dan Heath, *EDGE: Value-Driven Digital Transformation* (Crown Currency, 2019), 176.

Before you can acknowledge differences, you need to be aware of them. In *Jam Cultures*,[16] Kramer identifies four forms of difference awareness, describing how they are experienced (spoiler alert: only one offers the benefits of true diversity):

Corresponding

"We know we are different but we prefer to ignore it. We look to recognize ourselves in the other. We primarily focus on our similarities and tend to reduce something new to something we know. We wonder what our joint passions are."

Hierarchical

"We're different and that's fine, as long as it's clear who's in charge here. We need someone to tell us whether something's true or not true. That does require all of us to believe this person."

Contrasting

"Difference is competitive, leading to a tug of war. In this arena you have to be very sure of yourself to prove your point. You seek a position of power. You prefer to resolve tension by making others defer to your rules."

Complementary

"Our mutual differences complement each other and we're better off united. We look for synergy. We turn parties into partners."

Difference is viewed from a personal perspective, but it also happens from a group perspective, where a "group" might be at the level of the team, the collective, and beyond. Think about the groups you are a member of—they might map to organizational lines or they might not—and about groups you aren't. How do you see those differences?

Undertaking this practice personally has taught me a lot over the years. As a white, middle-aged, mostly male-presenting person from a middle-class background, it's been incredibly easy for me to assume that everyone views relationships as I view them. I've prided myself on the fact that in almost all cases, I view differences as complementary, and when I've slipped into other viewpoints, I've tried to catch myself and learn.[17] Being curious (and frankly, learning to shut up and listen—more on that later) has taught me a lot about how others view me and the differences between us. The two viewpoints rarely tally, at least not when we start working together.

These relationships are point to point, and importantly, the views on differences go both ways. My awareness of a difference between me or my group and you and your group in no way guarantees that you will reciprocate the awareness. A classic example

---

16 *Jam Cultures*, 77. This specific formulation is based on the work of anthropology professor Arie de Ruiter.

17 Remember my story from "When Others Are Taking the Decision" on page 320, where I just wanted to tell the teams taking a decision I agreed with what to do? That was clearly a slip into a hierarchical mode.

is that I, from my lofty traditional architect chair, see differences between me and all teams as complementary while they likely view the reverse relationships with me as hierarchical; this might be despite certain individual one-to-one interpersonal relationships being different.

In short, it's complicated.

Given all this awareness, only the latter complementary viewpoint works for us truly *valuing* differences and working with them. How then to bring the complementary perspective into your practice of architecture?

Feeling safe enough to contribute.   The focus of inclusion efforts—acknowledging and welcoming difference—needs to be at the heart of your advice process: in the advice conversations, in either the ADR's comments or face-to-face discussion, such as at advice forums.

When people feel included, they will feel safe to contribute. In our case, they'll feel safe to participate in the architecture advice process. When this happens, you have an opportunity to get the right people collaborating to deploy their unique differences in complementary ways.

To protect and foster the safety required for individuals and groups to have creative conversations, you need to look to those who have safety to give. That means those who already have it.

Those who traditionally held the formal positions with the power to make decisions are one group that has this safety in spades. However, other groups also hold the same power, but informally. These are made up of the individuals that reflect the "in-groups" of your wider society; in my experience, they are white, middle-class, educated, straight, and male. They still command greater safety to participate irrespective of where they sit in the formal organizational hierarchy.

Members of both these formal and informal groups have an additional task to perform. On top of their contributions to the advice process, they should "invert their participation mode."[18] This means if you are used to participating in discussions by talking, leading, and having your written pronouncements followed to the letter, then swap your method of participation to listening, following, suggesting, and questioning. This can be difficult, especially when the advice process is first adopted and trust is still growing.

Strategies for participation inversion range from the very simple (shutting up and making space in the silence for others to speak and waiting longer to speak the higher your perceived place in the hierarchy) to the slightly more involved (echoing and

---

18 The phrase comes from Open Spaces.

boosting ideas of others and welcoming rather than patronizing those who partici-pate) to the actively inclusive (suggesting someone share something because you know they have experience in that area). As participants who formerly filled the architectural practice space become more comfortable with leaving it open for others, they can use their spare brain space to become facilitators of coalescent argumenta-tion techniques.[19] Or, they can play the role of creativity sponsors, taking inspiration from some of the ideas in "Sharpen Context and Options with Advice" on page 309.

Personal Experiences with Inverting My Participation Mode

The first steps on this participation-inversion journey are often the hardest. How you choose to actively become inclusive and foster safety in others can be very personal. For example, I'm on the autistic spectrum. On the one hand, being able to see and understand differently helps me be better at my job: I'm great at focusing deeply, I spot patterns *really easily*, and I love learning new things and solving problems. On the other hand, it makes some things more difficult.

In particular, I tend to interrupt people when I get excited or have a new thought. I can see how this makes others less likely to share their thoughts with me, making them feel unheard. Unfortunately, my tendency to interrupt is most prevalent in real-time scenarios, such as during advice forums. There and in other face-to-face design sessions, I can be both the person advocating most strongly for inclusion *as well as* the person getting most in its way.

I've developed a personal strategy to combat my selfish interjections. First, I look out for myself itching to interrupt and remind myself to stay quiet. Second, I try to actively listen to the other person. Third—and this one's silly but practical—I make memes that reflect what I've picked up while listening to others.[20] This demonstrates that creativity is valued and that it's acceptable to have fun while doing the important work of software architecture.

While I've gotten better at reducing my interruptions over the years, it still happens. When it happens too much—typically, when I get excited about the progress a group or collective is making—I ask friends, colleagues, and clients to just interrupt me back

---

19 These techniques are the ones you saw back in Chapter 8, in "Coalescent Argumentation: An Alternative to Adversarial Argument" on page 187.

20 You know, classics like "Malicious Advice Mallard" (*https://oreil.ly/MHSwn*), "Success Kid" (*https://oreil.ly/WPIv0*), and "Philosoraptor" (*https://oreil.ly/EroyN*). I have developed a nice sideline in "yay for remember-ing the social contract" cheerleading memes, which helps, too. I like to think it encourages people to try just that little bit harder if they know they will get a terrible awesome meme out of it. However, I steer well clear of memes that are divisive. There are plenty of inclusive memes out there that don't punch down at a certain group. That's not to say that you can't take the mickey out of yourself, but it needs to be clear that's what's happening.

and tell me to shut up.[21] Don't be afraid to ask for help. If you suspect you are neurospicy, then this might include professional help. My diagnosis helped a *lot* of things make sense, and even knowing that something is harder for you than for everyone helps.

As contributions increase, differences within the collective will become increasingly evident. This is precisely what you want, but for good-faith conversations to be meaningful, participants require a shared desire to be understood and to understand others. According to Min-Sun Kim's Conversational Constraints Theory,[22] we all share five universal needs when participating in such conversations, irrespective of our cultural background:

Clarity
> Do people understand what I'm saying?

Consideration of others' feelings
> Am I not hurting or offending anyone?

Avoidance of negative evaluation by the other
> Do people see me how I want to be seen? Do I come across as trustworthy?

Space (minimizing imposition)
> Do I occupy too much (or not enough) verbal and nonverbal space? Do I talk too much, or am I too quiet? Am I infringing on someone's personal space? Am I too distant?

Effectiveness
> How do I get what I want? How do I ensure I won't get turned down?

We all consider these elements while conversing with one another, but it's unlikely that we consider them from a perspective of balance and inclusion. In fact, we typically consider them from the perspective of how we are perceived in relation to our place in the hierarchy. For example, those higher up will want to appear "correct" and will look to occupy more space than those "below" them in the hierarchy. "Effectiveness" for them is directly related to what they say is happening.

But for broad participation to arise, a collective focus on these five points with the goal of balance and inclusion is required. The *EDGE* criteria for truly diverse teams even includes "facilitators who are adept at encouraging wide participation." When

---

21 You all know who you are, and I'm grateful to you every day for keeping me grounded.

22 Min-Sun Kim, *Non-Western Perspectives on Human Communication: Implications for Theory and Practice* (SAGE Publications, 2002).

---

everyone is aware of—and values—difference but also acknowledges these five universal needs, then broad conversations are possible.

If you are flipping your mode to listening, your role in this facilitation can still be an active one. Look out for these five universal needs at play in conversations and try to help all participants become aware of these forces. Help everyone find a way to make the differences complementary so that everyone benefits. If you are flipping your mode to participating, taking part and contributing your perspectives, experience, insights, and creativity are sufficient.

The result is a greatly increased chance of everyone meeting their communication goals: people understand what they are saying, that they are considered to be participating in a trustworthy way, that they are not occupying too much space, and that the *collective* gets what it needs. This plays directly into the argumentation practice I described in Chapter 8.

When teams are diverse, participation is the most important thing because it means that everyone is contributing their unique outlooks and skill sets. It also means that the most basic level of safety is there because deploying your skills in a diverse team requires a degree of comfort around how this participation is welcomed.

But there is a significant hurdle to participation: you can't force it. Despite the fact that it would be great if a team member brought to bear a certain skill set or perspective, if that person doesn't feel so inclined, then it's not going to happen. And demanding their participation will certainly produce the opposite result.

Instead, participation needs to be encouraged. Encouragement begins with those with status (power) operating in an inclusive way.

Those with status can do this by being explicit about the fact that they are changing the more subtle rules of the game. Rather than drawing attention to the things you want to happen (certain people contributing), it is far more effective to focus on the things you don't want. Discuss openly the rules and behaviors that are excluding others. When you make a mistake yourself (personally, this is *frequently* my interrupting people), name it, apologize for it, and back up. If the contributor doesn't feel inclined to participate, let it go. There's always a next time. Even if it didn't fix it this time, it set the precedent that you value inclusion and that you are willing to use your privileged position to call this behavior out, even when it is behavior of your own making.

A thought-provoking blog post called "The Importance of Cultural Gardening" (*https://oreil.ly/Lym9k*) by Behzod Sirjani takes this further. As well as being full of suggestions for strategies for longer-term culture change, the post's metaphorical title is perfection. All inclusionary changes are not cutting down the whole tree nor lopping off structural or load-bearing branches (which some who currently have privilege will fear is happening). They are shaping things to grow in a fruitful direction, removing areas where two parts rub up against each other and cause friction and damage, and (most important) removing dead wood and making light and space for new growth.

"Light and space" is a particularly powerful concept. There are significant psychological benefits to feeling openly included in a group. If you *always* feel included, then you're probably unaware of them, but trust me, as someone whose autism makes them feel *very* included in some circles and *very* excluded from others, they are there. Trond Hjorteland calls this the "added benefit" of inclusion. Not only do you gain better solutions, but you also gain a secondary, longer-term benefit. Newly included participants feel part of something and that their ideas are considered; by being involved, they will also be more engaged and committed to what is decided on. This is even if they disagreed with part of it.

As you foster inclusion and consider differences from a complementary perspective, you will end up focusing on those differences. That's the whole point. That then allows everyone to find and bridge the differences, putting them to good use. Instead of pitting two ideas or perspectives against each other, where one wins and the other loses, you can examine if they might both be possible.

Such "it's both" thinking can be adopted easily by practicing the "yes, and…" approach. When using "yes, and…" you acknowledge the perspective of the other person. The alternative would be to say "yes, but…"—that immediately implies that you find fault in the other person's statement. Saying "yes, and…" conveys the fact that you hear and understand them, *and* you would like to continue and build on top of it. (You can read a lot more about "yes, and…" in Diana Montalion's book *Learning Systems Thinking*.) While it sounds simple, this is an incredibly powerful technique that improv actors use to keep creative spaces open, and it works in software, too.

For example, if someone says, "We need these systems to be cheap to run," you might reply, "*Yes, and* we don't want to restrict the freedoms of teams to make their own tech choices." Now compare that to "Yes, *but* we don't want to restrict the freedom of teams to make their own tech choices." Doesn't that sound negative? Phrased with "yes, and…" the tension between the two equally important needs is maintained. The design space to ensure that they can both be true is kept open, and more important, the power dynamic of who is stating what is defused.

Such "it's both" thinking is not a way to remove tension between needs and ideas. Deep dialogue does not erase conflict. Conflicts are a normal state of affairs in the constantly surprising world of software engineering, and from them, innovative and creative solutions blossom. Let's look at that more next.

Feeling safe enough to challenge.

> *Contrary to the popular myth, great teams are not characterized by an absence of conflict. On the contrary, in my experience, one of the most reliable indicators of a team that is continually learning is the visible conflict of ideas. In great teams conflict becomes productive.*
> —Peter Senge, *The Fifth Discipline* (p. 232)

One of the earliest failure patterns I identified in the advice process was the "off-grid decision": a decision that didn't follow the advice process and didn't result in a widely shared ADR. These decisions can arise for various reasons. There is always the possibility that the team or individual didn't realize they were deciding. Or they might have realized it was a decision but not that it was architecturally significant and therefore that there was a reason to follow the advice process and write it up as an ADR. Those are all fine and easy to fix, too: simply figure out where the misconceptions lay and reexplain.

There can also be a far more insidious reason for off-grid decisions when a decision is explicitly hidden, despite those involved fully understanding the advice process and the associated social contract. This problem is not one of inclusion. The deciders are deciding, but they are actively *avoiding* deciding out in the open. This is likely because they perceive an upcoming conflict that they want to avoid. They do not feel safe to challenge.

"Safe to challenge" is another way of saying that the participant feels safe enough to engage explicitly in a disagreement or in conflict with someone, but a conflict of ideas alone.

When decisions are off grid, that safety to challenge is missing. The lack of safety is *never* a result of some difference of technical opinion—remember, the advice process gives *all the power* and *all the accountability* to those making the options and taking the decision. There is instead something more subtle at play. Differences can exist between what groups people value, and conflicts can occur where these differences meet. Kramer identified five types of boundaries where conflict can occur:[23]

Vertical (across hierarchical levels)
    Others are above/below you in the generally agreed organizational or societal hierarchy.

Horizontal (across roles, areas of expertise, or departments)
    Others know different things or have different priorities from you.

---

23 *Jam Cultures*, 82.

Stakeholders (beyond the organization's boundaries [business partners, customers, job markets, etc.])
Others don't know as much as you do or have conflicting priorities to you.

Demographic (across various subgroups: gender, ethnicity, age, nationality, religion, sexual orientation, class)
Others see and experience the world differently from you.

Geographical (across distance and time zones)
Others are really far away.

Bridging and combining your differences productively involve incorporating as much of the carefully cultivated and protected diversity into your decisions as possible. The differences you want will arise at these boundaries, but they will most likely manifest technically. When you acknowledge differences and examine if opposing ideas can both be possible, you are keeping the creative space open and diffusing conflict between parties.

A great way to gain the benefit of all these differences at the boundaries is to be genuinely curious about them. Asking, "Why does that team have a different perspective?" flips the usual difference-is-a-problem narrative into one from which constructive and creative argumentation can flow. Curiosity is a great path to shared understanding, then empathy, and ultimately safety. It doesn't mean everyone has to agree, however.

Again, the best way to catalyze this shared understanding is for those who traditionally hold the power to put their own opinions and perceived norms up for scrutiny. These people can initiate and facilitate candid conversation about differences and similarities in viewpoints and ideas.

It's easy to forget that not everyone shares the same experiences and perspectives as you do. I've frequently seen architects assume that "everyone knows this and therefore feels as I do." Their assumptions are then shattered when they actually hear about the experiences and perspectives of others. It's eye-opening. A classic example of this is an older architect assuming everyone remembers historical lessons learned about certain legacy architectural styles. If most members of the development teams are 10+ years younger, this might have happened before they even entered the job market. In this case, the architect's view may turn out to be in the minority.

Beyond facilitating the acceptance and encouragement of differences, those with greater relative privilege in the collective can "lend" their privilege to other groups by explicitly being curious and keen to learn about others' viewpoints. This can lend credibility to those perspectives, resulting in their being listened to more fully.

As your collective becomes more practiced at collaborating openly and safely, and as the sense of safety—particularly to challenge—grows, more conversation will center on the common goals of the organization and the software systems. This is where the importance of organizational alignment comes in. In fact, Senge said that the essence of "the 'visioning' process lies in the gradual emergence of a shared vision from different personal visions. Even when people share a common vision, they may have different ideas about how to achieve [it]."[24]

These different ideas are where the tensions and conflict arise. Experiencing such differences in a group with high trust and high safety can be exciting and fun. But it can be scary at the same time.

Creative conflict creates uncertainty. Its goal is to bring together multiple viewpoints and ideas, and combine them in new and innovative ways that no individual could foresee. This uncertain world is where we software professionals live our lives and do our work. It's a fact of daily life.

No one likes too much uncertainty. And that's yet another important point of difference. One person's tolerance for uncertainty will likely be vastly different from another's. Therefore, ensure that, amid all the changes that the transition to the advice process brings, there is sufficient support to allow everyone to deal with the difference.

This is where psychological safety comes back in. Collectives practicing the advice process can protect psychological safety by reminding everyone of the one rule (anyone can make a decision) and the social contract (we'll all seek the appropriate advice from the appropriate advisers) and by ensuring that any cadenced rituals you set up, such as an advice forum, play their part.

Don't be surprised if, as a result of confronting the unknown, certain metaconversations arise about the advice process, various aspects of the collective, the culture that is developing, or remnants of your previous culture. As Kramer eloquently puts it:

> It's essential to create time and space for important conversations and real connection at regular intervals. We can create certainty by making explicit subconscious expectations and rules on participation and decision-making. It helps to make clear who has a say in what, what the status of a proposal is and how much room for influence there is. Is this proposal just a matter of testing the water or is it a mere formality? Clarity creates safety.[25]

---

24 Peter Senge, *The Fifth Discipline: The Art and Practice of the Learning Organization* (Doubleday, 1990), 231.

25 *Jam Cultures*, 200.

The more these metaconversations happen in a collective, the more the collective will bond and trust, and the more safety will grow. For this to happen sustainably, every voice needs to be valued and integrated into the collective wisdom.

Feeling safe enough to learn, including from failure.   Deciding requires learning, and learning works best when there is safety. Specifically, learning requires the safety to be wrong, and being wrong requires participants to feel safe to contribute and to challenge. Learning requires freedom from blame. If certain members of a collective get in the way of others' feeling all these things, then those members are preventing the others from learning. And if others can't learn, then how can your trust in them grow?

But if the required effort is put in, slowly but surely, as safety builds and trust increases, inclusion and participation in the practice of architecture will increase, too. Don't expect it to proceed in a steady, universal way, though. It might proceed in fits and starts, and even experience knockbacks. Blame is the social default when things don't go according to expectations, so that will need to be acknowledged and rooted out. Also, some will take longer to feel safe than others will. It's important to flow with this because, as I mentioned earlier, neither inclusion nor safety nor participation can be forced. If you do try to force them, you will end up having the opposite effect.

Instead, those with greater safety should try to attune their rhythm to the various goals and contexts of others. Slow down so that this tuning becomes easier, and only attempt to change procedures, never people. By doing so, you will see a positive change in those participating in the system.

This doesn't mean that you can't take a stand, but take a stand for inclusion; take a stand to break with out-of-date procedures and habits that hamper it. You can openly and vocally support positive steps and outcomes, and make room for curiosity and learning.

Break with your known as-is and start enjoying the unknown might-be. There can be joy and excitement in breaking ossified patterns that no longer work and in trying new things. Of all people, we software types should be able to embrace the opportunity to try something new; after all, our technologies change all the time, and we learn to cope with that, even enjoy it. Why can't we enjoy learning to master the architecture advice process? In doing so, we can recognize and acknowledge the tension and uncertainty, and then we can take the step together and do it anyway.

That is the main thing to fight for, above all else: whole-collective learning. You'll notice it starting to happen when failure becomes seen more positively, and you'll know it's achieved when the ideas of "failure" and "blame" are replaced by "learning" and "feedback."

The Transition for Those Who Must Share Their Power

So far, the focus of this chapter has been on those who, prior to the advice process, had little power to decide architecturally and on what those who had that power could do to include them in the practice of architecture. I have talked a lot about how those who previously held power can make sure it is evenly distributed. I made a significant assumption that these individuals are entirely willing and open participants in the effort.

However, as I've mentioned in previous chapters, this is not always the case. Sadly, for conscious or unconscious, benign or malicious reasons, almost all those who traditionally held both the power and accountability for architectural decisions have difficulty truly letting it go and letting others take it up in their stead.

Why won't that old system want to be swept away? Because it wasn't simply serving a functional role in the practice of architecture. It was also serving a social and ego-bolstering role to many involved. When you sweep away the traditional approach and the supporting centralized, hierarchical structures, you sweep away that support, too, and that can throw up defensive obstacles.

This section looks at those obstacles. It acknowledges fears of the power given away being misused and offers ways to counter this feeling in yourself as well as to support others. It also considers the darker side, conscious or unconscious, that can arise in individuals when they feel their power is threatened.

Fear Within Those Who Gave Power Away

While it can be scary to have responsibility for something for the first time, it can be equally scary to be the person who *used* to be responsible watching that newly anointed decider tackle a decision and fail. In fact, this is where I focus my coaching whenever folks are moving up the seniority tree and relying more and more on others.

Those who find this letting go the hardest are typically the ones who are the most competent at the practice of architecture. It's ironic that architects who would benefit most from the advice process approach are frequently those who have managed through sheer force of character and long, long hours to scale themselves and be everywhere all at once.

In this section, I'll talk about the fears faced by those who used to be solely responsible for decisions and how they could unintentionally affect others in the advice process. I'll also go over ways these people could overcome their fears.

Acknowledge fear of "bad decisions"

The most common reason people find it hard to let go of deciding power is the fear of "bad decisions." When you examine this fear more closely, you'll see that there is frequently an assumption from the person surrendering decision power that in all decisions, "I am right," and therefore "all those who disagree with me are wrong." I know how hard it is.[26] I've felt it myself, over and over. For the vast majority of decisions, there is no way of knowing who is "right" and to what extent until the decision has been taken, implemented by the relevant team(s), and is running in context, in production.

It is frequently a surprise to those who surrendered their decision power that they are *broadcasting* this fear, even when they don't intend to. But again and again, I've seen it exude from every pore, in person and on videoconferences. I've even seen it dripping from comments on ADRs and in emails. They all whisper, "You can do whatever you like as long as I agree with it," with a healthy dose of "If I don't agree, it'll fail expensively, but don't come crying to me when it does; I told you so."

It's a hard behavior pattern to unlearn, and those on the receiving end of it need to believe that it has genuinely disappeared. If you don't manage this, you are constantly undermining what safety to contribute—let alone safety to challenge and learn/fail—others may be fostering elsewhere.

A simple way to break away from telegraphing your fear is to learn to qualify statements, tempering your certainty. Rather than "This is a bad idea," share your degree of certainty. For example, "I am 90% certain."[27] Other personal hacks include consciously trying to offer advice rather than opinions, asking questions rather than making statements, and apologizing explicitly when you slip up. You can even elect to be silent for an entire advice forum, writing notes and providing these as advice comments afterward in written form. Frequently, the simple change in medium and distance this affords can give you time to be more careful about what you say and how you say it.

Celebrate all decisions

Once a decision has been taken, celebrate it, regardless of whether it had a positive or negative outcome and regardless of whether you agreed with it or not. Such celebration is important because every decision is a step forward in the collective practice of architecture, doubly so if you were personally uncomfortable about the decision.

---

26 In fact, this is how I felt when I advised a team to not use Lambdas. See "Sharpen Context and Options with Advice" on page 309.

27 For more examples of qualifying statements, read the Medium post "Strong Opinions Loosely Held Might Be the Worst Idea in Tech" (*https://oreil.ly/87Xq2*) by Michael Natkin.

If the decision had a positive outcome and you, as a previously accountable person, disagreed with it, make the fact that you were wrong clear. Make your personal learning explicit to everyone and admit your failing in the face of a larger success. Really celebrate the success.

If, on the other hand, the decision didn't work out as hoped, celebrate the fact that the decider felt confident enough to decide in the first place. Then, help everyone learn from the situation and use that to bolster the advice process still more. If you disagreed with the decision, don't remind people about this. Your advice will have been recorded during the advice process anyway, so there's no need to rub it in. The trust you have tried so hard to build will falter if the collective gets even a hint of a suspicion that you are of the mind that "this is fine until I see a decision I don't like."

Sometimes, a decision is neither a success nor a failure, and instead there is confusion about exactly what the outcomes were. If this is the case, there are two lessons to be learned. First, it is almost inevitable that advice that should have been recorded wasn't, or it wasn't articulated clearly, or it was provided too late in the decision process. If you are a steward of the advice process (and technically, everyone is), then this can be called out explicitly (the general fact it was missing, not the specific individual failing).

However, always protect against the updating of an ADR with the benefit of hindsight. That's a way to weaponize such written records of decisions in a way that does not reflect reality at the time, which will undermine trust catastrophically. Instead, use one of the standard mechanisms to learn lessons after an event, such as blameless postmortems and Agile retrospectives. The ADR remains as a record of what was known and believed *at the time*, but that's not to say that when this perception meets reality it can't be used as an opportunity to collectively learn.

Pay attention to who is deciding

How might you be confident that any fear from those who are used to deciding is not getting in the way of the advice process? It's when you see gradually increasing levels of participation from a broader and broader part of the collective.

Initially, you will likely notice increasing engagement in advice offering. Next, you will see more decisions coming from teams and not just from those who previously held some architecture responsibility. Subsequent to that, you will see teams moving more and more into decisions in the intermediate space, firming up boundaries between one another and decoupling in the same areas. Finally, you will see genuine attempts at decisions that have a significant chance of ending in failure. This indicates that people feel safe to fail and learn from the failure. It also shows that they're not afraid to admit to that failure. Contrast that with the situation where people deny that something was a failure. This self-deception arises from people's fear of losing something: their reputation, respect, credibility, compensation, position, or job. (A close cousin of this are decisions that are headed for failure but that no one is willing to admit. It's a classic example of sunk-cost fallacy arising from fear of failure.)

By paying attention to who is deciding, you can sense if you are transitioning power and accountability, however gradually. But if all you see week after week are the same old people making the same old architectural decisions, then you are failing to make a safe space for the practice of architecture. The fear is still there, and everyone will be picking up on it.

The fear of obsolescence

Despite the flowering of architectural decisions that the advice process will usher in, and the requirement to protect the architectural practice space, and all the advice that has to be offered, and the protection of psychological safety and of facilitation of learning, some who traditionally held decision responsibility and accountability can fear for their obsolescence. Aren't you just here to get it all set up and running, and then your job is done?

No. Remember, there are still those decisions to be taken at the system-wide, cross-team level. There are also the testable CFRs to capture and then ensuring that they are met. There are the other tools for strategic alignment to set up and maintain. There is more than enough architectural work to be getting on with.

The Behavior of Those Who Don't Like the Fact That Power Got Shared

Sometimes, unfortunately, darker forces can come into play, and a participant allows their fears to channel into behaviors aimed at disrupting the advice process. Let's turn now to how that fear might become channeled, the behaviors that might result, and the types of people who might fall into this trap.

Power plays

All this change can trigger insecurity, but it's an insecurity that can manifest in multiple ways. The specifics of this manifestation usually depend on the self-perceived position that the insecure person believes they hold. Everyone views themselves and their groups in relation to others in many different spheres: in the team, in the collective, in the organization, in their profession, and in their life. A significant change, such as adopting the advice process, can shake someone's world, calling into question their perceived position in it. Picture an architect who has put in years building their skills, slowly rising up the ranks, promotion after promotion. They got there on their merits and ability to architect better than anyone else. Now this hard-won power has been taken away. That's the kind of place this insecurity arises from.

An individual's reactions to insecurity can vary. They might attack, resist, deny, self-isolate, withhold participation or information, adapt, or mediate, or exhibit an ever-changing mix of some or all of these behaviors. All such tactics to increase their power or influence—colloquially known as "power plays"—by these individuals can be either explicit (challenges to those bringing in the process or appeals to "management" higher up the organizational hierarchy) or subterfuge (hidden in the informal power structures that shadow all explicit ones). While the explicit power plays are disruptive, they are actually easier to deal with. Open challenges can be tackled and backed up with suitable arguments and evidence points, which this book has been set up to provide.

Subterfuge power plays, on the other hand, are entirely different, mainly because they offer the saboteur plausible deniability. These individuals can *appear* to be following the advice process when in fact they are undermining it at every step. This is indeed powerful because the transition to a new process will undoubtedly have a high profile among senior and executive management, and if it is perceived to be failing, then the saboteur wins.

Types of sabotage

There are many sabotage attack vectors, but they fall into two broad realms of engagement: with the collective and process and with the execution of the decisions.

Examples of collective and process sabotage include:[28]

- Making "speeches"
- Bringing up irrelevant issues as frequently as possible
- Haggling over precise wordings
- Referring back to previous decisions and discussions
- Advocating for "caution"
- Worrying about the propriety of any decision ("Is this within our remit? Should we engage others from outside?")
- Failing to share (or hiding) essential information and expertise that only they hold
- Not routing others to experts that only they know of
- Misleading others (especially new joiners) as to the method of operation of the advice process

---

28 These all come from the precursor to the CIA's 1941 *Simple Sabotage Field Manual* (*https://oreil.ly/Gw2mk*). (Yes, *that* CIA.) It was declassified in 2008.

Examples of decision-execution sabotage include:

- Demanding explicitly written instructions
- "Misunderstanding" decisions
- Doing everything possible to delay implementation of decisions
- Looking for and working at unnecessary levels of quality
- Insisting on perfection in unimportant elements while allowing clear defects in essential ones
- Making "mistakes" in prioritization or location of work
- Preferring the work for decisions that arise from their power base
- Suggesting that decisions are reopened and revisited when nothing substantial has changed in the circumstances since they were originally taken

If you observe any of these actions repeatedly, call them out. It is important the first few times to double- or even triple-check that the process and social contract are understood by everyone. Also make sure that the advice process has replaced previous accountability structures and that redundant ceremonies and hierarchies have been replaced. Once those options have been exhausted, it's time to appeal to others yourself because you have someone either unable (hopefully) or unwilling (sadly, it can happen) to adapt to this new way of practicing architecture. In this case, they would be better off elsewhere in the organization.[29]

The advice process plus ADRs can neutralize sabotage

The advice process with the support of ADRs is well set up to repel power plays and sabotage. Here are three reasons why.

First, remember that advice is advice: the decider maintains decision responsibility and accountability. This is the greatest neutralizer of the charismatic saboteur who tries to withhold responsibility to decide in their area.

Second, remember that ADRs are a record of all advice provided and that those providing the advice are the ones obliged to ensure that it is accurately recorded. Also recall that ADRs progress through the stages of deciding *in the open*, and decisions are made with the information available at the time. When all participants are obliged to share openly, it is *far* harder to rewrite history. This is the greatest neutralizer of the information hoarder.

---

29 I have a short article that digs deeper into this topic (*https://oreil.ly/BKcqW*) on the site that accompanies this book if you want more tips on how to spot saboteurs.

Third, remember that in the advice process, not only can anyone decide, but also anyone can decide who decides. As long as they uphold the social contract, they are able to suggest any changes they think are necessary, including in team boundaries and ownership of various elements. Recall also that they are doing this out in the open, which greatly neutralizes the power of the uncaring individual, or at least leaves a trail of howls of complaint in ADR advice sections that are hard to ignore.

Transitions Are Uncomfortable

Transition causes upheaval, and that causes discomfort. But if change doesn't happen, then it's not a transition. Remember that not everyone is capable of changing at the same pace and that the discomfort felt will not be evenly distributed. Everyone has a responsibility both to speak up about their hopes and fears and to listen to and understand the hopes and fears of others.

While all need to do their best to relate to the individual experiences of everyone undertaking the journey with them, the fundamental nature of the change is not up for negotiation. The change has taken place, and power has shifted. Perhaps that is not something everyone can get behind. In that case, this way of organizing is not for them.

Yet again, there is a parallel of this focus on the collective over individuals in the Netflix culture. Netflix was famous for not tolerating "brilliant jerks":[30] individuals who ignored the Netflix social contract while thinking that their contributions in the form of code or ideas or something would give them a free pass from all that other "team" stuff.

A simpler version of this nontolerance of certain approaches to decision power results from adopting the advice process. There *will* be those who simply can't cope with or find a niche that satisfies them in this new order, and that's fine—not every way of working is for everyone. But be firm in communicating that the new way of working won't be changed simply to accommodate their needs in a way that compromises the overall systemic change. The whole point of the transition is to share power and accountability so that deciding can scale and teams can flow. If you don't achieve that completely and end up making concessions here and there for specific people for specific reasons, then all the upheaval of transition isn't worth it.

---

30 See slide 36 of the original Netflix Culture deck (*https://oreil.ly/q8fR-*). I've personally heard stories of well-known developers who worked there. They were offered the opportunity to change, to cut back on their "jerkness," but if it didn't work out, then they parted ways.

Conclusion

This chapter covered the key obstacles and forces that your software collective might encounter as you transition from a traditional to a decentralized, inclusive practice of software architecture.

I first described how those taking on decision power can experience this shift, what might get in its way, and how those who previously had the power and accountability can smooth and catalyze the process. I spent particular time on the topic of psychological safety and how it is of paramount importance when collectives want to decide, fail, and learn together.

Then, I looked at those who used to have sole command of the power and accountability of decisions and are now expected to share it. I acknowledged that fear is a valid emotion for such people before closing with the sad but necessary consideration of those who, either consciously or unconsciously, resent their loss of power.

When any of the circumstances discussed arise that require action to be taken, someone needs to make the first move. Taking such a first step is a demonstration of leadership, and that's where I'm going to turn next because, as with everything in this decentralized world, leadership can come from anywhere.

CHAPTER 16

On Leadership

With all the decentralization of power going on, you may have gotten the impression that there was no space in the advice process for leadership. But as Peter Drucker, the renowned 20th-century management theorist, is widely quoted as saying, "Only three things happen naturally in organizations: friction, confusion, and underperformance. Everything else requires leadership."

I completely agree.

As you transition to a decentralized approach to architecture, leadership is essential, and leadership *continues* to be essential once the metamorphosis is complete. In fact, just as a decentralized approach to the practice of architecture results in more architecture, the same can be said of leadership.

Yet I've barely mentioned leadership in the book so far. This chapter redresses that imbalance, starting by clarifying what leadership *isn't* before discussing leadership approaches that don't decentralize deciding and self-organizing, self-managing, self-sustaining teams.

I'll then clarify where this leadership is required during the transition to a decentralized approach to architecture. I'll show how it's not just in the practice of architecture but also in the deciding and in the creating and realizing of strategy. Leadership is also needed to establish and maintain the social contract as well as to foster a culture of inclusion and to establish and protect safety. (I'd argue this last one is the most important; otherwise, why did you even decentralize in the first place?)

Consequently, this chapter is primarily aimed at those who held and exercised power under traditional approaches. Why? First, the initial steps of transition to an advice process style of practicing architecture need to come from someone with power: the original leaders in traditionally structured organizations. Second, traditional leaders will have the most to unlearn before they can relearn, which is harder than learning alone.

Misconceptions About Leadership

Those who are used to leading in traditional hierarchical organizations may need to unlearn a lot, because leadership is one of those organizational factors that seems to be deeply misunderstood by virtually everyone, more so by those who depended on the hierarchy. Many conflate the idea of "leadership" with other roles and responsibilities: with managing, with hierarchical positions and certain job titles, or with a specific job of Leader. None of these is correct, but we think this because of how we are used to experiencing our organizations being run.

The aim of the advice process approach to software architecture is to break from this hierarchical hegemony and, just in your world that you collectively control, organize yourselves in an entirely different way. That extends to how you practice leadership. To do that, you need to be clear on what leadership *is not* before pulling together the relevant mindsets and practices to form a cohesive idea of the leadership that you can celebrate in your transition to your architectural practice and beyond.

Misconception 1: Leadership Is Innate

The biggest misconception is that leadership is based on some kind of innate quality. You hear talk of "born leaders"[1] far more than you should.[2]

Drucker flatly gives the lie to this in his essay "Leadership as Work": "[Leadership] has little to do with 'leadership qualities' and even less to do with 'charisma.'" He continues, "It is mundane, unromantic, and boring. Its essence is performance."[3] In Drucker's world, leadership is work. It has virtually nothing to do with charisma.

I've experienced this my entire life. I was an incredibly shy kid and very socially awkward, pretty much the opposite of someone you would describe as charismatic. I have no tales of leadership from the playground. I always took the back seat in group assignments at university, preferring to be an individual contributor. This continued into the world of work, right up to the point when I became line manager of a 36-person team. Up to that point, I thought I'd done a pretty good job of making it clear that I didn't ever want to lead anyone.

---

1 Usually men.

2 As I write this chapter in the politically uncertain times of 2024, I'm hearing it even more from demagogues and lazy commentators. It serves no one.

3 Peter Drucker, *The Essential Drucker* (Butterworth-Heineman, 2007), 203–204.

Rather than rely on my nonexisting innate leadership skills, I had to learn them, and learn them I did. It turned out that I enjoyed leading.

Misconception 2: Leadership Is Tied to Hierarchy

The second biggest misconception is that leadership is tied to specific parts of hierarchies. Specifically, if I am at the bottom of the hierarchy, I have no leadership skills, nor am I expected to have or exercise them. As I move up the hierarchy, I am expected to have increasing levels of leadership ability and to deploy my skills more and more as I reach loftier heights. In this conception, it is impossible to separate the level of leadership expected of a person and the level they hold in the organizational hierarchy.

Ironically, this conception is perhaps the easiest to dismiss. I am quietly confident that, in your career, you have experienced at least one "leader," perhaps very high up your organizational hierarchy, with *far* less than the required level of leadership skills you'd expect at their level. This is so common that there is a name for how it comes about: the Peter Principle,[4] which states that everyone rises to a level in the organizational hierarchy appropriate to their level of incompetence. This is particularly true of leadership skills.

When I was made a line manager, I was put into a position to lead people who were as skilled at leadership as I was at the time. Some were even keen to practice and develop their leadership skills. Yet, I was technically now "above" them in the hierarchy.

Misconception 3: Leadership Is Unidirectional

A third misconception about leadership is that it is unidirectional: leadership only flows one way—down. For every instance of leadership, there is a person who is the leader and someone who is the follower. This never changes. The two roles are fixed.

This is mixed in with hierarchical mental models. The leader is higher up the hierarchy. The follower is lower down, "below them." In this view, there is no space for leadership to flow in the other direction: from subordinates to those above them.

Not long after I took over the team, some of them asked whether I thought it was a good idea to start a podcast. At the time, I had a million other things on my mind,[5] and a podcast seemed very much a "nice to have" compared to all the other things on my plate. Months later, when I gave their suggestion proper consideration, I realized it was a great idea. In fact, it had the potential to help us with our recruitment target.

---

4 A great case study to read that tackles this is "Accelerating the Peter Principle in Healthcare" (*https://oreil.ly/4hUCi*) by Tom Olivo.

5 If you really want to know what this was, check out the first part of my talk "Organisation Refactoring and Culture Hacking" (*https://oreil.ly/ucsiK*) from JFokus 2020.

But because I'd assumed that leadership could go in only one direction, I'd not even considered that such a great idea could be put into action without my leadership—that it could be led by those who suggested it, and I could simply support.[6]

Misconception 4: Leadership Is Management

The last misconception to call out is probably the most insidious one: that leadership is just a form of management. This confusion may lead to many arriving at the other misconceptions. We also think management must be hierarchical, top-down, and therefore unidirectional.

In fact, management couldn't be farther away from leadership. As Ebenezer C. Ikonne makes clear in his book, *Becoming a Leader in Product Development: An Evidence-Based Guide to the Essentials* (Apress), management "focus[es] on the day-to-day activities required to ensure the organization functions properly and achieves its goals." Another way to say this is that management is concerned with stabilizing and optimizing the status quo. Leadership is precisely the opposite. Leadership's job is to *change* the status quo and find a better one. Leadership is all about change and the future. Leadership is about movement toward that. Therefore, it's intimately tied to learning.

In our advice process context, this brings up a key point: if teams are self-managing in their practice of architecture, then there is no one "higher up the hierarchy" for leadership to come from. Teams self-managing their architecture practice fit exactly into the definition of management I just shared. Via the advice process, teams can focus on the day-to-day activities of deciding required to ensure that they have the right architecture in place and that their parts of the software system can achieve their goals. They are stabilizing and optimizing their status quo.

But the advice process isn't just about teams being self-managing. I've also frequently suggested that teams need to be strategically self-organizing and self-sustaining. If, as I've argued more than once (most explicitly in Chapters 1, 9, and 14), the landscapes and climates in which our architectures live and evolve are constantly changing, we require a means to organize and sustain direction and movement. Direction and movement are sensitive to this technical landscape and climate as well as to the unique attitudes and aptitudes of each team.

Given all this, what, then, *is* leadership—specifically, leadership in the context of the architecture advice process with its core and supporting elements? What kind of leadership supports the transition to this new way of organizing and deciding that can be sustained in the long term?

---

6 This involved setting up meetings with the relevant peeps elsewhere in the organization (marketing, etc.) to check we wouldn't be making anything complicated for ourselves or anyone else in the organization. It turns out everyone loved the idea.

What Leadership Is

Drucker offers a perfect place to start: "The foundation of effective leadership is thinking through the organization's mission, defining it, establishing it, clearly and visibly…The leader sets the goals, sets the priorities, and sets and maintains the standards…The leader's first task is to be the trumpet that sounds a clear sound."[7]

You saw this foundation in Part II when I described both the need and the means for the collective to find and maintain a minimal viable agreement on the shared direction and destination of their systems. Those concepts and tools offered the means for the collective to set and maintain goals, priorities, and standards, in which case, everyone is "leading." But what about the sounding of the trumpet? What does it represent?

The Center for Creative Leadership (CCL) defines *leadership* as "the process of producing direction, alignment and commitment (DAC) in collectives. Leadership occurs as a group agrees on what they intend to achieve, aligns on how they will work together, and commits to working with each other as they strive to achieve group goals."[8]

That's really concrete and clear. But notice that it doesn't specify who the "leader" in such groups is. Might the role be spread around? Yes. The CCL's definition of *leadership* places it as a responsibility of the group, not just of the leader. The position of "leader" and leadership are not the same. In this framing, everyone in a group has a part to play in achieving direction, alignment, and commitment. By this definition, there are concepts of leadership that might map really nicely to our idea of a decentralized, nonhierarchical, self-organizing, and self-sustaining approach.

Let's move on and consider four popular approaches to leadership that meet the CCL's definition. Although none of them fit our decentralized needs precisely, considering them will allow me to clearly define the requirements for an alternative ideal of leadership.

Deming's 14 Points

One of the most famous approaches to leadership is encapsulated in W. Edwards Deming's 14 points for management (*https://oreil.ly/RjbHA*). While these have nothing to do with software, they were the inspiration for the DevOps movement as well as for Lean manufacturing.

Many of Deming's points tell leaders to *stop* doing things, not start them. "Eliminate slogans, exhortations, and targets" is frequently quoted, but there are also "cease dependence on inspection to achieve quality" and "eliminate numerical quotas for the

---

7 *The Essential Drucker*, 203–204.

8 CCL, *The Center for Creative Leadership Handbook of Leadership Development*, 3rd ed. (Wiley, 1998), 20.

workforce and numerical goals for management."[9] However, there are five principles that are both directive and particularly relevant to our purposes.

The first principle, "adopt and institute leadership," states: "The job of management is not supervision but leadership. Management must work on sources of improvement…Focus on outcomes…must be abolished. Leadership put in place."[10]

Although this comes from a hierarchical point of view—"adopting leadership" is what "management" needs to do—I include it because of Deming's key point that "focus on outcomes" is *not* the realm of leaders (or managers who are leading, in Deming's perspective). Now, we tend to think that leaders, whoever they are, drive us toward outcomes. Deming had another view. Driving us to outcomes was the job of those doing the work. For us in software, that's building, running, and evolving a quality product that meets our customers' needs.

The second principle for your attention is "drive out fear": "No-one can put in his best performance unless he feels secure…'Secure' means 'without fear, not afraid to express ideas, not afraid to ask questions.'"[11]

I hope this brings to mind Chapter 15's discussion of safety. This *is* the job of leadership, as Deming sees it. Leadership takes active steps to ameliorate the fear of everyone in the group. It's *not* the job of those who might be scared (for whatever reason) to "stop being scared and get over it" and to "participate." It *is*, however, the job of leadership to ensure that fear has no place to be and that contributions are welcomed.

The third relevant principle is "break down barriers between staff areas." This is a smartly crafted call for increased empathy and working better together. "Why not get acquainted with the customer?" Deming suggests. "Why not spend time in the factory, see the problems and hear about them?"[12] Fundamentally, this allows everyone to have an appreciation for what everyone else is doing.

The fourth relevant principle is "institute a vigorous program of education and self-improvement." It doesn't need much explanation, but I want to make clear that leadership ensures that everyone is learning—not simply learning facts, but also setting the example of "self-improving."[13]

---

9 W. Edwards Deming, *Out of the Crisis* (MIT Press, 1982), 23–24. This is easier said than done, actually, and once you know about it, you'll never listen to a member of your executive team or, in fact, anyone in a "leadership position" the same way again.

10 *Out of the Crisis*, 54.

11 *Out of the Crisis*, 59.

12 *Out of the Crisis*, 62. This is possibly (though I have no evidence for this) the origin of Toyota's "Gemba walk" practice, which requires that senior leadership simply walk the floor, not doing anything other than observing manufacturing taking place and learning from it.

13 *Out of the Crisis*, 62.

The final relevant Deming principle is "put everybody in the company to work to accomplish the transformation." Deming says, "The transformation is everybody's job."[14] Note that he's not only saying that everyone has to change, but he's also making clear that *the act of transition is everyone's job*, not just the job of those who are traditionally leaders.

There's a lot in all of these principles that is relevant for the transition to the architecture process and beyond, but I include these specific principles for their focus on the transition. Deming was trying to get American manufacturing "out of the crisis," after all. Despite the fact that he was focused on a very different industry, one with incredibly different dynamics, and he was writing close to half a century ago, his principles are still relevant because they focus on the power of leadership to effect a much-needed transformation. Most importantly, this was a transition to a new way of interrelating, working, thinking, and learning.

Servant Leadership

Another approach to leadership had a significant amount of momentum and mindshare when it first came out, and still does today: servant leadership (*https://www.greenleaf.org*), first proposed by Robert K. Greenleaf.

The goal of a servant leader is to serve others. This manifests as servant leaders looking to share their power for the benefit of the team, putting the needs of coworkers first, and helping them to both perform and develop to their fullest potential. Instead of subordinates working to serve their leader, the servant leader's sole focus is on serving their subordinates. This approach to leadership differs from traditional approaches to leadership where a leader's main focus is the thriving of their organization.

From our perspective, there are a few problems with the servant leader approach. It assumes that there is a hierarchy and power and that leadership is unidirectionally top-down. It also assumes that leaders distribute power as they see fit. This implies that the existing hierarchical power structures are fine; they just need a little rebalancing.

Perhaps the most incompatible assumption is that leadership needs to bias itself *either* toward the goals of the organization *or* to the development of everyone in that organization. In the words of the wee girl in the Old El Paso taco commercial: "Why not both?"[15]

---

14 *Out of the Crisis*, 86.

15 If you've never heard of this meme, drink deep from the fountain of meme knowledge (*https://oreil.ly/w2Ofz*).

Despite these drawbacks, there's a valuable aspect of servant leadership worth pulling out for our practice of architecture. Servant leadership makes clear there are two parts to leadership: a *strategic* part that's future focused, ensuring that the organization is headed in the desired direction, and an *operation* part that focuses on people in teams, ensuring that they collectively have what they need to feel safe, learn, and grow.

Adaptive Leadership

An issue many have with mainstream leadership philosophies is that they don't move fast enough for the modern world. They don't have a transformation mindset built into them. There is, however, an approach to leadership that puts transformation at its heart: Ronald Heifetz and Marty Linsky's adaptive leadership.

To be "agile" in software has always meant to be open to change, whatever the precise flavor of your approach, and that is precisely what adaptive leadership is about (ironically, we're going to adapt this definition of what it means to be *agile* even more). In fact, the authors of *EDGE* argue that the essence of adaptive leadership is contained in the Agile manifesto: "people and their interactions, delivering actual products and services (code), adjusting and learning, and customer focus."[16]

You could argue that the five software revolutions could be summed up as "being digital" (though I've intentionally avoided this as it's too narrow a conceptualization of the change taking place in software), and the focus of *EDGE* is all about driving toward "digital" organizations with adaptive leadership concepts at their core. But there's more to the revolutions than that. The revolutions share the push for change in many of the fundamental ideas around how we conceive of, build, and evolve software (now "digital") products and services that have been embedded for a long time—most notably, the outdated belief that the future can be predicted and managed.

Given this, adaptive leadership's primary aim is to refocus the predominant mindset of standard leadership from plan-do (though acknowledging that at times this is still appropriate), shifting the balance significantly toward envision-explore. This then becomes the primary mindset of the adaptive leader.

The legacy of decades of plan-do leadership makes this shift to adaptive leadership's envision-explore alternative difficult. Plan-do falsely offers promises of certainty while envision-explore directly acknowledges the significant possibility of failure. The authors point this difficulty out, admitting, "'I don't know' has not [historically] been a path to managerial success."[17]

---

16 *EDGE: Value-Driven Digital Transformation*, 191.

17 *EDGE: Value-Driven Digital Transformation*, 193.

When working in nonhierarchical, decentralized, sociotechnical systems, it's essential to be honest about this lack of control and predictability. While the *EDGE* authors assume there's a hierarchy present in adaptive leadership, unlike servant leadership, their approach to this "digital" mindset doesn't have a permanent "leader class" baked into it. They recommend leadership goals to be adopted by any leader, whoever they are and wherever they reside in the organization. In fact, if you make this leap—seeing the potential of leaders being everywhere—two key possibilities open up. First, the work can go to the place best suited for it, and second, leaders of that work can *arise* anywhere.

Give the work back to the people

All work moving to the place best suited for it is an aspect of adaptive leadership worth examining. Ikonne tackles it explicitly in *Becoming a Leader in Product Development*. "Work" for us is everything, including the work of architecting and deciding on architectures. Unfortunately, in adaptive leadership, this movement of work doesn't happen on its own. Instead, people are "empowered," and that's problematic.

"I am not a fan of the corporate-speak usage of the word *empowerment* because it avoids the real issue," says Ikonne. "Many organizations do not need to empower their people; instead, they need to liberate or free their people to handle adaptive work."[18] For too long, too much management/organizational thinking has considered those doing the work to be fancy machines that can be "managed." This was always based on false premises,[19] yet it has persisted, even into the world of knowledge work, such as software development and product delivery.

While "empowerment" is a step away from linear, mechanistic viewpoints, it is still affected by the legacy of this problematic concept. With empowerment, the freedom of doing a piece of work is handed to those doing it, but not the setting of the goals and outcomes for that piece of work nor its boundaries. I am empowered to deliver an outcome that someone other than me defines.

In the language of Shoshannah Zuboff, which I've been using in this book, empowerment is "you decide," but in a maximally adaptive world, you really also want "you decide who decides" because that is where leadership lies.

To fully achieve this conceptual shift, you need to jettison perhaps the most insidious mental models of not just leadership but also standard hierarchical organizational structures: specifically, the idea that there is an ossified organizational hierarchy and that this hierarchy serves to direct work, recognize and reward certain activities, and

---

18 *Becoming a Leader in Product Development: An Evidence-Based Guide to the Essentials*, 253.

19 See Diana Montalion's potted history in her talk "Systems Thinking for Software Professionals" (*https://oreil.ly/1877i*).

communicate information.[20] For us, this step ought not to be too difficult as we are only taking it with regard to the practice of architecture.[21]

Leadership can come from anywhere

The second possibility unlocked by adaptive leadership arises because it acknowledges that leadership isn't tied to hierarchy. Instead, adaptive leadership stresses the importance of informal authority. Ikonne explains: "Informal authority is the authority conferred on you by others because they trust you, respect you and believe that you have their best interest[s] at heart."[22] Informal authority, then, is authority that isn't conferred on someone simply because of the position they hold in an organization.

In many ways, this is simply acknowledging what really happens with leadership these days. Increasing numbers of us are realizing that the nature of the work we do—knowledge work—is less compatible with the means deployed to organize and then manage it. (I'll come back to this in detail in Chapter 17.) Many of us are simply less inclined to "do as we are told" because it seems self-evident to us that what we are told to do won't work. This is particularly evident in software. Many times, I've witnessed teams trying to avoid implementing an architectural decision that was impossible and they knew it. This disconnect is happening because we are all now increasingly better educated, both formally and informally, as to how software systems work. Many more of us are increasingly distrustful of authority wielded without explanation.[23]

Although I didn't mention it at the time, this antihierarchical, decentralizing force can be detected behind each of the five software revolutions. Outdated ideas of control, predictability, planning, and "management" are proving less and less effective. The concept of a "traditional" architect is an example of this. They are a dying breed because they are finding it increasingly hard to uphold the authority they have been given and to deliver on what they have been told they are both responsible and accountable for.

The alternative ways to organize and work—generative, expansive, respectful, exploratory, collaborative, fluid, open/porous, networked, feedback seeking and driven—are

---

20 I wrote about the various capabilities an organization offers, including these three, in "Your Organisation Viewed as a Collection of Capabilities" (*https://oreil.ly/85XWp*).

21 It is entirely possible to go farther. The techniques laid out in this book that I have specifically deployed for the practice of architecture can, and have, been deployed far more generally, company-wide. If you're interested in this, I encourage you to learn about it more, but this book contains all you ought to need to deploy this in your practice of architecture.

22 *Becoming a Leader in Product Development*, 239.

23 Hierarchical power wielded with expectation of complete subservience has other noticeable effects in these circumstances. Many subordinates eventually become servile after not being listened to. They literally do what they are told—no more and no less. They are simply waiting for orders. "Quiet quitting" (where someone doesn't leave an organization explicitly but contributes only the bare minimum) is an example of this.

finding places and ways to thrive. This book is an attempt to offer one such alternative, in the very specific world of software systems.

While adaptive leadership offers many of the elements you need, it is unfortunately still too tied to the idea of a hierarchy, which we saw was a pervasive fallacy. But what would it look like if you were to take many of the ideas of adaptive leadership to their logical conclusion and consider everyone to potentially be a leader?

Leader-Leader Leadership

The leader-leader perspective is described by L. David Marquet in his book *Turn the Ship Around!: A True Story of Turning Followers into Leaders* (Penguin). It takes place in the most unlikely of places—a US Navy submarine[24]—and tells the story of how he transformed a failing vessel under his command. The pivotal point in his thinking—and the trigger for his new leadership approach—comes after he gives a clearly impossible-to-follow order that his crew attempts to enact anyway. As the book progresses, we see his diagnosis of the hierarchical mindset that led to this crisis and how it might be transitioned to something entirely different.

In Marquet's diagnosis, the submarine was suffering from a "leader-follower" mindset, and because they were treated like followers, the crew acted like followers, doing exactly what they were told even when they knew it was futile or impossible. Sound familiar?

The dysfunction happened, Marquet argues, because his "leader-follower" approach was only ever intended to extract *physical* work. Crewing a nuclear submarine, where the important work is all *cognitive,* was very different. Leader-follower has problems coping with this. As Marquet points out, in leader-follower when the work is cognitive, "We're taught the solution is empowerment, but the message 'it takes me to empower you' [is] fundamentally disempower[ing]."[25] What he needed was an alternative that appropriately spread power, without the need for anyone to explicitly offer it to others. That alternative was "leader-leader" leadership, which gave everyone full control of and responsibility for their actions without it having to be offered.

Despite the great differences in domain, such challenges should sound very familiar. Decentralized architecture practice is another example of highly cognitive knowledge

---

24 I've worked hard to keep the military—in the form of metaphors, examples, and more—out of this book for a variety of reasons, but I feel justified in including this work. Not least because it is written with a humility and a focus on humanity that I don't think people would expect from a book about the Armed Forces. My challenge would be: if Captain Marquet can do this in his world, then what's stopping you from at least trying it in yours?

25 L. David Marquet, *Turn the Ship Around!: A True Story of Turning Followers into Leaders* (Penguin, 2013), xxii. Marquet's book is the most famous anecdotal proof point of research by Kurt Lewin in the 1930s and Wilfred Bion in the 1950s.

work—arguably more so, because the *only* thing we work with is abstract, ephemeral code. It should come as no surprise then that leader-follower, empowerment-based approaches to leadership fail with the architecture advice process in just the same way they did on Marquet's submarine.

Leader-leader works in the same way as the advice process. If anyone sees the need to lead and feels inclined to do so, then they can take that leadership role, and with it the power and accountability required. The act of deciding under the advice process is leadership, but there is so much more.

Marquet isn't arguing for less leadership; he's arguing for more. "Leader-leader is fundamentally different…At its core is the belief that we can all be leaders, and in fact, it's best when we are all leaders."[26] Just as the architecture advice process results in far more "architecture," leader-leader results in more leadership. In both cases, it allows the right leadership to emerge, when and where it is required.

From this framing of leadership, all the elements required by a decentralized approach to architecture come together: both for the transition to the advice process and for sustaining it for the long term.

Challenges with Transitioning to Leader-Leader Leadership

What precisely then is the role of leadership in transitioning to a decentralized architecture process? Marquet outlines a transition strategy that is applicable. Like all strategies, it is enacted in steps.

The primary job of a strategic leadership transformation is to foster a culture of leadership. This will initially fall to those who have the most leadership experience (perhaps not skills, but experience). It means they can model this new mode.

The advice process and associated supporting and aligning forces give everyone the opportunity to lead collectively. But this won't appear on its own. You need the first steps of transformational leadership to ensure that it appears. This is the organizational leadership strategy you need, and it must explicitly take the concept of leadership and transition it.

As you take these first steps, you will face a series of challenges.

Leadership challenge 1: Let go of the controls

If you are leading the transition to a new way of practicing leadership, your first challenge will seem like a paradox: your job is to let go of the controls and all other supporting mechanisms. Not just performatively. You *really* need to let go.

---

26 *Turn the Ship Around!*, xxii.

This means taking some big leaps that I've already talked about concerning the advice process. You are no longer responsible for making and taking decisions—the advice process has that covered. Neither are you responsible for top-down monitoring—eliminate it from your to-do list. Everyone is responsible for their own performance.[27]

"But, but…Andrew, you talked in Chapter X about keeping an eye on the long tail of decisions, and then in Chapter Y about the throughput of decisions?!?" Correct, I did, but the top-down monitoring by a fixed individual higher up the hierarchy is removed.

In the traditional approaches, much of the reassuring bureaucracy was built up to prevent mistakes. Every time a problem occurred, another check or template section or bureaucratic step got added, which everyone had to comply with. More and more of people's lives became about critiquing errors rather than setting everyone up for success. The fear of negative outcomes and their management and control had taken over, at the expense of accomplishing positive ones.

However, if you remove the need to appease the bureaucracy, then everyone is free to focus on the real goal of their work. The transitional leader's new role has two parts. First, explicitly acknowledge that everyone feels exposed without the false comfort provided by top-down supervision. Second, encourage everyone to keep pushing for decentralization, flow and feedback, learning, and (dare I say it) excellence. To do this is to notice—and allow—the collective to develop what Marquet calls the "lifeblood… of initiative and risk-taking,"[28] helping everyone celebrate both failure (as learning) and success.

As the transitional leaders let go of these controls, they will not only be aware of the tension that they themselves feel, but they will also be absorbing part of the tension of others, both in the collective and beyond. This is the early leadership job of holding space—the space for the learning and failure that I described previously. What is *not* a transitional leader's job is to have all the answers. (This is perhaps the hardest part of letting go, given what I noted earlier from *EDGE* about "I don't know" not being the best pathway to managerial success in traditional organizations.) Answers fill the space, preventing the learning and failure that everyone needs.

With the adoption of the advice process, the challenges and problems of building, running, and evolving software systems become the collective's problem. The space that leadership in these early stages creates by focusing on everyone's inclusion, contributions, and challenges can then be filled by what Jitske Kramer describes as

---

27 *Turn the Ship Around!*, 96. This might also call to mind Deming's third principle: "Stop depending on inspections."

28 *Turn the Ship Around!*, 46–47.

"everyone's emotions, thoughts, ideas, concerns, wishes and beliefs."[29] These are all the natural results of a decentralized, diverse collaboration. Such results mean that psychological safety will be starting to build for many.

Leadership challenge 2: Prioritize safety over specific decisions

Inclusion of as much of your collective's inherent diversity as possible is the goal if you want to achieve the best decisions. As Kramer makes clear, leadership's next role in transition is "[to] stop explaining why change is important and stop making recommendations on how inclusion could be done better. Instead, listen to each other's personal stories, talk about differences and similarities. Increase intimacy and discover shared passions."[30] Such conversations mean drifting away from the specific decision at hand and into the nuances of personal experience. They will happen in different ways, in different places, and at different paces as the different aspects of the collective diversity feel safe to express themselves.

I've never found it necessary to make *explicit* space for such interactions during the transition. It seems to arise naturally as a course of the day-to-day work of software. That's not to say that it wouldn't be necessary for your organization, and if it is, ensure that everyone feels the safety and space to do it.

What I do is pay attention to when a discussion about an architectural decision needs to have more space for a safe conversation about difference created and then allow for that. This might mean space in the "there and then." It might equally mean a separate conversation is spun off. That's fine. It's all part of the process. The key point is that the need for that time is identified, acknowledged, and given space to be.

This brings us back to boundary zones[31] where differences between collective members become evident and conflict typically takes place. In Chapter 15, I was writing in a way that suggested that these zones exist at clearly identifiable boundaries, between teams, between levels in the organization, between the organization and its customers, partners, and stakeholders, and so on. But these boundaries are never absolute, and sometimes other, extra-organizational views of the world come into play. It is a natural tendency for us to see familiarities in some and dissimilarities in others, and such bias is incredibly contextual. Perspectives on in-groups and out-groups and who is a member of both can be very fluid. Paying attention to the outside world and acknowledging that it can create divisions between members of the collective are essential.

---

29 *Jam Cultures*, 202.

30 *Jam Cultures*, 268.

31 Kramer also refers to them as "liminal zones."

Wherever these boundaries of difference lie, it is the job of inclusive leadership to look out for and then both stretch and bridge these boundaries. To do so, Kramer offers this list of tasks:[32]

- Counteract groupthink
- Unite people with different areas of expertise
- Encourage and facilitate the exchange at the edge of the differences

You can't achieve such boundary stretching and bridging by applying the same rules to everyone in a given situation. Nor can you stand on the sidelines and hope that social and cultural (in terms of the organization and beyond, in society, nationally, and internationally) differences will be handled by those directly involved.

The second goal of leadership in the transition is to curb the impulse to step aside and look for a neutral, distant, or even indifferent perspective. Architecture is a collective act, and these differences have an impact on all of us—maybe not directly or immediately, but eventually, they reach everyone. Leaders get involved, but as Kramer notes, to prioritize and protect safety. "Destigmatizing failure" on page 396 was an example of this kind of leadership. But other, smaller steps can be taken that move toward the same ends. Another suggestion in the previous chapter was to qualify your statements with degrees of confidence: "I'm 80% sure this will be the likely outcome because of…" and the like. Why is this so effective?

You want everyone in the collective to pay attention to the facts and figures in front of them, not your opinion. You also want everyone to be aware of, value, and, most important, *share* their hunches and gut feelings. These could be uncertainties, fears, and concerns as well as innovative ideas and hopes. Leaders can set this in motion by being willing to let everyone be aware of their lack of certainty. When this is laid out in the open, it becomes clear that something collective is being built and that no one yet knows all the answers. This relates back to the Deming principle to drive out fear that *EDGE* also talked about.

As this culture of uncertainty and questioning becomes more valued, you will likely begin to see other benefits.[33] Mistakes—which inevitably happen—will increasingly be seen as the opportunities for learning that they really are.[34] A questioning attitude rather than one of "following" will start to emerge, too. This is exactly what you need in the world of complex, interconnected, sociotechnical systems, making them truly resilient. (Or dare I say, antifragile?) You need this when your systems and the environment

---

32 *Jam Cultures*, 81.

33 *Jam Cultures*, 199.

34 *Jam Cultures*, 125.

in which they find themselves are constantly changing. You don't want obedience, the hallmark of the old, leader-follower world. You need effective knowledge work.

This all takes courage, but the collective will be grateful for it. As the collective transitions and as safety grows, this will happen more and more, until everyone truly values the benefits of real diversity and true inclusion in your software architectures.

These first leadership steps (the ones kicking off the transformation) will be taken by those who traditionally held the power. But you will know it is working as more of the collective feels greater safety to step up and lead in these ways, too. You will start seeing a blossoming of leader-leader in more and more places. The perfect way to value and protect this is in the third leadership challenge.

Leadership challenge 3: Implement "I intend to"

Despite all of these aforementioned benefits *and* the fact that hopefully *everyone* understands that great benefits can come from moving to a leader-leader mindset and way of working, it can still *feel* scary for everyone involved.

Luckily, there's a trick to overcome that. It again comes from Marquet. It's called "I intend to,"[35] and it is a very simple way to turn passive followers into active leaders. It is also the best way I know to encourage those who traditionally held the controls of leadership to let go.

"I intend to" is rooted in the idea that most people and teams most of the time know exactly what they need to do next, and when they don't, they know how to find out. Despite coming as a surprise to few (if the organization didn't think someone was competent, why did they hire or promote them in the first place?[36]) this can be a hard pill to swallow. Why? Because the hierarchical assumption is that subordinates need to constantly be monitored and prodded and told what to do.

This mental model is *very* persistent in virtually everyone who works in organizations, both the supervisors and the supervised. But it *can* be broken down by instituting the practice of "I intend to."

The practice is very simple. Anyone can do anything that is part of their responsibility, but if they are going outside their day-to-day activities, then they state clearly and openly what they intend to do before they do it.

For example, if a team wants to start a new practice of running blameless postmortems, they should just decide to do it and let everyone know by announcing, "We intend to run a blameless postmortem on this incident at this day and this time." Or a team

---

35 *Turn the Ship Around!*, 50.

36 Unless we *know* they got promoted or hired for reasons other than attitude and aptitude, but surely that would never happen, right?

might think of setting up a new lunch-and-learn or book club and would announce it in the same way: "We intend to…" These are a bit innocuous, but the idea can be taken a lot farther. You might realize that the disaster-recovery process needs to be enacted, for example, and you would announce this broadly in the same way: "I intend to…" Or you've noticed something that looks suspiciously like a security breach, and you might announce, "I intend to enact the incident-response process."

This announcement might then lead to one of two things. There might be no response, in which case it is assumed that everyone is fine with this step being taken and so the individual or team is free to proceed. Alternatively, someone has a reason why they should not take the announced step.

The "I intend to" approach has multiple benefits:

- Leadership spreads but in a way where everyone feels safe, both those taking it up and those letting go of it.
- Everyone knows what significant steps outside the day-to-day are taking place.
- Letting something happen means no one besides the person or team making the suggestion needs to do anything.
- Stopping something from happening is easy. Someone, anyone, just needs to say "stop" and provide their reasoning.
- If something stops, then the right people from the collective can huddle together with the right context and the right skills and take appropriate action.

This means that the latent competence in the collective can finally see the light of day. Traditional leaders no longer feel pressure to be the smartest, most experienced, or most responsible people in the organization.[37] They can step back and let the wealth of untapped potential that the collective has access to start making its way into the light.

You see a lot of this implicitly in the practice of sharing the *writing* and doing of spikes and ADRs as a part of advice forums and the advice process, but "I intend to" takes this power to act farther, into the realm of organizing and doing.

Just as with decisions, it *can* be tempting during this transition stage for those of us who are more used to leading to interject lightly on these announcements—not saying "no" per se but adding a little extra secret sauce. If you feel an urge, notice it, name it, and channel it elsewhere or just simply sit with it. But don't act on it. Don't add anything extra. Why? Because by embellishing at this transition stage, you are subtly taking control and ownership of the decision again, removing it from those who just tried to take it. But what if they have the right idea but sound as if they are

---

37 This can be an exhilarating experience for a traditional leader. That's not to say that you're suddenly without knowledge or experience or responsibility, but you're no longer carrying the weight of all of it on your shoulders.

going to go about it in the wrong way? That's fine; they'll learn. Perhaps your "right way" that they're not following isn't such a good way of approaching things after all.

Leadership challenge 4: Trust, then verify (but only if you need to)

The "I intend to" tip leads us to the fourth and final transitional leadership challenge: that of trusting others to learn to lead, letting them solve their own problems, and supporting the systemic outcomes and learning that result.

The trusting part is what you just saw in microcosm. If someone is going to lead and there is no valid reason to stop them, then simply leave them to it. Trust them. This doesn't mean that you agree with them. You might not. But unless there is a reason to stop them, then stay out of it for now.

When others have taken on the mantle of leadership, by all means verify the outcomes. But be careful: you don't want it to come across as if you are marking homework.

If the step toward leadership was a success, then celebrate it, in exactly the same way you would a step into deciding. If it was less so, still celebrate the fact that leadership is spreading and then contribute some leadership of your own to increase the chances that next time, new leaders feel more inclined to step up and more confident in their actions.

To do this, help the new leaders understand why something might have not worked out as the new leaders intended. Transitional leaders can talk those who are new to leadership through their thought processes and alternatives. This might include experienced leaders talking about the outcomes they personally would have aimed for and constraints they know might exist (people's time and access to resources are the two classics, but also consider the landscape that was collectively shaped by the CFRs and strategic directions from the principles and radar blips). It can also help for the experienced leaders to describe their mental models that they would have used to address the problem. A big part of leadership is seeing the world in a different way, and such support makes leadership more effective.

It can also be very instructive for experienced leaders to describe their priorities, what they would have been happy to see fail, and what they would have defended at all costs. This allows new leaders to see that accepting potential failure and priority of focus are also aspects of leadership.

Resisting the urge to provide solutions during this transitional stage allows leadership to spread, and it can be the most important step in leadership transitions. Traditional leaders might not even think about the action of providing solutions because it is a habit or it comes easily to them. They're so experienced in leading that they don't have to stop and think about it. They just notice something and act. Those stepping up to leadership need to build this skill. Therefore, those with more experience need to let others have both the time to learn to read situations that require leadership and the space to try things and fail at them. I've mentioned previously how hard this "letting go so that others might fail" step is for those who are used to leading. Experienced leaders will go through many emotions as they do this, and that's for them to experience because if they don't let go, leader-leader leadership can never emerge in your collective.

When it does, transitional leaders can step back. You have collectively taken yet another step toward a truly self-managing, self-organizing, and self-sustaining collective.

The Need for Ongoing Moral Leadership

Leader-leader is the most appropriate model of leadership both for the transition to and the ongoing use of a decentralized practice of architecture. But leadership isn't only critical during the transition. It continues to be important as long as systems are being built, deployed, and evolved.

So what does leadership do here? Where is it most effective, and where is it a distraction? There's an appropriate quote from Dennis Bakke, the originator of the advice process at AES:

> Today, there is almost too much focus on leadership, mainly because it is widely thought to be the key to economic success. In fact, the degree to which a leader can actually affect technical performance has been substantially overstated…on the other hand, the importance and impact of moral leadership on the life and success of the organization have been greatly under-appreciated.[38]

The advice process means that outside leadership to inspire technical performance is no longer necessary. Anyone or any team can lead themselves directly by taking appropriate decisions. But what of moral leadership? The advice process also shows why it is so important.

Moral leadership—by which I mean leadership that protects true diversity and promotes psychological safety—ensures that the decentralized deciding and practice of architecture continues and that power imbalances don't creep back in. Moral leadership ensures that the broadest set of voices feel safe enough to contribute, fail, and learn. Moral leadership both lives in and protects the cultural space you cleared for yourselves that I described in Chapters 7 and 15. Moral leadership offers the greatest opportunity for the best deciding to take place.

---

38 *Reinventing Organizations*, 369.

Moral leadership knows its job is never done. Remember, you're building software that's never been created before and releasing it into a world that's totally unpredictable. Remember also that all this is happening within a highly dynamic sociotechnical system. Moral leadership helps chart a path through these unknown and unknowable waters.

Therefore, moral leadership should feel free to roam far and wide within the organizational boundaries set by the transition to the advice process. (I'll come back to this fit within the organization in Chapter 17.) Moral leadership allows everyone to lead in all areas where they think it is appropriate: in interpersonal relations, in the ways of working, in the subtle ways in which culture is manifesting or not manifesting, in the presence or absence of one or more of the supporting elements I laid out in Part II.

Let's see how moral leadership manifests in real life: first, when moral challenges arise, both during the transition and afterward; second, in being sensitive to the culture(s) currently in your collective; and third, in ensuring that no "leader" ever has to hold a permanent position.

Responding to Moral Challenges

As a software professional, you're used to facing technical challenges on a daily basis. Moral challenges are different. These are the times when leadership is needed more than ever.

Ronald Heifetz, Marty Linsky,[39] and Alexander Grashow provide four archetypes for such moral challenges, which all share a need for individuals to alter their current values, beliefs, or behaviors.[40]

- A gap between articulated values and actual behaviors
- Competing commitments
- The need to speak the unspeakable
- Work avoidance

When such moral challenges present themselves, leadership can respond in multiple ways. Ikonne categorizes these responses into four types:[41]

---

39 These are the same Heifetz and Linsky who are behind adaptive leadership.

40 *Becoming a Leader in Product Development*, 233.

41 *Becoming a Leader in Product Development*, 235–237. Three of the four are maladaptive, and only one is generative. See if you can spot it.

Cultural trap

"We have always done it this way" (intentionally ignore new information).

Natural selection

"We will get lucky" (new info is recognized but not used).

Serendipity

"Flavor of the month" (a copycat approach to adaptation because "everyone else is doing it" and any feedback from the change is ignored or discarded).

Maximal adaptive capacity

"Getting it just right" (leaders absorb new information and then use what they learn as the basis of changes, even if the new information and the changes it causes challenge current beliefs and values).

Moral leadership is understanding the nature of such challenges when they arise and mobilizing the appropriate response. The only "appropriate" response for moral leadership is the last one: maximal adaptive capacity. It is the only one that continues the steps that the transition began toward this new, decentralized, sociotechnical system for practicing architecture and building, running, and evolving software. This can pose challenges both during and after the transition, when sustaining the collective.

Challenges during transition to the advice process

During a transition to a decentralized practice of architecture, moral challenges arise over and over again, all over the place, at all levels of detail, and in all manner of circumstances.

It may be a small challenge. For example, someone wants to schedule a new recurring meeting, and all but one say "yes," that works for them, but you notice that the person who voted "no" has a regular school run to do at that time and can't change it. Sensitive, appropriate moral leadership notices this and moves to take the pressure of asking for an alternative off that person alone.

It may also be a larger event. For example, the transition to the advice process is scaling up, and new teams are being staffed. Someone gets out the old spreadsheets used for planning team allocations last time and sets up a meeting invite to plan it with the usual suspects invited. It is an act of moral leadership to point out that this spreadsheet didn't work last time and is unlikely to work this time. The same moral leader also knows that they ought to invite new people but that the diary slot has been selected in the same way as last time. New people won't be able to participate, so it'll fall back once again on the usual suspects to do the work. Moral leadership here points this out and looks for an alternate way to go about the staffing, one that includes the right people and protects against the return of old power imbalances.

Challenges when sustaining the advice process

The work of moral leadership doesn't stop when transition is complete. In adaptive sociotechnical systems, no condition is permanent; you simply transition to a mode of constant but lower-level change. That's why adaptive leadership is called *adaptive* and why it considers itself agile. Because change is still happening, moral leadership continues to be required at every level to ensure that the four archetypes of moral challenges are guarded against and that the necessary ongoing change is happening.

Both during transition to and subsequent sustaining of the advice process, you will see challenges coming from two particular areas. I'll look at both in turn before I close.

Be Sensitive of—But Not Beholden to—All Your Current Cultures

As this transition and then sustaining of the decentralized deciding and practice of architecture happens, it is important for all leaders to pay attention to all of the current collective cultures. Why *cultures* (plural)? Well, you are not only (hopefully) in the process of building a culture of radical inclusivity, which, as I laid out in Chapter 15, has the express intention of building a safe and inclusive space for all skills, viewpoints, and experiences to be heard. You also ought to expect different teams to manifest their own subcultures as they learn to take up the mantles of responsibility and accountability.

This is a potent mix, and it's a mix that everyone stepping up to lead needs to be aware of. The broader the scope of that act of leadership, the more aware that person ought to be.

The most evident aspect of this will be the difference in levels of comfort for uncertainty. Times of transition have higher levels of uncertainty, but uncertainty comes from the amount of difference that immediately preceded it. If things weren't ideal but in a predictable way, and now things are better but are unpredictably better, it's not surprising that leaders will get pushback on the pace of change—most likely the change in mindsets and behaviors.

Be sensitive to such levels of comfort. Acts of leadership are not inherently moral. Leadership can be harmful and destructive. And it can cause this damage even if its intentions are potentially good.

Therefore, with the ultimate goal of the organization in mind, leaders need to balance these concerns and tread carefully. Actions won't always be popular, either—leadership is *precisely* the act of taking steps of change that cannot be popular in all circles— but leaders should listen to make sure the change and expected outcomes are the ones that manifest and that there are no unforeseen harmful results.

There Are No "Permanent Leaders"

As you put into action what I've described in this chapter, there is one final thing to look out for: "permanent leaders" arising within your advice process bubble.

Watch out for single people becoming associated with specific roles. For example, rather than referring to the "tech lead," everyone *always* thinks of "Anne the tech lead" to the exclusion of anyone else. If this is happening, you are in danger of slipping back into the "staffing by job title" failure mode that I highlighted in Chapter 15. When this happens, a strong association is forming between the role and the person. This can be the top of the slippery slope into the cultural trap I mentioned earlier.

But doesn't this naturally happen? Well, yes, in most cases it does. But there are very simple ways to guard against it:

- Try to think about the roles and not the person—use this when going on annual leave or when folks cover for each other.
- Make sure at least two people can lead on anything.
- Enforce rotations on key roles (such as who gets to host an advice forum) when a certain time limit is reached.

The last bullet, enforcing rotations, sounds like a harsh one. How will there ever be any continuity? Well, if you're concerned, consider what happens when colleagues leave the team or organization. Rather than sticking your head in the sand and hoping it doesn't happen, celebrate this impermanence of everyone in their roles intentionally.

Conclusion

Leader-leader is the kind of leadership that you need to both transition to and sustain your decentralized way of practicing software architecture. You need to acknowledge that leadership can come from anyone, irrespective of their position, perceived charisma, and relationship to those they are leading.

In doing so, your new practice of leadership will become accessible to everyone, as and when they need it. To succeed, leadership must defocus from the technical challenges and disassociate from managing, allowing teams to do that for themselves. Instead, leadership needs to focus on the moral challenges, holding space, and creating safety so that failure can be an asset and learning a celebration.

But what about the rest of your organization? How does this fit when it comes into contact with more viewpoints and mental models? And what about scale? How wide can this go? For that, you'll need to turn to the final chapter.

CHAPTER 17

Fitting the Advice Process Within Your Organization

After all this talk of adopting the architecture advice process, you may have forgotten that it takes place within your wider organization. While that's not your primary concern at the outset, the decentralized culture and structures of trust and feedback that you collectively rely on will continuously be in contact with other cultures and other ways of organizing within your organization. You'll need to pay attention to those contact points.

If you don't figure out what these contact points are and how they interact, collaborate, contradict, and coevolve with your advice process practice, you'll come into conflict with them. Sadly, because decentralized, trust-based approaches are a less familiar, minority way of organizing, when such conflicts arise, the advice process almost always loses out to creeping bureaucracy and hierarchy.

This final chapter examines those contact points, considering them from the early stages of adopting the advice process. It contains perspectives and strategies for ensuring that your decentralized approach to architecture can coexist or perhaps even coevolve with the surrounding organization. Most importantly, it shows how to avoid their coming into conflict with each other without asking either side to compromise.

The Software Engineering Subculture

The advice process needs to be able to exist within your organization's current software engineering department for it to be established and thrive.

Until software engineering came along, organizations tended toward more explicit monocultures. When you consider that *culture* is "the pattern of basic assumptions that a given group has invented, discovered, or developed in learning to cope with its problems of external adaptation or internal integration,"[1] you can see why all organizational problems tended to be experienced and solved in similar ways across all departments prior to the advent of software. Not only that, but whenever overarching cultures got results for an organization, they tended to be reinforced by senior leadership, again amplifying their uniform nature.

But senior leaders don't have to endorse a single, uniform culture. Multiple subcultures can coexist or at least be tolerated.

Frederic Laloux says that for trust-based cultures like those arising from the advice process to thrive, "the only make-or-break factors are the worldview held by the top leadership and the owners/board of the organization."[2] If senior leadership and the board understand and advocate for trust-supporting cultures, then you will succeed. If they don't, then you will fail.

Can multiple subcultures coexist within a single organization? Yes. While senior leadership still has the power to explicitly forbid them, if they work, and work well, then senior leadership will be comfortable with their coexistence despite their differences from the culture in the rest of the organization.

There is an example of this right under our noses. Software engineering already has a very distinct culture type, distinct even from the rest of the IT departments that typically house it. A distinct culture type that has coexisted alongside other parts of organizations for decades. Let's examine why this is and why those outside of software engineering appear to tolerate it. It's a result of four interrelated reasons that have to do with differences in our basic assumptions.

Reason 1: Software Development Doesn't Follow Standard Mental Models for Creation

The first reason is that software development doesn't follow the standard mental models for how organizations create products and services. A department that produces software will not have the same process as one that produces coffee makers. A physical product can easily take months to develop, manufacture, and ship. A software product or service can, too, but it's also possible to have new code in front of an entire user base within minutes. This is because some activities are inconceivably easy in software, such as releasing a new app version to millions of phone handsets globally. Other times, a change can be inexplicably complex or unpredictable. As I write, the impact of the CrowdStrike antivirus update (*https://oreil.ly/cLJwe*) is a prime

---

1 Edgar Schien, quoted in Jeffrey K. Liker, *The Toyota Way: 14 Management Principles from the World's Greatest Manufacturer* (McGraw-Hill, 2003), 229.

2 *Reinventing Organizations*, 369–370.

---

example of this. For this reason, software engineering cultures are distinct. Not only are the problems different in software, but we solve them differently, too.

Reason 2: Rates of Change in IT Departments Are Far Greater Than Anywhere Else

The second reason layers on top of the first. The differences in rates of change between IT departments and the rest of the organization are seen as necessary and reflective of the wider world. The pace of change in software has always been faster than anything else organizations face, whether that change is embraced or not. Consider how fast the entire user interface of your favorite social media site updates compared to the last time there was a significant change in a core piece of your organization's bureaucracy, such as purchasing. This is associated with a corresponding difference in comfort with that change velocity. Software people tend to be far keener to try the next shiny thing rather than choose the boring old technology than their organizational peers outside tech are.[3] This significant difference in pace affects the perception of problems that culture is there to resolve.

Reason 3: The Touch Points Between Software Engineering and the Rest of the Org Are Few and Distinct

Third, the touch points between software engineering and the rest of the organization are few in number and relatively distinct. This has led to organizations being largely comfortable managing technology functions at arm's length via things such as budgets, high-level roadmaps, and the like.[4] There is an unspoken understanding that anything more detailed will likely prove to be vastly wrong because of all the variation, both in the product- or service-creation process and in the willingness to adopt new ideas and practices. There are, however, a small number of figureheads or peacekeepers, known as "enterprise architects" and "product managers," who bridge both worlds. Yet again, the clear difference in recognition of and approaches to problems is clear for all to see.

---

3 The fact that we techies need to be reined in sometimes gave rise to the famous blog post by Dan McKinley, "Choose Boring Technology" (*https://oreil.ly/1Y9mI*).

4 This isn't to say that there aren't extensive frustrations when IT departments and software arms of organizations fail to deliver, just that even the reasons for the failures are never expressed in terms that everyone understands and agrees with for all the reasons I listed previously.

Reason 4: The Cultural Divide Between Software Engineering and the Rest of the Org Is Already Accepted

The fourth reason brings all this together. It is the fact that the preexisting cultural divide between software engineering and the rest of the organization is consequently already distinct and generally accepted. We "techies" think and act—and frequently dress—differently. It's practically expected of us. Perhaps this is due to the fact that software is still the new creature in the organizational jungle. Perhaps it's because of the combination of all the reasons I've already listed.

Taken together, this is why software engineering departments "going their own way" is already largely prebaked into organizations. As far as the rest of the organization is concerned, a shift in the practice of software or systems architecture doesn't feel like much of a leap.

I believe this is why I've never had any higher-level pushback on this way of organizing. In fact, the plans are usually warmly received as they aim to resolve many organizational tensions arising from failed, more traditional attempts. Add to this the fact that every time I've implemented the advice process (and every time I've heard about its implementation elsewhere), senior observers view the results positively. They experience a more transparent, more explicit, and more honest way of building, running, and evolving software systems. The advice process offers greater organizational alignment, improved management of variability, and a sustainable way to practice architecture everywhere. What's not to like?[5]

Although organizations generally accept that software engineering departments will operate differently from the rest of the org, that acceptance has a limit. Things can go wrong when the software teams and architecture function don't live up to the expectations and implicit organizational contracts that the rest of the organization has of them. Touch points between the software and nonsoftware areas are vulnerable and should be given special care.

However, if these touch points are managed, it is highly likely that the number of people adopting and practicing the advice process in your organization will grow, though that in turn can bring its own challenges.

Advice Process Bubbles

It is of utmost importance to give the architecture advice process a distinct practice space—one with a clear boundary separating those adopting the new ways of working and thinking from not only the rest of your software development department but

---

5 This is best exemplified in the experience report (*https://oreil.ly/wOonV*) I cowrote with Noush Streets and Kamil Dziublinski, CTOs at Xapo Bank, about their adoption of the advice process.

also the wider organization. This bounded space is an "advice process bubble." It is a place for your new sociotechnical system.

A bubble offers a simple way to represent the distinct freedom of practice and culture the advice process brings without disregarding the context of the wider organization. While the bubble makes clear where the practice area stops, outside forces still influence what goes on inside the bubble. While a bubble's boundary is explicit, it's not impermeable. Neither are bubbles opaque.

The idea of a bubble allows you to start small, perhaps as a personal practice or a single team. A bubble allows everyone involved time to learn what a transition to the advice process means for them and how the process fits with their existing software, skills, and culture. A bubble also offers the protection required for participants to develop the safety that is conducive to the advice process.

Figure 17-1 shows a very simple representation of an advice process bubble. Note how similar it is to a system context diagram from Chapter 14 in that it shows the teams practicing the advice process within the bubble, surrounded by all the other systems, actors, and key dependencies that are outside your sphere of influence but that you depend on or have a relationship with. (This similarity will increase as I consider how a bubble operates in more depth.)

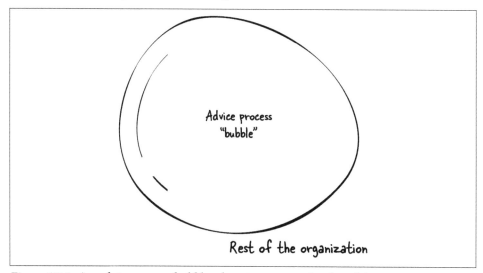

Figure 17-1. An advice process bubble where teams practice the advice process, surrounded by the rest of the organization where everything continues as usual

Let's take a closer look at what this advice process bubble is. First, I'll describe how a bubble appears to those outside, in the rest of the organization. Then, I'll spend a little time on how those inside bubbles should self-organize how their bubble is set up.

Finally, I'll discuss how those inside the bubble and those outside can interact constructively.

Bubbles Are Evident Only to Those Looking for Them

To those adopting the advice process *inside* a bubble, things—perhaps everything— ought to feel very different. But to those *outside* a bubble, everything ought to look and feel very similar—ideally, exactly the same—at least with regard to how they continue to go about their working lives and the expectations they have on the bubbled teams.

This is important because there are studies that suggest that this kind of hybrid model of organizing will attract pushback from those who are not adopting the new way of organizing and working.[6] This happens for many reasons that I won't go into here. Regardless, it is important not to give a reason or means for those outside any bubble to sabotage it.

This can be achieved by not giving those outside with their existing practices any reason to think of those within the bubble as receiving special treatment and, therefore, no reason to resent its existence—that is, at least until the implementation of the advice process has had a chance to prove itself and is in less danger of being swept away.

This approach makes the presence of bubbles less obtrusive for those outside them. However, that's not to say that a bubble's operations should be secretive; in fact, it's the opposite.

Because of the transparent way the advice process works, the artifacts produced by its day-to-day existence will still be available for *all*, but only for those who go looking. Artifacts should not be shoved in the faces of those outside a bubble, but they must be easily and freely available to anyone who wants to see them without their having to request access. Ideally, it should be as simple as clicking a hyperlink. This serves a double purpose. First, such transparency builds trust. Second, written communications and records of decisions are a powerful antidote against those who might look to undermine any change in how things are run—aka saboteurs.

From the outside, those in bubbles will appear to the casual observer as if they are simply engaged in yet another program of work, looking after just another set of products or services. Maybe to those looking more closely, bubble teams will likely be more effective, suffer less from variability, have better DORA metrics, and will fundamentally be enjoying themselves more (meaning that retention and career

---

6 The white paper "Modern Forms of Laissez-Faire Organization" (*https://oreil.ly/JeQaa*) by Donald W. de Guerre and Merrelyn Emery covers this well.

progression are probably noticeably better and even that absences are lower). But this quiet success won't be obtrusive.

Inside bubbles, the clear difference in culture and organization will be apparent. There will be a focus on safety, an absence of permanent hierarchy, and a fluidity of roles. There will also be a valued importance of experimentation and of learning. Most importantly, the architecture will be cleaner and clear in code, and it will have the appropriate degrees of flexibility in the appropriate places.

Bubbles Self-Organize

I've spent a lot of time in this book talking about how to engender a new culture of architecture practice but little about the new means of organizing. I've focused on what to *remove* and what *not* to do. This was intentional. The key point is that bubbles should be free to self-organize. This will be irrelevant while there is only one team within a bubble, but as soon as there are two or more teams, then the questions around organization arise.

When you first transition to an architecture advice process, you will likely be coming from a hierarchical model where individual contributors are grouped under line managers, who in turn are grouped under one or more tiers of middle managers, who in turn sit in departments that live under executives, who themselves are under a CEO or equivalent. This hierarchical model serves to group people together, allocates work and responsibility, and transmits communications down—and maybe up—the organization. It also offers a means for recognition and advancement: the higher up the hierarchy you are, the more senior you are, and the more power and responsibility you have.

There are limitations to this hierarchical model. Most notably, those at the lowest levels have the least power, and communications *across* the organization are terribly difficult. Because the hierarchy represents the means of organizing and communication as well as the distribution of power, its structure is very hard to change. Think of all the battles where "they took their team away from them." This is because your level in an organization represents how long it took to get there, and the longer it took, the less inclined you will be to give the power you have acquired away.

Yet there are positive aspects to hierarchy. First, because the model has been around for a very long time, people know what to expect from it. Second, it brings clarity to how your group is organized:

- It's clear to see what teams are responsible for *because responsibilities are fixed*.
- It's clear how skills and resources are distributed among those teams *because everyone has a job title matching their role*.

- Task allocation and team membership are coordinated *by the levels above.*

- Communication is predetermined *because it always comes top-down (and occasionally bottom-up).*

Unfortunately, these positive aspects are precisely what become problematic when hierarchical models are confronted with the unpredictable, unforeseeable demands of the postsoftware revolution world. In such a world, the answers to all these questions need to be much more fluid and responsive to the nature of the challenges facing teams right now. The best people to make those changes are those closest to the work.[7]

That's why alternative models of organizing for software engineering are required within bubbles: models that continue to provide clarity about areas of responsibility, distribution of skills and resources, allocation of tasks and team membership, and means of communication, in a way suited to modern software engineering and in a way that allows the teams to update the structure as and when they need to.

While team and organization design is outside the scope of this book, and there are many methodologies to draw upon,[8] the point to take away is that the best people to organize within advice process bubbles are those living inside of those bubbles and practicing the advice process.

Collective org design within bubbles

How the collective inside an advice process bubble goes about their org design can have a significant impact on their practice of architecture and the systems that result.[9] Imposing a new team topology from above on collectives trying to self-manage isn't going to give you what you need because that's falling back to hierarchical ways of thinking and the opposite of self-organizing. The same goes for dynamically reteaming some of them without their input. If you want teams to be self-managing, self-organizing, and self-sustaining, they need to undertake this work themselves. Everyone who joins an advice process bubble will need to go through the same activity.

There are 60 years of social science research backing up the fact that teams that self-manage need to self-organize, too. Open systems theory, which grew out of sociotechnical systems design, makes clear that those who will undertake work (in our

---

7 If you're thinking, "But what about the Spotify model?" (*https://oreil.ly/3NICF*) remember first that Spotify itself says not to adopt it. Also bear in mind that it simply layers additional mechanisms on top of a hierarchical approach. The problem isn't being tackled at source. Instead, sticking plasters of additional organizational complexity are simply being layered on top.

8 These days there are whole books dedicated to the core aspects of this, *Team Topologies* (IT Revolution Press) being the first among them, as well as *Dynamic Reteaming* (O'Reilly). I recommend you have a look at both of them if you've not done so already.

9 I'm not just talking about team and communications structures here. I also mean societal power structures.

---

case, building, running, and evolving software systems) need to also design how they will organize and operate. During these acts of organization design, all participants are equal, and the focus is on real business needs, management priorities and parameters, and the logistics of designing the work. Participants analyze their work, design new adaptive structures, and plan in detail the action steps required to implement these org designs.[10] An equivalent of this democratized org design can be achieved by collectives applying the Team Topologies or Dynamic Reteaming approaches, participating collectively in designing their initial topology in a way that answers the key questions in the previous subsection.

Org design is an ongoing process

As with all other forms of design, org design is iterative, and the collective within an advice process bubble should be sensitive to feedback on the design. Although org design can happen on a large scale, all at once across multiple teams, org redesign can also happen on a smaller, piecemeal scale. For example, an advice process decision can look to rehome a single part of a system, moving it from one team to another. Effectively this is the superseding of an earlier, layer 3 decision (self-governing and connected communities, discussed in Chapter 14). These org redesign decisions likely arise because of a two-way "conversation" between the decisions of right now and the earlier, underlying decisions that initially split up the work.

Your org design inside the bubble will be a mix of both these large- and small-scale redesigns. The evolution of systems, their responses to product changes, and the effects of technology evolution *should* have an impact on the number and responsibilities of teams. The collective *should* be continually looking to improve how they organize, evolving in a similar fashion to their software systems. Teams *shouldn't* be afraid to split, merge, and change direction (and required skill set) dramatically in the world of evolving architecture.

Bubbles Are Permeable

Just like real bubbles, advice process bubbles are at greatest risk of being compromised when they are most fragile. For advice process bubbles, this fragility is highest in the early weeks and months of adoption. Holes come about when external patterns, activities, and mental models seep in, sidelining the advice process. This happens because everyone inside the bubble is learning new (and unlearning old) ways of seeing, thinking, and acting. To protect the new practice and culture developing within the bubble, everyone needs to pay particular attention to what they do and how they do it.

---

10 These are known as "participative design workshops." Learn more on the Open Systems Theory website (*https://opensystemstheory.org*).

Slipping back to old ways is incredibly easy, but you can't protect your advice process practice space by shutting out the outside organization completely because a bubble needs to be permeable. An advice process bubble membrane is permeable in the sense that, although it acts as a barrier that protects your advice process practice space, it still allows certain artifacts and environmental factors to pass through. This happens in both directions. For example, those outside the bubble will still pass in their requirements for the systems they are looking for, and those within the bubble will want to contribute to external architectural principles, technology radars, shared strategic codebases, and the like. Those in the bubble will also emerge from it to socialize and participate in cross-organizational ceremonies, such as the recognition of contributions and achievements, hiring, leaving and letting go, festive parties, and so on.

Furthermore, the broader environmental forces that affect your organization will have an impact on a bubble and the teams within it. Consider the impact of a product that isn't profitable or the effects of a global pandemic. Both require an organization-wide response that will affect how everyone works and what everyone works on, including those inside an advice process bubble.

There are also expectations, both evident and not so evident, from those outside of the bubble. These expectations pass through the porous surface of the bubble and affect the advice process. Some of them relate to the aspects I have already listed, but some reflect more general concerns. Paying attention to these expectations is the best way of ensuring that your software engineering subculture continues to fit within the wider organizational culture and that your bubble doesn't get holed.

External Expectations on Those Within the Bubble

External expectations on bubbles exert the greatest external pressures. After all, advice bubbles exist within the space of those who practice software development and, on a greater scale, within an organization that expects you to contribute to its overall goals. Some expectations are self-evident, and some aren't. You need to be aware of all of them so that you can acknowledge and work on them.

Self-Evident Expectations

Let's start with the self-evident expectations from those outside of the bubble. There are three of them, and they can roughly be summarized as "we expect you to do your job building, running, and evolving software systems." Those within the advice process bubble can meet these expectations simply by following the advice process and successfully practicing software architecture.

Expectation: Systems meet requirements and align to the vision and goals

First, those outside the bubble will expect those within to deliver software products and services. This means fulfilling user stories and delivering CFRs. Bubble or not, everyone works in the same organization and ought to be pulling in the same direction, and your job is to build software.

As described throughout this book, this is ideally done by product-aligned, self-managing, self-organizing, and self-sustaining teams. However, I have also rolled out the advice process to organizations that have far more traditional approaches to planning and tackling work and will expect the same from those in the bubble. In all these circumstances, teams within the bubble can be expected to participate in the same planning ceremonies and still work their way through backlogs. Regardless of how you get there, there will be an expectation that code will get written, tested, and run up in prod.

More broadly, those outside the bubble will also expect you to follow or contribute to the organizational vision, product roadmap, goals, milestones, priorities, and so on. Bubbles can do this by understanding, contributing to, and making real the technology strategy through the investments, established architectural principles, and other supporting elements that I discussed in Part II.

Expectation: Systems are predictably delivered and securely operated

Second, teams within a bubble will be expected to do all this building, running, and evolving their software systems in a *sustainable and cost-effective fashion*. Another way to say this is that those outside bubbles expect software that doesn't expose the organization to undue risk, be that commercially, legally, or reputationally. If this contradicts the first expectation, then it is expected that those inside bubbles will say so.

There should be no issues with how those in the bubble predictably deliver and securely operate systems. Those inside the bubble will be free to feed back learnings from prod and use techniques like spikes. Ideally, teams in the bubble are practicing continuous deployment, but alternatives such as continuous delivery or even continuous integration won't suffer in any way from adopting the advice process approach.[11] Neither will your approach to managing and supporting infrastructure, however you choose to go about it—though I hope you're somewhere on the journey toward self-service, team-owned, cloud infrastructure.[12]

---

11 Even if you only integrate once every six months, deploy once a year, and release once a decade, this will still work for you. But I'm trying not to think about the circumstances that have led you to this.

12 In my experience, it works really well when infra teams also use the exact same architecture advice process to build their self-serve infrastructure platforms.

There shouldn't be a mismatch in the expectations regarding how secure and cost-effective the systems ought to be, either. Irrespective of how architecture is practiced, affordable services running securely ought to be a given.

Expectation: Accountability and responsibility are explicit and transparent

The third and final self-evident expectation is that those within the bubble will exhibit transparency, responsibility, and accountability. This means that there ought to be no surprises with how the building, running, and evolving of their systems is progressing.

By following the advice process, teams will be building, running, and evolving their software explicitly and transparently for the whole organization to see in generally available ADRs. This happens irrespective of whether they only engage people within the bubble for advice or if they roam farther afield and engage those beyond the bubble's membrane. This general availability of all ADRs not only satisfies the needs of the curious but also ensures that broader organizational standards of responsibility and accountability are met.

Less-Evident Expectations

The self-evident expectations are all directly related to the delivery of software, so they shouldn't be a surprise. But there are other expectations that the organization will have of those within an advice process bubble. These expectations are less directive and less explicit, but they go deeper and relate to frequently unconscious mental models of "how things are done." These less-evident expectations will directly affect your delivery and running of software if you don't work to manage them.

What follows is the list of standard expectations that I either come across or hear about regularly from others. It's by no means exhaustive, but it will give you an idea of the areas to consider from your perspective as well as the means to identify them if you've stumbled upon one that is unique to your organization.

Expectation: Those in bubbles can answer basic hierarchical questions

No matter how a bubble collective chooses to (re)organize itself, everyone *outside* will still expect a ready answer to their hierarchical questions of "who works for who," "who reports to who," and "who works with who." The outsiders will ask these questions precisely because the hierarchical approach to organizing is the only one they know.

The last question is the easiest to answer. Those within an advice process bubble will likely still use the concept of teams, so the answer to "who works with who" will be something like "these people here are in this team, and those people over there work in that team."

As for "who works for who," the answer will be whoever sets an individual's pay and agrees on their recognition and promotion. This will very likely be someone—or more than one person—outside a bubble, and that's fine.

That leaves the question of "who reports to who." This will most likely be the figurehead of the product or program of work that an individual is engaged in. This might be a product manager or a delivery manager. Given the scope of a bubble, these folks will likely also live outside the bubble. That's fine, too.

The point is that the presence of an advice process bubble shouldn't hinder the ability of those in that bubble to relate to hierarchical questions and be understood by their colleagues on the other side of the bubble membrane. They just might need to do a little translation.

Expectation: Appropriate skills are available in sufficient number and depth

There will also be a general expectation that everyone in a bubble has the aptitude (i.e., skills) to undertake the work expected of them, both now and, to a certain extent, in the future. This translates into the expectation that either (1) teams will ensure those skills develop on the job or (2) team members will be freed up to attend training courses.

Associated with this will be the expectation that everyone in the bubble will participate in the organization's approach to recognition and development. This process can take a variety of forms. I've participated in many of them, run a bunch, and helped design more than a few. It's a general rule that many recognition approaches are antipatterns, embedding and ossifying the idea that to progress you need to have longer tenure, act in a way that recognizes and defers to the values of the hierarchy above everything else, and be responsible for managing greater numbers of colleagues. None of these have to be the case.

Let's see what bubble collectives will likely need to consider to meet the expectations about their required levels of aptitude.

Explicitly define the behaviors and contributions valued inside the bubble.   First, you will do well to define the behavior and contributions that are valued within a bubble because everything else follows from this. Bear in mind that the behaviors and contributions that benefit the advice process are *not* the same as the behaviors and contributions that are traditionally recognized and rewarded in software circles. For example, "knowing things no one else does" and "being correct" are less valued in the advice process while listening, co-creating, and admitting and learning from failure are more valued. The first step to protect this difference within bubbles is to collectively decide on what these behaviors and expected contributions *are*. The second step is then to make them explicit by writing them down and publishing them for everyone in a bubble to see.

Despite the hierarchical implications of its name and structure, the "Capgemini Engineering Grade Ladder" (*https://oreil.ly/ry4wI*) I created with my teammates is a good example. Even though it only applies to developers, this document exemplifies a few things that are relevant to defining the behaviors and contributions valued inside an advice process bubble.

First, as you gain experience, the scope of both ownership and impact increases. It is, in effect, a maturity model. Second, the "glue work"—the less glamorous work that needs to happen to make a team successful—is explicitly described as being valued.[13] Third, there is an increasing emphasis on deciding and architectural skills (e.g., awareness of tech trends, ability to communicate options, and CFRs).

Certain things are explicitly *not* included in the grades. First, there's no mention of the time someone has to spend at a certain grade. Anything that you would usually associate with time, such as implicit levels of experience, is already captured in the statements about scope of impact and ownership, up to and including things running in production. Second, the grades don't mention specific technologies and say little about specific flavors of practices. This is because these weren't the aspects we wanted to emphasize. Technologies come and go all the time.[14] Finally, although the grades were created specifically for developers, there are frequent mentions of other roles. This indicates that the primary unit of success is that of a team and not of an individual playing a fixed set of roles. Altogether, the ladder is a good example of how defining your team's most valued behaviors and contributions allows a collective to be explicit about its intentions.

Explicitly recognize progress and reward achievements. Bubble collectives can ensure that they have the appropriate amount and depth of these skills available by recognizing progress and rewarding achievements toward them. By making it clear to everyone what progress truly is valued, you stand a far greater chance of seeing those behaviors and skills develop.

This is why tools like bubble behavior and contribution definitions prove so valuable. They not only make what everyone is aiming for clear but also can be used when creating development plans, when seeking and offering feedback, and when evaluating progress. This turns the words into actions.

In my Capgemini example, the grade ladder made it clear that long-term impact and collaboration were most valued. This clarity made it easy for everyone to plan to develop the valued skills, safe in the knowledge that these efforts would be noted. It

---

13 The term *glue work* comes from Tanya Reilly's famous talk and blog post, "Being Glue" (*https://oreil.ly/hf3LB*).

14 This also meant that we didn't have to constantly update to the latest JavaScript framework nor that those who specialized in the older, less-exciting technologies (the ones that were still valuable to our clients) would be penalized.

also discouraged individuals from going "goblin mode" and delivering short-term "value" at the expense of the overall long-term success.

Explicitly assist in hiring and onboarding new joiners.   While developing the skills and behaviors of those already in bubble collectives is important, that's not the only source of those skills and behaviors. There will also be new joiners, from either outside the organization or internal transfers. Both groups need to be onboarded so that they have the same understanding of the expectations placed on them that everyone else already shares. Again, an explicit grade ladder can help significantly with this.

A grade ladder allows potential candidates to see what kinds of skills and behaviors are valued and what they might be asked about in interviews. Consequently, they can prepare to bring their best selves. A grade ladder also enables candidates to figure out in advance what kind of role they might be interviewing for, and it allows the bubble collectives to locate them, skills- and attitude-wise, in the same way. Finally, if someone is hired and they join the team, the grade ladder can remind them what skills and behaviors everyone is looking for, enabling them to set their personal goals and ask for targeted feedback.

All of this offers bubble collectives the means to explicitly identify, recognize and reward, and supplement the required skills and behaviors that members are expected to have. Most importantly, it's explicit to *everyone* in the bubble, and everyone in the bubble can play a part in creating and maintaining it.

Expectation: Bubble inhabitants participate in org-wide ceremonies

The third and final less-evident external expectation picks up where the second one leaves off. Those in the bubble will be expected to participate in ceremonies and processes alongside others not inside the bubble. For example, a performance review process will most likely expect to compare the contributions and achievements of those inside the bubble to those outside it. Salary pots (allocations of money for things like pay increases and one-off bonuses) will also probably be allocated in a blanket fashion. Other aspects of organizational membership and recognition (i.e., redundancies) will likely originate outside of a bubble but will affect those inside the bubble, too.

The Capgemini engineering grades allowed us to explicitly rate everyone against their peers outside the boundaries of the bubble membrane. While we had no choice in this because it was the mechanism used company-wide, we still had flexibility to make things work for us. For example, while the nine-level grade system represented an agreement cross-company for representing ourselves and our skills, it left lots of room to maneuver. We just had to make sure that our maturity-model grades mapped to their equivalents appropriately.

> ### What Happens in the Bubble Shouldn't Negatively Affect What Happens Outside It
>
> While many things inside the bubble can be different, it's important to remember that practices and behaviors inside the bubble don't seep out of it. The practices are one thing, as are the shifts of power. I always make it very clear that this way of working applies only to those in the bubble and that teams joining the bubble do so with the agreement of all concerned.
>
> Everyone in the bubble needs to be clear that you cannot act in the bubble as if the rest of the organization and the outside world don't exist. Because the bubble intentionally operates transparently, the collective always needs to be conscious that what happens inside it can spread, affecting those outside, too.
>
> The prime example of this is open salaries where everyone knows what everyone else gets paid. Although this might work in many organizations, it would not work if only a subset of that organization adopted it. Instead, semitransparency, such as open salary-setting mechanisms tied explicitly to open grade ladders, can be a significant step toward this.

Bubbles Present an Interface Independent of Implementation

Although a bubble's membrane provides a bounded, safe space to practice the advice process, it also acts as an interface between those inside and outside of the bubble. Thinking of this relationship as an interface between new and legacy systems is a very fruitful way to conceive of it. The bubble is your new system, and it is surrounded by one or more legacy systems that place expectations on it. These expectations manifest in the form of API-like touch points and hand-offs that the bubble will have with the surrounding organization. You simply have a number of legacy APIs you have to support. Just as with working with legacy APIs, the idea is to do everything required to ensure that the legacy system or systems continue to work in completely the same way they always have. The legacy systems—or in this case, the rest of the organization outside your bubble—shouldn't even notice anything is different. This goes right up to and includes honoring the names of things (artifacts, roles, etc.) in the outside world. Being an interface comes with expectations that make sure the two subcultures (subsystems) can work together.

The Bubble's Interface Contract

You can think of bubbles as having interface contracts. Interface (aka API) contracts outline how different pieces of software or services should interact with one another.

These agreements define the rules, specifications, and expectations for data exchange, functionality, and communication so that the various systems can work together.

When you have an advice process bubble, your bubble's interface contract will cover four important elements:

- What a bubble will do (the external expectations I covered in the previous section)
- What information will be exchanged across the bubble membrane
- What the people outside the bubble will call things
- What the expectations around service levels are (e.g., how frequently things will be done, how long they will take, the quality of the results, etc.)

The contract focuses only on how the bubble will interact with the outside world. Meanwhile, the internal "implementation" includes the advice process and any supporting elements. Just as with software, hiding your implementation allows you to keep control of how you structure and do things. That belongs to the collective inside the bubble and is not up to anyone outside of it.

Treating the bubble's membrane as an interface enables you to retain your own reserved names for things (what your roles are called, what practices are used, and the artifacts that are produced as a result). You can protect the culture developing within the bubble without being subjected to the countervailing culture and mindsets beyond. You can be explicit about this difference in names and practices if you need to, but don't negotiate or surrender control of how you organize within your bubbles to the surrounding organization. If that happens, you will be unable to self-organize.

Make the Valuable Translation Work Explicit

Both contracts and the creation of artifacts that aid in the translation between systems are critical to the success of an interface. This seemingly supplementary work is critical for the bubble to operate on its own. It is the epitome of *glue work,* the less glamorous work that needs to happen to make a team successful.

Translation work can be technical. For example, it could include creating additional artifacts such as architectural overview diagrams or even historical narratives of the key architectural decisions that led up to the current systems of the kind I mentioned in Chapter 6.

Translation work will also include everything nontechnical involved in moving things back and forth across the bubble membrane. What this specifically entails will come directly from your org's expectations. For example, you may have to reshape inputs prior to a performance review cycle because you want to have additional steps for 360 review. This could involve batching up continual review outcomes from inside the bubble to meet the less frequent review cadence of the rest of the organization. It could even involve translation of the within-bubble grades into grades that exist in the rest of the organization.

Make the translation work explicit by creating one or more roles and zero or more circles to collect these roles, allowing everyone, inside and outside the bubble, to see and realize the value of this work. Translation work can and should be explicitly added to your circles and roles representation of the advice process bubble. An example of this is shown in Figure 17-2.

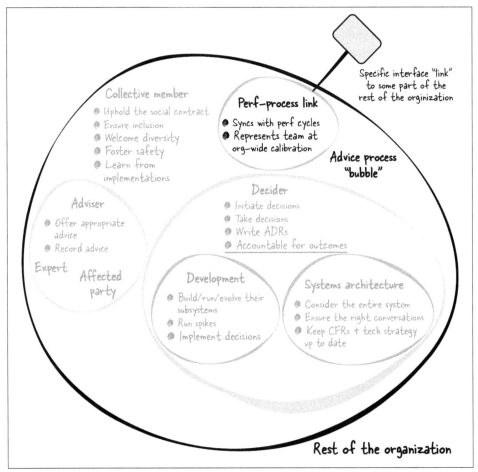

Figure 17-2. An additional circle with responsibilities for linking into the wider organization's performance management process has been added to the advice process bubble

All of these translations may sound a little strange and a little wasteful, but this is actually a standard approach that I and other colleagues have used in organizational transformations. It works because you can't have an impact if you talk to people in a language they don't understand. Such translations are typically undertaken by those with outside or cross-team roles (e.g., architecture), taking, for example, the form of supplementary orientation pages on the wiki, or reports in Jira set up to present data in a format that matches general reporting requirements, or copying performance review output into a format that the rest of the organization recognizes. It's beneficial to keep track of the amount of this additional work. Remember, your primary focus should be on the continuous delivery of value to users of your products or service(s), not on translating what you've done and plan to do for the benefit of those outside the value stream.

By performing these translations, those playing link roles remove any impact the different subculture inside the bubble might have on the rest of the organization. More importantly, they properly separate bubble cultures and how they organize from the culture and ways of organizing in the rest of the organization. This means that those in the bubbles can do things differently. The interface/implementation split means bubbles aren't obliged to create the artifacts or participate in ceremonies in the same way. They obtain the freedom to innovate *without* breaking the rest of the organization and upsetting everyone unnecessarily. Just like the equivalents in software, the bubble internals are free to change as they need. Many of those changes will come about as bubbles grow.

Growing Bubbles

You should always start your adoption of the advice process on a small scale as part of a team (if you personally don't have deciding power already), or perhaps as an individual (if you have deciding power), or ideally in a collaboration between these two. This allows those practicing this new way of architecture to get used to the process and develop a new culture. Later, assuming things inside a bubble go well, the bubble can incrementally take in more teams, becoming gradually less ad hoc and more established. As this growth happens, you will want to bear in mind how fast it is happening, how the culture within the bubble is changing, and most importantly, that the core goals of architecture continue to be served.

Incremental Growth, Team by Team

As more and more teams join an advice process bubble, you will likely want to make improvements in how you go about self-organizing. Growth spurts that add one or more teams to an advice process bubble signal a great opportunity for the collective to reevaluate how everything currently works. This can lead to changes in how the interfaces work and how contracts are fulfilled. It can also lead to changes in the interfaces themselves, and even in the world outside the bubble.

Such changes typically come about for positive reasons because the advice process is not only becoming established but also bearing results. Not all necessary changes will come from positive sources, though. It is possible that those outside bubbles will try to sabotage them by requesting detrimental changes.

Positive changes to bubble interfaces

As bubbles become more established, it is worth periodically asking, "Are all the elements that everyone *thought* they would need actually needed?" You see this "adding more elements than you need" a lot. Bureaucracy is great at adding but terrible at taking away. When you take a fresh look at what is *really* needed, it is amazing how much is simply there because "it's how we've always done it."

Again, just as you would look to improve a contract and interface between two software services when both parties are inclined to do so, you should do the same for bubble interfaces. Remember, changes to dependencies and interfaces are architecturally significant, and changes should engage all those who are affected and those with expertise. It should come as no surprise to you then that you can use the advice process supported by ADRs to make changes to the bubble interface, gather advice, and capture those changes.

But changes might go further, stretching into the rest of the organization.

Coping with external-expectation sabotage

Sometimes, as bubbles grow, people outside bubbles that are opposed to the advice process will use interface challenges as a means of sabotage, placing the most onerous expectations they can think of in the hope that they will overburden a bubble and make it fail. The bubble collective should initially counter this by simply stepping up and meeting the challenge, no matter how onerous. After a period of time doing this, they should point out how things might be done better. The best angle for this is to point out the waste inherent in what the bubble collective is being asked to do.

Even when you suspect sabotage, the best way to go about this is with magnanimity: use techniques such as the "five whys"[15] to get to the root of the request and then work a solution back from there. This allows for great innovation and is the basis for many improvements, both within and outside the bubble.

A classic example of a challenge is when you hear "but regulations dictate that…" The challenges come in the form: "you can't work like this because regulation X says you need to do process Y rather than the advice process." In these cases, you will likely uncover that what is being asked for is "industry-standard response to regulation X"

---

15 The five whys handbook (*https://oreil.ly/iFe24*) from the socialized UK National Health Service contains one of the best explanations I've seen.

as opposed to "a valid, organization-specific response to regulation X that allows us to work in the way that suits while still meeting the regulations." Getting to the underlying details of the challenge then allows the bubble to self-organize around it in a way that is minimally detrimental to the architectural practice.

Ensure You Protect the Core Goals of Your Architectural Practice

The advice process will likely spread to an increasing number of teams and supporting roles within your organization, but you must achieve this without compromising your new approach to practicing architecture. Recall the core goals of your decentralized, feedback-prioritizing, postrevolutionary architectural practice that you want to protect:

- Involve the appropriate people in decisions while keeping this number as small as possible
- Maximize the entitlement to initialize, make, and take decisions
- Maximize trust so that people feel the need to involve themselves in decisions where they have a stake
- Minimize the need for explicit sharing

The advice process with its social contract protects your decentralized practice by developing a climate of safety and a culture of learning. It's able to do this because ADRs assist in deciding, transparently recording both advice and decision outcomes. Where additional support is needed, advice forums can optimize the practice of advice seeking and offering, with further alignment offered by elements such as testable CFRs, actionable technology strategy, architectural principles, and a tech radar.

Each of these supporting elements complements the four goals rather than compromising them. But if you want to keep bringing the advice process to more and more teams, then at some point even these additional elements will start hindering rather than supporting because of the sheer amount of everything. Does that mean there is a limit to growth? Kind of. It depends on how you look at it.

Dividing Bubbles When They Get Too Big

As your advice process collective starts to take on more and more teams and individuals, you may be asking yourself, "How big can this go?" Although the spread of the advice process is often the goal, growth isn't always the right way to get there. Sometimes, bubbles need to split in order to keep growing the overall number of people using the advice process.

Nothing Can Grow Forever

It is a seemingly universal assumption that increasing a system's size is the *only* way to get more out of it. But nothing can grow forever. "Limitless growth" is a failure mode. For example, increasing only the number of people (or other key moving parts) in a system ignores other systemic aspects, such as the need for increasing communication, that are required to support those numbers.[16] Eventually, everything collapses under the combined weight.

However, it is a commendable goal to want to bring the advice process to an increased number of teams. So what if instead we split bubbles when they become so big that they threaten the four core goals of architectural practice? What if there were many bubbles, each independent of the others as much as they are of the organization, but also appropriately connected?

Divide a Bubble When the Core Goals of Your Architectural Practice Are Threatened

Perhaps you never have to divide a bubble; a single bubble can grow impressively large. I've seen 10 teams and multiple floating architects use a single one to practice architecture. We made heavy use of the regular cadence of the advice forum and automation to focus the right people's attention on the right ADRs and spikes, and we kept conversations focused using the principles and radar blips, but nothing felt strained.

Despite this, you always need to pay attention to how things change as you grow. Although it's possible to work within one giant bubble, you don't need to. Multiple smaller bubbles may be beneficial.

You can tell when you ought to split a bubble when you start to see the following warning signs, each of which is the result of one of the four core goals of architecture practice failing:

- Trust stops building or even decreases as it takes longer to take decisions despite all the advice being in, or decisions go off radar, or people seem increasingly scared of failure.

- Decisions are taking too long. It is taking too long to get all the required advice on decisions, and cross-system roles are finding it hard to stay on top of all the decisions that are being taken.

---

16 The reason we all think this way seems to arise directly from the capitalist idea of growth being an end unto itself. Think I'm kidding? The philosopher Mark Fisher quipped in his book *Capitalism Realism* (Zero Books) that "it is easier to imagine the end of the world than the end of capitalism." We see this every day when we acknowledge that we cannot simply continue consuming at such a rate and that the planet's resources are finite, yet we continue to follow the doctrine of growth as the only show in town.

- Advice forums are repeatedly covering cross-team ADRs that many of those attending have little or no interest in.

- Decisions are increasingly having to be explicitly shared after they have been taken.

All of these are symptoms of the collective practicing the advice process being too large. All of them can be solved by dividing the bubble collective.

How to Divide Your Bubble

When a bubble divides, members of one bubble can still visit the forums and read the ADRs of other bubbles. In fact, they might need to participate in order to offer advice. But what about all the other aspects that will be affected by the split?

Dividing teams

Once you realize that a bubble will benefit from being divided, you have to identify where to divide it. This is the most important and complicated part of bubble division.

Dividing an advice bubble along purely technical or departmental lines is generally a mistake. This kind of division tends to cement the silos already in your organization and takes teams farther away from the end users and organizational value delivered by their systems. This is the same kind of thinking that split "frontend" from "back-end" teams.

ADRs, Bubble Splitting, and Fracture Planes

I'm sometimes asked if ADRs should be written when a bubble is splitting. While I've not covered it here, there is no reason why it wouldn't work. You may also wonder if the fracture planes for decisions that I listed in Chapter 13 apply to bubble splitting, too. Again, I haven't done this myself so haven't included it. I would watch out for a slackening in the general understanding of what an architectural decision is if you did this. That's not to say don't try. One of the reviewers of this book, Vanessa Formicola, has had great success with *social* decision records (*https://oreil.ly/sq_Hi*) for exactly this purpose. If you are thinking along similar lines, in these or other areas, that's amazing! It's that kind of curiosity and willingness to experiment that led to this book.

The ideal divisions are typically along the lines of products or programs of work, in accordance with the fifth revolution: stream-aligned teams.[17] If a collective shares a set of milestones or dates, then that's a pretty good indication that you have the right lines.

What about dividing along "platform" or "shared services" team lines?[18] It might sound as if such teams have their own bubbles. I'd only advise this when the (internal) product value of the platform or shared service is firmly established *and* its capabilities are largely or wholly self-service *and* consumers of the platform's services are in more than one bubble. Otherwise, keep them in the same bubble as their main customers, the other engineering teams.

You may be tempted to start a new bubble whenever a new team adopts the advice process, but I'd counsel against it. Starting a new team within an existing bubble lets the new team experience how the advice process, ADRs, and any supporting elements are working *in your organization*. Of course, teams outside the bubble may have already been exposed to the workings of the advice process, either as attendees to an open advice forum or because they were consulted for advice, but there is no substitute for participating in, and not just observing, the advice process.

Finally, don't ever split a bubble down the middle purely for the sake of making the advice process more manageable. Instead, split off a small subset of teams along the previously mentioned fracture lines, making sure there is more than one team in both new bubbles. (Aside from when you are starting the transition to the advice process and there is only one team in a single bubble, the value comes when teams are collaborating.)

After you've determined where a bubble should be split, decide which teams will stay in the original and which will live in the new one. Although some roles may continue to serve both bubbles, such as system architects, ideally this isn't the case. If possible, those who are playing architecture roles shouldn't have more than one home bubble.

When the division initially happens, keep the expectation contract and interfaces between the bubbles and the rest of the organization the same. This has multiple benefits: the new bubble doesn't have to do anything extra in regard to the outside world when it is first created, and the rest of the organization will see the two bubbles as the same—perhaps even as a single entity. It will feel no different to them having one bubble or two.

---

17 Gartner (*https://oreil.ly/tP3Jo*) defines a *value stream* as "the sequence of activities necessary to deliver a product, service or experience to a customer, internal or external."

18 I'm thinking here of the team type described by Matthew Skelton and Manuel Pais in *Team Topologies*.

Dividing the advice forum

After you split the bubble and teams move into their new bubbles, the advice forum is the next thing to split. Each bubble should have its own forum time slot, invitees, and agenda. Each bubble's forum should be convened by parties within that bubble. Care should be taken not to overlap their scheduling because some nonbubble advisers, at least those playing "expert" roles like InfoSec, will want to attend them all.

Dividing ADRs

When a new bubble is formed, it can continue to add to the previous ADR library or create a separate one. The reason you might split them is there are distinctly different narratives to programs of work that teams are engaged on. If the decision is taken to have the legacy and greenfield work in the same program of work, then perhaps the ADR library will remain shared. But if it is decided that the programs of work should be split, then it is unlikely the ADRs will overlap much, and the libraries can be split. However you go about it, remember that ADRs are immutable records, so there is no need to edit anything in those that were written before the bubble split.

Finally, if there is no reason for ADRs themselves to be stored together (for example, if ADRs from one bubble share little to nothing with ADRs from the other bubble), then they can be separated. Remember, split or not, all ADRs should be readily accessible to all to maximize their value.

Architectural principles don't divide initially—they get copied

Because they are there to align everyone, architectural principles should be the same across bubbles. When a bubble splits, simply link to a shared original. Again, they will likely stay the same, but if principles do begin to diverge, typically for the reasons outlined in "Updating and Maintaining Principles" on page 269, then that's fine.

The technology radar doesn't divide

The technology radar is the final element to consider. There ought to be only one shared tech radar across all the bubbles as it is organization-wide and reflects the reality of the current tech landscape and the guidelines regarding working with tech within it.

When a rescan is due, bottom-up nudges to add blips and move the rings they live in can be incorporated from all bubbles. When a new team joins a bubble, they may have a bunch of blips to add to the radar because they come from a completely different part of the organization. A mini radar-updating sweep can be held just for them if it seems necessary. Alternatively, it can wait until the next general sweep.

Staying Aligned Across Bubbles

When bubbles are split, people are sometimes concerned about how to ensure that all the teams continue to maintain their alignment with the wider organization and with one another. Remember that the minimal possible level of alignment comes from the testable CFRs I discussed in Chapter 9. Some of the CFRs will likely apply organization-wide (e.g., legal and regulatory, security, cost, and others). Others may apply only to a single product or suite of products. In those cases, they won't have applied to teams from other products when they initially joined their first bubble, and they can now be moved out of the bubble to their new home with the team(s) that they do apply to.

Remember, everyone doesn't need full alignment—only the minimal amount to remain viable. One of the main reasons I suggested the splits I have is because they are likely to keep the teams together for shared reasons they care about and allow things they don't care about to diverge.

Protect and Encourage Differences Between Bubbles

To close, I'll remind you of one of the key themes running throughout this book: the sense that from difference comes creative power, and that power needs to be honored and protected. This fights against the tendency that many will feel to make things the same.

This "same is good, difference is bad" mentality holds a particular resonance for those of us who work in software. We painfully overuse the adage "don't repeat yourself" (aka DRY), for instance,[19] to the extent that we forget what it really means: it is only about *knowledge* in our code.[20] Our desire to find similarities and abstract them out to make everything more similar is a strong one.

This means that as the number of teams working in bubbles increases, you'll notice that those who have a broader oversight and remit will want things to be *the same across all bubbles everywhere*. This is because that's the traditional way for them to be able to keep doing what they're doing without collapsing under the cognitive load. While this makes sense and we can empathize with it, it's both impossible and undesirable.

What you want instead is to protect and encourage differences. In so doing, you will free everyone from unnecessary conformity and allow everyone to build, run, and evolve the best software and systems they are capable of. If that's not the goal of the practice of software architecture, I'm not sure what is.

---

19 The concept of DRY was first formulated by Andrew Hunt and Dave Thomas in their book *The Pragmatic Programmer*.

20 This was eloquently explained by Mathias Verraes in his blog "Dry Is About Knowledge" (*https://oreil.ly/6bf-p*).

Conclusion

The fit of the advice process with the surrounding organization is *essential* for the software systems architected to thrive. This concluding chapter showed how to ensure that fit is conscious and deliberate.

It showed how to think about the advice process practice space as a bubble, but one firmly rooted in the context of the organization. I also described how to understand the expectations the organization will have on you and how to meet them. I also discussed how to grow your architecture practice bubbles gradually, without losing anything that made your practices work.

Finally, I talked about how to scale by dividing, allowing your practice to remain true to the four core goals of an architecture practice while taking on a larger and larger remit. In so doing, you will maintain the hard-won space you cleared for a decentralized, feedback-driven, collective architecture practice. You will be able to thrive in the variability-strewn, postrevolutionary world of Agile, cloud, DevOps, product thinking, and stream-aligned teams. You will ensure a place for everyone to contribute and learn, and you will realize a sustainable architecture practice that works for the entire organization, now and for the future.

This is all I have to offer for now. I hope I brought together a complete enough set of information to entice you to begin, practice, retrospect, learn, and ultimately craft your own flavor of the architecture advice process. As you go about this, keep looking for alternative ways to unlock an approach to architecture practice that works best for your collective. Keep experimenting and please, please disagree with me whenever you find a better way.

When you do, I've only one request to make. Share what you learn and create as much as you are able, in blogs, talks, podcasts, books, and more.[21] That way, we can all gain inspiration from your achievements, furthering our collective endeavors.

Thank you for reading.

---

21 I've made a space for this sharing on the site that accompanies this book. Find out how you can get involved at *https://facilitatingsoftwarearchitecture.com/community*.

Index

versus effectiveness guarantee, 210-213
least surprise principle to detect, 216-219
maintaining during bubble division, 466
O-AA mechanisms for, 215-216
of teams, 16, 45
Andreesen, Marc, xx
antagonistic advice, seeking, 109
any other business (AOB), advice forum, 182
ARBs (Architecture Review Boards), 102, 162
architects, xix-xxi
adjusting to advice process roles, 322-323
as advice offerers versus decision takers, 96
as advice process initiators, 84
as deciders in advice process, 86-90
decision taking versus developer team,
101-104
integrating into advice process, 107
inverted hierarchy role, 366
as organization goals sources, 248
swamping of by traditional architecture
practice, 18
as takers of decisions, 101-102
traditional architecture practice roles, xxii,
3-7
and trust in advice process, 104
workflow problem in starting with, 84-92,
189, 196
Architectural Decision Records (ADRs),
115-157
in advice forum, 183, 188-190
advice process role, 136-146, 161
and architectural principles, 245, 267, 269
in coalescent approach, 188-190
and conceptual thread of decisions, 362
curating, 156-157
drafting to support deciding, 125-136
explicit accountability in, 164
framing context, 302-306
lifecycle of, 150-153
managing, 153-156
recording advice forums, 184
spiking of, 354-360
for splitting large decisions into smaller
ones, 339
structure, 117-125
taking decision and completing, 146-150
writing during bubble division, 463, 465
architectural principles, 239-272

from CFRs, 244
characteristics of, 242-244
as complement to advice process, 245, 267
copying for bubble division, 465
examples, 240-242
feedback from decisions, impact of, 267-269
principles workshop, 246-264
technical strategy effects of decisions, 271
updating and maintaining, 269-271
wiki for sharing workshop results, 264-267
Architectural Principles Hub (wiki page),
264-267
architecture advice forum, 179-207
ADRs in, 183, 188-190
agenda for, 180, 182
alternative flavors, 206
benefit of cadence, 202-204
centralizing coordination in, 191, 195-198
decentralizing execution, 195-197
deep domain expertise, centralization for,
197-198
for feedback to inform architectural principles, 268
group dynamics in, 190-195
kicking off advice process with, 204-206
offering and receiving of advice, 184, 191
opening of session, 183
recording advice in, 184
sociotechnical dynamics, 185-195
spikes in, 360
splitting bubbles, 465
versus traditional architecture meeting,
181-182
transparency for social cohesion and trust,
198-202
architecture advice process, 69-99
accountability in decision taking, 96-97,
162-164
adoption of, 101-113
ADR's role in, 136-146, 161
(see also Architectural Decision
Records)
advice seeking and social inclusion, 309-310
and alignment of organization, 209-211, 215
applied to your organization (see bubbles,
advice process)
architectural principles as complement to,
245, 267

About the Author

Andrew Harmel-Law is a tech principal at Thoughtworks, specializing in domain-driven design, org design, software and systems architecture, Agile delivery, build tools, and automation. Andrew's experience spans the software development lifecycle and many sectors.

Andrew is also an author and trainer for O'Reilly, having written not only this book about facilitating software architecture but also a chapter about implementing the Accelerate/DORA four key metrics. Andrew also runs regular online training sessions such as "Domain-Drive Design (First Steps)" and "Architecture Decision Making by Example." What motivates Andrew is the humane delivery and sustainable evolution of large-scale software solutions that fulfill complex user needs. Andrew understands that people, architecture, process, and tooling all have key roles to play in achieving this. Andrew has a great passion for open source software and its communities. Andrew has been involved with OSS to a greater or lesser extent since their career began; as a user, contributor, expert group member, or paid advocate—most notably as one of the Jenkins JobDSL originators (*https://oreil.ly/ZHWQ4*).

Andrew enjoys sharing their experience as much as possible. This sharing is seen in not only formal consulting engagements but also informally through mentoring, blog posts (*https://oreil.ly/Rec4F*), conferences (keynoting, speaking, and organizing) (*https://oreil.ly/g09EM*), and open sourcing their code.

If you want to reach out to Andrew, you can try LinkedIn (*https://linkedin.com/in/ andrewharmellaw*), Mastodon (*https://twit.social/@ahl*), Bluesky (*https://bsky.app/ profile/andrewhl.bsky.social*), or (if you must) Twitter (*https://twitter.com/al94781*).

Colophon

The animals on the cover of *Facilitating Software Architecture* are two-barred cross-bills (*Loxia leucoptera*). A North American version—currently listed as the same species—is known as the white-winged crossbill (two-barred crossbills tend to be a bit larger than their North American counterparts).

Two-barred crossbills inhabit the Palearctic, mostly in Russia. Their preferred habitats involve spruce trees and cones, which are their source of food. They use their unusual beak shapes to open the cones. Fun fact: two-barred crossbills are three times more likely to have lower beaks crossing to the right than to the left.

The male plumage is red while the female is yellow-green. The female typically builds the nest, lays three to four eggs, and incubates them. After the eggs hatch, the chicks are fed by both parents until they fledge 22 to 24 days later; they then remain with their parents for up to six weeks.

Many of the animals on O'Reilly covers are endangered; all of them are important to the world.

The cover illustration is by Karen Montgomery, based on an antique line engraving from *British Birds*. The series design is by Edie Freedman, Ellie Volckhausen, and Karen Montgomery. The cover fonts are Gilroy Semibold and Guardian Sans. The text font is Adobe Minion Pro; the heading font is Adobe Myriad Condensed; and the code font is Dalton Maag's Ubuntu Mono.

O'REILLY®

Learn from experts.
Become one yourself.

60,000+ titles | Live events with experts | Role-based courses
Interactive learning | Certification preparation

**Try the O'Reilly learning platform
free for 10 days.**

Milton Keynes UK
Ingram Content Group UK Ltd.
UKHW010916071224
452148UK00002B/3